A Short History of the
Italian People

THE HAPPY CITY

From a fresco in the Palazzo Pubblico of Siena

JANET PENROSE TREVELYAN

A Short History
of the
Italian People

FROM THE BARBARIAN INVASIONS
TO THE PRESENT DAY

*

REVISED EDITION WITH AN EPILOGUE BY
D. MACK SMITH
Fellow of Peterhouse, Cambridge
Author of 'Cavour and Garibaldi'

AND A FOREWORD BY
G. M. TREVELYAN, O.M.

LONDON
GEORGE ALLEN & UNWIN LTD

First published by G. P. Putnam's Sons, 1920
Second Edition, revised and enlarged. 1926
Third Edition, revised and enlarged, 1929
Fourth Edition, revised and brought up to date
published by George Allen & Unwin Ltd, 1956

PRINTED IN GREAT BRITAIN
in 10 point Pilgrim type
BY THE EAST MIDLAND ALLIED PRESS, LTD
KETTERING, PETERBOROUGH AND ELSEWHERE

TO THE DEAR MEMORY
OF A LITTLE BOY
THEODORE MACAULAY TREVELYAN

*To whom the Heroes of Old Rome
were as the playmates of today
I dedicate this book*

FOREWORD BY
G. M. TREVELYAN, O.M.

My wife's *Short History of the Italian People* is a political not a social history. It was first published in 1920 by Messrs. Putnam and went through three editions; in the last of these (1928) she carried down the story to the period of Mussolini's power. The book has since fallen out of print, but as it does not appear to be replaced by any other similar work Messrs. Allen & Unwin suggested that they should bring out a new edition. As my wife is no longer able to do hard historical work herself, it has been continued to the fall of Mussolini by my friend Mr. D. Mack Smith, Fellow of Peterhouse, Cambridge, the author of *Cavour and Garibaldi* (1954).

Most of the original illustrations are reproduced. In order to contain the maps within a single page of the demy 8vo format (since folding maps are now out of the question) it has been necessary to turn the 'leg' of Italy straight up and down the page instead of at the customary angle. The compass directions are clearly indicated.

AUTHOR'S PREFACE

MY sole intention, when I embarked upon the task of writing this book twelve years ago, was to present to English readers, in as concise a form as possible, a story which was then all too little known to most of them. The pressing need for a 'Short History of Italy' in the English tongue was borne in upon me as early as the year 1902, when I endeavoured to give a series of lantern lectures on Italian history to London school children at the Passmore Edwards Settlement. Since then the need has been in great part met by the appearance of the slender volume entitled *Italy, Mediæval and Modern*, written by Miss Ady in collaboration with three other Oxford lecturers; but although this summary presents the case with admirable clearness, it still perhaps leaves room for another interpretation, based on the long-continued ruminations of a single mind. The shortcomings of the following attempt will be obvious to every reader, but at least it is the result of a deep and growing love for the subject, of many wanderings in the by-paths of Italy, and of an inherited affection for her present population. For a summary of this nature, which is admittedly only an introduction to the subject, I have not thought it necessary to attempt any original research; I have not studied in the archives of Italian towns; I do not claim to have made new discoveries. But I have endeavoured, by using the work already done on each period by Italian, British, French, and German scholars, and by illuminating it with the sayings of contemporary writers, to present a narrative as near to the truth as it was possible for me to make it. Whether I have succeeded in the task is for others than myself to judge, but if I shall have helped my countrymen to bestow a more generous attention on a branch of history neglected both in English and American education, if they will go beyond this sketch and study the story of Italy in the detail it deserves, I shall ask no other reward for my labour. The history of Italy should take its place in all our higher schools, no less than that of France, Greece, and Ancient Rome, for in the brilliance of its incidents, the richness and variety of the human types that it presents, it is surely unsurpassed in all the European scene.

My thanks are due to many friends for their assistance,

encouragement, or helpful criticism; but principally to these four : Miss L. P. de Castelvecchio, Miss Melian Stawell, Dr. Edmund Gardner, and Professor Thomas Okey, who, by reading different portions of the book in manuscript, have all given me invaluable help.

J.P.T.

Chelsea, London,
February, 1919.

CONTENTS

ILLUSTRATIONS

MAPS

CHAPTER I

Italy in the Century Preceding
the Barbarian Invasions

WHEN the Emperor Diocletian, towards the end of the third century
A.D., set himself to reorganize the government of the known world,
his stout heart may well have quailed before the magnitude of the
task before him. The preceding fourteen years had witnessed a succession of six Emperors, some of them men of exceptional courage
and ability, of whom three had been assassinated by their troops,
one had been killed by the hardships of campaigning, another by
lightning on the borders of Persia, and the last still remained to be
dealt with and removed. That task successfully accomplished,
Diocletian turned his attention to the greater problem before him,
and the conclusion at which he arrived was that in order to save
the Empire its constitution must be fundamentally remodelled. His
memorable division of the whole into four parts, together with his
thorough reform of the administration, enabled the machine of
government to run for another century and to resist the shattering
blows of the barbarian wreckers for many years longer still.

The three associates to whom Diocletian deputed the sovereignty
of Europe and Northern Africa were all men of considerable experience and capacity. The eldest of them, Maximian, an unlettered
soldier better suited to carry out the suggestions of his patron than
to initiate a policy of his own, received with the title of 'Augustus'
the 'dioceses' of Italy, Spain, and Africa; Constantius Chlorus, the
most popular of the younger generals, was made 'Cæsar' of Gaul
and Britain, while Galerius, a man of vigorous but cruel temper,
was set to guard the Danube frontier with the title of 'Cæsar' of
Mœsia and Pannonia. Diocletian himself, an 'Augustus' like Maximian, kept the whole of the East, with Egypt and Thrace, and was
tacitly acknowledged by each of his three partners as the guiding
spirit of the confederation. He was indeed one of the most accomplished bureaucrats that have ever left their mark on the world's
history. With the chaotic spectacle of the last hundred years before
his eyes, he saw that the real danger lay in the abuse of power by
independent generals, and he therefore initiated an elaborate system of divisions, in which the higher and lower officials should act

B

as checks and counter-checks on one another, and thus prevent the abuse of authority. One of his first acts was to curtail the over-grown power of the Prætorian Prefect, an official who, originally the commander of the Prætorian Guards, had gradually become the general factotum and often the assassin of the Emperor, with practical control over military, judicial, and financial affairs. Dio-cletian divided this great office also in four, giving a Prætorian Prefect to each of his new quarters of the Empire,[1] and at the same time considerably reducing the military power at his disposal.

The scheme of division was, however, carried much further than this. Thirteen great 'dioceses,' each as large as a country of modern Europe, were carved out of the four Prefectures and placed each under its Vicarius or vice-prefect, while these were further sub-divided into provinces, all of them far smaller than the ancient provinces, and administered by governors who were responsible to the Prætorian Prefect but were otherwise absolute within their respective districts. Thus Diocletian hoped by multiplying the holders to divide the substance of power, and, by this organized hierarchy of ranks, culminating in the Cæsars and the Augusti, to ensure a regular and peaceful development for the State. Amid the tumults of the years which succeeded the abdication of Diocletian the machine still ran, though with some groaning and stumbling. But it had one most serious defect—that it vastly increased the expenses of administration. Each of the provincial governors, as well as the Vicarii and the Prætorian Prefects, maintained an osten-tatious court which had to be paid for out of the revenues of the province, and the multiplication of subordinate offices of all sorts was so enormous that the poet Claudian, at the end of the fourth century, complained that the receivers of public money almost outnumbered the payers of it.

To meet this immense burden of expense, every effort of the government was directed towards maintaining the system of taxa-tion in all its terrible efficiency. The general principle of Imperial taxation in the fourth century was that the central government sent down an edict, or *indiction* (frequently followed by a *super-indiction*), to the capital city of each diocese, stating the amount required from that area; that this total sum was then divided among the provinces and subdivided among the towns (the units of collec-tion), while the unfortunate town-councillors, or *decuriones*, were made personally responsible for the sum required. This office, in

---

[1] Side by side with these four Prefectures, the office of Prætorian Pre-fect of Rome also continued to exist, with authority independent of that of the Prefect of Italy; it was a survival from the days of Augustus.

common with many others, had already been made hereditary, simply because no sane man would voluntarily have undertaken the burdens it entailed, and the heaviest penalties were imposed upon the *decurio* who sought to evade his obligations. Thus the once coveted position of municipal senator had gradually become a mere object of terror, and the hapless *decurio* would frequently settle as a serf on the estate of some neighbouring grandee, and implore his protection against the Imperial vengeance.

In the collection of the taxes, extortion and violence were the order of the day, especially in the levying of contributions in kind for the maintenance of the army; and until stopped by an edict of Constantine, torture was freely employed in extorting the impositions on trade and industry which were exacted every fourth year. Perhaps the best evidence of the exhaustion which the methods of imperial taxation produced is the fact that we frequently find remissions of taxation granted to certain districts—a phenomenon which attests the complete inability to pay on the part of the regions in question.

Italy fared no better than other parts of the Empire in the matter of taxation, for the much-dreaded land-tax, long the bane of the provinces alone, was imposed on her by Diocletian. Nor did she gain any compensating advantages under the new system. Rome was no longer the seat of empire, for Maximian fixed his residence at Milan, within striking distance of the barbarians beyond the Alps, and the Roman Senate, which ten years before had actually elected an Emperor from its own number, sank into complete insignificance. Nor was Maximian an easy master, for in the first year of his reign he quelled the mutinous spirit of the Romans by a series of executions and confiscations which struck terror into the hearts of any would-be leaders of rebellion. Not until the abdication of Diocletian and his elder colleague in 305 did the rising discontent break out in a revolt—headed by Maximian's son Maxentius—against the new Cæsar appointed by Galerius. The remnant of the Prætorian Guards supported Maxentius; Severus, the unpopular Cæsar, was captured and forced to commit suicide [306], and the Romans enjoyed for six years the presence of an Emperor of their own choosing,—whose cruelty and licentiousness, however, soon made them regret their choice. A party among the Senate began to look for help towards the young ruler of Gaul, Constantine, son of Constantius Chlorus; Maxentius himself provoked a conflict, and in 312 the Gallic Cæsar decided to stake his fortune on an invasion of Italy. He met and defeated two armies sent for-

ward by Maxentius at Turin and Verona, advanced on Rome by the
Flaminian Way, and at the great battle of the Milvian Bridge annihilated the last army which his adversary could muster. Maxentius
was drowned in the Tiber, and Constantine found himself master
of the West.

He remained for two or three months in Rome, settling the affairs
of Italy, exterminating the brood of Maxentius, giving magnificent
games in the Colosseum, laying the foundations of the Basilica of
St. Peter, and erecting a triumphal arch to himself—which, however, in the absence of contemporary talent, had to be adorned by
stripping the reliefs from the Arch of Trajan. He made Rome
obedient for the future by distributing the few remaining Prætorian
Guards among the frontier legions, and the efficacy of this measure
was proved by the absolute quiescence of the ancient capital during
the remainder of the century. While Constantine was spending the
rest of his energetic life on the frontiers, in civil war against his
rival Licinius, in founding his 'New Rome' on the Bosphorus, and in
effecting his memorable revolution in the religion of the Empire,
Old Rome relapsed into a state of inglorious peace, living on the
mere shadow and sound of her ancient greatness. Even the consuls
were no longer elected by the Roman rabble, but appointed by the
Emperor, wherever he happened to be, and their sole duty towards
their nominal capital was that of providing games in honour of
their election in the Flavian amphitheatre. All real power was in
the hands of the Prætorian Prefect, whose duties were to maintain
order, to preside at all meetings of the Senate and in his own
supreme court of justice, to see to the upkeep of the public works—
an immense item in such a city as Rome—and to superintend the
enormous distributions of free corn by which the poorer population
was fed and propitiated.

The condition of that population in Rome, and indeed in all
Italy, was, as far as we can now ascertain it, one of the utmost
degradation. Agriculture had been declining ever since the days of
the early Empire, owing partly to the crushing-out of the peasant
owner through the increase of large estates worked by slave labour,
partly to the regular importation of slave-grown corn from Sicily
and Africa. Towards the end of the fourth century a remission of
taxation was granted, on the ground of barrenness and depopula-
tion, to 330,000 acres in the province of Campania,[1] once the most
fertile region in Southern Italy. Meanwhile the imported corn was
used to feed the idle populace of Rome, and naturally the poorer

[1] Not to be confused with the so-called *Campagna*, the comparatively
barren district immediately around Rome.

inhabitants of the country flocked into the town to share this bounty, thus further denuding the soil of its proper cultivators. A glimpse into the life of Rome in the latter half of this century is given us by Ammianus Marcellinus, an honest officer of household troops who accompanied the Emperor Julian on his Persian campaign [362-3], and who, years afterwards, employed his leisure in writing the history of his times. His picture of the life of the Roman nobles is both curious and repulsive:

Followed by a train of fifty servants [he writes] and tearing up the pavement, they drive along the streets with the same impetuous speed as if they travelled with post horses; and the example of the Senators is boldly imitated by the matrons and ladies, whose covered carriages are continually driving around the immense space of the city and suburbs. . . . In their journeys into the country, the whole body of the household marches with their master. The baggage and wardrobe move in the front, and are immediately followed by a multitude of cooks and inferior servants, employed in the service of the kitchens and of the table. The main body is composed of a promiscuous crowd of slaves, increased by the accidental concourse of idle or dependent plebeians. The rear is closed by the favourite band of eunuchs, distributed from age to youth, according to the order of seniority. . . . When the lord has called for warm water, if a slave is tardy in his obedience, he is instantly chastised with three hundred lashes; but should the same slave commit a wilful murder, the master will mildly observe that he is a worthless fellow, but that if he repeats the offence he shall not go unpunished.

The same writer then describes how the idle populace spent their days lounging in the baths and open spaces, discussing nothing but the prospects of the coming races, swearing that the State would fall if this or that colour were victorious. The games indeed were still the one absorbing passion of Roman society, and although Constantine made some attempts to discourage the slaughter of gladiators in the arena, the practice continued right down to the end of the fourth century, and some writers think even far into the fifth.

Indeed, when we consider that besides the demoralizing effect of the games, the whole fabric of Roman society was rotten with slavery—that not only agriculture, but every industry in the towns and all domestic service was performed by slaves, and that the vices of the irresponsible upper class increased in proportion to their idleness, it is difficult to see any redeeming feature, any hope or promise in the Italy of the fourth century. Yet one new influence there was which seemed to contain the seed of better things. In the year 312, soon after the battle of the Milvian Bridge, Constantine had gone to Milan to meet his fellow-Emperor Licinius, and had there drawn up with him the celebrated Edict which gave peace to the Christians after the long and terrible persecution of Diocletian. Twelve years later, when he had crushed Licinius and become sole Emperor, he issued circular letters to the provinces calling upon all his subjects to embrace the religion of their ruler, and in 325 he summoned the famous Council of Nicæa to decide how that religion should truly be defined. The fourth century was therefore the first in which the Christian Church acquired political power, and it is interesting to see what effect the organization which embodied the new spirit of charity and brotherhood had on the existing social system. The final suppression of the gladiatorial shows is universally admitted to have been mainly the work of Christianity; the leaders of the Church constantly and vehemently denounced them as *sinful* (not merely as inhuman or brutalizing), forbade their flocks to attend the games under pain of exclusion from the Eucharist, and refused to admit into the Church any gladiator who would not swear to give up his profession. It is true that very many Christians failed to live up to these high standards, and the Fathers were continually complaining of the way in which the faithful could be seen flocking to the amphitheatres; but once the whole weight of the hierarchy was thrown into the scale against them, their suppression was only a question of time. It is said, indeed, that they were brought to a dramatic conclusion on the occasion of the Emperor Honorius' visit to Rome in 404, when the heroic monk Telemachus sprang into the arena to try and part the combatants, and perished under a shower of stones from the angry spectators.

In this direction, then, and generally in the higher value it succeeded in attaching to human life, the Church of the fourth century gave a real lift to the civilization of its day. In the fundamental abuse of slavery, however, it does not appear to have been of much service, though here again the Fathers always inculcated kindness to the slave as to a fellow man. But the Church did not attack the system as such, and the weakness of its attitude is seen in the very slight improvement in the laws regarding slaves under Constantine and his successors. A master was still at liberty to torture his slave to death, if he had no *intention* of killing him, and a slave was still incapable of contracting a legal marriage.

Perhaps indeed the main contribution of the Christian Church to the life of Italy at this time was the interest which it gradually aroused in its own internal affairs—in elections to the Papacy, and in the doings of certain of its great men. Since the abandonment of Rome by the Emperors the old interest in political matters had died away, and it seemed as though Rome would sink to producing nothing but gladiators and charioteers. Yet little by little the innate political sense of the Romans began to express itself anew in the ardour with which they threw themselves into ecclesiastical affairs. The Arian Controversy—the central event of the fourth century throughout the East—though it never succeeded in convulsing Italy, was yet of immense importance to the rising power of the Papacy, for the Bishops of Rome emerged from it with a character for spotless orthodoxy, and the city of Rome had had the honour of sheltering within her walls the great Athanasius himself, during his second exile from Alexandria [341]. More than this, we seem for the first time to catch the tone of true Papal haughtiness in the answer of Pope Liberius to the Arian Emperor Constantius, when the latter sent to demand that he should renounce communion with Athanasius [356]. Liberius replied by pronouncing a solemn anathema against all Arian heretics, by casting the Emperor's gifts out of St. Peter's as polluted offerings, and by choosing exile rather than submission. So vehement was the clamour which his banishment aroused in Rome that in the next year Constantius was compelled to allow him to return. Ten years later, the position of Bishop of Rome had become so much coveted that a disputed election, between Damasus and Ursicinus, produced a civil war [366] extending over many months, and the successful candidate, Damasus, waded to the Papal throne through the slaughter of hundreds of his rival's adherents in the basilicas of Rome.

But as yet the Papacy had produced no one commanding figure, for the great Jerome, long secretary to Pope Damasus, was disappointed in his hopes of succeeding his patron. The greatest Italian of the fourth century was, however, though not a Pope, a Churchman, for in 374 the clamorous voice of the Milanese called Ambrose, their civil governor, to fill the vacant Bishopric of Milan. In the character of Ambrose the virtues of the Roman administrator and of the Christian idealist are blended. A man of high rank himself, being the son of a Prætorian Prefect of the Gauls, he had all the knowledge of the world necessary for the manifold duties of his position, and this was no doubt of great assistance to him in his dealings with the 'Augusti' of Italy, whose residence at Milan frequently brought them into contact or conflict with their formidable Bishop. But in the most famous incidents of his life his Christian fervour—with all the limitations and exaltations of the fourth century—predominates over everything else. Now he is engaged in a bitter struggle with the Arian Empress-mother Justina for the possession of the basilicas of Milan, using such language as a later Pope might have used towards a rebellious Hohenstaufen; now he is prevailing upon the Emperor Theodosius to rescind an order he had issued for the punishment of certain riotous Christian monks in the East, who had destroyed a Jewish synagogue; now he is refusing, with a loftiness of soul that does him lasting honour, to hold communion with the Gaulish bishops who had ordered the execution of Priscilian—the first heretic to be put to death by Christian hands for the Christian faith which he held [385]. But, after all, Ambrose lives, and deserves to live, in the popular imagination by one episode alone—his infliction of penance on the great Theodosius for the massacre of Thessalonica [390]. In an access of rage the Emperor had sent the fatal order that the murder of the Governor of that city (a Goth named Botheric) should be avenged by an indiscriminate massacre, and seven thousand persons had been slaughtered at the games. No doubt the fact that the Governor had been an Arian heretic, while the Thessalonians were orthodox 'Romans,' had its full influence on the mind of Ambrose; but in any case his action was as bold as it was dramatic. Theodosius was at that moment at Milan, and Ambrose sternly exhorted him to repentance, declaring that he could not celebrate the Eucharist in the presence of one with so great a load of blood-guiltiness upon his head. The Emperor submitted, and in the newly built basilica which occupied the site of what is now the *Duomo* he humbled himself before the Christian Bishop, stripping himself of his Imperial insignia and imploring for absolution with many tears. It is the first of those memorable scenes of the abasement of the temporal before the spiritual power by which the Catholic Church has so well succeeded in striking the imagination of Europe.

So the life of Italy moved on in this last century of peace before the storm, its centres of interest gradually becoming wholly different from those of the old Imperial days. Emperors were proclaimed and died, but seldom came to visit Rome; the final division of the Empire into two parts, the East and the West, was effected under Valentinian I. and his brother Valens, without sensibly influencing the condition of Italy [365]; the campaigns on the Rhine, the Danube, or in Persia were discussed in the Baths of Caracalla much as we should discuss a 'little war' on the Indian Frontier. But at last an event occurred which must have been received even in Rome with a feeling akin to panic: it was the crushing defeat

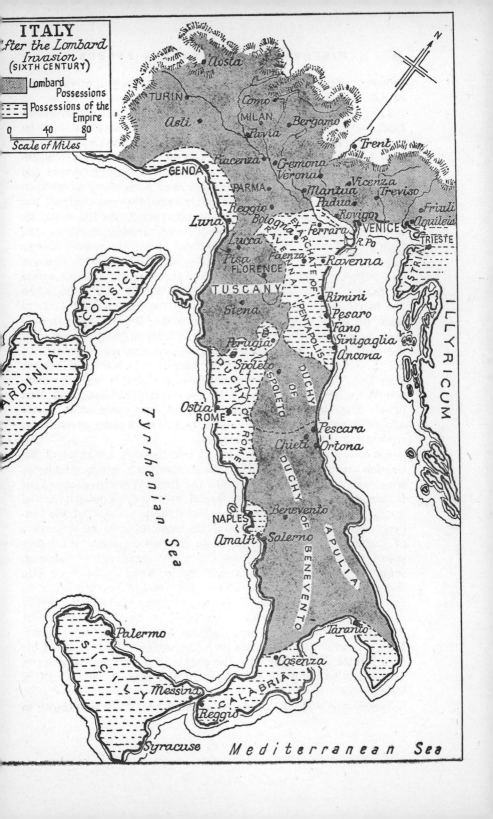

ITALY
after the Lombard
Invasion
(SIXTH CENTURY)

Lombard
Possessions
Possessions of the
Empire

0   40   80
Scale of Miles

N

Aosta
TURIN
Como
MILAN
Asti
Pavia
Bergamo
Trent
Piacenza
Cremona
Verona
Vicenza
Treviso
GENOA
PARMA
Mantua
Padua
Friuli
Reggio
Bologna
Rovigo
Aquileia
Luna
Ferrara
VENICE
TRIESTE
Lucca
Faenza
R. Po
Pisa
Ravenna
FLORENCE
TUSCANY
Rimini
Siena
Pesaro
Fano
Perugia
Sinigaglia
Spoleto
Ancona
CORSICA
SARDINIA
DUCHY OF ROME
DUCHY OF SPOLETO
PENTAPOLIS
EXARCHATE OF RAVENNA
ISTRIA
ILLYRICUM
Ostia
ROME
Pescara
Chieti
Ortona
Tyrrhenian Sea
NAPLES
Benevento
Amalfi
Salerno
DUCHY OF BENEVENTO
APULIA
Palermo
Taranto
Cosenza
SICILY
Messina
CALABRIA
Reggio
Syracuse
Mediterranean Sea

inflicted on the Emperor Valens by the Goths in 378, at the battle of Adrianople.

Long the standing menace of the Empire in Trajan's province of Dacia beyond the Danube, the Goths, who in their gradual migration had split into three—Visigoths, Ostrogoths, and Gepidæ—were now being hard pressed in their turn by the Huns; they had implored the Emperor Valens to grant them a passage across the Danube, and, once on the Roman side, had been stung to madness by the weak Emperor's faithless policy towards them, had gathered their forces in overwhelming numbers and annihilated him and his army under the walls of Adrianople. Fortunately, however, the barbarians did not use their victory well, though they were able to advance up to the very gates of Constantinople; and the Romans still possessed two leaders who were capable of stemming the tide of disaster. These were Gratian, son of Valentinian I., who, when the battle was fought, was already on the march from Gaul to assist his uncle Valens, and the good soldier Theodosius, son of a Spanish general of that name who had been unjustly beheaded at the order of Justina, Valentinian's widow, two years before the battle. These two now divided the Empire between them, all but Italy and Africa, which were already under Justina and her young son Valentinian II. Gratian took the West, Theodosius the East [379]. The Goths were partly harassed into submission, partly adopted into the body-politic and settled in the Balkan provinces as fœderati; and Italy breathed again.

But civil war brought her at length into the very vortex of affairs. Gratian was murdered in 383 by an usurper from Britain, Maximus, who, though at first content with the three Western 'dioceses' of Britain, Gaul, and Spain, soon began to covet the inheritance of young Valentinian, and in 387 invaded Italy and forced the Emperor, his mother and sisters to fly in terror to seek the protection of Theodosius. Theodosius gallantly married the sister of his suppliant, advanced through Pannonia to the head of the Adriatic, found the usurper Maximus shut up in Aquileia, besieged him there, captured and beheaded him. He restored Valentinian II. to the nominal Empire of the West, but left him really at the mercy of his barbarian army and of its Frankish chief, the ambitious Arbogast. When the time was ripe, Arbogast had his young master killed in some athletic games with the soldiers [392], invested his own secretary Eugenius with the purple, and sent ambassadors to Theodosius to acquaint him with the sad event of the death of Valentinian.

Theodosius bided his time, but at last he set forth once more to chastise the rebellious West [394], and this time, though the task was more difficult, he accomplished it more thoroughly. Again he crossed the spurs of the Julian Alps and saw the plain of Aquileia lying below him, but now it was filled with a vast army of Gauls and Franks, and in the first day's battle his ten thousand Visigoths, who bore the brunt of the fight, were almost annihilated. But on the next day the Emperor, miraculously assisted by a sudden storm of wind that sprang up behind him and blew the blinding dust in the faces of the Franks, drove all before him. The puppet-Emperor Eugenius was seized by some of his own soldiers and dragged before Theodosius, who allowed one of his guards to behead him in his presence. Arbogast the Frank fled into the mountains and there fell on his own sword, leaving the stage clear for the conqueror.

This battle between East and West was significant for many reasons, but perhaps chiefly for this, that it was the last struggle in Italy between Paganism and Christianity. The rhetorician Eugenius, otherwise a mere respectable nonentity, goes down to fame as the last Emperor who favoured the Olympian gods and allowed their worship to be celebrated with splendour in Rome. The altar of Victory, removed by the orthodox Gratian, was replaced in the Senate-house, and Eugenius set up, in the mountain passes by which Theodosius must march, bronze statues of Zeus armed with golden thunderbolts. But it was the last flicker of the Olympian lightning. Theodosius, the orthodox Spaniard, entered Rome, closed the newly opened temples, banished the priests, and extinguished the flame of Vesta. Paganism was condemned to live on underground, but it took its slow revenge on the new faith by bequeathing to it the spirit of polytheism, and after many days the rites of the ancient gods lived again in the worship of the saints.

So the great-hearted Theodosius conquered, reigned for four months alone, and died [395] in that very city of Milan which had witnessed his noble humiliation before St. Ambrose. He left the Roman world—though he knew it not—in the utmost peril. Only a strong man could have continued with success the policy he had so largely adopted of *using* the barbarians. Necessity had driven him to do so after the battle of Adrianople, but it is probable that he carried it too far. He loved his tall, fair-haired warriors, and among the ten thousand Visigoths whom he carried to the battle of the Julian Alps was a certain young chieftain of the name of Alaric. Most of the ten thousand were slain, but Alaric remained, and had cast his first glance upon the fair plains of Italy. And now the government of the world had passed into the hands of two spiritless boys, Arcadius at Constantinople, Honorius at Milan.

CHAPTER II

The Barbarian Invasions

THOUGH Theodosius himself was gone, he had bequeathed to his eleven-year-old son Honorius a guardian who, for thirteen years, made head against the enemies of Rome. This was the Vandal Stilicho, a soldier who had risen to fame and fortune under the fighting Emperor, had received his favourite niece, Serena, in marriage, had been appointed *Master of the Horse and Foot*, and was finally left as regent of the Western Empire. So long as he lived the Visigoths were held at bay, either by arms or by treaty; when he fell, Italy lay defenceless.

The first years of his reign were occupied in a cautious game of fence between himself and Alaric (now acknowledged King of the Visigoths), who had taken up an advantageous position for harassing either Empire in the north-western corner of Illyricum. In the year 400 the Gothic King invaded Northern Italy, but was eventually defeated by Stilicho and forced to retire again to his former point of vantage. Stilicho was inclined to treat with him and win him over to the service of the Empire, but his own position was beset with difficulties, for as a Vandal he was exposed to the jealous suspicion of Honorius' Italian courtiers, and the rise of an upstart Emperor in Gaul had forced him to withdraw the legions from the Rhine and so to let in a flood of new barbarians [407]. At length a mutiny broke out against him among the Roman legions at Pavia [408]. Stilicho fled to Ravenna, the lagoon city at the mouth of the Po, which was to be the Empire's last stronghold in Italy, but was there overtaken and beheaded by a troop of Imperial horse. Honorius had turned against his guardian, and had struck down the one bulwark that stood between Rome and the advancing tide.

Scarcely had the news of the murder reached the Gothic camp than Alaric set his army in motion, marched by the well-known route into Venetia, and this time struck straight for Rome. He did not waste men in an attack on the strong walls built by Aurelian against the Allemanni a hundred and forty years before, and repaired since his first invasion, but immediately sat down to enforce a strict blockade. He soon had the city at his mercy, for no help came from the Imperial coward at Ravenna, and when the swarming population of Rome was almost reduced to cannibalism the Senate sent forth an humble embassy to enquire the besieger's terms. The Goth simply demanded all the gold and silver in the city, all the precious movables, all the barbarian slaves. 'What then,' asked the horrified ambassadors, 'do you intend to leave us?' 'Your lives,' replied in disdain the honest conqueror. He was prevailed upon, however, to modify his demands to a more manageable figure, and on the receipt of 5,000 pounds of gold, 30,000 of silver, 3,000 scarlet hides, 4,000 silken tunics, and 3,000 pounds of pepper, he and his chieftains consented to raise the siege.

Then ensued a period of wearisome negotiations with Honorius, who would consent to none of the terms of peace proposed by Alaric, even though the Senate implored him to do so; and at last, when a conference to which he had been summoned at Rimini proved fruitless, Alaric lost patience, and returned to lay siege to Rome once more [409]. But this time the Senate was quite willing to come to terms, without any reference to Honorius, and accepted his request that the Prætorian Prefect Attalus should be·raised to the purple as his puppet-Emperor. An embassy was sent to Honorius to acquaint him with the fact, and he, who had just signed away Spain, Gaul, and Britain to the usurper Constantine, cheerfully acquiesced in this new insult. But Attalus was a Greek, and in his heart despised the yellow-haired barbarians, so that Alaric found his puppet growing more and more unsatisfactory. At last, after a ten months' reign, he summoned him to his camp at Rimini, and there formally degraded him in sight of the Gothic veterans whom he had slighted. The diadem and purple robe were sent to Honorius, and it seemed as though the last obstacle to a reconciliation had been removed. But with incredible folly Honorius still rejected all Alaric's fairest offers, and nothing was left to the barbarian but to turn south once more and wreak his vengeance in grim earnest on the Eternal City.

He had not long to wait. Probably the Senate again tried negotiation, but this time in vain, and within a few days of his arrival his men found a weak spot at the Salarian Gate, and broke in by it in irresistible swarms [Aug. 24, 410]. They set on fire the Palace of Sallust near the gate and then spread over the city to plunder and kill. But the meagre accounts of the sack which have survived expressly tell us that no systematic massacre was organized and that Alaric gave strict orders to his men to respect the right of sanctuary in Christian churches. The basilicas of St. Peter and St. Paul especially were soon filled with a panic-sticken crowd of refugees, who remained there in trembling safety during the three days' sack that Alaric allowed his army. But over the rest of the city the Goths roamed unchecked, giving vent to all those native passions which had been so painfully repressed during the marchings and countermarchings of the last two years. Temples, palaces, and private houses were ransacked for their treasures, no doubt with a joyous accompaniment of killing and outrage which had been too long denied to these half-tamed Teutons. St. Augustine, who saw and conversed with many of the fugitives in Carthage, speaks of 'so great a carnage that the bodies could not even be buried,' but on the whole the ecclesiastical writers—practically our sole authorities for the events of the sack—dwell more upon the mitigations of its horrors produced by the barbarians' awe of Christianity than upon those horrors themselves. At any rate it seems clear that no very great destruction of buildings occurred, for the burning of the Palace of Sallust is the only specific case mentioned by any contemporary historian. Yet the mere fact of the fall of the sacred city was sufficient to produce the direst consternation throughout Christendom. A multitude of fugitives who had fled both before and after the siege spread themselves over all parts of the Mediterranean coast. St. Jerome in his cave at Bethlehem gave shelter and commiseration to a large band of exiles, once members of the proudest families in Rome, now wanderers reduced to beggary. The pagans vehemently declared that the catastrophe was due to the insults heaped upon the ancient gods, and their clamour became so loud that Augustine himself was moved to answer them in his great work of Christian apologetics, *The City of God*.

Meanwhile the authors of all this panic and upheaval marched leisurely south along the Appian Way, encumbered with a long train of treasure-laden wagons and a horde of new-made slaves. Alaric probably intended to cross by Sicily to Africa and chastise the Governor of that province, who had been withholding the supplies of corn from Rome, ever since the unlucky Attalus had been raised to the purple. But he advanced no farther than the toe of Italy. There fever seized him, and he died, and his warriors turned aside the waters of the stream Busento, and buried him in its stony bed. They killed the slaves who dug the grave, that no human lip might betray the secret of his burial-place, and the bones of Alaric still rest unknown, far from his home by the broad Danube, beneath the murmur of that slender southern stream.

Among the high-born captives whom the Goths carried with them from Rome was the princess Galla Placidia, daughter of the great Theodosius and half-sister of Honorius. This maiden of eighteen was beloved by Athaulf, Alaric's brother-in-law, whom the Goths now proclaimed as King in place of the dead chieftain. Abandoning Alaric's scheme for invading Africa, Athaulf remained for nearly two years in Italy, and then marched north [412] and across the Maritime Alps into Gallia Narbonensis, the future Provence. There he settled down with his nation and married his fair captive [414], thus uniting the noblest houses of 'Gothia' and 'Romania.' But within a year [415] they were wandering again, this time over the Pyrenees into Spain; their infant son Theodosius died, Athaulf was murdered, and his successor sent the widowed queen back with great pomp to the borders of Gaul, and there consigned her to the care of Rome. Behind her the Visigothic kingdom was soon firmly established on both sides of the Pyrenees, from the Loire to the Mediterranean, there to do good service when the time came against the invading hordes of the Huns.

After two years of widowhood Placidia married the general Constantius, Honorius' latest favourite, and by him became the mother of the last and most worthless emperor of the Theodosian line, Valentinian III., and of that princess Honoria of whom the legend runs that her ring summoned Attila, the Scourge of God, to be her champion against Christendom.

Honorius dragged out his futile existence until 423, and after a brief usurpation on the part of one Joannes, Placidia was restored by the troops of the Eastern court, and reigned at Ravenna for five-and-twenty years in the name of her son Valentinian. Her memory pervades the beautiful dead city of the marshes, for she gathered to her court many holy men and many skilful workers in mosaic; and though much of her work has perished, here and there some gem-like fragment remains to give the traveller of today a glimpse of the piety and taste of that distant age. So important a part, indeed, does Ravenna play in the troublous century of which we are now speaking, that it may be well to try to reconstruct some image of the watery stronghold which Honorius first made the seat of Imperial government. In the first place Ravenna was then, as Venice is now, a city of lagoons, for at high tide the sea still flooded her streets, and at low tide they were filled with the muddy waters of the Po, one branch of which swept round the walls, while another flowed through the city in a maze of canals. But the steady deposit of mud brought down by the sluggish river has in the course of centuries raised the whole level of that coast, so that now Ravenna stands high and dry, and the Adriatic can only be seen —six miles away—from the tops of the highest *campanili*. In

Placidia's day, too, the town was connected by a causeway with the port and arsenal of Classis, built by Augustus as the head-quarters of the Adriatic fleet, and still a flourishing harbour-town as late as the ninth century. Go to it now, and you will find only the colossal sixth-century church of Sant' *Apollinare in Classe*, tenanted by one solitary custodian, while all around stretches the dead-flat marsh, green in spring with the rice-crops raised by the patient Romagnuols, and on the seaward side the view is closed by the black line of the Pineta. A melancholy place, fit to be connected in our minds with the passing away of an old order. For the days of the Empire of the West were numbered, and the reign of Galla Placidia sheds but a fitful light of peace and civilization over its closing years.

She died at Rome in 450, on the eve of the new storm. Her reign had been remarkable for two things—the conquest of Africa by the Vandals, a Teutonic people which in the general loosening of the nations had gradually pressed southward from its home by the Baltic across Gaul and the Pyrenees into Spain: and the rise to power of the general Aëtius, 'the last of the Romans.' This man had gained his experience in long warfare against the Visigothic king-dom of Southern Gaul, but he was now confronted by a far greater danger, and had the wit to combine with his brave foes to ward it off. The Huns, that foul and savage people which inspired a greater sense of horror and disgust among their contemporaries than any other of the wandering nations, were on the move once more, and in their long march of 350 years from the north of China had now reached the gates of Roman Gaul. For seventy years they had been established in Dacia (the modern Roumania and Transylvania), having thence, as we have seen, driven out the Visigoths, and for eighteen they had been ruled by one of those born conquerors who, like Alexander, Akbar, Napoleon, appear from time to time and 'haste stormfully across the astonished earth.' Attila made his power felt as far as the islands of the Baltic in the North, China in the East, Persia in the South-East, while towards the court of Constantinople under the feeble Theodosius II. his attitude was that of an insulting bully. Now, in 450, on the accession of a more manly Emperor at Byzantium, the soldier Marcian, Attila turned his thoughts towards an easier prey, the crumbling Empire of the West. Declaring as one of his pretexts for invasion that he was the betrothed of the princess Honoria, and as such claimed half the dominions of her brother Valentinian, he set his hordes in motion in the spring of 451, but for some obscure reason marched for the

THE MAUSOLEUM OF GALLA PLACIDIA, RAVENNA

Rhine, not Italy, and burst with irresistible force into North-Eastern Gaul.

Unopposed he pressed on as far as Orleans, but there received his first check at the hands of Aëtius and the Visigoths; and it was during his retreat from this city that Aëtius and his allies—Visigoths, Franks, Armoricans, and Burgundians, came up with him in the Catalaunian Plain, between the Seine and the Aube, and there crippled him with so immense a slaughter that he was glad to retire in safety across the Rhine. He returned to his stronghold in Hungary for the winter, meditating schemes of revenge; the Goths marched south to their new capital, Toulouse; Aëtius to Italy.

With the spring of 452, Attila was again in motion, and this time he made for Italy. Marching by the road across the Julian Alps which had already served Theodosius and Alaric, he found his passage barred by the strong fortress of Aquileia, and was obliged to stop and lay siege to it. The garrison which Aëtius had placed there resisted bravely, but at last the Huns battered in the walls, burst into the trembling town, and destroyed it so completely that it was practically blotted out from the map of Italy. The same destruction was meted out to three more cities and probably many nameless villages along the Venetian coast; and it is no wonder that at the news of his approach the panic-striken peasants fled in hot haste to that group of lagoon-guarded islands which was one day to be Venice. Attila passed on unopposed into Lombardy, marching along the foot of the Alps as far as Bergamo, and then down through Milan and Pavia to the Po, but there, strangely enough, he turned eastwards again, as though in doubt whether to press on to Rome or no. While in this state of indecision he was met on the banks of the Mincio by an illustrious embassy from Rome, headed by Bishop Leo—the first of those grand mediæval Popes with whose imposing figures we shall make a nearer acquaintance later on. Whether the barbarian was in truth awed by Leo's saintly presence, whether there were rumours that Aëtius was bestirring himself in his rear, or whether the mysterious fate of Alaric filled his successor with a vague dread, the result of the interview was that Attila retired from Italy. And all who have visited the *stanze* of Raphael in the Vatican will remember the famous legend which represents the defenders of the Holy See, St. Peter and St. Paul, appearing in the air with naked swords to ward off the barbarian from the Sacred City.

Thus Italy was saved from utter ruin, for in the next year Attila was cut off by an untimely death on the night of his nuptials with the damsel Ildico, and his empire immediately fell to pieces under

C

the numerous sons whom he left to contest the sovereignty. As soon as the danger was passed away, the wretched Emperor Valentinian plucked up the courage to rid himself of the man whom he had only tolerated so long as he had need of him—Aëtius; he enticed him into his palace at Rome, and there murdered him with his own hand [454]. But Aëtius was soon avenged, for three months afterwards two soldiers of the Emperor's guard, favourites of the dead general, stabbed Valentinian as he was watching the games in the Campus Martius, and not a hand was lifted to defend him. Worthless as he was, however, his death had a sensible effect in hastening the next catastrophe of Rome. Since the retreat of the Huns the most formidable disturbers of the Roman peace had been the Vandals, whose conquest of Africa under their King Gaiseric had been the chief event of Placidia's reign. This very savage race was now let loose upon Rome by the folly of Valentinian's successor, the elderly official Petronius Maximus, who insulted the dead Emperor's widow Eudoxia by forcing her to marry him within a month of her husband's death. In despair the proud Empress—herself a daughter of Theodosius II.—appealed to Gaiseric, and the astute Vandal needed no second summons. Just three months after the accession of Maximus the barbarian fleet arrived at Ostia [June, 455], and at the news the mob of Rome rose in wild fury, assaulted the Imperial palace, and tore the hapless Emperor limb from limb. Once more the defence of the city was undertaken by Pope Leo, but this time with only partial success. Gaiseric agreed that there should be no killing and no torturing of the captives to make them reveal their treasures, but whether these promises were kept or not, the Vandals certainly enjoyed a fourteen days' pillage of the defenceless town, and loaded their galleys at leisure with the spoils which Alaric had left. They bore away with them to Carthage not only the Empress Eudoxia and her two daughters, but also the sacred vessels of the Temple of Jerusalem which Titus had brought in triumph to Rome, and a good half of the gilded copper tiles of the Temple of Jupiter Capitolinus.

The period of twenty-one years between Gaiseric's sack of Rome and the fall of the Western Empire is that to which posterity usually applies the name of the Phantom Emperors. It is an epithet that well suggests the mockery to which the Roman Empire had now sunk, though no doubt the full-blooded individuals to whom it is applied felt their own struggles to be hot and living enough. It is not our intention to enter into the details of their brief careers; but it may be well to state their names, their dates, and the manner in which they were severally driven from the stage. First, then, came the Gallo-Roman Avitus [August, 455—October, 456], made Emperor by the Visigoths and accepted by the Senate in the chaos which succeeded the retreat of Gaiseric; he was deposed after a reign of fourteen months by the 'Patrician' Ricimer, a general of Suevo-Visigothic origin who had lately risen to the command of the forces. For sixteen years after the fall of Avitus, Ricimer wielded the supreme power in the State; a bold and unscrupulous soldier of fortune, playing only for his own hand, he was yet Rome's sole bulwark against the Vandal, and never permitted while he lived another descent in force upon her coasts. He made and unmade successively three Emperors: (1) Majorian, soldier and lawgiver [457—461], whose care for the harassed provincials sheds the one gleam of good government over this troubled epoch; he was however deposed and put to death at Ricimer's order on his return from an unsuccessful expedition against the Vandals; (2) Severus, an absolute cipher, of whom it can only be said that he was made Emperor in November, 461, and died either naturally or by poison in 465; (3) Anthemius [467—472], a distinguished Byzantine general whom Ricimer accepted from the hands of the Eastern Emperor Leo in return for a solid contribution in ships and men towards a great expedition against the Vandals; he quarrelled with Ricimer in 471, was besieged by him in Rome and put to death, July, 472. At the time of the siege Ricimer had already proclaimed a fourth Emperor—Olybrius, a Roman Senator who had married one of the daughters of the exiled Empress Eudoxia; but he did not live to destroy him, for he was himself carried off by a sudden illness but a month after he had slain Anthemius. Three more phantoms are still to pass before Italy will have learnt to acknowledge a barbarian ruler under his own name, without the expensive fiction of an Emperor to cover his actions.

On the death of Olybrius, two months after that of his patron, a long delay occurred before the Byzantine court again decided to send its nominee, one Julius Nepos, to assume the government of the West. In the interval, the Burgundian auxiliaries, headed by a nephew of Ricimer, had raised *their* puppet, a certain Glycerius, to the throne; but when Nepos landed at the port of Rome in the spring of 474 the poor puppet willingly submitted to be consecrated with the episcopal oil and sent to Illyricum as Bishop of Salona. His successor reigned but fourteen months, after which he too fell a victim to the commander of his troops, the 'Patrician' Orestes, and was forced to fly from Ravenna to that very city of Salona to which he had consigned his predecessor. There he lived on for five years in a state of precarious royalty, while the last act in the drama of the Western Empire was being performed across the Adriatic.

Orestes, a man of some courage and ability, who in the course of a varied career had once been Attila's Secretary of State, kept the allegiance of his turbulent troops—the real masters of Italy— for just a year from the flight of Nepos, and caused them to acclaim as Emperor his young son, Romulus. They nicknamed him August-ulus, and so it happens that the handsome boy who closed the long line of Roman Emperors united in himself the names of the first King and of the first Emperor of Rome. The immediate cause of his downfall was a demand on the part of the troops to have one third of the land of Italy made over to them—a demand which Orestes flatly refused. They mutinied against him, choosing for their chief a young barbarian adventurer named Odovacar; besieged him in Pavia, captured the town, and dispatched the luckless Patrician [Aug., 476]. Romulus was found cowering at Ravenna, but the conqueror spared his life and assigned to him the beautiful villa reared long ago by Lucullus on the Bay of Naples, with a liberal allowance for his youthful needs. One thing only was required of him: to signify his abdication to the Senate, and to authorize that body to send the Imperial insignia to Constantinople, with a humble message to the Emperor Zeno stating that in future one Emperor would be sufficient both for East and West.

CHAPTER III

The Kingdom of Theodoric

THE tall barbarian who had thus risen with little trouble to be ruler in Italy was sprung from one of the lesser Teutonic tribes which had owned the sway of Attila, and had then won their freedom at his death. The son of a Scyrian chief named Edécon, Odovacar lives in history as the first man who had the courage to brush away the fiction of a Western Empire, while keeping tight hold on the substance of Imperial authority. He had called himself king even before the murder of Orestes, but being anxious to stand well with Byzantium he sent the above-mentioned embassy to the Emperor Zeno, together with a request that the latter would bestow on him the title of Patrician. Zeno had no wish to quarrel with the leader of so many seasoned warriors, but with true Byzantine trickery he declared that such a title was not his to give while the rightful Emperor of the West, Julius Nepos, still lived; and at the same time addressed the letter in which he stated this opinion 'to the Patrician Odovacar.' More than this shadowy recognition Odovacar never received, but his relations with Byzantium were not unfriendly for the first ten years of his reign, since he refrained from all aggressive acts, and Zeno's vanity had no doubt been flattered by the gift of the Imperial insignia.

Within his new kingdom Odovacar's first action was to make his promised grant to the troops of one third of the land of Italy. This was in reality but an extension of the existing right of the soldiers to occupy one third of the houses in which they were quartered; but it was naturally not carried out without a great deal of discontent on the part of the ousted proprietors—a discontent which bore evil fruit for Odovacar in his time of need. For the rest, he upheld all the elaborate machinery of Roman government, and made use of certain excellent ministers, such as Cassiodorus senior, Pelagius, and Liberius; he ruled in fact as one of the later Emperors might have wished to rule—by the arms of barbarians over a peaceful and tax-paying land. Yet he is branded as 'tyrannus' by all Roman writers; unwelcomed by the Italian people, unacknowledged by the Eastern Emperor, his throne was secure only so long as Byzantium had not the strength or the opportunity to crush him; and that breathing space did not even last his lifetime.

For after the Visigoths and the Vandals, it was now the turn of the next great Teutonic invaders, the Ostrogoths, to descend upon Italy, and to found there a kingdom whose splendour and whose fall have made it one of the grand tragedies of history. Long subject to the all-conquering Huns, the Ostrogoths had actually fought against their Visigothic brethren at the battle of the Catalaunian Plain, but on the break-up of Attila's empire they had won for themselves the region of Pannonia, between Danube and Save, and under their kings of the god-descended 'Amal' lineage had proved troublesome neighbours enough to the Empire of the East. At last, after one of their fierce raids across the Save, the Emperor Leo agreed to pay them all their arrears of tribute on condition that the sole heir to their kingship, a boy of seven named Theodoric, should be sent as hostage to Constantinople [461]. Thus for ten years the future King lived at the court of Byzantium, much favoured by the Emperor, learning the value of civilization and its ways, but yet too true a Goth to waste his time in bookish studies. Years afterwards, when he had come into his kingdom, he used to trace his signature through a gold plate perforated with the letters THEO, and there is no evidence that he ever knew how to read.

He returned home in 471, became sole king of the Goths three years later, transferred his people's quarters to the rich land at the mouth of the Danube [474], and lived for fourteen years on terms of uneasy neighbourhood with Byzantium—now in high favour at court, now burning and harrying up to the very gates of Constantinople. Zeno bestowed on him the titles of Patrician and Consul, and at last, in 488, the much-harassed Emperor bethought him of the old expedient of setting one barbarian to crush another. 'He exhorted Theodoric,' says Procopius, 'to march to Italy, and coming to grips with Odovacar, to win the western kingdom for himself and the Goths.' Theodoric closed with the offer, set forth in the late autumn of 488 with his whole people,—amounting perhaps to 250,000 souls,—beat the Gepidæ on the way in his own old lair between Drave and Save, and in August, 489, descended on the Isonzo, the frontier of Italy, and there found Odovacar and his host drawn up to dispute the passage.

It cost the Goths four years of war to subdue the 'tyrant' Odovacar, but at length he was driven within the walls of Ravenna and there closely besieged. Finally he surrendered in February, 493, on suspiciously liberal terms. Not only was his life assured to him; he was to share the kingdom with Theodoric. The conqueror entered the impregnable city, invited his fallen foe to a banquet at the palace, and there with his own hand dealt him so true a blow that he fell cleft from collar-bone to hip. 'Why, the wretch cannot have had a bone in his body,' laughed Theodoric in glee, while his followers joyously made an end of Odovacar's bodyguard.

But, the tyrant safely disposed of, Theodoric's native barbarity was put under restraint, and he devoted all his energies to the pacification of the country. He was anxious to obtain recognition from Byzantium and sent an embassy to Zeno to ask for the 'royal apparel,' but Zeno died at this juncture and it was not until four years later [497] that Theodoric obtained from the new Emperor Anastasius the 'ornaments of the palace,' which Odovacar had dispatched to Constantinople. No Imperial attributes, however, were conferred by this gift, and Theodoric lived and died a mere 'King' of the Ostrogoths, with the additional title of 'Patrician' under the Roman Emperor. So far his position hardly differed from that of Odovacar, but the superior genius of the Ostrogoth built from these elements a remarkable structure, the Gothic Kingdom of Italy, which became the admiration of his contemporaries and has continued ever since to excite the interest and curiosity of the historian.

Theodoric took up his residence at Ravenna, where the noble church of Sant' Appollinare Nuovo, a fragment of his palace, and the massive mausoleum which he built to contain his bones still remain as memorials of his rule. Odovacar's best ministers were invited to serve under his successor; and a commission with Liberius at its head proceeded to carry out the arduous task of settling the Gothic veterans on the land of Italy. This was done as far as possible according to the military divisions of the host—by families, 'hundreds,' and 'thousands,' so that the cohesion of the nation should not be broken by too scattered a distribution. The land they occupied was the 'third part' already seized by Odovacar's men, and now for the most part left vacant by the death of its owners; but as the Goths exceeded Odovacar's partisans in numbers it was also necessary to make a further division between Goth and Roman. The newcomers of course took possession of the 'coloni' or serfs whom they found upon the land. Their settlement was thickest in the east, the centre, and the Lombard Plain, but they maintained garrisons in Sicily and throughout the south, and held the Dalmatian coast in considerable force.

Theodoric's reign in Italy lasted three-and-thirty years, from 493 to 526, and seemed on the surface to be the dawn of a new era of prosperity and strength for the unhappy country. Even a pro-Byzantine historian admits that 'the Romans called him a second Trajan or Valentinian, in whose footsteps he followed.' The abiding

note of his rule was *justice*—justice towards Goth and Roman, towards Jew, Arian, and Catholic; and the success of this policy for
the first thirty years perhaps blinded its author to the hollowness
of his real position. For in truth Theodoric was strong only so long
as Byzantium was weak—and we may add, so long as the Churches
of Rome and Byzantium were divided by the feud of Arian and
Catholic, as was the case until the accession of a Catholic Emperor in 518. Till then the Arian King of Italy could afford to
despise the Papacy, unsupported as it was by the Byzantine Emperor. In 498, in fact, the King was called in, Arian though he was,
to arbitrate between two rival candidates to the Papal throne. In
other matters also his undertakings prospered, and in 500 he made
a triumphal progress to Rome, harangued the people in the Forum,
presided at the games in the Circus Maximus, and renewed the
distributions of corn,—sure roads all to the favour of the Roman
mob. More enduring monuments of his visit were the repairing of
the walls and the Imperial palace, for which he authorized the use
of twenty-five thousand bricks a year; the partial draining of the
Pontine Marshes, and (probably) the issue of the famous *Edictum
Theodorici*, an abbreviated code of Roman law, taken mainly from
the Code of Theodosius II., and intended, as the epilogue states,
'for the common benefit of all, whether Barbarian or Roman.' Thus
was the rude Goth brought within the sway of civilization, for
even in cases between Goth and Goth the Edict was the standard,
while for the Roman population the Roman law was left in its full
vigour.

It was soon after this memorable visit to Rome that Theodoric
took as his chief minister the younger Cassiodorus, a man whose
name is inseparably associated with that of the great King in this
earnest attempt to make barbarian rule acceptable to the Italians.
In his office of *Quæstor* Cassiodorus was practically Theodoric's
Secretary of State, and when we remember that not only was the
King unlettered, but that Latin was a foreign tongue to him, it will
easily be seen how important such a post could be made. Fortunately, however, the interpreter-secretary was an honest man, and
in the invaluable collection of his official letters which has survived[1]
we see through all the amiable verbiage of the writer how sincere
was his longing that Goth and Roman should live together in peace
and good fellowship, how deep was his sense of Italy's good fortune
in having found a master like Theodoric. Cassiodorus lived on to
serve Theodoric's daughter and grandson, and the first of the more

[1] The *Variæ Epistolæ*, collected and edited by Cassiodorus himself about
538. See T. Hodgkin's condensed translation: *The Letters of Cassiodorus.*

democratic kings whom bad times called to the surface; but when the long and bitter war had fairly begun, when his dream of a kingdom of Italy had been finally shattered, the old statesman retired to his native Calabria, and there on the heights of Squillace built a spacious monastry, known as *Vivarium* from the artificial fish-ponds which supplied its food. For already the saintly Benedict had established his 'rule' at Monte Cassino, the mother of western monasticism and so provided for Cassiodorus a model for his own foundation. But the ex-minister of Theodoric was not satisfied with the contemplative religious life alone, and laid posterity under an inestimable debt of gratitude by the rule which he laid down that his monks were to spend a part of each day in copying, adorning, and binding the works of ancient writers, both Pagan and Christian. 'To this simple but brilliant idea,' writes Professor Bury, 'of taking advantage of the unemployed energy that ran to seed in monastic society for the spread and transmission of learning, both profane and sacred, we owe the survival of the great bulk of our Latin literature.' Cassiodorus lived on for five-and-thirty years in his happy retirement at Squillace, leaving a local as well as a European fame. A Calabrian magnate of the Napoleonic era was wont to speak of him with fond familiarity as '*quel gran signorone.*'[1]

Theodoric's affairs prospered both within and without his Italian kingdom, for among the barbarian tribes beyond the Alps his prestige stood very high, and by an elaborate system of intermarriages he connected himself with nearly all their ruling families. Thus he himself married the sister of Clovis the Frank, and gave his own to the King of the Vandals; one daughter was married to the King of the Visigoths, another to the future King of the Burgundians. But when in spite of these alliances the treacherous Frank overran and nearly wiped out the Visigothic kingdom of Toulouse [509] Theodoric stepped in and saved the remnant, and thenceforward exercised a substantial protectorate over his grandson Amalaric's dominions in Spain and along the coast of Gaul. Yet even at the height of his power, when he was obeyed from Gibraltar to the Danube and from Dalmatia to Sicily, the old King must have sighed for a son to whom to leave his crown. He had but one legitimate child, his daughter Amalasuntha; the husband whom he chose for her, a distant kinsman of the Amal lineage, died young, and one baby grandson was all that Theodoric had to look to as the inheritor of his Italian kingdom.

[1] This was G. Pepe's father. *Mems. of Gen. Pepe*, ch. xvii.

And in truth the outlook had suddenly grown dark and sullen as the great Ostrogoth drew towards his end. The Emperor Justin, who had ascended the Byzantine throne in 518, and still more his famous nephew Justinian, were bent on undermining Theodoric's position in Italy, and to this end concluded first a close alliance with the Papacy, and then proceeded to enter into correspondence with the malcontents in the Roman Senate. Of these there appear to have been an increasing number. Never heartily reconciled to the barbarian rule, the haughty nobles of Rome had always been the most difficult of Theodoric's subjects to deal with, and now found a willing listener for all their grievances in the crafty Justinian. In 524 a conspiracy was discovered, made memorable to posterity by its implications to Boëthius, the 'Last of the Ancients.' Whether Boëthius had in truth been intriguing with Byzantium, he was thrown into prison at Pavia, and there in the long months of his captivity wrote his famous book, *The Consolation of Philosophy*, which became the most popular philosophical work of the Middle Ages. Already by his translations from Aristotle he had assured the survival of the Greek philosophy, as Cassiodorus had assured the survival of the Latin classics; but the fate of Boëthius was more tragic than that of his great contemporary. He was condemned to death by the Senate at Theodoric's command, together with his father-in-law Symmachus, and probably executed under circumstances of atrocious barbarity.

These two judicial murders were closely followed by an equally calamitous adventure. Exasperated at the news that the Emperor was initiating a new and severe persecution of the Arians—his own co-religionists—Theodoric in anger summoned the Pope to Ravenna and ordered him to proceed immediately to Constantinople, accompanied by a suitable embassy, to inform the Emperor that unless he made reparations to the Arians he would himself wreak his vengeance on the Catholics of Italy. The Pope, scared and browbeaten, departed on his mission [525], effected something with the Emperor, but in Theodoric's view not enough, for on his return he was thrown into prison at Ravenna, and there, to the horror of all men, died [May, 526]. It was the deathstroke to Theodoric's already crumbling reputation. Soured and disappointed, his work of reconciliation wasted, haunted, it is said, by remorse for the death of Symmachus and Boëthius, the old King felt his end approaching. But, mindful at the last of those true foundations of his greatness which he seemed but now to have forgotten, he summoned the Gothic nobles round him, and after presenting to them their boy-king Athalaric, exhorted them all to live in peace with the Roman Senate and the

Emperor. Then he expired, and two generations had scarcely passed away before the Catholics were gravely consigning his soul to the burning crater of Lipari.

The history of the next nine years is bound up with that of the princess Amalasuntha, mother of the eight-year-old king, and it forms the first chapter in the downfall of the Gothic kingdom. An extremely able and gifted woman, speaking Greek and Latin as fluently as Gothic, Amalasuntha was the embodiment of the Romanizing spirit which had influenced a section of the Goths, but in proportion as she Romanized she lost the confidence of her only real support, the Gothic people. She brought up her son Athalaric more as a student than as a Teutonic hero-king, until at last (probably in 532) the Gothic nobles at Ravenna broke out into angry remonstrance, and insisted on withdrawing him from his mother's tutelage and on giving him Gothic youths of his own age as his companions. The boy thus became a rallying-point against his mother for the leaders of the nationalist party. Their hostility threw Amalasuntha more and more into the arms of Justinian. She sent to inquire from the Emperor whether in case of need Theodoric's daughter might obtain from him a safe asylum, but at the same time she planned a bold and terrible stroke for regaining her own ascendancy at home. Three Gothic nobles of the highest rank were simultaneously murdered by her orders [533]; and it seemed as if Amalasuntha would succeed in riding the storm. But her triumph was short-lived. Athalaric, worn out by drunkenness and vice, died at the age of sixteen [October, 534], and even the daughter of Theodoric could scarcely claim as yet to reign in her own right over a nation to whom the 'monstrous regiment of women' was a thing unknown. To strengthen her position she summoned to Ravenna the only male offshoot of the royal house still living, her cousin Theodahad, and formally proposed to him to share her throne, on condition that he should only be King in name, while she continued to govern as before. Theodahad accepted the proposal, but once the formal letters announcing the event were despatched to Justinian, the new King began to make common cause with the kinsmen of the three murdered nobles. After a few month of hollow partnership he had the Queen seized and carried off to a lonely island rising out of the lake of Bolsena, and, while protesting to Justinian that not a hair of her head should be touched, he secretly allowed her enemies to follow her and fulfil their revenge. They crossed over to the island stronghold, brushed past the cowardly guards, and murdered Amalasuntha in her bath [535].

These events had been closely followed and turned to account by the busy brain of Justinian. On hearing of the imprisonment of Amalasuntha he had sent an ambassador to Italy to assure her of his especial protection, and now at the news of her death, posing as champion of the murdered Queen, he declared war on Theodahad, for it happened that just at this moment Justinian found himself in a better position for offensive war than any Byzantine Emperor since Theodosius. He had discovered a great general, by name Belisarius, who had returned only the year before from the conquest and extinction of the Vandal kingdom of Africa, and was now free to turn his arms against the usurpers of Italy. Belisarius landed in Sicily in the summer of 535 and was soon master of the whole island.

Early in the next year he advanced northwards through Calabria, welcomed as a deliverer by the population, but at Naples he encountered a determined resistance from garrison and people combined. Still Belisarius made himself master of the town, and the loss of Naples spurred the Gothic people into action. At an armed assembly on the Pontine Marshes the cowardly Theodahad was declared deposed and a simple warrior named Vitigis acclaimed as King [August, 536]. Theodahad fled from Rome towards Ravenna, but was overtaken and killed on the Flaminian Way; and the new King, leaving but a slender garrison in Rome, decided to retire and concentrate his forces at Ravenna. But behind his back the Pope invited Belisarius into the city, and the Gothic garrison, too weak even to check his advance, marched out by the Flaminian Gate as Belisarius entered by the Asinarian [December, 536].

Too late did Vitigis perceive his mistake in letting Rome slip so easily, and in March, 537, he advanced against it with every available man that he could muster, amounting in all, says Procopius, to 150,000 horse and foot. The long siege of Rome that followed was made distastrous for future ages by the cutting of the aqueducts— a measure of war by which Vitigis hoped to reduce the garrison, but which turned his camping-ground instead into a malarious marsh. By that one fatal deed the Goths did more to plunge Rome into the squalor of the Middle Ages than all their good government had done to avert it. Belisarius conducted the defence with admirable skill, and Justinian was sufficiently aware of the importance of Rome to dispatch reinforcements to his lieutenant before it was too late. By December, five thousand men had arrived at Ostia; Belisarius made an energetic *sortie* to divert the enemy's attention from them, and the next day consented to receive an embassy from the discouraged Goths to enquire the Emperor's terms of peace. In vain the envoys reminded Belisarius of the commission given to Theodoric to conquer Italy, and of the uniform justice of his rule; the general doggedly replied that Theodoric had been sent to conquer Odovacar, not to set himself up as 'tyrannus' in his place. An offer of Sicily, Naples, and an annual tribute was contemptuously rejected, and all that Belisarius would grant was a three months' truce to enable Vitigis to send an embassy to Justinian. During the truce the Gothic King decided in discouragement to raise the siege of Rome. On March 21, 538, one year and nine days after the first arrival of the Goths, the remnant of their host retreated over the Milvian Bridge, Belisarius lashing them on in one last furious sally.

The back of the Gothic resistance was now broken, though for another two years they made a gallant fight for the plain of the Po. But by the spring of 540 Belisarius had won all but the impregnable Ravenna, which, like Theodoric, he only entered at last by guile. Tired of their incompetent King Vitigis, some of the Gothic chiefs conceived the bold idea of making Belisarius himself Emperor of the West, and the general, feigning consent to the proposal, entered Ravenna as a friend and ally. Then he threw off the mask, placed Vitigis in honourable captivity, and in May set sail for Constantinople with the king, the nobles, and the treasure of the Goths as his spoils of war.

Thus Italy was reunited to the Empire ; but the Gothic nation was not yet vanquished. Under the young hero Totila, whom the chiefs chose for their King in the autumn of 541, the aspect of affairs was completely reversed, and by 543 the whole of central and southern Italy, including Naples, was reconquered by his arms. This result was greatly assisted by the disgust of the Italians at the robbery to which they were immediately subjected by the Byzantine tax-gatherers. They began to regret the mild sway of Theodoric, and did what they could to help his successor by paying to him the rents due to their absent landlords. Rome, however, stood firm, though Totila appealed in a letter to the Senate to the old loyalty of the Romans towards Theodoric, and pointed out to them the miseries they had reaped by their change of masters. In the spring of 544 his preparations for besieging the capital were so far advanced that Justinian in alarm sent Belisarius once more to Italy, but this time without troops or money, for Belisarius was out of favour with the crowned circus-girl Theodora, Justinian's wife. He could accomplish nothing, and in the autumn of 545 Totila laid formal siege to

Rome, where after three months he was admitted by treacherous sentries, tired of the long privations of the siege.

King Totila entered the starving city, sunk now in the lowest depths of misery. But having no faith in walled cities, which had already wrought his people so much ill, he soon resolved to evacuate it and demolish the walls, and a rumour even ran current that he intended to destroy the city itself. Belisarius lay stricken with fever at Portus, but he heard the rumour, perhaps even saw the glow from some burning houses in the Trasteverine quarter, and addressed to the Gothic King a noble letter, which does honour alike to writer and receiver.[1] But Totila was soon far away, fighting a Greek detachment in Lucania, and Belisarius reoccupied the deserted capital and hastily rebuilt the walls. Totila returned in a rage to the assault, only to be beaten back at all points; and with his prestige much lowered he retired to carry on small operations in the centre and south, till the recall of Belisarius in the spring of 549 enabled him to appear once more before Rome. Well provisioned and under a gallant general named Diogenes, it seemed as though Rome were again impregnable, but once more did treacherous sentries, this time at the Pauline Gate, surrender her by stealth to the Goth. And once within the walls, Totila did not repeat his former mistake. By every means in his power he encouraged the scattered inhabitants to return; he restored the buildings that had perished in the first siege, he gave splendid games in the Circus Maximus.

---

[1] ' . . . Of all the cities scattered beneath the sun, Rome is confessed to be the greatest and most notable. For neither was she built by the energy of a single man, nor has she quickly attained to so much grandeur and beauty. No, a long line of Emperors, the united efforts of the best of men, time in abundance, wealth without stint, have all been needed to bring together there so many skilful workers and so many treasures from all quarters of the earth. Those who built the city, as thou now seest her, little by little, left her as a monument of the virtue of mankind to all posterity, so that any injury done to her would seem like an outrage against mankind of all ages. For it would rob our ancestors of the memorial of their virtues, and our posterity of the sight of their works. Confess therefore that one of two things must happen. Either thou wilt be worsted by the Emperor in this present war, or thou wilt conquer, if that be possible. Art thou victor, thou wilt in destroying Rome, good Sir, destroy not what is another's, but thine own. Preserving her, thou wilt enrich thyself with the finest possession on the earth. If on the other hand the worser lot fall to thy share, by saving Rome thou wilt lay up for thyself a rich debt of gratitude with the conqueror, but by destroying her thou wilt forfeit all claim for mercy, nor wilt thou derive any advantage from thy deed. Finally, there is the reputation, in sure proportion to thy works, which in either case awaits thee with mankind. For as his deeds are, such is the name by which a king will live.' (Procopius, De Bello Gothico, iii., 22.)

Then he departed to complete the reconquest of Italy and Sicily, even of remote Corsica and Sardinia, and by the end of 550 he could boast that his sway over Italy—all but three or four coast towns —was as absolute as that of Theodoric had ever been.

But Justinian's hatred of the Goths only slumbered, for with magnificent obstinacy he had refused even to see the ambassadors frequently sent to him by Totila, and now at length [551] he sent forth another expedition which was finally to crush the upstart and his people. It was under the command of the eunuch Narses, a wizened old man of seventy-five, who yet displayed all the qualities of a military leader. With admirable skill he marched his army round the head of the Adriatic to Ravenna (still in Imperial hands), and then plunged into the Apennines, in order, like a good strategist, to seek out and destroy his enemy. The decisive battle was fought in a high mountain valley on the Flaminian Way, between Scheggia and Tadino, and resulted in the rout of the Goths and the death of their king.

But Totila made a good end. Before the two armies had joined battle he rode out into the open space between them, and, wishing to gain time for certain reinforcements to arrive, gave the two hosts an extraordinary display of Gothic horsemanship.

Dressed in a suit of armour richly embossed with gold [says Procopius] with purple favours and other kingly ornaments streaming from helmet, javelin, and lance, he was most wonderful to behold. Mounted on a splendid charger, he skilfully performed a rhythmical dance in the space between the two armies. He wheeled his horse in swift circles, now this way and now that, and as he rode he hurled his lance in the air, seized it again as it came quivering down, and passed it rapidly from hand to hand. Now he would lie back in his saddle with legs apart, now he would bend to one side, now to the other, displaying all the accomplishments in which he had been trained from childhood upwards.[1]

But though this performance enabled the last detachment to come up and take part in the battle, the charges of Gothic horse broke in vain against the dismounted lancers of Narses' centre, while from the flanks they were shot down by the Roman archers. At nightfall all was lost, and the king himself, unrecognized amid the general rout, was struck in the back by a pursuing barbarian of Narses' army. His comrades bore him painfully to a village many miles from the field, and there they laid him down only to die. But the remnant, still unbeaten, found one more champion, the brave

[1] Procopius, De Bello Gothico, iv.

Teias, to lead them in a despairing effort to relieve Cumæ, where the Gothic treasure lay hoarded. For two months this little band held the Imperial army at bay, but at last it was overwhelmed and Teias killed in a two days' battle near the foot of Vesuvius. One thousand men, all that was left of the heroic army, demanded of Narses a free passage out of Italy with their arms in their hands, and the general consented,

> For he feared that they still could sting.

So they vanished across the Alps, those unconquerable men, and it seemed as though the best hope of Italy vanished with them. Historians of all ages have indulged in fond speculations as to the probable fate of Italy if the Gothic dynasty had taken root and flourished, and many have pictured her saved from all the degradation and misery of the Dark Ages. Yet even were it conceivable that the proud nobles of Rome could have submitted permanently to barbarian rule, or that Arian and Catholic could have become welded into a single commonwealth, or that Justinian could have recognized the virtues of his foes, should we not willingly give all the seven dark centuries for the Campanile of Giotto, or the Campo of Siena? And it needed the misgovernment of those seven centuries to produce the vigorous growth, the independence, the wickedness and glory of the *Cities*, those eternal protests against the barbarian, under whatever name he came. If Italy had passed too easily from the despotism of the emperors to the protection of a Gothic overlord, she might never have developed that spirit of local self-reliance and pugnacity which produced Florence, Perugia, Pisa, and the cities of the Lombard Plain. So although we may regret the extinction of the Ostrogoths as a *race*—for they could not but have strengthened the stock with which they mingled—the extinction of their dynasty is a less melancholy matter, for it was the first step in the long process by which the mediæval cities were made.

Photo: *Ricci, Ravenna*

THE EMPRESS THEODORA AND HER COURT

From the mosaic in the church of San Vitale, Ravenna

CHAPTER IV

The Lombards, the Popes, and the Franks

WHEN the victorious Narses had reduced the last remaining Gothic garrisons, at Cumæ and at Lucca, he was left to repair as best he could the ruin caused by twenty years of war. There is evidence that he laboured earnestly and successfully at the rebuilding of certain cities, especially of Milan, and that he endeavoured to carry out the benevolent intentions of his master Justinian, who, now that Italy was reconquered, issued a 'Pragmatic Sanction' authorizing some much-needed reforms in the administration. Yet the name of Narses is inseparably connected with by far the most fatal calamity which Italy had yet endured—the invasion of the 'unspeakable nation'[1] of the Lombards. The connection is probably merely fabulous, for only one out of four contemporary writers mentions it,[2] but the substance of the famous legend is that the General, out of pique at his recall by the Empress Sophia, wife of Justin II., sent an invitation to the 'Langobardi,' to come and take possession of Italy. In itself it is more probable that the Lombards, like the Visigoths before them, descended into Italy as soon as the back of its defender was turned, for certain it is that they appeared in Venetia under their King Alboin in 568, the year after Narses' departure, and spread, with practically no opposition, over the whole vast plain which now bears their name.

This truly barbarous race, 'fierce with more than the ordinary fierceness of Germany,' as a writer of the reign of Tiberius described them, had in the course of six centuries or more wandered south and east from their Scandinavian home, until at last, after annihilating the Heruli on the plains of Hungary [508], and the Gepidæ in Pannonia [554], they found themselves on the threshold of Italy [567]. They entered it as conquerors—not, like the Ostrogoths, to drive out a 'tyrannus' and set up a legitimate rule, but to possess the

---

[1] *Gens nefandissima*, the usual epithet applied to the Lombards by successive Popes.

[2] The *Liber Pontificalis*, in its Life of Pope John III., between 580 and 590. The other three are Gregory of Tours, Marius of Aventicum, and the anonymous '*Annals of Ravenna.*'

land, regardless of any interests save their own. Alboin established his headquarters at Pavia, which became the Lombard capital for two hundred years, and in 570 he crossed the Apennines and conquered Tuscany, with much slaughter of Roman landowners. Two of his followers, Farwald and Zotto, penetrated further south and laid the foundations of the great Lombard 'Duchies' of Spoleto and Benevento. The former of these embraced the greater part of what we now call Umbria and the Marches, with the sea-coast between Ancona and Pescara, but its importance lay in the fact that it commanded two of the three roads[1] connecting Rome with Ravenna, and was therefore a constant source of danger to the relics of Roman rule. The Duchy of Benevento was of still greater extent, for it included the whole of southern Italy except the two peninsulas and the meagre strip of territory which formed the Imperial 'Duchy' of Naples. Both of these principalities, however, maintained a state of semi-independence towards the King at Pavia, and together with the border Duchy of Friuli (the Lombard bulwark against the incursions of still ruder races like the Avars), frequently caused him trouble and annoyance.

The condition of the subjugated population is a question which has engaged the eager attention of many scholars, both German and Italian. The Lombard settlement differed from the Gothic in that the conquerors took, not a third of the land, but of the produce, so that the Italian landowners were reduced to the condition of tributaries, each with a Lombard 'guest' (hospes) quartered upon him. This arrangement naturally curtailed the freedom of the Italian 'host,' who would probably be held to his land so as to enable it to yield the largest possible tribute, and we find in fact that in the Lombard codes of law the Italian occupied an intermediate position between the slave and the freeman, and was called by the otherwise unknown name of 'Aldius.' In the towns, however, there is much evidence to show that Roman officials and institutions lingered on, though many cities were made subject to Lombard 'Dukes,' and others were placed under the authority of the King's representatives, the *Gastalds*. But the Roman law continued to exist for suits between Roman and Roman, and the titles 'Judex,' 'Consul,' 'Exceptor,' etc., are frequently met with even for Lombard towns in documents of the seventh and eighth centuries. Naturally, too, in the districts remaining Roman the old institutions continued in full force, and the constant example of these towns would do much to keep alive the civic organization in the Lombard cities.

[1] The other went through Perugia, which remained Roman (except for a brief interval from 593—9).

Of this so-called 'Roman' territory the *Exarchate of Ravenna*, with the adjoining region of the *Pentapolis*,[1] was by far the largest in extent, though Lombard encroachments gradually reduced its area. It was directly administered by the Exarch or Viceroy, who was the Emperor's representative for the whole of Italy. He it was who appointed the dukes, or military governors, of Rome and Naples, who made peace or war with the Lombards, who even had the right of confirming the election of the Popes. He represented all that was left of Imperial Italy, but his authority gradually waned before the young and rising power of the Popes, and he was extinguished at last in the clash between Lombard and Frank, which a Pope was to bring about. Over the extreme south of Italy the Byzantine influence was still strong, and Sicily remained wholly under the Empire, but a noteworthy tendency of the unsettled times was the increasing independence of the 'dukes' of Naples and Rome, who were sometimes elected tulmultuously by the people instead of appointed by the Exarch. Towards the end of the Lombard period, indeed, the 'exercitus Romanus' under its 'duke' plays an important part in the three-cornered quarrels of Pope, Exarch, and Lombards, and the evolution of the mediæval Roman republic, with its frequent antagonism towards the Pope, is already foreshadowed.

Meanwhile King Alboin had been murdered by his wife Rosamund, in revenge, it is said, for being forced to drink to the King's health out of a goblet fashioned from her own father's skull [573]. Then after the short reign of Clefo there followed an interregnum of ten years, during which the land was divided between some thirty-six independent dukes. But pressure from the Franks at last induced them to elect another king, and their choice fell [584] on Authari, son of Clefo, who by his marriage with Theodolinda, daughter of Garibald, Duke of Bavaria, laid the foundation of a lasting dynasty among the Lombards. For not only was the Queen's hold on the affections of her new people so great that on the death of Authari [590] they invited her to choose his successor by bestowing her hand on whom she would, but her orthodox Catholicism was of inestimable value in bridging the gulf between her Arian subjects and the old civilization into which they were now thrust. For though she did not actually succeed in converting either her first or her second husband (whose name was Agilulf), her only son, Adelwald, was baptized according to the Catholic rite, and her relations with the champion of Rome and of orthodoxy, Pope Gregory the Great, were uniformly cordial. Legend even relates

---

[1] Consisting of the five cities of Rimini, Pesaro, Fano, Sinigaglia, and Ancona, with the territory behind them.

that the Pope sent her, as a mark of his especial favour, one of the
nails from the True Cross which Helena, mother of Constantine,
had brought from Jerusalem, and that she had it beaten into the
thin circlet of iron which gave its name to the famous 'Iron Crown
of the Lombards.'

But the dealings of Pope Gregory the Great with the Lombards
as a whole were not usually of so friendly a nature as this. Elected
Pope in 590, after three years spent as Papal Nuncio in that best of
all schools of worldly wisdom, the Byzantine Court, Gregory found
himself, through the impotence of Exarch and Emperor, the sole
bulwark of Rome against the 'unspeakable' invaders. Twice during
the first three years of his Pontificate was Rome threatened by
Lombard armies, the first under Ariulf, Duke of Spoleto, the second
under King Agilulf himself. But each time the intrepid Pope succeeded in overawing the invader by a personal interview, and in the
case of Ariulf he even went so far as to negotiate [592] a separate
peace—a stretch of Papal power which gave great offence at Constantinople. Gregory's efforts, indeed, were all directed to arranging
a lasting peace with the Lombard King, for the miseries of a constant state of warfare touched no one more closely than the Pope,
who was responsible for the welfare of those vast estates known as
the 'Patrimony of St. Peter,' lying scattered all over Italy and supplying the bulk of the Papal revenues. But the sullen jealousy of the
Exarch Romanus, and the strained relations with Constantinople
produced by certain heretical acts of the Emperor Maurice, for a
time frustrated all Gregory's attempts, and it was not until the
spring of 599 that a comprehensive peace was arranged between
Agilulf, the Exarch, and the Pope, and including the Dukes of
Spoleto and Benevento. Herein the Pope served Italy well, but the
position of responsibility in which he was placed by the Lombard
wars led directly to that increase in the power of the Roman See
which has had so many and such dubious results for Italy. When
Gregory died in 604 he left the Papacy infinitely stronger than he
found it, and his successors were not slow to follow and improve
upon his example. Just 150 years after the death of Gregory his
policy culminated, as we shall see, in the conversion of the 'Patrimony of St. Peter' into the 'State of the Church.'

In the first half of the seventh century the Lombard kingdom
grew and prospered at the expense of fragments of Roman territory
left unconquered by Alboin. Agilulf won Cremona, Mantua, and
the whole of the remaining course of the Po, while his son-in-law
Rothari [636—652] made the still more important conquest of the
Ligurian coast, with Genoa and all the cities between Ventimiglia

and Luna. This king Rothari seems indeed to have found his position so secure that he was able to devote his attention to codifying the laws of the Lombards, and the result of his labours is a most curious document, highly instructive as to the manners of these latest backwoodsmen who had swooped down upon the land of Virgil. The code deals pre-eminently with criminal offences, though there are also sections on inheritance and the position of women, and the crimes contemplated range from murder to the cutting off of the hairs of a horse's tail. The principle adopted is throughout that of composition in money, in order to avoid the blood-feud, and each free Lombard seems to have had his price, or *weregeld*, which must be paid by his murderer on conviction—half to the king's court and half to the dead man's relations. No table of the *weregelds* of free Lombards has survived, but we know that the price of murdering an Aldius, or semi-free Italian, was 60 *solidi*, while a foreman swineherd was valued at 50 *solidi*, his underlings at 25 apiece, and a 'rustic slave under the farm labourer' could be killed with impunity for even less. In the same way there was an elaborate tariff of compensation of wounds, of which one specimen may be quoted. In the case of breaking the bones of the head (for which the fine was 12 *solidi* per bone) 'the broken bones are to be counted thus, that one bone shall be found large enough to make an audible sound when thrown against a shield at 12 feet distance on the road.'

Thus King Rothari guarded the safety of his subjects, and died in peace—the last Lombard king to profess the Arian heresy. He was succeeded [653] by Aripert, nephew of Theodelinda, and he by his two sons [661], who tried the dangerous scheme of reigning at Milan and Pavia respectively. The plan worked ill, and a quarrel between the brothers gave a pretext to Grimwald, the energetic Duke of Benevento, to march northward and seize the crown [662]. His reign coincided with the one serious attempt of Byzantium to reconquer the western 'diocese,' for early in 663 the Emperor Constans II., grandson of the great Heraclius, landed at Tarentum, determined to drive out the Lombard usurpers. But he failed to take Benevento, which was gallantly held by the King's young son; part of his army was annihilated at Forino, and he was glad to push on by way of Naples to Rome, where he was received with servile apprehension by Pope Vitalian and the civic authorities. He had already won a character for ferocity by his treatment of the aged Pope Martin I., who had differed from him on the question of the Two Wills in Christ and had therefore been dragged to Constantinople, and subjected to such hardships that he died. Now, however, the Emperor contented himself with stripping the city of all the treasures he could carry away, especially the copper tiles from the roof of the Pantheon, and after a twelve days' sojourn he departed for Sicily, where he abode for five years, oppressing the unhappy provincials. At last, however, his career was cut short by an aggrieved valet, who for some private grudge struck his master on the head with a copper soap-box as he sat in his bath, instantly killing him [668].

The reign of Constans II. marks the lowest point in the dealings of Rome with her Byzantine over-lords. Henceforth a marked increase in local patriotism begins to show itself, and the Liber Pontificalis continually mentions the existence of three Orders—clergy, army, and people—who control the Papal elections and whose leaders govern the city. When the grandson of Constans, Justinian II., tried to repeat the experiment of summoning a rebellious Pope to Constantinople, this civic militia, aided by the 'army' of Ravenna, rose in fierce tumult against the envoy and hustled him ignominiously out of the city [692].

On the death of Grimwald the Lombard crown had returned to the family of Theodolinda, in which it now remained until the year 712. But at that date a revolution brought to the throne a man of new blood, Liutprand, son of Ansprand, and with the reign of this remarkable personage we enter upon the most prosperous period of the Lombard monarchy. Not only did Liutprand make a thorough revision of the Code of Rothari, modifying its provisions in the direction of a far greater regard for human life, not only did he subdue the turbulent Dukes of Spoleto and Benevento to his will, but his lot was cast in the days of the Iconoclastic Controversy, from the confusion of which he all but succeeded in shaping a Lombard Kingdom of all Italy.

In the year 717 a strong man at last ascended the throne of Constantinople in the person of Leo the Isaurian, commonly known as the Iconoclast. He performed for Eastern Europe the same service as Charles Martel was shortly to render to the West—that of inflicting a defeat on the successors of Mohammed. But contact with Mohammedanism in the heyday of its strength only led him to perceive the degradation of the Christian rite, and he determined to do what in him lay to purge his religion from the charge of idolatry. His celebrated Edict for the destruction of sacred pictures and images was promulgated in 726. The decree reached Ravenna in 727 and there produced a tumult in which the Exarch Paulus was killed, so that the adroit Liutprand was enabled to push his conquests in the East, where Bologna and the cities of the Pentapolis soon surrendered to him. Meanwhile the Roman See was worthily occupied by Pope Gregory II., who while opposing a firm resistance to the impious designs of Leo, exerted all his influence to uphold the civil authority of the Emperor. He must have seen only too clearly that a revolted Italy would fall an easy prey to the King of the Lombards. Thus he intrigued with the Dukes of Spoleto and Benevento for the recovery of the Pentapolis, and his action produced a strange league between Liutprand and the new Exarch Eutychius [730]. Advancing through Spoleto, Liutprand joined the Exarch before the walls of Rome, and the city lay at his mercy. But once more was the influence of the Pope sufficient to quell the spirit of the barbarian; Gregory came forth to meet the King, and Liutprand humbly offered up his royal robes and crown at the shrine of St. Peter, while persuading the Exarch to agree to the Pope's terms of peace.

In the next year [731] the valiant old Pope died, to be succeeded by yet a third Gregory, who continued the profitable policy of dividing the Lombard house against itself, while opposing the Iconoclastic decrees with obstinate persistency. In 739 this Pope, in the course of his wars with Liutprand, made the first of those memorable appeals to the Frankish rulers of Gaul which were to exert so decisive an influence upon the course of Italian history. But the time was not yet ripe, and Charles Martel, Mayor of the Palace, refused the Pope's appeal. Gregory died without having recovered certain territories seized by Liutprand, and a new Pope, Zacharias, was left to confront the victorious King unaided. Without hesitation he adoped the old expedient of a personal interview. Accompanied by a long train of ecclesiastics, he journeyed fourth to meet the King at Terni, and there addressed him so persuasively on the merits of peace that Liutprand gave back large portions of the Papal Patrimony which had been absorbed by the Lombard state. All these territories were handed over to 'Peter, Prince of the Apostles,' with no mention of Emperor or Exarch, and there is little doubt that the Pope exercised real sovereignty within their boundaries.

Soon after these events King Liutprand died [Jan., 744], and after the short reign of his nephew, Hildebrand, the crown passed to the family of the Dukes of Friuli—first to Ratchis [744—49] and then to his hot-blooded brother Aistulf, with whom the downfall of the Lombard monarchy began.

Yet Aistulf's reign opened in a blaze of glory. Within two years

of his accession he had taken the hitherto impregnable[1] Ravenna
[751], and was issuing edicts from the Palatium of the Exarchs. Nor
was the Exarchate ever restored to life. It was the final extinction
of Byzantine authority in Upper Italy, but the sequel was to show
that Aistulf's act was to open the way not to Lombard but to
Papal supremacy along the Adriatic sea-board. Next he was insis-
ting on the payment of a poll-tax by the inhabitants of the *Ducatus
Romæ*, and threatening Rome herself with destruction unless his
demands were complied with. The Pope (Stephen II.) appealed in
despair to his nominal lord the Emperor, who had already sent a
futile embassy to Aistulf on the subject of the Exarchate; but without waiting for a reply he wrote, with a truer instinct, to the real
arbiter of the West, Pippin, son of Charles Martel, whom his barons
had just proclaimed King of the Franks. In this first letter the Pope
merely asked for an interview, to which Pippin eagerly assented,
sending a duke and a bishop to escort the Pope to Frankland. But
Stephen was already revolving that great scheme for the aggrandizement of the Papal See which was to influence the course of Italian
politics down to our own day. Probably he already fancied that he
had authority for his dreams in the marvellous fable of the Donation of Constantine, which was the contribution of the eighth
century to the great forgeries of history. The work of some pious
scribe in the Papal Chancery, writing between the years 750 and
770, this celebrated document purported to give the sequel to the
legend of Constantine's cure and conversion by Pope Sylvester, and
takes the form of a decree in the name of the first Christian Emperor. Much of it is taken up with the Emperor's gracious ordinances concerning the raiment to be worn by the Roman clergy
and their horses, but the crucial paragraph contains these words:

Wherefore, that the pontifical crown may not grow too cheap, but
may be adorned with glory and influence even beyond the dignity
of the earthly empire, lo! we hand over and relinquish our palace,
the city of Rome, and all the provinces, places, and cities of Italy
and the western regions, to the most blessed Pontiff and universal
Pope Sylvester; and we ordain that they shall be governed by him
and his successors, and we grant that they shall remain under the
authority of the holy Roman Church.

The first mention of the Donation occurs in a letter of Pope
Hadrian to Charles the Great in 777, so that if Stephen was already

[1] It had once been raided (probably in 740) by the Lombards under
Hildebrand, but they had promptly been expelled again by the *Venetian*
militia.

acquainted with it on his journey into Frankland, he did not as yet venture to appeal to it in his dealings with the King. But his conduct throughout those dealings seems to justify the supposition that, whether he knew it to be a forgery or not, he was already inspired by a knowledge of its contents.

His first meeting with Pippin occurred at Ponthion in Champagne, and there the Pope extracted a preliminary promise from his host that he would 'restore to him the Exarchate of Ravenna and the rights and territories of the Roman Republic.' Thus cautiously did the Popes proceed in their acquisition of the 'Western regions.' Then followed a solemn coronation of Pippin as King and *Patrician* in the Abbey of St. Denis—the latter title, which had been borne by the Exarchs, conferring some vague right of protection over the Roman territories. Lastly a great assembly of the Frankish nobles was held [July, 754] at Quierzy (Carisiacum) near Soissons, and a treaty with the Pope agreed upon which has received the name of the *Donation of Pippin*. Though the document itself has disappeared, it must have contained a promise to hand over to the Roman Republic (*i.e.*, to the Pope) the territories which the 'unspeakable Aistulf' had lately seized.

It now only remained for Pippin to put his promises into execution. In March, 755, he crossed the Mont Cenis, drove Aistulf back to Pavia, and soon extorted a promise from him to restore Ravenna and certain other cities to the Roman Republic. Hereupon the Pope returned to Rome and Pippin to France, but the Frankish host had scarcely disappeared before Aistulf showed that he had no intention of carrying out his pledge, and by Jan., 756, he was closely besieging the walls of Rome. In this sore strait Pope Stephen sent forth a memorable cry for help, the 'Letter of St. Peter,' in which he made the Apostle exhort the Frankish King with the most awful conjurations to come to the rescue of 'this my city of Rome.' Pippin obeyed the command, bore Aistulf to his knees with very little trouble, and this time secured the fulfilment of his demands by sending the Abbot Fulrad, accompanied by certain Lombard officers, to all the surrendered towns,[1] whence he conveyed their keys to the Shrine of St. Peter in Rome. Two officers of the Imperial household, sent by their master to request the restoration of the Exarchate to *him*, returned to Constantinople empty-handed.

The last act in the drama of Lombard dominion was the eighteen years' reign [756—774] of Desiderius[2]—a disappointing personage

---

[1] Twenty-three in number, including the coast-line from Comacchio to Sinigaglia, but without Ancona, which was surrendered later by Desiderius.

[2] The 'King Didier' of Charlemagne romance.

who, while attempting to play a great game in Italian politics, showed no gleam of statesmanship in carrying it out. He lived to be matched against three Popes—Paul I., Stephen III., and lastly Hadrian I., and the only weapon which he used in his endless wrangles with them was the seizure or restoration of the unhappy towns of the Pentapolis, whose inhabitants must often have cursed the treaty which made them such a bone of contention between Pope and King. Meanwhile King Pippin died in 768, and was succeeded by his two sons Charles and Carloman; but the latter only lived three years, and the Frankish nobles decided to pass over his two young sons and acknowledge Charles as sole lord of the Franks. Carloman's widow, Gerberga, fled with her boys to the court of Desiderius [772] and furnished the Lombard with a new cause of quarrel against his rival. Desiderius haughtily demanded of the new Pope, Hadrian I., that he should crown the sons of Carloman, and on his refusal seized almost all the cities of the Pentapolis and then advanced on Rome. But once more the Papal threat of anathema was sufficient to turn back the Lombard, and Desiderius retreated to face a still more formidable foe in the north. For at last, in response to Hadrian's appeals, Charles the Frank was on the move. He descended from the Alps on Pavia, where King Desiderius was soon blockaded, and at Easter of the year 774, Charles determined to leave his camp and visit Rome. He was received by Hadrian with solemn pomp in the atrium of St. Peter's, the gigantic Frank ascending the long flight of steps on his knees, and kissing each step as he advanced. Charles then confirmed the Donation of his father Pippin, recognizing the Pope as Sovereign of the Exarchate, the Pentapolis, and the Ducatus Romæ. But soon he was back at Pavia, pressing the siege of the exhausted city, and in June Desiderius at last surrendered, and was sent to end his days in a Frankish monastery. The Lombard monarchy was at an end, and henceforward Charles styled himself 'Rex Francorum et Langobardorum, et Patricius Romanorum.'

But the entry upon the Italian scene of this, the greatest ruler of the Middle Ages, did not produce so marked a change in the life of the people as might perhaps have been expected. The Lombard organization of the land was left almost undisturbed, save that in the towns the Gastalds were for the most part replaced by Frankish Counts; and the reforms which Italy gradually shared with the rest of the Frankish Empire related chiefly to the administration of justice, and did not long outlast the lifetime of their author. But in this department the improvement was, so long as it endured, real and beneficent. Soon the spectacle was regularly witnessed of the progress of the two *Missi Dominici*, or Royal Commissioners, through the towns of Upper and Central Italy on their yearly rounds of inspection; their function was, broadly speaking, to hold the rapacious counts in check, and to hear and redress the grievances of the weak. Their authority rested not on present force, but on the fear of the distant King's censure, and it therefore needed an arm as long as Charles's to make that authority effective. Under his weak successors the *Missi* continued to represent, though at rarer intervals, the shadow of a central power, but in the welter of nascent feudalism their office was doomed to decline and disappear.

Twice again [781 and 787] during the long Pontificate of Hadrian did the affairs of Italy require Charles's presence, for the Pope was continually assailing him with querulous complaints against all manner of enemies, from the Lombard Prince of Benevento to the 'most wicked Neapolitans and the Greeks hateful to God.' But it was reserved for Hadrian's successor, Leo III., to play the part which hastened the climax of early mediæval history. A street affray [Apr. 25, 799] in which the Pope was unhorsed and wounded by the faction of Hadrian's nephews led to the intervention of the Frankish 'Patricius,' for Leo fled to Paderborn in Westphalia and there implored the King's vengeance on his assailants. Charles decided to send a Frankish commission to Rome to investigate the case; Leo returned under its protection, and a formal trial was held in the Triclinium of the Lateran, at which the Pope's would-be murderers were pronounced guilty. Sentence was reserved, however, for a more exalted judge, since Charles himself had announced his intention of spending Christmas of the year 800 in Rome. He arrived towards the end of November, heard Leo take a solemn oath of self-expurgation from the charges brought against him, and banished the two chief conspirators to France.

Whether the Pope had already planned the bold stroke that was to follow, it is hard to say, still harder whether any shadow of it had crossed the mind of the heroic Frank. Yet many circumstances had combined to force the two chief actors in the drama into the positions which they now took up. The Byzantine throne had for the last three years been disgraced by the usurpation of the she-wolf Irene, who had deposed and blinded her own son, Constantine VI., so that the Roman Empire seemed in men's minds to be in abeyance. Then came the wholly unique position in which Charles stood towards the Roman Church through the events of the last thirty years; the need for a visible head of the Christian State to sustain the visible head of the Church, the yearning for a strong ruler clothed with the ancient authority of Roman Emperor. But whatever the motives, the scene in St. Peter's on Christmas Day of the year 800 is stamped for ever on the imagination of posterity— the tall Frank clad in the white *chlamys* and sandals of a Roman Patricius, kneeling in prayer at the high altar, the white-robed Pope crowning him as he rises 'with a very precious crown,' and the deafening shout ringing through all the packed basilica—'Carolo Augusto a Deo conorato magno et pacifico Imperatori vita et victoria !' That shout was taken up and answered by the waiting multitude without, and as it swelled and died away it proclaimed to a listening world that the Roman Empire was not dead, but lived again for the salvation of mankind

CHAPTER V

The Beginning of the Middle Ages

THE Empire of Charles the Great, which in the minds of his contemporaries seemed to open so fair a prospect for the future of Western Europe, was destined to a rapid and melancholy decay. Indefatigably as the great Emperor worked in the last fourteen years of his life to bring order and strength into the administration, fortune and the tendencies of the time were all against him. His two capable elder sons, Charles, King of the Franks, and Pippin, King of Italy, both died before their father, and at the old Emperor's death in 814 the sole heir left to inherit his vast dominions was his youngest son Louis, whose too monkish disposition earned him the title of the Pious. During his long and troubled reign the forces of disorder surged up again unchecked. In Italy, nominally ruled by his son Lothar, power fell more and more into the hands of dukes and counts who built castles and carried on private war, while the bishops and abbots adopted the practice of granting lands in exchange for military service, and so became in their turn feudal magnates. That tendency towards the localization of power, which Charles had done his best to check by the institution of the *Missi Dominici*, now carried all before it, and the occasional irruption of the royal authority, never strong enough to enforce peace, only served to embitter the strife. Italy, in fact, lapsed into an anarchical type of feudalism, to which her still dominant Lombard population suited itself with alacrity. For the Lombard element had only been partially submerged by the coming of the Franks, and in the south the great duchy of Benevento maintained complete independence from the Frankish Empire. But the tendencies towards anarchy and subdivision became just as strong in the south as in the north, for the duchies of Salerno and Capua split off from that of Benevento during the ninth century, while the weak rule of Byzantium over the coast districts favoured the rise of semi-autonomous maritime republics such as Naples, Amalfi, and Gaëta.

Meanwhile a powerful stimulus to these disruptive forces was given by the renewed barbarian invasions of the ninth century. Italy was caught between the waves of Saracen conquest from the south and of Magyar conquest from the north, and, except at a few rare moments, could not oppose an united front to either. All through the eighth century the Arab conquerors of Northern Africa and their Berber subjects (collectively known by the name of Saracens) had sent out plundering expeditions to Sicily and Southern Italy, but it was not until the ninth century that they definitely undertook the conquest of Sicily. It took them fifty years [827—878] to subjugate the island, for the Byzantines defended it with unwonted energy; but at last Syracuse fell, and Islam was supreme from sea to sea. A remarkable incident of the conquest was the aid given to the Moslems by a Neapolitan fleet at the siege of Messina in 843, so little as yet had Christendom grasped the notion of combining against the common foe. Shortly after this, however, the needful impulse towards union was given by an outrage against the *sanctum sanctorum* of Christianity, the Shrine of St. Peter. A formidable Saracen fleet sailed up the unguarded Tiber, and, while refraining from an attack on the Aurelian Walls, the raiders fell upon the open suburb of the Borgo, plundered St. Peter's at their leisure, down to the silver plates upon the massive doors, and only retired on the approach of a Christian force under the Count of Spoleto. The news sent a thrill of horror throughout the West, and a new Pope, Leo IV., determined to prevent a repetition of the insult by enclosing the Borgo in a wall as stout as that of the city itself. The work was pushed forward with energy, and meanwhile the Pope succeeded in combining the navies of Amalfi, Gaëta, and Naples in an attack on the Saracen fleet, which suffered a crushing disaster off Ostia [849]. The prisoners taken alive were brought to Rome and set to labour at the new walls, and soon the famous Leonine City was completed [852], the walls were sprinkled with holy water in a dedicatory procession, and inscriptions placed above the three gates.[1]

The ninth century, while it witnessed the decline and extinction of the Carolingian line of Emperors, produced a succession of able Popes, who not only maintained but extended the already formidable pretensions of St. Peter. The Emperor Lothar I., grandson of Charles the Great, had endeavoured to assert the Imperial authority over the Papal elections by laying it down, in a *Constitutio* of the year 824, that although the Pope should be *elected* by the clergy and people of Rome, he could not be consecrated without the approval of the Emperor conveyed by his *Missi*. The condition appears to have been adhered to so long as the Carolingian Emperors preserved the power to enforce it, but with their decline the independence of the Papacy emerged once more and was exempli-

---

[1] The most conspicuous remnant of Leo's fortifications is now the round tower on the top of the Vatican Hill, known as the 'Torre dei Saraceni.'

fied by the reigns of two such Popes as Leo IV. and Nicholas I.
[858—867]. The untiring activity of this latter Pope has earned him
with many the title of the Great. He goes down to fame as the last
Pope to interfere in the internal affairs of the Byzantine Patriarch-
ate, as the winner of a new flock—the Bulgarian kingdom—for the
Roman fold (greatly to the indignation of the Greeks), as the stern
upholder of the marriage-vow against the weak King Lothar, grandson of Louis the Pious, and above all as the patron and promulgator
of the Forged Decretals of Isidore. This amazing collection of documents, the work of a pious monk of the Rhineland writing about
852, purported to be a complete series of the letters and decrees of
the earliest Popes, from Clement to Melchiades, together with the
Acts of a large number of (fictitious) councils, and the text of the
Donation of Constantine. Its tendency throughout was to exalt
the clerical at the expense of the temporal power, and above all to
raise the authority of the Pope high above all others. Nicholas I.
eagerly welcomed the pious fraud as soon as it was brought to his
notice; he used it in crushing a refractory Frankish Archbishop,
and it maintained its position in the Church almost unchallenged
down to the Reformation.

Under the later Carolingians, whose family feuds brought the
dynasty to an unhappy end in 888, the unity of the Empire founded
by Charles was never maintained. The three great divisions of
Germany, France, and Italy began to be marked off, and the title of
King of Italy, which Charles had bestowed on his son Pippin, was
always held by one of his descendants, though the authority which
it gave became more and more shadowy. On the extinction of the
Carolingian line this title was striven for by the Lombard and
Franco-Lombard dukes, marquises, and counts whose power had
flamed up again in the absence of a superior force, and under the
two Dukes of Spoleto, Guido and Lambert [889—898], a revival
of the Lombard kingdom was practically achieved. Their territories
stretched northwards beyond the Apennines and included Milan
and Pavia, but on the north-east they were held in check by the
powerful Duke of Friuli, Berengar, whose feudal rule stretched as
far west as the Adda, and on the south-west by the Marquis of
Tuscany. Both Guido and Lambert had themselves crowned Emperor as well as King of Italy by subservient Popes, but a rival
claimant to the Empire existed in the person of Arnulf, an illegitimate Carolingian, who descended into Italy in 896, and was
crowned by Pope Formosus. His triumph was short-lived, however,
and on the return of the Spoletan party to Rome in the following
year the corpse of the pro-German Pope (who had died in the

interval) was solemnly exhumed and set up for trial before an ecclesiastical synod. The scene is described by the contemporary *Chronicle of Farfa*, and remains one of the most vivid pictures of the manners of that age. After the condemnation a rush was made for the body, the pontifical vestments were stripped off, and the three fingers which were wont to be raised in blessing hacked away; then the naked mummy was dragged through the streets by a yelling mob of clergy and people and at length hurled into the Tiber. Its vicissitudes did not even end there, however, for it was cast up on the shore of the river and piously buried by a nameless monk; and a few months afterwards a reaction in Roman politics produced repentance and a solemn re-committal of the poor remains to their previous tomb in the atrium of St. Peter's. And, in vindication of the canonicity of his election, the images of the saints which Formosus had set up in the basilica bowed their heads in reverence as the corpse passed by.

On the confused and violent period [896—951] which prepared for the coming of Otto the Great it is impossible to do more than touch, yet two or three figures emerge from the chaos, of sufficient interest to arrest our attention. Two Popes, Sergius III. [904—11] and John X. [914—28], and two women of high birth and infamous reputation, Theodora and her daughter Marozia, ruled Rome for the first quarter of the tenth century, laying the foundation of that feudal aristocracy of Rome which was to be the pride and torment of the Papal city throughout the Middle Ages. Theodora was the wife of one Theophylactus, 'Consul and Governor of the Roman Senate,' and also the mistress of Pope John, while Marozia was the mistress of Pope Sergius, and afterwards married Alberic, Duke of Spoleto, who had dispossessed and murdered the last heir of the Lombard line. During Pope John's reign this clan, with the Pope's assistance, displayed unusual vigour and ability in forming a league of all the scattered units of the south—Byzantines, Lombards, and Neapolitans—against the Saracens established on the river Garigliano, and in 916 the robber-fortress was destroyed and the Moslems were permanently expelled from the district south of Rome.

But in the north, Duke Berengar of Friuli had been far less successful in stemming the irresistible tide of Hungarian or Magyar invasion, and during the whole of this period hordes of these ferocious savages wandered about Italy, striking terror wherever they went, but incidentally causing a healthy change in the habits of the townspeople, who were obliged to build walls in self-defence and to organize a civic militia. Berengar assumed the title of King of Italy in 900, and was crowned Emperor by Pope John in 915, but nine years later he was murdered by his Lombard nobles, and no claimant to the Western Empire arose for more than a generation. Pope John was shortly afterwards removed from the scene by Marozia and her second husband, Guido of Tuscany, who threw him into the dungeons of St. Angelo and there had him strangled. Rome was for some years entirely at the feet of Marozia, who called herself 'Senatrix' and placed her son John on the Papal chair [931]. The crimes of this adventurous lady, however, led directly to one of those remarkable episodes of the Middle Ages which proved, ever and anon, that the city of Rome still preserved some remnants of the spirit of order and of true political life which had caused her greatness in ancient days. Marozia had a son by her first marriage, named, like his father, Alberic; and this youth succeeded in expelling his mother and the 'King of Italy' whom she had taken as her third husband, Hugo of Provence, in a sudden riot arising out of the wedding-feast. He passionately called the Romans to arms, taunting them with submitting to the yoke of a *Burgundian*, and drove King Hugo ignominiously from the city. From that moment Alberic reigned supreme, and for twenty-two years he maintained his authority against all comers, under the title of 'Prince and Senator of all the Romans.' He was the first to organize the civic militia in definite regiments, corresponding to the twelve 'regions' of Rome and commanded by *Banderesi* or standard-bearers, and in many fights with King Hugo's forces the Roman militia proved their strength. He relegated the Pope to the sphere of spiritual authority, and after his brother John's death was careful to bestow the tiara on none but docile, unassuming monks, who would not protest against his seizure of the Temporal Power. But Alberic was more than a mere despot; he was a zealous reformer in ecclesiastical affairs; and indeed the state of corruption into which the Benedictine monasteries had fallen during the ninth century warranted the most drastic remedies. In France the greatness of the evil had worked at last its own cure, and the great Abbey of Cluny had arisen in 910, with a rule modelled on that of Benedict, but stricter in many points. Alberic now invited Odo, the Abbot of Cluny, to visit Rome, and with his aid succeeded in introducing order and discipline into all the monasteries in Roman territory. A monument of his labours still exists in the Priory of Malta on the Aventine, which was originally Alberic's palace, and was presented by him to Odo for the purpose of founding a monastery.

Towards the end of Alberic's reign the course of events in the north had once more become favourable to the intervention of a

E

Transalpine master. King Hugo had been dethroned by a Berengar, Count of Ivrea, in 945, and on the death of Hugo's more popular son Lothar a little later [950], Berengar had sought to coerce Lothar's beautiful widow, Adelheid, into a marriage with his own son, Adalbert. But Adelheid escaped, and united with Pope Agapitus (who perhaps chafed at Alberic's control) in sending an urgent invitation to the great Saxon King, Otto I., to come and settle the affairs of Italy. Otto came [951], gallantly married the distressed queen, forced Berengar to hold his kingdom as a fief of the German crown, but was prevented from entering Rome by the mere refusal of Alberic to admit him within the walls. Ten years later, however, the aspect of affairs had changed; Alberic was dead, Berengar was once more powerful and hated, and the Papal chair was occupied by Alberic's young son, Octavian, who as John XII. scandalized Christendom by his hunting and his amours, and by the mad freaks which led him to ordain a deacon in his stable and to quaff toasts to the Devil. It was at John's summons, however, that Otto came for the second time, for Berengar had occupied the Papal territories in the north. The tyrant fled at his approach; at Pavia Otto received the Iron Crown of Italy, and in Rome he suffered himself to be anointed Emperor of the Romans by the scapegrace Pope [962]. Thus was the Empire revived in the person of one who could make good its claims, but the Romans scowled at the foreigner, and on his departure for the north they broke out in fierce revolt, which it needed all Otto's energy to quell. He returned, determined to enforce his authority; held an Assembly in St. Peter's [963], which deposed the Pope, and forced the Romans to accept a *Privilegium* which bound them 'neither to elect nor consecrate a Pope without the consent of the Lord Emperor Otto and of his son, King Otto.' This was the beginning of the period of Imperial control over the Papacy, which was to be constantly asserted during the next hundred years and to lead at last to the irresistible reaction under Gregory VII. But even in Otto's lifetime the Romans would not accept his nominees, and rebelled once more against him in 966. Otto returned in wrath to Rome, hanged the twelve Captains of the Regions, and ordered the Prefect of the city to be hung by the hair of his head from the equestrian statue of Marcus Aurelius[1] before the Lateran. Rebellion was quelled by these measures, but the Imperial claim to regulate the Papacy was one which Rome never accepted save at the sword's point.

Otto the Great died in 973, having caused his son Otto to be crowned Emperor during his lifetime, and having married him to

[1] Believed throughout the Middle Ages to have been that of Constantine.

the Byzantine princess, Theophano. But the second Otto's career was brief and tragic. In 982 he was confronted by a formidable league of Greeks and Saracens in Southern Italy, marched with all his force against them, was defeated and barely escaped with his life, only to die a year later in Rome, on the eve of a new expedition. He was buried in the atrium of St. Peter's, and his tomb may still be seen in the crypt. His infant son Otto III., already crowned King of the Germans, and one day to be hailed 'the wonder of the world' by his dazzled contemporaries, was brought up in Germany under the guardianship of his Greek mother, and during his long minority Rome fell under the sway of the 'Patrician' Crescentius, who ruled the city with something of the absolutism of Alberic. But two Papal revolutions in quick succession, attended by frightful atrocities, at last aroused the conscience of Northern Europe. At the Council of Rheims in 991 the Bishop of Orleans openly spoke of the Pope as Antichrist, and when at last the young King was able to set out for Italy he came as the deliverer of an oppressed and groaning Church.

His first act, on the opportune death of the existing Pope, was to appoint his cousin Bruno of Carinthia (who took the name of Gregory V.) to the vacant chair; and the nomination of this, the first German Pope, proclaimed to the world the new Emperor's intention of maintaining his grandfather's supremacy in the Papal elections. The Pope, a fervent ascetic, was twenty-three years of age, the Emperor sixteen; between them they dreamed of reforming the world against the coming millennium—that thousandth year of the Christian Era, to which the faithful looked with so much anxious hope and dread. They began their rule with unexampled clemency towards turbulent Rome, but facts soon showed them that in Rome force must be met with force. Scarcely was Otto's back turned than his hated 'Saxon' Pope was expelled by the 'Patrician' Crescentius; an Anti-Pope was set up, and Crescentius and the nationalist faction defied the Saxon tyrants. Otto and Gregory returned together in the spring of 998, and at their coming the trembling Anti-Pope fled, while Crescentius shut himself up in the castle of St. Angelo. Then Otto showed that he could be as cruel as any of his Byzantine ancestors; the Anti-Pope was caught, brought back to Rome, and deprived of eyes, nose, ears, and tongue; Crescentius, after a brave defence, was beheaded on the battlements of St. Angelo, and his body hung on a gallows in the Neronian Field.

But, having struck hard, Otto showed his yearning to heal and recreate. On Gregory's death he summoned his learned tutor Gerbert, whose knowledge was so portentous for that ignorant age that he was widely believed to be in league with the devil, and made him Pope under the name of Sylvester II. Together the new Constantine and the new Sylvester were to purify the world, and to set a new Rome at the head of a regenerated Christian empire. One of Otto's seals bears the inscription *Renovatio Imperii Romani*. He took up his abode on the Aventine, and but for one brief return to Germany, where he opened the tomb of Charlemagne and gazed on the remains of his great predecessor, he spent the rest of his short life in Italy. Half Byzantine as he was by blood, he imported an Eastern ceremonialism into his Court; sat alone at a semicircular table at the upper end of his hall; wore the crimson and purple of a Roman Emperor. But this mystical spirit impelled him also towards the wave of religious asceticism that was passing over Italy at this time. He became an ardent disciple of St. Nilus of Gaëta and St. Romuald of Ravenna; and when Rome had cast him out, early in 1001, by one of her periodic revolutions, he made his way to Ravenna, and spent Easter in the monastery of St. Apollinaris at Classis. And there, on the north wall of the deserted basilica, may still be read a record of his piety, in the inscription that relates his pilgrimages and his penances.[1] Otto III. died at the age of twenty-two, in the Sabine fortress of Paterno, and in the next year his saintly Pope Sylvester followed him to the grave—carried off in the body, so said the Romans, by his constant ally the devil. Thus ended the attempt of the idealist Græco-German to regenerate the world.

---

[1] Otho III. Rom. Imp. Germ. ob patrata crimina austeriori disciplinæ Sancti Romualdi obtemperans emenso nudis pedibus ab urbe Roma ad Garganum montem itinere basilicam hanc et cœnobium Classense XXXX diebus pœnitens inhabitavit et hic cilicio ac voluntariis castigationibus peccata sua xpinsea augustum dedit humilitatis exemplum et imperator sibi templum hoc et pœnitentiam suam nobilitavit   año P. C. M.

CHAPTER VI

The Normans in Southern Italy; Henry IV. and Hildebrand

THE first attempt of the transalpine rulers to reform the Papacy had ended in gloom and failure, and for forty years after the death of the last Otto the Tiara became the sport of contending factions in Rome, chief among them the Crescentii and the Counts of Tusculum, who were descended from Alberic. In the north the empire was carried on by two vigorous German princes, Henry II. and Conrad the Salic [1013—1039], whose incursions into the affairs of Lombardy produced a rising spirit of nationalism which greatly fostered the growth and independence of the towns. But it was in the south that the first half of the eleventh century witnessed the most remarkable events, for it saw the coming of those Norman adventurers who were so soon to make of it one of the most imposing kingdoms of the Middle Ages.

The condition of this unhappy country at the beginning of the eleventh century was such as to offer an ideal prey to some enterprising conqueror. The ancient Lombard Duchy of Benevento had gradually become parcelled out into several smaller princedoms, usually at war with one another, of which those of Capua, Salerno, and Benevento were the most important; the Byzantine Empire, which had never renounced its claims to sovereignty, had succeeded in driving the Saracens out of Apulia, and had applied the name of 'Theme of Lombardy' to the whole of that region; the republics of Naples, Gaëta and Amalfi (nominally subject to Constantinople) carried on a lucrative traffic with Sicily and the east, and waged endless wars with the Lombard princes, while roving bands of Saracens traversed the country, taking service with this prince or that and infinitely increasing the general unrest. Into this cauldron of strife there came, in the year 1003, a band of forty Norman pilgrims, newly returned from the Holy Land, whose prowess in repelling a Saracen raid on Salerno induced the prince of that city to invite them into his service. From this time onwards the numbers of the Normans were continually increased by the arrival of small bodies of adventurers, until in 1022 the aspect of affairs was changed by the coming of three sons of the Baron Tancred de

Hauteville. In 1025 these doughty champions accompanied the
Byzantine General Maniaces in an attack on the Saracens of Sicily,
and there performed such prodigies of valour that on their return
to the mainland they deemed themselves justified in seizing several
towns of Apulia as the reward for their services. They bestowed
the title of Count of Apulia on William Bras de Fer, the eldest of
the brothers, and organized a military constitution for the new
state, whose capital was Melfi [1043]. Shortly after this [1047] they
were joined by Robert, the fourth brother, who was one day to
make his surname of *Guiscard* (the Weasel) famous throughout the
east and west. He arrived in time to take part in the great struggle
against the Pope and the western Emperor which was to decide the
fate of the Normans in their new dominion.

For in the year 1051 Pope Leo IX., partly through the voluntary
offering of the inhabitants and partly by an advantageous exchange
with his ally, the western Emperor, had acquired the city of Benevento in full sovereignty, and the dispossessed Lombard prince had
called in the Normans to plunder and harry his former possessions.
Pope Leo immediately organized a league to extirpate the brood of
robbers, borrowed a few hundred Swabians from the Emperor
(giants who despised the Normans for their smallness of stature),
and took the field in person at the head of a motley host of thirty
thousand Lombards and Italians. He met the Normans at Città in
the Capitanata, and though these could only muster three thousand
horse and a few hundred infantry, they had soon completely routed
the Pope's Italians and slain the Swabians where they stood [1053].
Leo himself fell into their hands, but with politic courtesy they
humbly implored his pardon for their victory and conducted him
back in state to Benevento, where they succeeded in obtaining from
him the confirmation of their conquests, past and future. This
treaty was the inauguration of the Norman rôle of Protectors of
the Church which was to bring them so much honour and profit
during the rest of their career.

Fortified with the Papal blessing, Robert Guiscard now set himself to win the Calabrian peninsula, while his brother Humphrey
consolidated the Norman rule in Apulia. On Humphrey's death
[1056] Robert had himself proclaimed Duke of Apulia and Calabria,
and three years later he was solemnly confirmed by Pope Nicholas
II. in all his conquests *as a vassal of the Church*, and in return swore
an oath that the Normans would always maintain the Church in
her possessions, and support the canonically elected Popes.

This treaty with the Norman leader marks an important step in
the development of the Reformed Papacy, which had at last arisen

on the ruins of the Tusculan family. The reform had been chiefly the work of two men, Hildebrand the monk and Henry the Emperor, and was of such vast importance to the history of the Middle Ages that it may be well to glance at the manner in which it was brought about. The family of the Counts of Tusculum had succeeded in placing three Popes in succession on the sacred chair, their reigns extending from 1012 to 1045, and had brought the Papacy at last to such a depth of degradation in the person of Benedict IX. (who was elected in 1033 at the age of twelve) that even Rome was disgusted, and a synod of Roman clergy resolved to seek the intervention of the young German King Henry III., son of the Emperor Conrad the Salic. Benedict, against whom the Romans had already raised one Anti-Pope, Sylvester III., had recently sold the Papacy, in exchange for the revenue of St. Peter's pence from England, to a well-meaning priest who took the name of Gregory VI. [1045], and whose merit was that he selected the young Tuscan monk Hildebrand to be his confidential chaplain. But Benedict soon reasserted his claim and occupied the Lateran, while Sylvester held St. Peter's and Gregory St. Maria Maggiore, so that at Henry's coming there were three Popes in Rome. He sternly brushed them all aside (Gregory confessing his simony and retiring of his own accord), and presented the Romans with a German Bishop, Swidger of Bamberg, as their Pope (Clement II.), who proceeded to crown Henry first as Emperor and then as Patricius of the Romans. It was this latter title that was considered to carry with it the power of appointing to the Papacy; it had been borne by the exarchs, by Pippin and Charlemagne, and more recently by Crescentius, and the ancient privilege was now confirmed by the decree of a synod investing Henry with the right of nomination. Henry exercised it wisely and well during his short life; on Clement's death he appointed the saintly bishop of Toul (Leo IX.), whose reign saw some effective steps in the direction of church reform, and when Leo also died he sent another German bishop to Rome as Victor II. [1055] before his own career was cut short by death at the age of thirty-nine [1056]. Never again did the empire and Papacy attain to such a unity of purpose as under Henry III., but by his work of reformation the great Emperor had indeed undermined his own office, for he had raised up in this new and self-respecting Papacy a power against which the might of his successors was to shatter itself in vain.

The two main objects which the Reforming Popes, inspired by the sleepless activity of Hildebrand, had in view were the enforcement of celibacy on the secular clergy and the suppression of simony. The former was enjoined by the decrees of synod after synod, and was taken up in Lombardy with fanatical zeal by the party of the *Patarines*, or *Beggars*, who as the democratic and Papal faction soon found themselves in fierce conflict with the Imperial interests of upper Italy, and thus may not unfairly be called the ancestors of the Guelfs. In this branch of his work, in fact, the iron will of Hildebrand did at last overcome the mass of opposition which he encountered from the married clergy, and the Catholic Church has, from that day to this, maintained the position which he took up. But in the suppression of simony he gradually found himself involved in a contest with the whole secular power, for a crusade against the buying and selling of spiritual offices inevitably became a crusade against the appointment of bishops and abbots by secular princes—who generally exacted an equivalent for the coveted gift. Thus the first note of rebellion against the Imperial claims was struck in 1059 by the famous decree of the Lateran Council under Nicholas II. (who had made Hildebrand Archdeacon of Rome), by which the election to the Papacy was vested in the Cardinal-bishops and Cardinal-priests of the Roman territory, with only a vague reservation of the rights of 'Henry at this present time King, as well as to his successors who shall have received this right in person from the sacred chair.'

King Henry IV. was at this time only nine years old, and therefore could not resent this infringement of the rights bequeathed him by his father. But two years later, when Hildebrand had actually carried out the decree by causing the Cardinals to elect Anselm of Lucca to the vacant chair as Alexander II., Henry was invested with the insignia of the Patriciate by a deputation of anti-reforming Roman nobles, and presided at a council of German and Lombard bishops which pronounced Alexander deposed and elected an Anti-Pope in his stead. The strife was patched up later on and Alexander was recognized, but the scene must have made a deep impression on the mind of the young King. It set the tone of his future dealings with the Papacy.

At last, on Alexander's death in 1073, Hildebrand was himself elected Pope by the unanimous voice of the cardinals, supported by the acclamations of the people. He took the name of Gregory VII. The conduct of King Henry had already begun to cause him anxiety, for in a dispute concerning the Archbishopric of Milan he had invested the candidate of the anti-reforming party with the ring and staff, while the 'Patarines' had made a canonical election, confirmed by Alexander. Gregory, therefore, at the first Lenten

Synod [1075] which he held in Rome, proclaimed his policy in no uncertain tones. Investiture by laymen was for the first time directly condemned, and the penalty of anathema threatened against any who should practise it. Henry replied by appointing German bishops to the sees of Spoleto and Fermo, and by investing yet another archbishop of Milan, though his former nominee was still alive. Gregory rebuked him for these offences in a grave letter dispatched at Christmas 1075, and accompanied the letter by a verbal message citing him to appear before the Lenten Synod in Rome to answer for his conduct. Henry, strong in the momentary support of his nobles, who had assisted him in suppressing the rebellion of Saxony, summoned a council of German bishops to meet at Worms, and there openly defied the Pope. A decree of deposition was signed by all the bishops, and sent to Rome with a letter addressed to Gregory by the King himself.

How darest thou [wrote Henry], who hast won thy power through craft, flattery, bribery, and force, stretch forth thine hand against the Lord's anointed, despising the precept of the true Pope, St. Peter, 'Fear God, honour the King'? Condemned by the voice of all our bishops, quit the Apostolic Chair and let another take it, who will preach the sound doctrine of St. Peter, and not do violence under the cloak of religion. I, Henry, by the grace of God King, with all my bishops, say unto thee 'Get thee down, get thee down.'

But the fulminations of the King were answered by the more terrible and far more effective fulminations of the Pope. In the presence of the Lenten Synod, which had heard with indignation the decree of the Council of Worms, Gregory pronounced sentence of excommunication and of deposition against King Henry, and released his subjects from their oath of allegiance [1076]. No such thunderbolt had ever fallen on the head of a Christian King. Its effects were immediately felt in Germany, where Henry had never attained to his father's authority with the great nobles; Saxony revolted anew, vassal after vassal withdrew his support from the King [1076]. At last, in October, a Diet was held at Tribur, and humiliating terms of reconciliation were imposed upon Henry. Unless he had obtained absolution in person within a year from the pronouncement of the ban, the sentence of deposition was to take effect, and meanwhile he was to exercise none of the pre-rogatives of royalty. Henry was fain to submit, and, in the dead of winter, hearing that the Pope had started north on his way to preside at the Diet of Augsburg (where the fate of the kingdom was to be decided) he resolved to meet him on the way, and wring absolution from him at any cost. The cost was heavy indeed. At Henry's approach Gregory retreated to the castle of Canossa, the stronghold of his firm friend and ally, the Countess Matilda of Tuscany, and thither Henry followed him, intent only upon his quest. It was an unusually bitter winter, and the snow lay drifted deep in the mountain valleys, but Henry approached the castle as a penitent, barefooted and clothed in a coarse woollen garment, and stood knocking for admittance at the gate. For three days [Jan. 25—28, 1077], he stood and knocked, before the priest within was satisfied, while even the Countess Matilda, prototype of the Guelfs of future days, shuddered at so abject a humiliation of the temporal head of Christendom. When at last he was admitted it was only to find that absolution alone was to be granted him, while the whole question of his deposition was to be left for the decision of the Diet.

Little advantage, in fact, had Henry gained by his performance at Canossa. His enemies were not conciliated, his friends merely disgusted. The Diet of Forchheim, which met in March, pronounced him deposed and elected Rudolf of Swabia in his stead. Civil war followed, but as soon as Henry showed a bold front his friends again rallied round him. Gregory hesitated long between the two rivals, greatly disappointing the Swabians, who hoped that he would have thrown all his weight into their scale. At last, however, after Henry's army had been routed at the river Unstrut [Jan., 1080], the Pope's doubts gave way, and he renewed the ban both of excommunication and of deposition against Henry at the Lenten Synod of March, 1080. This time, however, the King met ban with ban. At a great assembly of German bishops held at Brixen in June, Gregory was pronounced deposed, and Wibert, Archbishop of Ravenna, elected in his place. Shortly afterwards [Oct., 1080] Rudolf of Swabia was killed in battle, so that Henry's position was stronger than at any previous time. He resolved to use it in humbling the Pope. In the spring of 1081 he crossed the Alps into Italy, which he was not to leave for the next three years, and encamped with his army before the Leonine City. But Rome held firm for Gregory, and after a short siege Henry was obliged to retire into Tuscany, where he carried on a tedious war with the Countess Matilda. Meanwhile Gregory appealed in vain to his vassal Robert Guiscard; the wonderful Norman was engaged at this moment in his attempt to conquer the Eastern Empire, and would not come to the Pope's aid. At last, in June, 1083, Henry's men broke into the Borgo of St. Peter's, and Gregory fled in haste to the castle of St. Angelo. The Romans, weary of the interminable strife, implored him to make terms with the King, and it was at length agreed that a General Council should be summoned for November to arbitrate between the two. But nothing was further from the mind of Gregory than genuine arbitration; he summoned only such bishops as had not been excommunicated, thereby excluding the whole of Henry's party. Hearing this, Henry broke the treaty on his side by arresting some of Gregory's partisans on their journey, and the council ended in failure. The Roman populace were obliged to take matters into their own hands. Henry had departed on an expedition against Guiscard in Apulia (for the Duke had now returned from the east), when he was overtaken by Roman envoys imploring him to come back and take possession of the city. Overjoyed at this turn of fortune, Henry hastened back, occupied the Lateran, caused his Anti-Pope Wibert to be consecrated as Clement III. [March, 1084], and on Easter Sunday received the Imperial Crown at his hands in St. Peter's.

But his triumph was short-lived. The dauntless old Pope within St. Angelo may have been forced to look upon the bravery of his coronation pageant; he was even besieged in the fortress by the angry Romans, but meanwhile his messengers were hastening to Robert Guiscard, and this time the Norman saw his own interest in coming to his suzerain's relief. With thirty-six thousand men, including a large force of Saracens, he advanced on Rome, and Henry, who had but a small force, was obliged to evacuate his new capital and to retire, first into Lombardy, and then across the Alps. Behind him the Norman broke into the city by the Flaminian Gate, and treated it as the prize of war. Saracens, Northmen, and Calabrians spread plundering through the streets, and on the third day a rising of the Imperial party provoked a savage reprisal, during which the whole quarter between the Lateran and the Colosseum was destroyed by fire, kindled at the order of Guiscard. Gregory seems to have made no effort to stay the havoc and slaughter, and when at last it ceased he was obliged to retire with his deliverer into southern Italy, for Rome would harbour him no more. Sorrowfully he journeyed across the ravaged Campagna to Monte Cassino, and thence to Salerno, where after a year's sojourn he died. 'Henry and Wibert I absolve not,' he solemnly declared, 'nor the principal persons who by word and deed have abetted their wickedness and impiety, but all others I absolve and bless who freely believe that I have power so to do, as the Vicar of St. Peter and St. Paul.' And then in a nobler spirit, 'I have loved righteousness and hated iniquity: therefore I die in exile.'

So amid the curses of Rome and the glare of her burning streets, ended the first chapter in the long struggle between Emperor and Pope. It had been well for Henry, the seeming victor, if he could have followed his great antagonist speedily to the grave. But Henry was yet to endure twenty years of life, dogged by the implacable hatred of Gregory's successors; he was to be passed over, though the natural head of Christendom, as leader of the First Crusade; his two sons, encouraged by successive Popes, were to rise up in rebellion against him. At last, worn out by his incessant misfortunes, deposed by his unnatural son, he died in 1106, an old man though only in his fifty-seventh year. The Countess Matilda outlived him by nine years [1115], and left a will which was to add new flames to the fire of discord between Church and Empire for the next two hundred years. The whole of her vast possessions she bequeathed to the Church, drawing no distinction between the feudal lands which she held from the Empire and the 'allodial' estates over which her right of bequest was undisputed. To the ever-recurring quarrel on the right of investiture this fresh cause for strife was therefore added, but the confusion that ensued directly favoured the rise of the towns, and the earliest examples of communal constitutions are found among the relics of the Countess Matilda's possessions. In giving this unconscious stimulus to the emancipation of the cities the old *dévote* was building better than she knew, for she had passed on her quarrel to a force that carried with it the spirit of the age, that stood for freedom against alien domination. From the War of Investitures arose the Italian city-states.

CHAPTER VII

The Rise of the Cities, and their Conflict with Frederick Barbarossa

And many a warrior-peopled citadel,
Like rocks which fire lifts out of the flat deep
Arose in sacred Italy,
Frowning o'er the tempestuous sea
Of kings, and priests, and slaves, in tower-crown'd majesty.
SHELLEY, *Ode to Liberty*

BY the time at which we have now arrived—the beginning of the twelfth century—the cities of northern and central Italy had already achieved, through internal struggles which are for the most part unrecorded, that municipal independence which was to be both their glory and their ruin. The War of Investitures had proved, as we have seen, a direct stimulus to the process of emancipation, but in order to understand this process more fully it will be necessary to cast a brief glance at the history of the cities since we lost sight of them in the general feudalization of the country under the Carlovingians.

Charles the Great had hoped to secure the obedience of the cities by placing in each a *count* as the king's representative; but under the weak rule of his successors these counts were able to make their power hereditary, and to arrogate to themselves all the privileges of feudal nobles. So formidable had they become, indeed, in the anarchic times of the Italian or Lombard Emperors[1] [888—924], that these shadowy rulers bethought them of the expedient of delegating their powers to the *bishops* of the towns, and were the first to effect this change in some of the cities of Lombardy. Meanwhile the invasions of the savage Magyars had forced the inhabitants to provide for their own defence by fortifying their towns and by forming a regular militia. Otto the Great and his successors encouraged the transference of power from the counts to the bishops, who now in their turn began to grant away the lands outside the city walls to feudal vassals, or *Capitani*, while these again divided their fiefs among sub-vassals or *Valvassors*. In this way the bishops could command a large military force, but even so their power was less obnoxious to the emperors than that of the counts, for they could not make it hereditary, and as yet no one had challenged the Emperor's right of investiture, which for all practical purposes was one of nomination.

[1] See. p. 63.

By the end of the tenth century, therefore, the cities of upper Italy had all passed under the temporal rule of their bishops, and had once more begun to take an active and often a turbulent part in Imperial affairs. The long and bitter enmity between Milan and Pavia, for instance, arose from the hostility of the Pavesans towards the German kings, Henry II. and Conrad the Salic [1013—1039], whose part was at first taken by the Milanese under their great Archbishop Heribert. But when Conrad attempted to interfere with the privileges of the Archbishop in a quarrel between the *Capitani* and *Valvassors*, the Milanese turned on him in fury [1036], while the Pavesans took up his cause, and for two years Heribert and the 'people' of Milan defied the Emperor and prevented him from entering their walls. Conrad bequeathed the quarrel to the feudal nobles who remained faithful to him, but in the war that followed, Heribert invented the famous *Carroccio*, or sacred car, bearing the altar and banner of the Commune, and showed for the first time that civic patriotism was a match for the feudal forces of the countryside. This device was speedily adopted by the other Lombard cities, and to lose the *Carroccio* in battle became the mark of utter ignominy and disgrace.

The great-hearted Heribert died in 1045, and under the long reign of his successor Guido, Milan, and indeed the whole of Lombardy, was convulsed by the controversy set on foot by the reforming Popes concerning the marriage of the clergy. The reformers (whose nickname of *Patarines* we have already mentioned),[1] led by Ariald a monk and Landulph a noble, roused the populace of Milan against their priests, who claimed the direct authority of St. Ambrose for the right of clerical marriage. Fierce fighting took place in streets and churches, but it was remarkable that whenever Rome interfered by sending her legates to support the reformers, the Milanese devotion to St. Ambrose awoke at once, and the mob rallied to the cry of 'Shall Ambrose submit to Peter?' For nearly thirty years the city was in a chronic state of disturbance, and the authority of the Archbishop (who sided on the whole with the anti-reformers) dwindled to the vanishing-point. From 1065 to 1075 Milan was ruled by the fanatic reformer Herlembald, brother of Landulph, and after his death the episcopal power was still further weakened by the War of Investitures, which produced rival claimants to the sees not only of Milan but of most of the other Lombard towns. In the strife of Pope and Emperor the people seized its opportunity, and by the first or second decade of the twelfth century the cities had almost all developed a full-blown constitution. At the head of the

[1] See p. 72.

state we find the Consuls, variable in number, annually elected and usually drawn from the noble class; then comes the *Consiglio di Credenza*, or Privy Council, and below that the *Gran Consiglio*, often consisting of several hundred of the free but non-noble citizens, so many for each quarter of the town. The ultimate authority was the great mass of the free citizens assembled in the public square (the so-called *Parlamento*), but this was only summoned in times of emergency, and was only expected to endorse by acclamation the decisions arrived at by the higher councils.

No sooner, however, had the cities achieved their liberty than they turned their new-found strength against one another. The pugnacity of the Lombard Communes has become a by-word of history, and only at one supreme moment of danger did they ever combine against a common foe. Even then their union was but temporary, and we shall be obliged to record the melancholy fall of city after city, first under domestic tyranny, and finally under the yoke of the foreigner. Their feuds arose sometimes from disputes over water-ways and trade-routes, or over the boundaries of a diocese or of a feudal fief, but often from the mere arrogance of the stronger cities, which early acquired a passion for crushing their weaker neighbours. In 1100 Cremona attacked and subjugated Crema; Pavia did the same with Tortona, and both the conquered towns placed themselves under the protection of Milan. From 1107 to 1111 Milan carried on a furious war with Lodi, and finally razed the town to its foundations and distributed the inhabitants among six undefended villages. Next she turned her arms against Como, and after ten years of bloody war forced her to submit to paying the taxes and serving in the armies of her rival. It is no wonder that, when the day of retribution came, both Lodi and Como were found in the ranks of the German invader.

While the cities of the north had thus emerged into a state of complete individual freedom, a directly opposite tendency was at work in the less fortunate regions of the south. There the successors of Robert Guiscard were extinguishing the last relics of republican independence, and laying the foundations of that grinding feudalism which was to drain the lifeblood of the country for seven long centuries. Guiscard himself had subdued, by the year 1080, the last Greek cities of the Apulian coast, from Bari to Tarentum; the republic of Amalfi had bestowed on him the title of duke, on condition that her municipal freedom should be respected; and he and his nephew Richard of Aversa had also acquired the three remaining Lombard duchies of Salerno, Benevento and Capua. But the exploits of the two Rogers, father and son, were perhaps still more remarkable. The elder (himself the youngest of the sons of Tancred) succeeded, after a war of twenty-eight years [1062—1090], in winning the whole of Sicily from the Saracens, and ruled the island according to the law of its various inhabitants—Greeks, Saracens, and Normans—with rude justice until his death in 1101. The younger, as able and energetic as his father, but with more of the tyrant's temper, lost no opportunity of extending and consolidating his dominions. In 1127, on the death of Guiscard's grandson William, he set sail for the mainland and forced the reluctant barons to acknowledge him as Duke of Apulia and Calabria, and three years later [1130], taking advantage of a Papal schism, he bargained with the Anti-Pope Anaclete II to bestow on him the title of king, in exchange for the support of the Norman arms. But many of the more northern barons refused to march with him against the lawful Pope (Innocent II.); they allied themselves with Naples (still a practically free republic, though under the suzerainty of the Eastern Empire), and took part in the long and gallant resistance of that city to the forces of King Roger [1135]. The Emperor Lothar was induced by St. Bernard to intervene [1137] on behalf of Pope Innocent; he advanced with overwhelming forces; the Pisans sent a fleet of a hundred galleys to the relief of Naples, and Roger was obliged to bow for the moment before the storm. But on the speedy retreat of Lothar he returned with an army of Saracens, wreaked a savage vengeance on the revolted districts, and by a stroke of good fortune managed to possess himself of the person of Innocent [1138], from whom he wrung a formal recognition of his regal title and of his right to Naples. The republic, deserted on all sides, sent to offer him the ducal crown, and whether out of respect or fear, Roger allowed her to retain many of her municipal institutions. But he had already extinguished the privileges of Amalfi, and the extinction of those of Naples was only a question of time.

After this humiliating adventure, Pope Innocent was called upon to face a still more formidable situation at his very doors. The republican spirit had spread to Rome, and the chronic discontent of the populace with clerical rule found expression in a revolution [1143] which installed a senate once more upon the Capitol. The immediate occasion of the rising was a war with Tivoli in which the Pope had adroitly reaped all the advantages won in battle by the city militia, but it was made famous by its association with the name of Arnold of Brescia, the reforming monk who came to support the young republic with his eloquence and his enthusiasm. Long a pupil of Abelard at the University of Paris, Arnold yearned for a return to the ancient inwardness of the Christian faith, and had imbibed the sternest notions on the subject of the wordliness and corruption of the priesthood. In his native Brescia he had already led the revolt of the people against the temporal rule of their bishop, and he was now to dedicate the rest of his life to a crusade against the usurpations of the Papacy. His doctrines were condemned and he himself was banished from Italy by the Lateran Council of 1139, but having patched up a reconciliation with Pope Eugenius III. (a disciple of St. Bernard), he hastened to Rome in 1146 and devoted himself, under the auspices of the new-made Senate, to the task of rousing the popular feeling against the *Dominium temporale*. Eugenius was obliged to spend most of his reign in exile, or in those Latin or Tuscan towns which now, in the general anarchy, had reverted to their primitive tradition of hostility to Rome; and the Eternal City was ruled by a *Patricius* and a senate of fifty-six burghers and members of the lesser nobility. The greater nobles mostly sided with the Pope, or else with impartial shrewdness seized the towns and villages which had belonged to the territories of the Church.

Thus matters went on for nine years, until the patriots were confronted by an alliance between the two strongest forces of the age. In 1152 Frederick of Swabia, nephew of the last King Conrad III., was elected King of the Germans; in 1154 our countryman, Nicholas Breakspear, became Pope as Hadrian IV. The interests of these two, divergent on most points, were at least identical as against revolutionaries such as Arnold of Brescia. Hadrian expelled the prophet by means of the Church's most terrible weapon: he laid the interdict upon Rome until the people consented to Arnold's banishment. Frederick, after his first campaign in Lombardy, was approaching Rome for his coronation [1155], and readily consented to purchase the Pope's goodwill by seizing Arnold at the Tuscan fortress in which he had taken refuge. Arnold was handed over to the Papal prefect, who condemned him to death, and thus the first Italian to protest against the temporal power expiated his heresy on the gallows. His body was burnt and the ashes scattered in the Tiber, that no relic of the heresiarch might remain to encourage his disciples. But the Roman Senate still survived, and when Frederick gave an unfavourable answer to its envoys and refused to take even the customary oath to respect the liberties of the people, the gates of the city were barred against him, and his coronation was hastily performed [June 18, 1155] without popular acclamation, in St. Peter's, the Papal stronghold. During the banquet following, the Roman militia made a desperate onslaught on his camp beside the

F

Leonine walls, and though the attack was repulsed, the new-made Emperor soon found it convenient to retire before the summer heats to Germany.

Frederick of Hohenstaufen, Duke of Swabia, King of the Germans and Imperator Augustus, was in many ways the ideal embodiment of the Germanic hero-king. Unmatched in bodily prowess, a firm and just master towards the turbulent lords who had so often made his predecessors' reigns a burden to them, filled moreover with the lofty ambition to leave a great name in history, he was a leader whom his Germans could follow to war with an enthusiasm unknown since the days of Otto or Charles. But there was a dark strain of cruelty in his nature, and his destiny led him to pit his strength against a force which he could neither understand nor respect—the pride of the self-governing Communes of Italy. To him the burghers were merely rebellious subjects, who had to be brought back to a sense of their duty, while to them he appeared as a monster of tyranny whose red beard reeked with the blood of their brothers and compatriots.[1] The quarrel first arose through the complaints made to him at the Diet of Constance [1153] by two citizens of Lodi against the violence of the Milanese, and Frederick resolved to combine his coronation journey with a thorough settlement of the affairs of Lombardy. Thus it occurred that, when he arrived before Rome in the summer of 1155, much had already happened in the north; the territories of Milan had been ravaged for the first time; Asti, for certain offences against the Marquis of Montferrat, had been sacked; Tortona, for its alliance with the Milanese, destroyed to its foundations; and a deep division, founded on ancient feuds, had been drawn between the Imperialist cities, headed by Pavia and Cremona, and the republican, headed by Milan. It was this division amongst the Lombards themselves that enabled Frederick for so long to hold the balance between them; when at last they combined, not even he could stand against them.

His second campaign, in 1158, was provoked by the continual arrogance of the Milanese, who, not content with rebuilding Tortona, had just destroyed Lodi for the second time, owing to the contumacy of the Lodesans in refusing to swear an oath of unconditional fidelity to Milan without the clause 'saving our allegiance to the Emperor.' Frederick determined to chastise these insolent subjects; his army, swelled by the militias of the Imperialist cities, amounted to some hundred thousand men, and after choosing the

[1] The Italians first called him Barbarossa after the siege of Crema [1159]
(see p. 83).

site for a New Lodi in a strong position on the Adda, he sat down
to invest the immense circuit of the walls of Milan [Aug. 6, 1158].[1]
The siege was marked by many deeds of heroism and cruelty on
both sides, but the pinch of hunger was felt within the walls from
the very first days, and after only a month's resistance a capitulation was arranged [Sept. 7, 1158] to the satisfaction of both parties.
The Milanese were to pay an indemnity, to give three hundred
hostages, and to restore their freedom to Lodi and Como, but they
retained the right of electing their own consuls, subject only to the
Emperor's confirmation. The lull produced by this compact, however, was not of long duration, for Frederick was shrewd enough
to see that his authority needed reinforcing by a more general
arrangement, and for this purpose he summoned a diet to meet at
Roncaglia, at which the vexed question of the *regalia*, or Imperial
prerogatives, was to be settled. Here he obtained from the doctors
of Bologna University (on which he had always showered his
benefits) a decision eminently favourable to his interests; even the
appointment of the consuls was declared to be an Imperial right,
and Frederick only remitted it in the case of those cities which had
stood by him most loyally. Here too was first instituted the office
of the *Podestà*, or Imperial representative for the administration of
justice in each diocese, the peculiar feature of whose office was that
its holder was bound to be a native of some other Commune, in
order to secure impartiality. Unpopular at first, the Podestà became in time an integral part of the polity of the towns; his election reverted to the Communes themselves, and his jurisdiction
insensibly paved the way towards the rule of the despots.

The result of the new laws of Roncaglia was to set Lombardy
once more in a blaze [1159]. The Imperial Chancellor was driven
out of Milan by an angry mob when he came to replace the consuls
by a Podestà, and the town of Crema resisted with equal energy
Frederick's orders to demolish its fortifications. Upon this the
Cremonese, implacable enemies of the Cremascans, persuaded
Frederick to attack the impudent town, and the year 1159 was
marked by the seven months' siege of this insignificant fortress—
a siege at which Frederick earned immortal infamy by his device
of tying fifty Cremascan prisoners (some of them children) to the
front of one of his moving towers, so as to ward off the missiles
of the besieged. The device failed, for the Cremascans sacrificed

---

[1] Since the campaign of 1154—5 the citizens had thrown up a new ram-
part to enclose the suburbs which had grown up outside the Wall of
Maximian; it was surrounded by a moat of running water and was pierced
by eighteen gates and posterns.

their sons to their freedom; the tower was driven back, and the bodies of the mangled hostages were removed in the evening by the shame-struck Germans. But the end came at last, and in January, 1160, Crema surrendered, on condition that its population of some twenty thousand souls should depart in peace, carrying such of their property as they were able. Behind the long procession the Cremonese sprang like wolves upon the empty town, seized whatever was movable, and set fire to the rest.

But Milan was still unsubdued, and until the summer of 1161 Frederick had no adequate army with which to undertake its reduction. Then, however, his Germans once more poured down the passes to join him, and this time Frederick made no direct attack upon the walls, but contented himself with a systematic destruction of all crops, vines, and fruit-trees within a twelve-mile radius of the town, and with cutting off the hands of all peasants seized in conveying provisions into it. These measures, aided by a disastrous fire which destroyed the city granaries, proved effectual; in February, 1162, the consuls began to sound Frederick as to terms of peace. But Frederick would have nothing but unconditional surrender; Milan must trust to his clemency alone. An imposing ceremony was therefore arranged, in which the *Carroccio*, escorted by the militias of the six gates bearing crosses in their hands, was brought forth to the Emperor's camp near Lodi, and its mast lowered before him in sign of homage; the citizens fell on their knees before the Imperial throne, and raising their crosses aloft, cried aloud for mercy. But Frederick's face remained impassive, and he merely commanded them to return to their city, whither he would send his commissioners to take from them the oath of allegiance. He then retired to Pavia, and summoned a Parliament consisting of the deadliest enemies of Milan to decide upon her fate. The decision was soon arrived at: Milan must be destroyed, and her inhabitants parcelled out amongst four undefended villages. Eight days' notice of the sentence was given, and at the end of that time [Mar. 26, 1162] Frederick led his army once more towards the now deserted city, and entered it by a breach in the walls. He gave the signal to fall on, and the men of Lodi, Cremona, Pavia, Novara, and Como, together with the *Capitani* of Seprio and Martesana, each took possession of the gate and section of the wall allotted to them and set themselves exultingly to the work of destruction. Then they spread into the town itself and sacked the houses, while some of the streets were set on fire, but a certain awe restrained the pillagers from destroying churches and convents. Yet the devastation was complete enough, and for five years the proud city of Milan lay ruined and deserted, whilst her people, scattered amongst squalid villages or hostile cities, drank the cup of adversity to the very dregs.

Meanwhile in another quarter events had occurred which were to have an important influence on the struggle between Frederick and the cities. In 1159 the valiant English Pope had died, on the eve of a formidable contest with Frederick on the subject of his encroachments on the Papal territories. A double election followed, the Imperialist cardinals (with whom this time the Senate made common cause) choosing an open-handed noble who took the name of Victor IV., while the Papal party (numerically the stronger) chose Alexander III. Neither Pope could maintain himself in Rome, but Frederick at once took up Victor's cause and had his election ratified by a Synod at Pavia, while Alexander, though obliged to fly to France [1162], maintained from his exile the spirits of the struggling Communes. England, France, and the Norman King of Sicily recognized him as lawful Pope, and even in Germany he had a strong party. On Victor's death, however, the Imperial Chancellor in Italy set up another Anti-Pope (Paschalis III.), but as this puppet was unknown and unpopular in Rome the Senate began to incline towards Alexander, who with the help of William of Sicily made his return to the Lateran in November, 1165.

On receipt of this news Frederick resolved on war, and within a year [Nov., 1166], he had again crossed the Alps, intent on installing his own Pope in the Lateran by force. He arrived before Rome at the end of July, 1167, and after a bloody battle in and around St. Peter's felt himself master of the situation. The Senate made terms with him at the price of expelling Alexander; Paschalis was conse-crated with all due form in St. Peter's, and Frederick might flatter himself that he had regained the position of Henry III. towards the Church. But at this moment his triumphs were swept from his hand at a single blow. Pestilence—the August fever of Rome—descended on his army: it was St. Peter's vengeance, so said the Romans, on the desecrators of his altar. With a wasted and stricken force Frederick retraced his steps towards the north. There he perceived that the tide in Lombardy had also turned against him, but, unable to withstand it now, he withdrew secretly across the Alps in March, 1168.

Italy indeed was already lost to him, though it needed the ex-perience of two more bloody campaigns before Frederick would admit the fact. But as early as 1164 the tyranny of the Podestàs whom he had appointed in the March of Verona had produced a league between the cities of Verona, Vicenza, Padua, and Treviso, with the secret support of Venice, and during the expedition to Rome the heads of this League were in active communication with some of the cities of Lombardy proper. The negotiations culminated in a secret meeting at the monastery of Pontida [April 7, 1167], at which the Veronese delegates agreed with those of Brescia, Bergamo, Cremona, Mantua, Ferrara, and the Milanese villages, to support one another with life and property until the privileges enjoyed since the reign of Henry IV. should be recovered. With uplifted hands the envoys swore that the first object of the League should be the rebuilding of the walls of Milan. Such was the celebrated Lombard League, which gradually increased in power until it included all the Communes (except Pavia) which had formerly been Imperialist, and finally expressed its strength by building a new city in the March of Montferrat which, in honour of the lawful Pope, it named Alexandria.

For six years after his hurried retreat in 1168, Frederick was unable to return to Italy. He committed his Italian affairs to the hands of his Chancellor Christian, Archbishop of Mainz, whose most notable enterprise, the siege of Ancona, miscarried in spite of the assistance of a Venetian fleet. But in 1174, he was free to return once more, and marched over the Mont Cenis at the head of a fine army. The whole winter was spent in the fruitless siege of Alexandria, which, though its walls were as yet only of earth bound together with straw, held out triumphantly till April, 1175, when the army of the League approached to its relief. Frederick raised the siege, and opened negotiations both with the Pope and the Communes, but though both parties disbanded their armies for the year, no settlement could be arrived at with the Papal legates. A desultory war broke out again, but as soon as the passes were open in the spring, Frederick's main force rejoined him, marching by Chiavenna and Como, and the decisive battle was at last fought [May 29, 1176], in the neighbourhood of Legnano, between the Imperialists on the one side and the militias of Milan, Piacenza, Verona, Brescia, Novara, and Vercelli on the other. At first the German charge carried all before it, but the Milanese *Carroccio* was guarded by two picked bodies of young men, named the Company of Death and the Company of the Carroccio, who had vowed to die rather than turn their backs. Their firmness converted the incipient panic into a victorious attack. The Imperial standard-bearer fell; Frederick himself was unhorsed and left for dead upon the field, while the Italian cavalry broke the last resistance of the Germans and pursued the fugitives into the deep waters of the Ticino. Long search was made among the dead for Frederick's body, but after some days the news spread that he had appeared after all at Pavia, safe but alone, and for a moment the Lombards felt their victory turned to dust and ashes.

But they need not have feared, for the Emperor had had enough. He saved his pride indeed by reconciling himself first with the Pope, whose mediation he desired in the negotiations with the cities, but thenceforward, to use a modern phrase, he recognized his subjects as belligerents. It was at length arranged that a conference between the representatives of the Emperor and of the Communes should meet under the presidency of Alexander at Venice—the only town which, having impartially supported both sides, could act as an acceptable intermediary. There in July, 1177, a truce of six years was agreed upon, pending a more permanent arrangement. At the end of the six years, though the hot-heads on both sides wished to renew the war, the truce was converted into the celebrated Treaty of Constance [1183], by which the Emperor retained only the right of *investing* the Consuls, leaving their free election to the Communes, and abandoned all criminal jurisdiction to the communal judges. His suzerainty was to be acknowledged by an oath of allegiance, which must be taken by all citizens between the ages of seventeen and seventy, and his ancient right of lodging and maintenance at the public expense during his coronation journey was reasserted.

Thus the twenty-two years war ended in an adjustment between the three most vital forces of the age, in the only manner which that age found possible—a titular subjection of the people to their lord, with a real independence, and a co-operation, expressed in the outward show of reverence, between the temporal and spiritual heads of Christendom. When on July 23, 1177, Pope Alexander authorized the aged Doge Ziani to invite Barbarossa to the City of the Lagoons, and when the proud Emperor knelt before his old antagonist and humbly kissed his foot, probably no one in the vast audience assembled in St. Mark's Piazza thought the ceremony anything but fitting. It symbolized the reconciliation between Church and Empire, without which mediæval thought could not conceive of a well-ordered world, and the fact that the Church stood for the moment as the ally and protector of the people gave a peculiar solidity also to the cause of freedom. Italian life stood at the threshold between old and new, but those two majestic figures of Pope and Emperor still held sway over its imagination, and were still to exercise, long after one of them at least had ceased to be a reality, the master-influence over its destinies and struggles.

CHAPTER VIII

Venice, Genoa and Pisa,
to the End of the Twelfth Century

THE choice of Venice as the scene of the reconciliation between Barbarossa and the Communes was the half-conscious recognition of her unique position among the cities of Italy. Secure in her strange isolation among the impregnable lagoons, never mastered by Hun, Goth, or Lombard, though owing her existence to all three, this city of refuge founded in the evil days of the decaying Empire pursued throughout her early history a course fundamentally different from that of the typical Communes of northern Italy. In a less marked degree the two other sea-republics of Genoa and Pisa withdrew themselves from the life of the mainland, and sought their fortune in the outer world; but these resembled the cities of the plain in one respect—that they early learnt to turn their arms against one another. Within the space at our command it will be impossible to follow out in any detail the fascinating story of these three republics, but no sketch of the life of Italy, however slight, can afford to pass unnoticed so remarkable an offshoot of that life.

The islands of the Venetian lagoon, though probably inhabited even in Roman times by a handful of hardy fisher-folk, received their first great accession of population during the invasion of the Huns under Attila, when Aquileia, Padua, and many other towns of the mainland sent forth their bands of fugitives to seek a safer home among the sea-waters. For the lagoons, sheltered from the open sea by the long low barrier of the *Lido*, were reduced twice a day to impassable mud-flats by the ebb of the shallow tide, and so protected the sandy islands they contained from all approach either from sea or land, save to the native-born pilot. Here then, safe from the land-loving barbarians, and receiving fresh strength from each great convulsion of the mainland (but more especially from the Lombard invasion), there gradually arose a chain of twelve small townships[1] scattered along the sixty miles of coast from

---

[1] The names of these townships, taken from north to south, are as follows: Grado, Bibbione, Caorle, Jesolo or Equilium, Heraclea, Torcello, Burano, Rivus Altus (Rialto), Malamocco or Metamaucus, Pupilia, Clugies Minor and Clugies Major (Chioggia).

Grado to Chioggia. Each township soon had its *tribune*, and each was inspired by feelings of fierce animosity towards its neighbour, but in face of the outside world these discords were held in check, and the tribunes always spoke of themselves collectively as the *tribuni marittimi*. By the time of Theodoric the islanders had already attracted attention by the peculiarity of their existence, and a famous letter of Cassiodorus to the tribunes dated September, 537, and asking for a supply of transports, gives the earliest description of the lagoon settlements:

'It is a pleasure [writes the garrulous Secretary][1] to recall the situation of your dwellings as I myself have seen them. Venetia the praiseworthy touches on the south Ravenna and the Po, while on the east it enjoys the delightsomeness of the Ionian shore, where the alternating tide now discovers and now conceals the face of the fields. . . . Here, after the manner of water-fowl, have you fixed your homes. . . . Like them there are seen amid the wide expanse of the waters your scattered dwellings, not the product of Nature, but cemented by the care of man into a firm foundation. For by a twisted and knotted osierwork the earth there collected is turned into a solid mass, and you oppose without fear to the waves of the sea so fragile a bulwark. . . . Your inhabitants have one notion of plenty, that of gorging themselves with fish. . . . One kind of food refreshes all; the same sort of dwelling shelters all; no one can envy his neighbour's home. . . . Your whole attention is concentrated on your salt-works. Instead of driving the plough or wielding the sickle, you roll your cylinders. . . . Therefore let your boats, which you keep tethered, like so many beasts of burden, to your walls, be kept in diligent repair.'

During the great march of Narses round the head of the Adriatic[2] the General made use of the flat Venetian boats to transport his supplies, and perhaps out of gratitude for this service he built, when the war was over, on the island of Rivus Altus, a church to St. Theodore, a few stones of which were recently found incorporated in the wall of St. Mark's northern transept.

By the end of the seventh century the feuds and jealousies which distracted the settlements had become so inconvenient that a General Assembly, or *Arrengo*, was summoned by the Patriarch of Grado to meet at Heraclea [697], and there at his advice it was decided to elect one supreme magistrate for the whole of the lagoon communities, to hold his office for life and bear the title of Duke or *Doge*. No limitations were as yet imposed upon the Dogeship.

[1] See Dr. Hodgkin's translation in *The Letters of Cassiodorus*, p. 515.
[2] See p. 47.

save that the tribunes were still retained as subordinate officials and that for the decision of peace or war the assent of an *Arrengo* was necessary. So absolute an authority naturally became an object of fierce rivalry between the different townships. Nor were the populace content with their new autocracy, and from 737 to 742 the experiment of an annual governor, or *Magister Militum*, was tried, but since this only led to still greater scenes of violence the Assembly reverted after five years to the Dogeship, which was now to endure for over a thousand years. Soon, however, a marked tendency towards hereditary succession began to show itself, and for nearly three hundred years the dukedom was all but monopolized by four powerful families—the Galbai or Heraclea [764—804], the Particiachi or Badoeri [811—942], the Candiani, alternating at first with the last-named, but predominating from 932 to 979, and lastly the Orseoli, who in the person of Pietro Orseolo II [991—1008] gave to Venice by far the most illustrious Doge that had as yet reigned over her. But the deep-rooted democratic feeling of the lagoon-dwellers had never cordially accepted the principle of heredity, and at last it asserted itself in a violent resistance to the attempt of the third of Orseolo's sons to seize the Dogeship—a resistance which ended in a formal decree [1032] of the *Arrengo* that in future both hereditary succession and the association of a Doge-Consort during the Doge's lifetime should be illegal. At the same time the first limitations to the Doge's power were made by giving him two ducal councillors, and by obliging him to ask the advice on important matters of a council of prominent citizens called the *Pregadi* or *Invited*.

Meanwhile in their relation to the outside world the Venetians had gradually attained to a position of formidable strength and independence. So long as the Exarchate endured, the lagoon townships owned themselves a part of it; but when the Franks had extinguished the last relics of Byzantine rule in northern Italy [774], the one care of the islanders was to hold aloof both from east and west, though they accepted the nominal suzerainty of Byzantium, as being the weaker and more distant power of the two. But the Frankish Empire did not relinquish them without a struggle. Pippin, whom his father Charles had made King of Italy, came in 810 with a powerful fleet and army to attack the lagoons; he penetrated northwards along the Lido as far as Malamocco (then the seat of government), but only to find the town deserted, for the inhabitants had judged it safer to concentrate at *Rialto*, that cluster of islands between the mainland and the Lido which was thenceforward to be

Venice. There, armed with 'bows and missile weapons,'[1] they bade the Franks defiance, until the approach of summer and of a Byzantine fleet together warned Pippin to retire. 'Ye are my subjects,' argued the defeated King to a deputation of Venetians, 'for ye come from lands that are mine!' 'Nay,' answered his stubborn opponents, 'we will be the Roman Emperor's men, not yours.' This six months' siege was the turning-point in the early history of Venice; it determined the future bias of the state towards Constantinople and away from the territorial lords of Italy, and by the choice it brought about of Rialto as the capital it laid the foundation of Venice as she is today. Angelo Particiaco, elected Doge in 811, built the first ducal palace on the site of the present structure, and in the reign of his son the new capital was hallowed by the rape of the body of St. Mark from Alexandria [829], and the erection of a basilica to do it honour—next to Narses's old church of St. Theodore.

During the ninth century the Venetians had a hard struggle to defend their home and their growing trade against Saracen and Dalmatian pirates, but the continuous warfare in which they lived favoured their development as a sea-power, and the advantageous treaties they obtained from Carolingian and Italian emperors show the increasing respect in which their state was held.[2] But it was not until the reign of Pietro Orseolo II. [991—1008], which followed on a period of stormy faction-feuds within Venice itself (during the Candiano dynasty), that the true period of Venetian expansion begins. This remarkable statesman not only concluded favourable commercial treaties with the Greek Emperor and with the Saracens, but adopted at last a decisive policy against the Slav pirates of the Dalmatian coast, whose depredations and demands for blackmail had become a curse to the state. A great expedition was fitted out in the year 1000; Lagosta, the pirate stronghold, was taken by assault, and the small trading towns along the coast hastened to recognize their protector as *Duke of Dalmatia*. From that time onwards Venice never abandoned her claim to police the opposite shore of the Adriatic, with its innumerable harbours and rocky islands. Her rule, as it gradually consolidated itself, was gladly accepted by the coast towns, which had maintained the traditions of Roman life amid the flood of Slav invasion during the seventh and eighth centuries; but when the Hungarian kingdom arose under the great St. Stephen [997—1038], Venice found herself involved in

---

[1] See the account of the siege in the *De Administrando Imperii* of the Emperor Constantine Porphyrogenitus, cap. 28.
[2] Guido of Spoleto (Emperor from 891—6) granted them the privilege of remaining under the jurisdiction of their Doge throughout his dominions.

a prolonged struggle with the Hungarians for the possession of Dalmatia, and only obtained a 'secure' title to those regions at the beginning of the fifteenth century.

So far did these successes spread the fame of Doge Orseolo that the romantic mind of his contemporary, Otto III., was filled with the desire to see and speak with him, and during the last year of the young Emperor's life—when Rome had cast him out—he paid a secret visit to the lagoons [1001] lodging in the newly completed *second* ducal palace,[1] standing godfather to the Doge's son and holding high metaphysical discourse with the Doge himself.[2] It is the first recorded visit of curiosity paid to the lagoon-city by a European sovereign.

In other respects Orseolo's brilliant reign added greatly to the lustre of the Venetian *Dogado;* one of his sons married the niece of the Greek Emperor Basil, another the daughter of the King of Hungary, and this second son also succeeded his father in the Dogeship. Throughout the eleventh century, indeed, the republic followed the lines laid down for her by Orseolo, keeping a vigilant eye on the Dalmatian coast, steadily expanding her commerce in the Levant; and the struggles of Pope and Emperor which distracted the mainland left her undisturbed. The advent of the Normans in the south, however, affected her more nearly, for when Robert Guiscard made his famous attack on the Eastern Empire by besieging Durazzo, the Emperor appealed for aid to the Venetians, and a great fleet under Doge Domenico Selvo sailed to the relief of the beleaguered port [1087]. At sea the islanders won a decisive victory [September, 1087], but its fruits were thrown away by the rashness of the young Emperor Alexius, who allowed himself to be defeated on land by a vastly inferior force of Normans [November, 1087]. Durazzo fell to Duke Robert in the spring, Thessaly was invaded, and after the episode of the expulsion of Henry IV. from Rome the tireless Norman returned again to the attack, and Alexius was obliged to purchase the further aid of the Venetians by the promise of important commercial privileges. Though defeated by the Normans at Corfu they exacted the full reward for their services, and in 1085 the Golden Bull of Alexius conferred on them the nucleus of a Venetian quarter in Constantinople, together with free access (exempt from customs duties) to all the ports of the Empire.

---

[1] The first was burnt down in 976, during a tumult ending in the death of Candiano IV.

[2] See the contemporary chronicle of Joannes Diaconus, Orseolo's chaplain, printed in Monticolo, *Fonti per la Storia d'Italia.*

Thus were Venetian interests already firmly established in the Levant when the period of the Crusades opened to her a new field of enterprise and of profit. The sagacity of her merchant population was never so abundantly shown as during this outburst of the religious fervour of Europe. She took no part in the first disorderly march to the Holy Land [1096]; she left the walls of Jerusalem to be breached by a company of Genoese engineers; but in 1099, unwilling to be left behind in the race for trade supremacy, she fitted out a fleet of two hundred sail under Doge Vitale Michieli, which in its piratical career stole the body of St. Nicholas at Myra, and finally assisted in the siege and capture of Haifa [1100]. Four years later, when the Genoese had safely established Baldwin I. on the throne of Jerusalem, the republic responded to his appeal for help by sending another fine fleet to assist at the siege of Sidon [1104]; and when the city fell she exacted as the price for her services a quarter of the conquered town in what amounted to full sovereignty. This concession was the model for many more of the same kind, and when the Venetians performed their crowning exploit of the conquest of Tyre in 1123, their Doge Michieli II. took care to secure beforehand a treaty from the barons of Jerusalem granting them a free quarter under their own magistrates in every city of the kingdom.

But the success of the Venetians in Syria had already roused against them the jealousy of the Greek Empire, now ruled by the energetic John Comnenus [1118—1143] son of Alexius. John's refusal to renew his father's Golden Bull led to a direct attack by Michieli's victorious fleet, during its return from the east [1123 —24], on several of the Greek islands, and had it not been for the rise of the Norman power under Roger II., which threw Venetians and Greeks once more together, the final catastrophe of Constantinople might not have been so long delayed. Even that danger, however, produced but a temporary alliance, during which the Venetians assisted the Emperor Manuel, son of John, to recover Corfu [1148]; but the mutual jealousy of the allied armies produced a dangerous collision between them, and the expedition ended in a treaty between Venetians and Normans which gave great offence to Manuel. In 1172 his long-cherished resentment found vent in the sudden seizure of the persons and property of all Venetian traders in Constantinople, and the expedition which the republic fitted out in hot haste to avenge the outrage proved a disastrous failure. The Doge who commanded it was murdered on his return by the angry populace [1172], and before his successor—the celebrated Sebastian Ziani—was chosen, important modifications had been made in the constitution. A deliberative assembly of 480 members, nominated for one year by twelve popularly elected deputies, and then naming its own re-electors, was created as a much-needed intermediary between Doge and Arrengo; it received the name of the *Maggior Consiglio*, or Great Council, and became the foundation-stone of the Venetian constitution. At the same time the ducal councillors were increased from two to six, in order still further to restrict the Doge's independence.

Meanwhile in the affairs of the mainland, Venice had sided on the whole with the Communes by secretly joining the Veronese League, prototype of the more famous Lombard League; but this did not prevent her, as we have seen, from sending a fleet to help the Imperialists at the siege of Ancona [1174]—a town which had provoked her jealousy by allying itself with Manuel. The exploit, though a failure, contributed to the reasons which induced both parties to accept her as the scene of the Congress of 1177, and Venice naturally emerged from that memorable transaction with greatly enhanced prestige. In 1175 she had already resumed friendly relations with Manuel, who was alarmed at her continued alliance with his Norman foes; she concluded a highly favourable treaty with Isaac Comnenus in 1185, and in 1187 her assistance was eagerly sought for by the organizers of the ill-fated Third Crusade. But it was not until the project of the Fourth Crusade was launched by Pope Innocent III. in 1198 that Venice, under the guidance of old Enrico Dandolo, saw her supreme chance, and by her characteristic qualities of sagacity and unscrupulous courage climbed to the topmost rank of European Powers.

Venice entered into the scheme as a purely commercial transaction; she bargained to transport the Crusaders to the 'Land of Outremer' for a certain price, and when in the summer of 1202 the full price was not forthcoming, the Doge refused to sail except on condition that the fleet should stop on the way to reduce the troublesome stronghold of Zara, now for the fifth time in the possession of the King of Hungary. Zara was taken and sacked, greatly to the scandal of the Pope—for the King of Hungary had himself taken the Cross; and while wintering there the leaders of the expedition received opportune proposals from the exiled heir to the Byzantine throne, young Alexius Comnenus, to the effect that if they would first restore him to his Empire he would do all in his power to assist the host on its journey to Palestine, would bring the Greek Church into subjection to Rome, and would pay vast sums for the further hire of the Venetian fleet. These seductive offers were accepted by Dandolo and by the Marquis Boniface of

Monferrat, though hotly opposed by the genuine section of the Crusaders. The fleet sailed in the spring for Constantinople, where the usurping Emperor, Alexius the Elder, saw its arrival with dismay; a combined assault, glorified by the heroism of old Dandolo, was delivered on July 17, which, though unsuccessful, produced the unlooked-for result of a revolution within the city by which the usurper Alexius was driven from the throne. Young Alexius entered his capital in triumph, and it only remained to carry out the terms of the agreement of Zara. But his treasury was empty, and the populace not in the mood to tolerate taxation, so that between his fears and his debts Alexius was obliged to invite the fleet to stay. Another winter was accordingly spent in inaction, in spite of the protests of Pope Innocent; but an ultimatum from the Crusaders on the subject of the money due to them at last produced a second insurrection, by which Alexius was dethroned and murdered and the 'Franks' driven from the city. Stung to fury, they returned to the assault and hurled their ships against the mighty sea-walls which had never till then been scaled. The first time they were repulsed; but at the second attempt the Greeks fled in panic, and the capital of Eastern Christendom lay a prey to the Soldiers of the Cross. How she was used by those champions has been too often told to need repetition here.[1]

It remained only to divide the spoils, and Venice emerged from the Fourth Crusade the mistress of an Empire. All the Greek islands, most of the Morea, Durazzo, Adrianople, a footing in Eubœa, and eventually Crete,[2] fell to her share, and she adopted the expedient of granting these possessions as feudal fiefs to certain of her nobles. Enrico Dandolo died in the city he had conquered, the first Doge of Venice to bear the proud title of 'Despot and Lord of one quarter and half a quarter of the Roman Empire.' He had done what Robert Guiscard and his Normans had striven in vain to do: he had shattered the Empire of Constantine, and by so doing had brought the Turk nearer by many days' marches to the heart of Europe.

The development of Genoa and Pisa into self-conscious city-states took place considerably later than that of Venice, and was due more directly than hers to the appearance in the Mediterranean of the Saracens, whose marauding fleets threatened the very existence of exposed communities such as theirs. We hear of a Moorish raid on Genoa in 936, of an attack on Pisa—only turned into a repulse by

---

[1] See Gibbon's account of the sack of Constantinople.
[2] Crete was actually assigned to the Marquis of Monferrat, but was sold by him to the republic for ten thousand marks.

the heroism of a woman—in 1005, and, in tardy revenge for this event, of a combined attack by the fleets of both cities on the Saracens established in Sardinia [1007]. This expedition, however, though successful as against the Saracens, led to the first war between the two cities themselves [1011—12], for the Genoese had been the subordinate partners in the venture, but refused to be content with a lesser share of the spoil. It was the beginning of the endless rivalries and quarrels between the two republics which are just as characteristic of their life as the gallant stand which they made against the encroachments of the Moors. Eventually [1050] the Genoese acquired in Sardinia the town of Algaria, while Cagliari was occupied directly by the Pisan Commune. The other towns were parcelled out among the feudal nobility of the Val d'Arno, who under their curious title of 'Judge' soon became independent princes. But this division of the island between Genoa and Pisa was naturally a fruitful source of future quarrels.

At this time Pisa was still decidedly the stronger and more ambitious of the two republics, and also the more aristocratic; her 'Ghibelline' traditions are well symbolized by the legend of the seven barons of Otto II., who came to solicit her aid in their master's war against the Greeks of southern Italy, and liked the town so well that they remained to found the seven noblest families of Pisa. When the great Countess Matilda, the champion of the Church against Henry IV., extended her dominion over all Tuscany and far into the Lombard Plain, she appointed her viscount to rule in the harbour town; but the Pisans sympathized in reality with the Emperor, and in return for their loyalty received a charter from him in 1081 confirming their 'ancient privileges,' and expressly recognizing as their representatives twelve *boni homines* elected 'in the Assembly.' Thus the Commune of Pisa already existed under a feudal over-lord, who happened to be of the Church party; and the Emperor, by adroitly flattering the spirit of freedom, won over the city to the Imperialist and future 'Ghibelline' side. Genoa, on the other hand, being left more to herself, developed during the tenth century a peculiar arrangement, by which her citizens were divided into *Companies* (generally seven in number), each with a consul at its head; each company could furnish its quota of galleys in time of war, and each went forth under the leadership of its own consul—who, however, acted also as consul of the commune. Under such an organization Genoa gradually acquired, during the eleventh century, a feudal suzerainty over all the Ligurian coast, from Ventimiglia to Porto Venere, but it was a suzerainty ill-defined and often disputed, as may be seen by the jealous stipulation made by the Genoese in one of their treaties with Baldwin, King of Jerusalem, that the ships of Savona, Noli, and Albenga should not be admitted into the Genoese harbours of the Holy Land [1104].

The exploits of Genoa and Pisa during the First Crusade were of the same general character as those of Venice, but perhaps in the first instance more disinterested, for a small force of Genoese under Embriaco the 'Hammer-head' actually built the catapults and moving towers by which the walls of Jerusalem were scaled [1099]. During the ten years following the establishment of the 'Latin Kingdom of Jerusalem' Genoa founded self-governing colonies in Acre, Cæsarea, Tripoli, Antioch, and Laodicea, while Pisa had the honour of supplying in 1100 the first Patriarch for the new kingdom, in the person of her pushing and energetic Archbishop Daimbert. Pisa also acquired quarters for herself in Jaffa and Tyre, but a more romantic instance of her crusading zeal was her spirited attack in 1113 on the Saracens established in Majorca and Ivizza, an enterprise in which her sons performed prodigies of valour and succeeded at last in driving the Infidel out of both islands. But the crusading adventures of both republics were sadly interrupted in 1119 by a bloody war which broke out between them on the subject of the right of nomination to the sees of Corsica; it continued for fourteen years with varying fortune, and was only ended [1133] by a papal compromise when, as already related, Pope Innocent II. stood in sore need of the Pisan galleys to help him in chasing King Roger back to Sicily.[1] The Pisans employed their galleys, however, mainly in the siege and sack of their ancient rival Amalfi [1135—37], and by the crushing blows which they dealt the brave little republic contributed their mite towards the ruin of the south.

During the great war in Lombardy neither Genoa nor Pisa took any active part, for both were in truth more intent upon their own incessant strife than upon the struggle of the inland towns for freedom. Their efforts were mainly directed towards maintaining neutrality with Barbarossa. When, however, after the first capitulation of Milan, Genoa sent no representatives to the servile Diet of Roncaglia, Frederick took offence at the omission, adopted a menacing tone towards the republic, and advanced as far as Bosco in order to coerce her. But at the news of his approach the whole population turned out to build a new wall round the exposed suburbs of the town, and the Emperor wisely moderated his demands. At the crisis of the war Genoa did not join the Lombard League, but she took the part of Alexander III. against the Emperor's Anti-Pope, and she sent

[1] See p. 80.

G

a secret subsidy towards the building of Alessandria. Partly out of jealousy towards Pisa, however, she warmly supported Frederick's Chancellor, Christian of Mainz, when he came in 1171 to settle the affairs of Tuscany, and great was her satisfaction when he pronounced the ban of the Empire against Pisa for refusing his arbitration in her quarrels with Lucca. At this time, indeed, Genoa was decidedly the more Imperialist of the two republics, and she reached the climax of her loyalty when Frederick himself, with his wife and son, came to visit her on his return to Germany after the Congress of Venice.

But the tyranny and bad faith of Frederick's son, Henry VI., entirely changed the current of feeling in the sea-republic. All through the long years of war in Lombardy Genoa's importance as a mercantile power had been steadily increasing, in spite of an almost continuous state of warfare between herself and Pisa; her establishments in the Levant brought a constant flow of wealth into the city; she was one of the principal partners in the Third Crusade. When therefore the young Emperor Henry VI., who had married Constance, heiress of the Norman kings [1186] and had been crowned in Rome in 1191, wished to assert his rule in Sicily, it was natural that he should turn for help to the Ligurian sea-port. By the promise of Syracuse and of unlimited trading privileges in the island he secured her alliance, only to repudiate all his pledges when her ships had won him Messina, Syracuse, and finally Palermo [1194]. The Genoese sailed home in wrath, and to mark their displeasure they solemnly expelled the Podestà whom they had borrowed from Imperialist Pavia, and resolved that thenceforward they would take their chief magistrate only from Milan or from some other city of the Lombard League.

In Tuscany too the Germanizing policy of Henry soon produced a counterpart to the more famous Northern League, and Florence, Siena, Lucca, and Pistoja headed the list of anti-German towns. But the 'proud mart of Pisæ' stood aloof; perhaps it was enough that her old foes Genoa and Lucca had taken the other part; but at any rate it is from this point that the local jealousies of Genoa and Pisa become merged in those larger hostilities of Guelf and Ghibelline, which, from the days of Barbarossa onwards, were to dominate and embitter the feuds of the Italian towns.

CHAPTER IX

Italy and the House of Hohenstaufen

Qua entro è lo secondo Federico. DANTE, *Inferno*, C. X.

THE marriage of Henry VI., the son of Barbarossa, with Constance, heiress of the Norman kings of Sicily, was, next to the battle of Legnano, perhaps the cardinal event of the Italian Middle Ages. Regarded by the old Emperor himself as the crowning triumph of his policy, it placed the Hohenstaufen dynasty at a height of power never before attained in Italy by the transalpine sovereigns, for it more than made up for the loss of supremacy in Lombardy, and it gave a foothold for the future reconquest of the whole peninsula. But it had one fatal blemish. The Norman kings had held their crown in fief from the Pope; would the German submit to the same arrangement? And if not, was it to be expected that the Popes would agree to being hemmed in on north and south by a hostile Power, ever threatening to engulf that apple of the Papal eye, the Patrimony of St. Peter? The course of events was to show that such a situation was indeed impossible, and could only lead to a titanic struggle between the two antagonistic forces—a struggle from which not even the greatest of the mediæval emperors could wring victory, but which led directly to the fall of the Hohenstaufen and the ruin of the Empire.

The brief career of Henry VI. [1190—1197] certainly went far to justify the fears of the Papacy, for after suppressing the revolt of Tancred the Norman in Sicily with inhuman cruelty he attempted to set up a strong German rule in Central Italy. Tuscany, with the disputed heritage of the Countess Matilda, was bestowed on his brother Philip, Spoleto with all the Umbrian towns on Conrad of Urslingen, the March of Ancona on his Seneschal Markwald. Throughout the patrimony he was more absolute than the Pope; even in Rome he had a party. But he died before he could consolidate his power [1197], and the crown of Sicily, together with many other claims as vague as they were disquieting, descended to his little son Frederick, who, by the irony of fate, was left at the death of his mother next year to the guardianship of his 'over-lord' the Pope. And it was a Pope who knew how to make the most of such a rôle, for in January, 1198, Cardinal Lothar, son of the Count of Segni, had been elected as Innocent III.

It was time indeed that the Chair of St. Peter should be occupied by a man of supreme ability, for the affairs of Italy, from the Papal point of view, were at the lowest ebb. Lombardy was seething with heresy, imported from the neighbouring Provence and taking the form of a mystical and democratic movement against the corruption and greed of the clergy. Expressed in its purest form by the preaching of Francis of Assisi, the doctrine of poverty was consecrated to the service of the Church by Innocent, who gave his approval to the foundation of the Franciscan Order in 1210; but this was not sufficient to allay the movement of revolt, which smouldered on in Lombardy throughout the thirteenth century. In addition to these more general anxieties, Innocent found the patrimony in the hands of German princes and feudal barons, while for over fifty years— ever since the evil days of Arnold of Brescia—no Pope had been able to call himself master within the walls of Rome. Even Alexander III., the protector of the Lombard League, who had seen the greatest potentate in Europe kneel at his feet, and at whose command the King of England had bared his back to the rod for the murder of Thomas Becket—even he had spent more than half his long reign in exile from Rome. For to the Senate of Rome the Pope stood in the same relation as did the Emperor towards the Communes of Lombardy, and since he had less material force at his command, he was more frequently worsted in his efforts to obtain supremacy. But in Rome the fight was already a three-cornered one, for the great vassals of the Pope—Frangipani, Pierleoni, Colonna, Tebaldi, and many more—would submit to neither Pope nor Senate, but from their towers within the city or their castles overlooking the Campagna maintained a predatory independence, ever ready to make or unmake a Pope, but never to render him obedience. It is indeed strange that amid the clash of these turbulent nobles the Senate was able to maintain itself at all; but the Senate had armed the militia of Rome, and in many a fight both within and without the walls the militia had proved itself a force to be respected. At the time of Innocent's accession the Senate had perhaps reached the height of its power, for it had attracted many of the lesser nobility to take office within its ranks, and in 1188 it had wrung a formal treaty from Pope Clement III.—as the price of his entry into the town—by which the Pope was recognized as overlord and retained the right of *investing* the freely elected senators, but otherwise claimed no jurisdiction within the city.

The real test of municipal independence in the Middle Ages lay in the right of making peace and war, and this was always freely exercised by the Senate. Indeed the new 'Senatus Populusque Romanus' reverted faithfully to the traditions of its prototype by the hatred it bore towards the Latin towns; especially Tivoli and Tusculum, which the Popes were accustomed to use as their strongholds when driven out of Rome. The Romans thirsted to see these insignificant rivals utterly destroyed, and in the case of Tusculum their thirst was gratified. They took advantage of the approaching coronation of Henry VI. to make a bargain with the Emperor, by which he was to hand over the defenceless town as the price of his admission into Rome; and three days after the coronation ceremony the German garrison in Tusculum was withdrawn, and the Roman militia fell on its prey [1191]. Not one stone was left upon another in the whole circuit of the town, and the visitor of today to the home of Cicero beholds indeed the carefully cherished relics of antiquity, but of mediæval buildings scarcely a trace.

It was the first aim of Innocent III. to regain possession of the patrimony of St. Peter, and in this task he was powerfully aided by the sudden death of Henry VI., which threw the Imperial party everywhere into confusion. The towns of Umbria, Tuscany, and the Marches gladly rose against their German overlords [1198] and rendered homage to Innocent's legates instead, and the Pope wisely refrained from interfering with their internal organization. He merely supplanted the Emperor as their feudal suzerain, and as yet there was no emperor in a position to dispute the bold aggression. The Donation of Pippin had become an accomplished fact. In Rome too Innocent was equally fortunate, for after a period of violent faction fights between Papalist and Republicans, the constitution was definitely set aside [1205] and instead of a Senate of fifty-six elected members the Romans submitted to the rule of a single senator, nominated directly or indirectly by the Pope.

Upon these successes of Pope Innocent there followed that unfailing source of profit to the Papacy, a disputed Imperial election. The candidates were Philip of Swabia, the quondam Duke of Tuscany, and Otto, the head of the house of Welf or Guelf. This clan were the traditional opponents of the Hohenstaufen—whose castle of Waiblingen in Swabia began about this time to give its name to the 'High Imperialist' faction known to history as the *Ghibellines*. Naturally Innocent favoured the Guelf, from whom he obtained, in return for the recognition of his election, the celebrated *Capitulation of Neuss*, by which the limits of the territories of the Church were defined[1] and all Imperial pretensions within those territories renounced. Probably Otto signed this document in light-hearted sincerity, but when at last he came to Italy for his coronation he found that in practice a Papalist Emperor was a contradiction in terms. He was hardly crowned before he began bestowing large tracts of the new made State of the Church on German and Italian nobles, and he soon resolved to extend his authority over the south as well—the inheritance of the Pope's ward, young Frederick. But this was more than Innocent could tolerate, and when the news arrived that Otto had crossed the Apulian border, the Pope indignantly launched the excommunication against his creature [November 18, 1210], barely a year after he had set the crown upon his head.

But he had a yet higher card than this to play. Frederick of Sicily, his ward and vassal, was now a youth of sixteen, and might be raised up against the perfidious Guelf. The German princes, always more inclined towards a Hohenstaufen than a Guelf, agreed to depose Otto, and in the autumn of 1211 they summoned Frederick II. to the throne. Otto hastened back to face the new danger, and in April, 1212, Frederick followed him across the Alps, to play the astonishing rôle of Papal candidate for the disputed crown. He was elected King of the Romans in December, and the next year, at Eger, confirmed all the provisions of the Capitulation of Neuss. But the Pope was not yet satisfied; so, after his coronation at Aachen, Frederick not only took the Cross for a campaign in Palestine [1215], but also made a solemn vow to bestow the kingdom of Sicily on his infant son Henry as soon as he himself should have been crowned Emperor. Thus the great Pope thought to have laid the threatening spectre of a union between the two crowns, and died before he was undeceived [1216].

Time passed away, however, and the Crusader still remained at home. Indeed there were far more engrossing matters to detain the young King in Germany, where it was not until 1218 that Otto's death relieved him of embarrassment. Then he was free to seek the Imperial crown, and in September, 1220, after renewing to a lesser Pope than Innocent, his promise concerning Sicily, he entered Lombardy on his way to Rome. Already, however, he had reduced his undertakings to waste paper by causing his son Henry, the youth-

---

[1] They comprised the ancient *Ducatus Romæ* from Radicofani in Tuscany to Ceprano on the Garigliano; the Exarchate, the Pentapolis (Rimini, Pesaro, Fano, Sinigaglia, and Ancona), the March of Ancona, the Duchy of Spoleto, and the lands of the Countess Matilda—in fact practically the 'Papal States' of modern times.

ful King of Sicily, to be crowned at Frankfort King of the Romans, or Emperor presumptive, thus securing for the future the very combination which Innocent had striven to prevent.

During the fifty years which had intervened between the wars of Barbarossa and the advent of Frederick II., the politics of the Italian cities had undergone a profound modification. In the great struggle against the first Frederick each town had whole-heartedly embraced either the republican or the Imperial cause ; now the two main currents were crossed and recrossed by endless party factions which had sprung up within the cities themselves. The reason for this change is to be found in the long process, carried on ever since the time of the first municipal wars, by which the feudal nobles were brought into subjection to the towns—a process which reached its climax in the last twenty years of the twelfth century. It was a struggle for life between the *municipia* in their new-found strength and the descendants of Lombard, Frankish, and German counts who possessed the countryside, and usually it resulted in the reduction of the noble to the condition of vassal of the town, forced to reside within its walls for a certain period of the year and to render it aid in time of war. But the consuls soon found that their new-made subjects proved themselves troublesome citizens; battlemented fortresses flanked by towers sprang up within the city walls, in revenge for the dismantled castles without, and in the absence of a superior coercive force the nobles formed a rallying-point for all the elements hostile to the city of their adoption. Thus the nobles subdued by Milan would ally themselves with the hereditary enemies of the Milanese,—Lodi, Como, and Cremona; those subdued by Pisa would offer their swords to Lucca or Genoa; those put down by the consuls of Florence would call in the consuls of Siena or Arezzo to their aid. Hence a blind and never-ending war, usually between the nominal factions of Guelf and Ghibelline—for wherever the coercing city was Guelf, the refractory nobles would of necessity be Ghibelline, and *vice versa*.

So exhausting had the strife become in the years succeeding the battle of Legnano that the cities almost with one accord adopted the expedient first introduced by Barbarossa at the Diet of Roncaglia—the rule of the *Podestà* or 'Head of the State,' a supreme magistrate, part judge, part policeman, whose duty it was to maintain order with the strong hand during the single year of his term of office.[1] He was always imported from another city, in order to secure impartiality; he might bring neither wife nor

[1] See p. 83.

relative with him, nor might he so much as eat or drink with any citizen, and when his term had expired he was bound to remain within the city for fifty days in order to answer any charges brought against him. But in return for these restrictions he had a free hand in the maintenance of order, and in the last resort he would proceed with his guard to the siege and demolition of towers and fortresses and the expulsion of their owners. The turn of the exiles, however, would come again in the long run; they would return with a Podestà of their own making and expel the leaders of the opposite faction, and these periodic banishments and re-entries became a familiar feature of the Italian revolutions. So evenly were the two parties balanced, that it was only when the Emperor took the field in person that the Ghibellines obtained a temporary advantage, and even then the Pope was always at hand to rally the Guelfs and breathe courage into them by his spiritual thunders.

Frederick's passage across Lombardy on his way to Rome in 1220 was uneventful, as the young King was only anxious to accomplish his Imperial coronation and to press on to Sicily, in order to reorganize the affairs of his southern kingdom. He appeased Pope Honorius III. at his coronation by recognizing anew the Papal suzerainty over the kingdom, and by undertaking to give it an administration wholly separate from that of the Empire. Many times did the good Pope exhort his 'beloved son' to depart on the Crusade, but Frederick found the task of governing his kingdom far too absorbing, and remained for six years in Sicily and Apulia, forming from the feudal heritage of the Normans a modern state of which he was the enlightened despot or Podestà. Gradually he brought the barons of the mainland into subjection and established the royal authority on a firm basis, while in Sicily he accomplished the still more difficult task of subjugating the Saracens of the interior, who had previously given him endless trouble. He finally deported twenty thousand of them in a body to the Apulian city of Lucera, where they lived under their own laws as a military colony and learnt to do their new master good service in time of need. For the Emperor Frederick was a man of wide understanding and culture; could converse in their own tongue with the Arab philosophers of Palermo, and made his court the meeting-place between the scholars of East and West and the centre of a new movement towards a vernacular Italian literature. The clergy looked askance at him as an atheist and free-thinker, but for the moment he was intent on consolidating his power and avoided all acute controversy. In 1223 he assumed the title of King of Jerusalem by his marriage with Yolande, daughter and heiress of King John of

Brienne, and in 1225 bound himself by solemn oath to start within two years on the Crusade. But one obstacle had still to be cleared away before he could set forth: the rights of the Empire must be asserted in Northern Italy and the co-operation of the cities in his enterprise obtained. For this purpose he summoned a Diet to meet him at Cremona in March, 1226, 'for the succour of the Holy Land and the readjustment of the rights of the Empire.' But the cities read a menace in the summons, coming from the grandson of Barbarossa, and before Frederick had even appeared among them they had renewed the Lombard League [1226]—ostensibly for the maintenance of the Treaty of Constance—and now sullenly refused to attend his Diet. The Emperor remained for four months in Lombardy, but after the failure of his negotiations he pronounced the Ban of the Empire against the recalcitrant cities in the cathedral of Borgo San Donnino, revoking all their privileges and more espec-ially the provisions of the Treaty of Constance. He then retired in great mortification to the south, beaten at all points in his first brush with the free citizens.

The well-meaning Honorius patched up a reconciliation between the two parties in the winter, and his death in March, 1227, was a real misfortune for Frederick. The new Pope, Cardinal Ugolino of Ostia, was a man old in years and bitter in spirit, to whom the half-measures of Honorius had long been a weariness and an offence. He took the name of Grerogy IX. His first act was to summon Frederick to start immediately for the Crusade, according to his vow, and the Emperor obediently assembled a large army at Brindisi in August, 1227, and actually set sail on September 8th. But within a few days he was back again at Otranto, having been, according to his own account, taken ill at sea; and in a transport of rage at the news, Gregory hurled the excommunication at the malingerer, accompanying it by an encyclical to all the bishops setting forth his case in the most violent terms. Frederick replied by a manifesto to the kings of Europe—a famous document in which for the first time he dropped the mask, and vehemently attacked his 'stepmother' the Church. His sentences fall like ham-mer-strokes : 'The Roman Church is like a leech ; she calls herself my mother and nurse; but she is a stepmother, and the root of all evils. Her legates go through all lands, binding, loosing, punishing; not to sow the seed of the Word, but to subdue all men and wring from them their money. . . .' In spite of all, however, and thwarted at every turn by the Pope, he went on with his prepara-tions for the Crusade, and actually started in June, 1228, with the Ban still upon him. For this piece of audacity Gregory excommunicated him afresh, sent two legates after him to forbid the crusading army to have anything to do with such a leader, and poured an army of marauders into Apulia. Even so, however, Frederick accomplished more in the East than any Christian prince since Godfrey of Bouillon; he obtained from Sultan Kamel the surrender of Jerusalem, Bethlehem, and Nazareth, and, without mass or benediction, placed the crown of the Latin kingdom upon his own head, in the Church of the Holy Sepulchre [March 18, 1229]. Then he hurried back to chastize the Pope's crusaders in Apulia, was greeted by a third excommunication from Gregory on landing, but at last, after driving the Papal armies before him across the Liris, brought the Pope to terms at San Germano [July, 1230], and wrung absolution from him at the price of important concessions to the Sicilian clergy.

The five years following the Treaty of San Germano were by far the most peaceful and productive in Frederick's life. He spent them mainly in Apulia, moving about between his castles at Foggia, Melfi, Castel del Monte near Andria, and Lago Pesole in the central hills, and here too he gathered round him those bands of scholars, troubadours, astrologers, and lawyers who made the court of Frederick II. famous as a precursor of the Renaissance. Frederick himself had imbibed a passion for knowledge from the Arab tutors who had guarded his childhood at Palermo, and his special tastes were geometry, medicine, and astrology; but he was also an enlightened patron of the nascent vernacular poetry, and has left a collection of very passable lyrics in praise of his mistress. Probably his greatest service to learning was his foundation of the University of Naples in 1224, with chairs for 'every branch of Law, for Theology, and all the liberal arts,' as he wrote to its older rival, Bologna; and it was here that the professional jurists were trained by whose help he was able to accomplish his greatest reform—the suppression of the criminal jurisdiction of the feudal nobles. For within the limits of his southern kingdom, Frederick ruled with an absolutism to which he never attained in Germany; he issued his great codification and revision of the Norman and Lombard laws—the so-called Constitutions of Melfi—in 1231, and he saw to it that none but royal judges properly qualified should administer the new code. In his reorganization of the finances he relied partly on *collecta* from the tenants of the vast domains of the crown and on contributions in kind from the non-royal lands, but largely also on customs duties and on monopolies, the value of which he was quick to recognize. His edict embodying these proposals was submitted to a great assembly of all the estates of the realm held at Melfi in 1231, but the wording of the edict makes it clear that the Emperor-King was the only fount of authority, and that the estates had at most a consultative voice.[1]

These institutions of Frederick II. were of permanent value, for not even the unheavals caused by the French invasion sufficed to overturn them. To a modern eye, however, they are counter-balanced by the savage edicts against heretics of the years 1224 and 1232, which Frederick issued partly to propitate the Pope, partly as a blow to the seething democracy of Lombardy, the hotbed of the heretical sects. Frederick, the scoffer and free-thinker, the favourer of Jews and Mohammedans, was the first temporal ruler in Italy to enjoin his officials to assist in hunting out suspected heretics, and to prepare the stake for them when convicted.

In 1234 Frederick assisted Pope Gregory in putting down a for-midable rebellion of the Romans—who had never heartily acquies-ced in the arrangement made with Innocent III.—and in the next year [1235] was obliged to go to Germany, where his son Henry had revolted against him, allying himself with Milan and certain other towns of the Lombard League. It filled the Emperor's cup of wrath against the Lombards, which had been mounting ever since the disastrous transactions of the year 1226. And now, too, he was joined at Augsburg by the evil genius of his later years, Eccelino da Romano, a Ghibelline of the Trevisan March who had lately made himself master of Verona, and who coveted the Emperor's help against his rival Azzo d'Este, champion of the Guelfs through-out the March, and Podestà of Vicenza. His counsel turned the scale in favour of war: 'Italy,' wrote Frederick to the Pope in June, 1236, 'Italy is my heritage, and all the world knows it.' It was his declara-tion of war against both Pope and Lombards; the time had come for him to assert the ancient might of the Empire, and to exact the same obedience from centre and north as he already enjoyed in the south. Nothing, of course, was further from the intentions of the League than to grant this, and a war began, more bloody and still more long drawn out than that which had wasted the great plain in the time of Frederick's grandsire. It was not long before the Em-peror, by the help of ten thousand Saracens, drawn from his colony of Lucera, wiped out the stain of Legnano by his signal defeat of the Milanese at Cortenuova [November, 1237], and the capture of their *carroccio*. But in the next year his whole army was held up for nine weeks before the heroic little town of Brescia, which even then he was unable to take, and the Guelfs raised their heads once more. Behind them too there now arose the figure of their cham-

[1] See Winkelmann, *Kaiser Friedrich II.*, ii., 267 fol.

pion, the Pope, who, weary of his fruitless efforts to make peace on his own terms, entered the field with his own peculiar weapons— excommunication and the new-made Orders of St. Francis and St. Dominic. He launched the ban against the Emperor on March 20, 1239, and by means of the 'Third Order,' founded in a moment of exaltation by the sweetest of peace lovers, he enlisted the common people against the Emperor.

But in temporal arms the Emperor still prevailed, and by the middle of 1240 he had occupied almost the whole of the States of the Church, and threatened to march on Rome. The dauntless Gregory, however, summoned a general Council to meet in the Lateran at the following Easter, and arranged with the Genoese to convey its members to Rome. Frederick determined to frustrate this scheme at all costs, and ordered his faithful Pisans to attack the Genoese fleet at sea and capture its episcopal freight. This was accomplished at a battle off the Tuscan coast [May, 1241], and Frederick became possessed of the persons of three Papal legates and of near a hundred bishops and abbots from Lombardy, France, and Spain, whom he sent for safe keeping to his Apulian castles. Gregory did not long survive this blow, but died in Rome in the August heat of 1241, while his arch-enemy lay encamped on the Alban Hills.

But the idea of a general Council to support the Pope in his great struggle did not die with him. His successor, Innocent IV.,— chosen after an interregnum of nearly two years [1243],—was a Genoese of the noble house of Fieschi. He was reputed a Ghibelline, but the Emperor's famous remark on hearing of the election— 'I have lost a good friend, for no Pope can be a Ghibelline'—proved all too true. Frederick by this time desired peace, but neither party trusted the other in the negotiations, and Innocent at length baffled the Emperor by flying secretly to Genoa and thence to France, where he summoned the long-delayed Council to meet at Lyons in June, 1245. Its verdict was a foregone conclusion. Scarcely any German bishops made their appearance; Frederick himself was only informally invited, and scorned the invitation. He sent indeed one of his most distinguished jurists, Thaddeus of Suessa, to plead his cause, but no impression could he make on the assembled bishops. On July 17, in the old cathedral of Lyons, Innocent pronounced the Emperor excommunicate and deposed, and absolved his subjects both of the Empire and of the Sicilian kingdom from their oath of allegiance.

The days were past in which the Emperor could have met defiance with defiance, set up an anti-Pope as his grandfather had done, and boldly faced his enemy. Nor had the time arrived in

which a monarch could have led Europe in a struggle against the
Papacy itself. Innocent IV., secure behind the rock-barrier of the
Alps, was master of the field, and could even afford to reject the
offers of mediation put forward by his host, St. Louis of France.
He preferred instead to set up a rival king to Frederick's son Conrad in Germany, to promote a plot among the Apulian barons
against the life of their master, and to preach a crusade against the
Emperor at a moment when St. Louis needed that Emperor's aid in
a Crusade against the Infidel. Frederick still made repeated overtures of peace, but all was of no avail, and early in 1247 he began
to meditate a march on Lyons, won over the Count of Savoy to his
side by giving him one of his daughters in marriage, and advanced
as far as Turin. Thence, however, he was recalled to Lombardy by
a great catastrophe in his rear—the defection (instigated by some
of the Pope's kinsmen) of the important city of Parma, hitherto one
of the few centres of loyalty in Lombardy. The siege detained him
for eight months, and was marked by deeds of cold-blooded cruelty
on either side, for Frederick was by no means free from that dark
taint in the blood of all the Hohenstaufen, and the sentence of Lyons
had finally soured his temper. At last a victorious sally of the
Parmesans, in which they made off with the Imperial crown itself,
forced him to raise the siege [February, 1248], but even so his
marvellous energy still gave him the upper hand in Lombardy and
Piedmont. In the next year, however, his fortune darkened; his
great minister and favourite, Peter di Vinea, was arrested on a
charge of brewing poison for his master; his eyes were put out, and
he dashed out his brains against a pillar to save himself from further torments. 'This Peter,' cried the Emperor in despair, 'whom I
thought a rock, and who was the half of my life, has plotted my
murder. Whom can I trust henceforth?' In May his gallant son
Enzio was defeated and taken prisoner by the Bolognese, who held
him as a state prisoner for twenty-two years, till his death in 1271.
The news of his capture reached Frederick in the south, whence he
was directing a bloody war that devastated Umbria and the
Marches; the whole country groaned in the agonies of the struggle.
'The wolves gathered together in mighty multitude round the city
moats,' writes the good friar Salimbene, 'howling dismally for ex-
ceeding anguish of hunger; and they crept into the cities by night
and devoured men and women and children who slept under the
porticoes or in wagons.' The north lay maimed and exhausted
under the tyranny of Eccelino, who arrogated to himself the title
of Imperial Vicar; the rancorous hatred of the Pope towards his
great enemy shut out all hope of peace. At last the Emperor's

health failed beneath the bodily and mental strain of the long war; he fell seriously ill in November, 1250, and died at his hunting lodge in Fiorentino, a few miles from the fortress of Lucera. He was absolved by the Archbishop of Palermo, and made in all respects 'a good end,'—rumour even declared that he died in the garb of a Cistercian monk. But in the popular imagination he was long thought of with awe as Antichrist, and was expected to return again to fulfil his cup of wickedness; like Nero, the world could not believe him dead. His contemporary Salimbene half shared these views, yet the picture he has left of him shows us rather a very human, sinful, brilliant man, whose greatest fault was that he was born out of due time.

Of faith in God he had none [writes the friar[1]]; he was crafty, wily, avaricious, lustful, malicious, wrathful; and yet a gallant man at times, when he would show his kindness or courtesy; full of solace, jocund, delightful, fertile in devices. He knew how to read, write, and sing, and to make songs and music. He was a comely man and well-formed, tho' of middle stature. Moreover he knew how to speak with many and varied tongues, and, to be brief, if he had been rightly Catholic, and had loved God and His Church, he would have had few Emperors his equals in the world.

[1] See Mr. Coulton's translation in *From St. Francis to Dante*, p. 241.

CHAPTER X

From the Fall of the Hohenstaufen to the 'Babylonish Captivity' of the Papacy

Biaus Chevalier et preus
Et sage fu Manifrois,
De toutes bonnes teches
Entechiés et courtois.

En lui ne falloit riens,
Forsque seulement fois ;
Mais cette faute est laide
En contes et en Rois.   ADAM D'ARRAS.

OF the six sons of Frederick II., only Manfred, Prince of Taranto, his bastard and favourite,[1] was present at the Emperor's death-bed, and to him Frederick bequeathed the regency of Apulia and Sicily in the name of Conrad, the legitimate heir. The figure of Manfred, as it stands portrayed for all time in Dante's *Purgatory*—'biondo era e bello e di gentile aspetto'[2]—will ever be one of the most attractive in that many-coloured age. Half poet, half paladin, he combined his father's courage and enlightenment with a blither spirit, and while vigorously patronizing the industry and commerce of his kingdom, he reigned over his court as a King of Troubadours, dressed ever in green, the colour of hope. He had co-operated loyally with his half-brother Conrad, King of the Romans, when the latter came to take up his Italian inheritance; but when Conrad died at Lavello in the prime of his youth, Manfred proclaimed himself Regent for his young nephew Conradin, and four years later assumed, or usurped, the crown of Apulia and Sicily—thereby giving hope of a national dynasty, divorced for ever from the German line. Circumstance forced him, however, to become the champion of the Ghibellines rather than the King of Italy, for the Popes would make neither truce nor pact with the 'brood of vipers,' as they charitably termed the Hohenstaufen. As his power increased he sent his 'Vicars' into Lombardy, Romagna, and Tuscany, and it was under the command of one of these, Count Jordan of Anglano, that the Ghibellines of Siena, aided by those of Florence under Farinata degli Uberti, won the famous victory of Montaperti [September 4, 1260], over the Florentine Guelfs. It was the first time that Tuscany became the central battle-ground of Italian politics, but in truth this apparently local struggle, arising out of the

---

[1] His mother was Bianca Lancia, a Piedmontese lady of noble birth.
[2] Canto III.

jealousy between the democratic *commune* of Florence and the great Ghibelline clan of the Uberti, was fraught with consequences for the whole of Italy. It extinguished for the time being the supremacy which Florence—whose traditions had been Guelf ever since the days of the Countess Matilda—had built up in Tuscany since Frederick's death; the city was forced to submit to a Ghibelline Podestà, Count Guido Novello, who styled himself Manfred's Vicar [1260—66]; and a Ghibelline League was formed between Florence, Pisa, Siena, and other lesser towns which completely reversed the balance of power in Tuscany and even threatened the Patrimony of St. Peter.

At this juncture [1261], Pope Alexander IV., the comparatively mild successor of the vindictive Innocent, died and was succeeded by a Frenchman, who took the name of Urban IV. In his hands the policy of calling in a French deliverer to exterminate the 'brood of vipers'—a policy first conceived by Innocent IV., but honourably resisted at that time by St. Louis of France— took final shape. The deliverer was found in the person of Charles, Count of Anjou and Provence, the needy and unscrupulous brother of King Louis; and to him Urban offered the crown of Sicily and Naples [1262], while the Romans, independently of the Pope, bestowed on him the Senatorship of their city [1263]. Charles and his wife Beatrice, daughter and heiress of Raymond Berengar IV., last Count of Provence, caught eagerly at these proposals; the Countess pledged her jewels to fit out the expedition, and an army of thirty thousand men was soon collected, drawn by the dazzling prospects of lands and booty which the Count held out to them. To these inducements was soon added that of the remission of sins, for Pope Clement IV.. the successor of Urban, formally elevated the expedition to the rank of a crusade. Legates were sent to demand money from the Churches of England, Germany, and France, but little was obtained except from the French clergy, and at Whitsuntide, 1265, the Pope welcomed an almost penniless champion into Rome. Manfred meanwhile hovered irresolute in the Sabine hills. Already the preaching of the mendicant friars was beginning to take effect; some of Manfred's most trusted partisans deserted to the enemy's camp; the elaborate arrangements he had made for checking the progress of the Provençals in Lombardy melted away at the approach of the 'Crusaders.' In January, 1266, Charles was crowned King of Sicily in St. Peter's, and before the month was out he was hastening at the head of his ragged host of French adventurers, Florentine Guelfs, and Apulian turn-coats to seize the kingdom from his adversary. Manfred, afraid to trust his vassals in a waiting game, marched from Capua to Benevento to meet him, and there on the plain of Grandella, a little to the northward of the old Papal city, the two armies met in desperate shock [Feb., 1266]. Saracens and Germans fought well for Manfred, but were thrown into confusion at last by the French device of stabbing at their horses, and Manfred saw his reserve of Apulian vassals turn rein and fly at the moment he ordered them to charge. Almost alone he plunged into the fight, seeking death, and when night fell he lay unrecognized among the slain, while his men dispersed into the mountains, or were killed and taken in large numbers. After three days his body was found by a camp-follower and taken on an ass's back to the French Prince's tent, where it was recognized with tears by Jordan of Anglano and the other captives. But, being excommunicate, the son of Frederick II. could not be buried in hallowed ground, and a cairn was raised instead over his bones at the bridge-head, each soldier in Charles's host casting a stone upon his grave.[1] His wife and three little sons were seized by the conqueror and cast into prison, whence they never issued alive; Benevento, though a Papal city, was sacked with inhuman ferocity, and Charles then made his triumphal entry into Naples. But the kingdom soon found that he had come only to chastise it with scorpions. Confiscated fiefs were showered upon his nobler followers, while the humbler, clothed with official authority as tax-gatherers, customs-officers, judges, bailiffs, and what-not, spread themselves over the land like a swarm of locusts, exhorting its wealth in the King's name.[2] The wretched population soon sighed for the lost days of Frederick and Manfred, and nursing their wrongs in secret until—in Sicily at least—the day of retribution came.

Meanwhile the effects of Anjou's victory were felt far and wide throughout the peninsula, and a Guelf reaction set in in all but a few isolated towns. In Tuscany Count Guido Novello was ignominiously frightened out of Florence by a popular riot; the Pope conferred the title of Vicar-Imperial of Tuscany upon King Charles, and the Florentines themselves offered him the lordship (signoria) of their city for six years, with the privilege of naming the Podestà and the Captain of the People. Charles did not fail to assure himself of this advantage, and early in 1267 he sent eight hundred French cavalry into the town, and appointed Count Guy de Montfort as his Vicar. The Ghibellines disappeared into exile once more.

In Rome, however, the too close proximity of the conqueror,

---

[1] Giov. Villiani, bk. vii., 9.   Dante, *Purg.*, iii., 110.
[2] Sabas Malaspina, the Guelf chronicler, gives a vivid picture of the iniquities of the French after the conquest.

H

combined with the anti-Papal feeling that was never far below the surface, produced a movement in the opposite direction. Through the timid jealousy of the Pope himself Charles had been forced to resign the Senatorship of the city within three months of the battle of Benevento, but the Romans showed no disposition to consult the Pope as to their mode of government, and in the next year chose as their Senator a roving knight-errant of the royal house of Spain, Don Henry of Castile—a man eminently fitted both by his personal qualities and by the bitter hatred he bore towards his cousin, Charles of Anjou, to lead a reaction against him. His presence in Rome, and the hope he inspired in the anti-Angevin and Ghibelline remnant throughout Italy, made possible the next act in the tragedy of the Swabian line.

For there still remained beyond the Alps one offshoot of the 'poisonous race of Frederick'[1]—young Conradin, the nephew whom Manfred had supplanted nine years before as King of Apulia and Sicily. He had now reached the age of fifteen, and naturally became at Manfred's death the object of all the passionate hopes and aspirations of the defeated Ghibellines. Pisa and Siena, Verona and Palermo sent him their envoys, Don Henry declared in his favour, and in October, 1267, the high-spirited boy crossed the Brenner with a small army and journeyed via Verona, Pavia, and Savona to Pisa, which he reached in May, 1268. A rising of the Saracens of Lucera kept Charles busy in the kingdom, and Conradin was able to advance through Tuscany with little opposition and to make his triumphal entry into Rome on July 24, 1268. Within a month he and Don Henry were marching eastwards at the head of a gallant army to seek out their enemy on his return from the siege of Lucera and Charles was hastening northward and westward to meet them Swabian and Angevin faced each other at the river Salto, near Tagliacozzo, on August 23rd; Don Henry crossed the river and swept all before him by the fury of his charge; Conradin followed with the second line and appeared to have completed the rout of the French, when from behind a neighbouring hill, Charles of Anjou emerged with a picked body of eight hundred knights and fell upon the scattered Ghibellines, who were already busy pillaging his camp. Don Henry, returning too late from the pursuit was beaten off and fled to Monte Cassino, where the abbot arrested him, while Conradin escaped with five hundred men and arrived in Rome. Here, however, he sound found that none would harbour him. Hoping to reach Pisa by sea, he descended to the coast a Astura with about a score of German and Italian knights and pu

[1] Letter from Clement IV. to the Roman clergy, October 21, 1267.

off in a light galley—only to be overtaken and seized by the Guelf owner of Astura, Giovanni Frangipani. Sold by him to King Charles, he was first imprisoned in the Castle of Palestrina and then taken in chains to Naples, where after a mock trial he was convicted of high treason and beheaded, together with his brother-in-arms, young Frederick of Austria, on a scaffold in the market-place [Oct., 29, 1268]. Pope Clement raised not a finger to save him.

After a ruthless repression in Sicily, which had revolted under the leadership of Frederick of Castile, brother of Don Henry, Charles of Anjou felt himself at last secure upon his throne. The Romans had already elected him Senator for the second time [1268], and the Pope had confirmed the election for ten years. Master of Rome and paramount power in Tuscany, he now persuaded half the cities of Lombardy to bestow their 'signoria' upon him, and from a vassal prince called in to save the Pope he thus rose within four years to be the most formidable ruler in Italy. But his very strength brought about a slow reaction. A national and anti-French party appeared among the Cardinals, and in spite of Charles's opposition these succeeded after a three years' vacancy in electing an Italian, Tedaldo Visconti, as Pope. Gregory X. [1271—76] was a peace-maker; he strove hard to reconcile Guelfs and Ghibellines in Florence, though with poor success, and in order to provide for future Papal elections with due promptitude and freedom from pressure he issued from Lyons the famous decree establishing the *Conclave*. The Cardinals were to be immured in the palace of the last Pope, in whatever city he had died, and there kept on a diminishing scale of diet until the election had been made. Thus it was hoped to avoid such scandals as the long delay in Gregory's own election. As a counterpoise to Charles of Anjou, Gregory also favoured the rising power of the new King of the Romans, Rudolf of Habsburg, and invited him to come to Rome for his Imperial coronation. But Germany at last claimed her own, and throughout his life the hard-worked King never found leisure to cross the Alps and plunge into the cauldron of Italian strife.

The process of checking Anjou's power was carried still further by a great Pope of the house of Orsini, Nicholas III. [1277—80]. As a Roman noble, Nicholas resented Charles's interference in Roman affairs through his office of Senator, and at the expiration of the ten years' term conferred on him by Clement IV. [1278], the new Pope compelled him to resign it, while at the same time he issued a decree debarring any Emperor, king, prince, or foreign count from holding the Senatorship in future. With great astuteness, too, he played off the pretensions of Rudolf of Habsburg against those of Charles, and induced the former to make over the district of Romagna[1] in effective sovereignty to the Church, in exchange for the title of Vicar-Imperial of Tuscany, hitherto held by Charles. Two of the Pope's nephews were sent into Romagna to receive the submission of the cities, and even the proud and turbulent Bologna was obliged to do homage to the 'Bear-cubs.' From this time onwards the claim of the Church to rule Romagna was never abandoned, though it occasionally lapsed for lack of means.

Nicholas III., however, did not live to see the maturing of his schemes against the French dominion. It is probable that in the last year of his life he was privy to the great conspiracy by which a grandson of Manfred was set at last upon the throne of Sicily, but at any rate death removed the Nationalist Pope before the decisive moment had arrived. Many signs, however, were pointing to an upheaval at no distant date. Pedro, King of Aragon, who had married the daughter and heiress of King Manfred, was bound by the tie of common hostility against Charles to Michael Palæologus, the restorer of the Greek Empire of Constantinople; for Charles had espoused the cause of the last representative of the 'Latin' dynasty established in 1204,[2] and under that pretext was making vast preparations for the invasion and conquest of Greece. Pedro, sustained by subsidies from Palæologus, boldly prepared a counter-attack in the form of an expedition to win the crown of Sicily, and the ambassador between the two courts—perhaps indeed the life and soul of the design—was a certain noble of Salerno named Giovanni da Procida, once physician to Frederick II., then minister of Manfred, and now exile and confidant at the Court of Don Pedro. A few Sicilian nobles were probably also drawn into the plot, but long before the Aragonese fleet had weighed anchor from the port of Barcelona the train was fired by a far more terrible conspirator than the King of Aragon: the people of Palermo rose against their masters.

The revolution of the 'Sicilian Vespers,' so-called because it broke out at the hour of Vespers, on March 31, 1282, arose from a sudden outburst of rage on the part of a crowd of Palermitans, before whose eyes a party of Frenchman had ill-treated a young bride as she was going towards the church of Santo Spirito, without the walls. A long course of cruelty, insult, and extortion had prepared the way for such an outburst, and when an excited crowd poured

---

[1] The name of *Romagna* began to be given about this time to the Roman or Papal territories north of the Apennines of which Bologna was the centre.

[2] When the Venetians and 'Franks' took Constantinople. See p. 95.

back into the streets shouting 'Death to the French!' the town rose
with one accord, the citadel was stormed, and before morning
broke, the whole French population of Palermo—two thousand in
number—had been massacred without mercy. A provisional government was formed and the revolution organized; three bodies of
Palermitans marched out to raise the country eastward, southward,
and westward; and such of the French as escaped the slaughter that
followed fled hastily to the royal fortress of Messina. But on April
28, Messina followed the general example and declared it a republic,
and with the departure of the French garrison across the Straits the
whole island was freed for the moment from the foreign yoke.
But it was only the beginning of a twenty years' struggle. Alarmed
at the prospect of King Charles's vengeance, the Parliament of
Palermo formally invited Don Pedro of Aragon to take up his inheritance, the crown of Sicily; and with his arrival at Trapani on August
30 and coronation at Palermo the war assumed the dynastic aspect
which it had lacked hitherto. Charles was driven back to the mainland from before the walls of Messina by King Pedro's superior fleet,
and never succeeded in re-crossing the Straits; his eldest son was
taken prisoner next year by the Aragonese admiral, and he himself
died at Foggia in 1285, at the lowest ebb of his fortunes. But his
interests were left in good hands. In 1288 Pope Nicholas IV. absolved the younger Charles from all the conditions under which he
had obtained his release from captivity, and which included the
cession of Sicily to King Pedro's son James; and when James succeeded to the throne of Aragon, leaving Sicily to his brother Frederick, Pope Boniface VIII. stirred up a war between the two brothers [1297]. When, however, Frederick still held his own with the
Sicilians, who found in him a brave and loyal leader, Boniface
played his last card by calling in another French pretender, Charles
of Valois, brother of Philip IV., to win Sicily back for the Church.
Beaten in a guerilla war, Valois surrendered his shadowy rights in
the Treaty of Caltabellotta [August 31, 1302], and Boniface, upon
whom other storm-clouds were fast descending, was fain to recognize Frederick, the grandson of Manfred, as 'King of Trinacria.'
Thus the Swabian line reappeared in the Aragonese dynasty, which
maintained itself in Sicily for over a century, until Alfonso the
Magnanimous re-united the two crowns.

While these events were in progress in the South, the Papacy which
sought to control and guide them was hastening fast towards a
great catastrophe. Eight years before the recognition of Frederick
of Sicily, a long delay in the Papal Election caused by the friction

between the Cardinals of the Colonna and Orsini factions produced a most singular result. In despair at reaching an agreement, the Cardinals at last caught at the suggestion that a certain pious hermit of the Abruzzi, Fra Pietro of Monte Morrone, should be elected Pope, mainly on the ground that his sanctity had once enabled him to hang his cowl on a sunbeam in the presence of Pope Gregory X. and his court. His fame as a saint and miracle-worker had already spread far and wide throughout Italy, and he had gathered round him a small community of 'Spiritualists' or *Fraticelli*—rebels from the main body of the Franciscans, inasmuch as they desired to carry out the rule of St. Francis to the letter. A deputation of bishops was accordingly sent to inform the hermit of his elevation [July, 1294], and King Charles II. of Naples hastened to Monte Morrone to do obeisance to the saint, and to see that in worldly matters his own influence should be paramount. The bewildered old man was taken in procession to Aquila, where he was consecrated Pope as Celestine V., and in the autumn the King conveyed him by slow stages to Naples, in spite of the protests of the Roman Cardinals. Terrified by the hubbub of the great city, tormented by a sense of his own incompetence and by a haunting dread lest his election should have been but a glittering lure of the Devil, the unfortunate Celestine immured himself in a cell in the Castel Nuovo, and pondered in his heart the dream of abdication. He took counsel with one of the most sagacious of the Roman Cardinals, Benedetto Gaetani, and learnt from him that he might freely renounce the Papacy, since there were precedents for such a course. Probably, however, the edifying tale of the Cardinal's arranging a speaking-tube through which he addressed the poor visionary in the watches of the night as the Voice of God, commanding him to lay down the Tiara, is the fabrication of a later writer.[1] At any rate the outcome was that on the 13th of December, 1294, before a full assembly of Cardinals, Pope Celestine V. read a formal deed of abdication, laid down the Pontifical robes, and clad himself once more in the tattered gown of Monte Morrone. Once more the Cardinals assembled in Conclave, and this time they elected, as Pope Boniface VIII., that same Cardinal Gaetani who had so glibly encouraged the renunciation. King Charles II., irritated at the abdication of his creature, was won over to the new Pope by a promise of help with the affairs of Sicily, and undertook in return to arrest the wandering Celestine, who had escaped while being conveyed under guard to Rome. All agreed that an ex-Pope at large was too dangerous a rallying-point for heretics and *Fraticelli*, and he was accordingly arrested [June,

[1] See Tosti, *Storia di Bonifazio VIII.*, Note E. for the evidence.

1295] in an attempt to cross the sea and delivered to Pope Boniface for safe keeping. Imprisoned in a narrow cell in the Castle of Fumone, the old man died after a few months [May, 1296]—while passionate accusations of foul play were hurled at Boniface by his adherents. The Church canonized him within twenty years of his death, but his contemporary Dante, who could not forgive him for giving place to Boniface, relegated to the Outer Hell, among the mean souls who lived without either praise or infamy, the shade of him

che fece per viltate il gran rifiuto.

Boniface VIII., who assumed the Tiara at the age of seventy-seven, was elected as the person marked out by every quality to save the Church from the ignominious position in which the disasters of the last three years had left her. The event proved that he was to drag her down in his own fall. Violent and overbearing by nature, he attempted to rule the world with the sceptre of Gregory VII., but in doing so he failed to reckon with the spirit of rising nationalism in Europe. Sicily remained untaken, for all his efforts; the King and Parliament of England repudiated his interference with their internal affairs; the King and Parliament of France grappled with him and threw him. Nearer home, however, he at first achieved a signal triumph over his enemies. The great family of the Colonna, which included two cardinals among its members and owned a series of towns and fortresses in the Volscian and Sabine hills, early provoked the jealousy of Boniface, who as a member of the lesser nobility[1] could ill brook the pride and arrogance of such a clan. They were suspected of intriguing with Frederick of Sicily, and of the still more deadly offence of spreading doubts as to the validity of Celestine's abdication. In May, 1297, Boniface summoned the two Cardinals to clear themselves of these charges, and when they replied by a manifesto declaring the election of Boniface illegal, since Celestine could not abdicate, and appealing against him to a general Council, Boniface launched the excommunication against the Cardinals Jacopo and Pietro, with the latter's five brothers and their heirs, and proceeded to collect troops with which to attack them. In December he enlisted all Christendom in the struggle by proclaiming it a crusade; one by one the fortresses of the Colonna were stormed and their palaces in Rome burnt to ashes; at last only the Cyclopean walls of Palestrina, which sheltered the two Cardinals and Count Sciarra, still held out. Unsupported from outside, however, the Colonna were obliged to surrender, after a long blockade [September, 1298], and with cords round their necks they

---

[1] The Gaetani were merely *knights* in Anagni.

proceeded to Rieti to implore the Pope's pardon and their release from excommunication. Boniface received them with fair words, but immediately sent orders to his Vicar in Rome to demolish the whole town of Palestrina, except the Cathedral alone, and to drive the plough and scatter salt over its ruins. This order was literally obeyed, and to Pope Boniface belongs the glory of having destroyed all that was left of the ancient Præneste, as well as the mediæval palace of the Colonna and all the dwellings of their humbler dependants. Fearing for their lives, the Colonna fled into exile, and Counts Stephen and Sciarra found a ready welcome at the court of the Pope's ablest antagonist, King Philip the Fair of France.

The quarrel between Boniface and Philip IV. had first broken out in the year 1296, when Boniface by the famous Bull *Clericis laicos* had proclaimed the clergy immune from royal taxation, and Philip had replied by forbidding the export of gold to Italy. After a brief lull the dispute flamed out afresh in 1301, when the bishop of Pamiers, Boniface's Legate, was convicted of high treason by the royal court for intrigues against the King in Languedoc, and Boniface, to avenge the insult, issued the Bull *Ausculta Fili*, in which he warned the King in significant words not to imagine that he had 'no superior.' He haughtily summoned the clergy of France to a council in Rome in the following November [1302], there to pronounce judgment upon the King's proceedings. Philip dexterously circulated a garbled version of this Bull and burnt it publicly in Paris on February 11, 1302, and then, by a supreme stroke of policy, summoned the Three Estates to meet in April and obtained their enthusiastic consent to a decree forbidding the clergy to obey the Pope's command. Upon this Boniface published a Bull of excommunication against all who should go about to hinder the faithful from approaching the throne of the Apostles [June 29, 1302], and when Philip hesitated and seemed anxious to gain time Boniface followed it up with a threat of deposition unless the King should express repentance.

But by this time the King had made up his mind to act. His plan was to summon Boniface before a General Council of the Church at Lyons, and since he knew well enough that Boniface would not obey, he decided to convey him thither by force. Stephen and Sciarra Colonna urged him to strong measures, and he found a perfect instrument for the deed in his able legist Guillaume de Nogaret, whose grandfather had been burnt as a heretic in Languedoc. Nogaret laid a formal indictment against the Pope before King Philip at a council of prelates and barons in the Louvre on

March 12, 1303, and then proceeded with three companions to Italy, with the King's letters patent in his pocket, to organize the *coup de main*. He spent some weeks in Tuscany, drawing freely on the King's Florentine bankers, and intriguing with the discontented barons of the Campagna, many of whom were ill-disposed towards Boniface owing to the encroachments of his avaricious nephew, Count Peter Gaetani. Sciarra Colonna joined him with about five hundred horse, and the conspirators then proceeded to the neighbourhood of Anagni, where the Pope had taken up his summer quarters. Meanwhile King Philip had held a second and larger assembly at the Louvre in June, at which the Pope had been accused of a long list of crimes and the King had formally appealed to a council against him, and at the news Boniface resolved to act. It became known to Nogaret that a Bull of excommunication and deposition against his master was to be posted up on the door of the Cathedral of Anagni on Sunday, September 8, and he determined to anticipate the blow. At dawn on the 7th, Nogaret, Sciarra, and their troop, bearing the fleur-de-lys and the gonfalon of St. Peter, rode into the town and the inhabitants, whose Podestà had already been won over, gathered round the intruders shouting, 'Death to Boniface! Long live the King of France!' The Papal palace was easily broken into, and Sciarra and Nogaret soon found themselves in the presence of the aged Pope, who at the noise without had hastily clad himself in the Pontifical robes and was found seated on a throne with the Keys and Cross in his hands. Sciarra would have killed him then and there, but Nogaret interposed and sought to persuade the old man to come with him peaceably to Lyons. Boniface answered not a word, save to taunt his oppressor with his Patarine ancestry, and the dauntlessness of their victim seems to have struck confusion into the invaders' plans. Two days were wasted in inaction, and on Monday the 9th the populace of Anagni suddenly veered round and stormed the palace once more with cries of 'Death to the traitors!', while a troop of horse from Rome led by Cardinal Orsini arrived on the scene and completed the Pope's deliverance. Nogaret fled to Ferentino, and Boniface was conveyed to Rome, but, as Villani says, 'he did not therefore rejoice in any wise, forasmuch as the pain of his adversity had so entered into his heart and clotted there.' In Rome he found himself little better than a prisoner, for the Orsini watched him night and day. Frenzied with rage and bitterness, powerless to avenge his insults, suspicious of all who surrounded him, he shut himself into his rooms in the Vatican, and on October 12 his troubled spirit passed away. His enemies did not fail to circulate the darkest rumours of his death; he had been heard calling on the name of Beelzebub, they declared, and in his madness he had taken his own life by beating his head against the chamber walls. A prophecy attributed to his victim Celestine was repeated from mouth to mouth: 'Intrabit ut vulpis, regnabit ut leo, morietur ut canis.'

The real weakness of the fabric reared by Gregory, the Innocents, and Boniface was shown by the ease with which it succumbed to the blow of Anagni. Not only was no vengeance taken on the raiders by the weak Pope who followed, Benedict XI., but the arch-conspirator in Paris, King Philip IV., was left master of the field. The long-disputed election which followed Benedict's death in 1304 resulted in the choice of a Frenchman, Bertrand de Got, as Pope Clement V. [1305—13]; and at the King's suggestion he summoned the Cardinals to France instead of joining them at Perugia. The Tiara was placed on his head in the Church of S. Just at Lyons, and he then withdrew to the strong city of Avignon, which lay within the Provençal dominions of the King of Naples. The 'Babylonish Captivity' of the Papacy to the Kings of France had begun, and for over seventy years—save for the brief return of Urban V. in 1367 —no Pope was seen on the southern side of the Alps. Italy, the home of Empire and of Papacy, was left deserted by both, and in that strange freedom fell a prey to innumerable petty despotisms, which grew and flourished in the absence of a strong coercive hand to master them. It will now be necessary to retrace our steps some fifty years, and to follow the transformation of the Communes into the full-blown Tyrannies of the fourteenth century.

CHAPTER XI

The Rise of the Tyrannies:
the Rise of Florence

Chè le città d'Italia tutte piene
Son di tiranni, ed un Marcel diventa
Ogni villan che parteggiando viene. *Purgatorio*, Can. VI.

FOR sixty years after the death of Frederick II., no Emperor descended on the Italian plain. During that long interregnum the cities of Lombardy, Tuscany, and Romagna were free to follow out their destiny without external coercion,—though affected in varying degrees by every convulsion of Rome and the South,—and to evolve for themselves some solution from the endless chaos of civil war. For, as we have seen in a previous chapter,[1] the earlier animosities of city against city had become transformed by the end of the twelfth century into a blind intestine strife, owing its origin to the subjugation and absorption of the nobles of the *contado* by the victorious Communes. This process, though necessary to the very existence of the Communes, had produced a troublesome and unruly type of citizen who either schemed to monopolize all power into his own hands, or else was ever ready to make common cause with the enemies of his adopted home. Lastly, we saw how the continual antagonism between these 'Citizens and Co-citizens,' as a brilliant historian of the Middle Ages has named them,[2] though in origin a merely social struggle, was caught up into the mighty dualism of Guelf and Ghibelline and seemed to receive from it the doom of perpetuity.

These fierce domestic wars reached their climax during the forty years that followed Frederick's death. The fury of the struggle is incredible. Houses are sacked and demolished, women and children massacred, half the population of the town cast out into exile; but the victors live on in constant dread of reprisals, for the shifting kaleidoscope of feuds and alliances may at any moment give the exiles their chance of return. And return will mean the same treatment for the now dominant party. These roving bands of exiles— the *fuorusciti*, as the chroniclers name them—form one of the most curious phenomena of the time; they are political entities just as much as the towns that cast them forth, for they already

[1] See p. 103.
[2] J. Ferrari, *Hist. des Révolutions d'Italie*, Paris, 1858.

stand allied with every other unit of their party throughout Italy,
and often play an important part in the quarrels of some quite
distant town. Thus a large body of Guelfs from Florence and other
Tuscan towns, expelled after the battle of Montaperti, were called
in by their brethren of Modena and Reggio to assist in expelling the
Ghibellines from those cities—a task which the Florentines joyfully
performed by hard and bloody fighting on the Piazzas of the two
towns. 'For,' explains Villani, 'it is the custom in the cities of
Lombardy for men to assemble and fight on the piazza of the commonwealth.' Finally they joined the army of Charles of Anjou,
and on the field of Benevento won their right of re-entry into
Florence. Their return was the signal for the ruin of the opposite
party, for when King Charles sent them eight hundred men-at-
arms wherewith to maintain the Guelf sway in Florence, the
Ghibellines, so Villani tells us, 'departed from Florence without
stroke of sword, and some went to Siena, some to Pisa, and some
to other places.' So in like manner the Ghibelline nobles of Milan,
exiled in 1258, made common cause with the Ghibellines of Como
and the territories of Monferrat for nearly twenty years, and then
at last came back on an accidental turn of the tide, to find the mob
already sacking the houses of Guelfs.

It was only natural that in these endless wars the noble families
on either side should come to the front, and should in many cases
impose their names upon the struggle to the exclusion of the older
appellations. Thus Bologna was cleft to its foundations between
the *Geremei* and the *Lambertazzi*, the former Guelf, the latter Ghibelline; at Milan the issue lay between the *Della Torre* and the *Visconti*, at Como between the *Vitani* and the *Rusconi*, while Verona
was torn between the *Montecchi*[1] and the *Counts of San Bonifazio*,
Ferrara between *Salinguerra* and the *Marquis of Este*, Rimini between the *Parcitadi* and the *Malatesta*. The exigencies of the
struggle also produced, especially in cities where the *Grandi*, or
imported nobles from the countryside, made themselves particularly
obnoxious, a new official with the title of *Captain of the People*,
whose business it was to enforce the laws against the insolent gran-
dees, to lead and discipline the army, and generally to guide the
policy of the republic in the interests of his party. He is a partisan
and a leader of partisans, and for that reason he does not supersede
the impartial Podestà, who, however, falls to the second rank and
is retained merely as a figurehead and as the supreme judicial
authority of the Commune. The office of the Podestà is on the
wane; the *Capitano* will soon be all in all, and his appointment,

[1] Shakespeare's *Montagues*.

instead of being annual, will be extended to a five or ten years'
term or even raised to an unlimited *Signoria*. Being necessarily a
fighting man, he is frequently taken from one or other of the noble
houses that distract the town; in that case he has all the instincts
of a dynast, and with luck and courage on his side will succeed in
founding a despotism.

The wars in which Frederick II. had plunged the valley of the
Po had also provided a direct and powerful stimulus to the growth
of despotism in Italy. They had favoured the rise of military leaders
on either side,—territorial lords like the Marquis of Este, the Count
of San Bonifazio, and above all the infamous Ezzelino da Romano,
who between them acquired the mastery over all the cities of the
March of Verona in the course of the general war. Ezzelino, by
the help of the Ghibelline Montecchi, had been named Captain of
the People in Imperialist Verona as early as 1235, and during the
next fifteen years gradually extended his rule over Vicenza, Padua,
and the territories of the 'Trevisan March,' while his rival Azzo of
Este secured himself in Ferrara and thence upheld the Guelf cause.
The Emperor never interfered with Ezzelino's absolute rule over
the March of Verona, for his hands were too full elsewhere, and
the tyrant was therefore free to organize a reign of terror which
has hardly been surpassed for ferocity in all the annals of mediæval
Europe, and which left an indelible impression on the imagination
of his contemporaries. No family of repute in his dominions was
safe from his spies, his torturers, and his dungeons, and when his
castles became too few for the multitude of suspects he erected
eight new prisons at Padua, with cells so dark, airless, and filthy
that men were thankful to escape them by death. Into these dens
he thrust whole families together, often after long preliminary
tortures, and when at last they were opened on the deliverance of
Padua in 1256, it was found that they contained a miserable band
of blinded children. After the death of Frederick, Ezzelino redoubled his butcheries and began to lay his schemes for the conquest
of Lombardy; he entered into an alliance with the two Ghibelline
captains of Cremona, Oberto Pelavicino and Buoso da Doara, and
even intrigued with the nobles (the 'Co-citizens') of Guelf Brescia.
But the danger roused his enemies to action. In 1255 Pope Alexander IV. preached a crusade against the 'son of perdition and man
of blood, Ezzelino da Romano,' and a league was formed between
Venice, Bologna, Ferrara, and Mantua, and the exiles of blood-
stained Padua, to put an end to the monster and his cruelties
together. Ezzelino maintained himself for three years against the
League; seized Brescia by a *coup de main* in 1258, and next year

came near to doing the same with Milan, by the help of a band of her exiled Ghibelline nobles. But he had pushed on too far from his base; the Guelf armies surrounded him beside the river Adda, and, on September 16, 1259, in an attempt to force a passage eastwards at the bridge of Cassano he was overpowered, wounded, and taken prisoner. He lay for eleven days in the tent of his former ally Pelavicino, who had now joined the League against him, then tore the dressings from his wounds and suffered himself to bleed to death.

Italy had rid herself of the person of the tyrant, but the system he had founded remained. Verona, which he had ruled by a mixture of affability and terrorism for twenty-four years, now fell under the sway of a citizen of obscure family named Mastino della Scala, who was proclaimed 'Perpetual Captain of the Veronese People' in 1262 and founded the Scaliger dynasty; Ferrara remained devoted to the great House of Este, which never lost its hold upon the town for the next three and a half centuries; Mantua, after a period of furious party violence, passed from the Counts of San Bonifazio to the Bonaccorsi family in 1272, and from them to the Gonzaga in 1328.

Meanwhile at Milan, the ancient bulwark of freedom against foreign tyranny, events in 1237 had also tended towards the rise of a domestic despotism. When the Lombard army was routed by the Emperor on the field of Cortenuova, the Milanese fugitives, driven northwards into the mountains, were kindly received and sheltered by the Guelf lord of the Val Sassina, Pagano della Torre (a 'co-citizen' of Ghibelline Bergamo), and in return for this service his family were ever afterwards held in high honour by the popular party of Milan. Pagano's son Martino headed the opposition against the *Grandi*, who as usual had Ghibelline tendencies. In 1258 the antagonism grew to open war between the two parties, supported respectively by the Vitani and the Rusconi of Como; the Pope intervened and secured the banishment of the chiefs of both sides, but Della Torre boldly broke his exile, and, returning on a wave of popular enthusiasm, was hailed as 'Anziano del Popolo' and established the ascendancy of his party at Milan for the next twenty years. He was still, however, on bad terms with the Pope (Urban IV.), who, in 1262, revenged himself by appointing as Archbishop of Milan a member of the great Ghibelline family of the Visconti. Della Torre refused to receive the new Archbishop, in spite of a Papal interdict, and Visconti thus became a rallying-point for banished nobles and remained in exile from his see for fifteen years.

The invasion of Charles of Anjou tended still further to strengthen the position of the Della Torre, and Filippo, who succeeded his brother Martino in 1263, was acknowledged as *Signore* by many of the neighbouring Lombard cities. But at last the opportunity of the exiles came. A revolution in Como gave the Ghibelline Rusconi once more the upper hand, and by their aid and that of the Marquis of Monferrat, Visconti found himself able to assume the offensive and, in 1277, to advance upon Milan. Napoleone della Torre, who had somewhat alienated the affections of the Milanese, came forth with a small force of mercenaries to meet him, but fell into an ambush at Desio and was taken prisoner with five of his relatives. The communal army, marching out tardily to his support, made a virtue of necessity by joining hands with the returning Ghibellines, and Otto Visconti was welcomed by the mob with cries of 'Peace!' The Della Torre were given up to their enemies the Rusconi and chained within narrow iron cages in the castle of Baradello, where Napoleone died after eighteen months of direst suffering. Otto Visconti and his nephew Matteo ruled as undisputed lords of Milan, and founded that brilliant and crime-stained dynasty of which the *castello* and the cathedral stand today as the immortal monuments.

The tyrannies of the Visconti, the Scala and the House of Este were all of them examples of the *impartial despotisms* which were strong enough to impose internal peace upon the communes under their rule, and in that respect they marked a distinct advance upon the bloody affrays, the massacres and expulsions of the earlier *régime*. In external affairs the tyrant might be the champion of the Guelfs, like the Marquis of Este, or of the Ghibellines, like Visconti and Scala, but within the walls of the cities they ruled the feud was kept in check, the exiles were recalled, and the people encouraged to forget politics in the development of a new prosperity. At the best the new ruler proved himself a patron of letters, a fosterer of trade, a builder of churches and palaces; at the worst he but substituted the cruelty of a single master for the barbarous warfare of the past sixty years. There may have been less liberty, but civilization increased, and time was to show that the Rule of the Tyrants was to be anything but unfavourable to the emergence of genius in literature and art.

While the Valley of the Po was being slowly but surely carved into a series of strong and pugnacious principalities, the isolated but ever-vigilant Republic of Venice on the one hand, and the communes of Tuscany and the western coast on the other were following out lines of more or less divergent tendency. In Venice the ever-increasing wealth and power of her own native-born nobles—a far more truly patriotic caste than the feudal nobility imported into the cities of the mainland—produced an oligarchic type of government which was for centuries the admiration of Europe, while Florence, with her more complex population and interests, only attained a stable government through the clash of many revolutions. In the year 1297 Venice, under the guidance of Doge Pietro Gradenigo, assented to the famous measure known as the Closing of the Great Council, by which the privilege of belonging to that body (the sole fount of office in the State) was practically restricted to the existing members and their descendants for ever. The powers of the Doge were at the same time jealously hedged in, for despotism was of all things the most abhorrent to the resident oligarchy of the lagoons; and when after a disastrous war on the mainland the need for a stronger executive was felt, the Council, in 1310, supplied it by naming a Committee of Ten, which, armed with the most formidable powers, became in after years a name of mystery and terror to Europe.

Very different from the well-ordered egotism of the Venetian Republic was the fate of the brilliant but distracted communes of Tuscany and the Mediterranean coast. Faction at home and inter-communal jealousy were there the order of the day longer even than in Lombardy. Pisa and Siena maintained their Ghibelline traditions unimpaired throughout Frederick's reign, profited by the brief glory of Manfred, suffered from the advent of Charles and from their championship of Conradin, and received unwonted favours at the hands of the 'Ghibelline' Pope, Gregory X. Genoa, on the other hand, remained more aloof from mainland politics owing to her position behind her mountain barrier, but even there the great divisions crept in, and the common people, headed by the noble houses of Doria and Spinola, held mainly for the Ghibellines, while the Grimaldi and Fieschi, with a strong party among the bourgeoisie, held for the Guelfs. Whatever her internal politics, however, the hostility of Genoa to Pisa was inveterate and un-sleeping; and after the restoration of the Greek Empire of Constantinople in 1261, which profited Genoa at the expense of Venice and Pisa, a death-struggle between the two naval powers of the West became altogether inevitable. Their interests clashed in Constantinople, in Palestine, in Corsica and Sardinia, and at last, in 1284, both powers put forth their full strength in the great naval battle of Meloria off the Tuscan coast. The Pisans fought with desperate courage, but were overborne at last by superior numbers, and of their great fleet of over one hundred sail only twelve returned to port while 11,000 Pisan prisoners were dragged to fill the dungeons of Genoa. Naturally enough the mainland enemies of Pisa—Florence, Lucca, Prato, Pistoia, and Volterra—chose this moment to form a league against her for her utter destruction, and she was only saved by calling to the head of affairs one of her own Guelf nobles, Ugolino della Gherardesca, who was able to negotiate a peace at the price of some castles and territory. Pisa submitted to his rule unwillingly, for the people had no love for their Guelf 'co-citizens' and had already banished Ugolino and his party once before. But at this crisis the Count was indispensable for his very Guelfism, and he astutely sought to tighten his hold upon the city by placing every obstacle in the way of the release of the Pisan prisoners, whose return, he knew, would be fatal to his power. At last, however, the Ghibellines regained the upper hand, and Ugolino and his family were attacked and captured in the palace of the Podestà. He and his two sons and two grandsons were thrown into the Gualandi Tower, in the Piazza degli Anziani; Pisa, reverting to her Ghibelline traditions, called in the famous Romagnuol captain, Guido of Montefeltro, to lead her armies for three years, and on the day of his entry in 1288 the Archbishop ordered the door of Ugolino's dungeon to be locked from without and the key thrown into the Arno. The cries of the wretched captives were heard for several days, beseeching that at least they might be shriven, but not even that boon was granted them. Death at last ended their torments. 'And thenceforward,' says Villani, 'the said prison was called the Tower of Hunger, and will be always.'

But the history of Tuscany leads inevitably to that of Florence, and it is time that we followed in somewhat closer detail the doings of the great Republic of the Val d'Arno. In Florence, still more clearly than in the Lombard towns, the strife of Guelf and Ghibelline had had its origin in the struggle between the People, headed by the urban nobles who as *consuls* had ruled the Commune ever since the death of the Countess Matilda, and the feudal nobles of the countryside, who had gradually been subjected and brought to live within the city walls. Villani dates the beginning of the 'accursed parties' from a famous crime—the murder of young Buondelmonte by a party of nobles of the Amidei and Uberti clans, in revenge for a slight offered to a maiden of their kindred [1215]. But the crime was a symptom, not a cause of strife. The Uberti (whose very name betrays a Germanic descent) had already raised a rebellion against the consular government in 1177, and to their

I

influence was attributed the introduction, in 1193, of the Podestà, under whose rule the Consuls were gradually transformed into the Council of the Podestà, and the government became more aristocratic. Naturally, therefore, when the advent of Frederick II. gave a name to the dumb antagonisms of noble and burgher, or rather of Teuton and Latin, throughout Northern Italy, the Uberti and their friends were found among the Ghibellines, and the true Commune of Florence among the Guelfs. On Frederick's death the expulsion of his son Frederick of Antioch, who had captured the city by the aid of the Uberti in 1249, was celebrated by the establishment in 1250 of the First Popular Government, or *Primo Popolo*, in which the Guelfs were supreme, and the rights of the burghers defended by the introduction of a new officer—the Captain of the People. In Florence the Capitano was a strictly constitutional official, imported from without and holding office only for a year;—he was the leader of the popular militia, both of the city and the countryside, but possessed judicial as well as military functions and served in fact as the chief executive officer and figurehead of the *People* as against the nobles. The Podestà still subsisted as the official head of the Commune, with command over the cavalry and regular soldiers, and the juxtaposition of the two authorities did not necessarily produce friction, but rather a balance of power which led each section of the state to respect the other. Florence prospered exceedingly in the ten years following the establishment of this curious double government. At this time she coined the famous golden florin which became the standard of value for many centuries throughout the Mediterranean world. But her Ghibelline nobles still formed a dangerous and combustible element, and in 1258 their intrigues with Manfred produced a violent explosion in which the whole clan of the Uberti were driven out and went to take refuge at Siena, the Ghibelline stronghold. Farinata degli Uberti procured help from Manfred,[1] and craftily induced the Florentines, by promising to deliver Siena into their hands, to send out a great army into the Sienese territory; then, gathering Manfred's Germans and the Sienese militia, he fell upon them unawares at Montaperti and routed them at the bloody battle

Che fece l'Arbia colorata in rosso.

Farinata entered Florence in triumph, abolished the popular government, and set up Count Guido Novello, a bitter Ghibelline from the Upper Arno, as Podestà. But when the Ghibellines proposed to render Florence for ever harmless by razing her walls and

[1] See p. 111.

palaces to the ground, Farinata indignantly protested, and thereby
saved his city from the fate which had overtaken Milan just a
hundred years before.

The rule of the Ghibellines lasted only so long as the star of
Manfred was in the ascendant, and with the coming of Charles of
Anjou they were expelled by a counter-revolution, and the Guelfs
returned to power [1266]. The office of Captain of the People was
at once resuscitated, but between the Podestà and the Capitano
there now appears a central executive body composed of twelve
Anziani or Elders, two from each *Sesto*[1] of the City, who with
their deliberative council of a hundred 'Worthies of the People' are
collectively known as the *Signoria*. The two great functionaries are
also provided with two Councils apiece, those of the Capitano
being entirely composed of non-noble citizens, while those of the
Podestà include a proportion of nobles, and already the Guild-
masters, or Capitudini, have acquired the right to sit *ex officio* in
the Captain's Council.

This was the celebrated *Secondo Popolo*, the democratic government under which Florence succeeded so much longer than her
neighbours in staving off the advances of despotism; and though
the political power of the Podestà and Capitano was eclipsed later
on by that of the central executive, or *Signoria*, the two officers
themselves with their different councils subsisted until the beginning of the sixteenth century. In 1282, however, the twelve Anziani were replaced by a body of six Guild-masters, or *Priors of the
Arts*, whose admission to the highest position in the State expresses
the importance acquired by the trading guilds of Florence. They
were only allowed to hold office for two months, probably in order
to guard against the danger of despotism, and during their term of
office lived in the Palazzo Pubblico and took no meals with any
other citizen. Thus Florence bade fair to become a true republic of
craftsmen, but there still existed certain unhealed social troubles
which prevented her from following unchecked so peaceful a
development.

First, the proscription of the Ghibellines in 1267 led to the formation of a regular party organization named the *Parte Guelfa*, which
undertook the administration of confiscated goods, and since we
hear that 3,000 Ghibellines were banished and deprived of their
possessions in the years 1268 and '69, the new society must at once
have leapt to great wealth and influence. The spoils were at first
divided equally between the Commune, the Party, and individual

[1] Florence was early divided into six sections, five on the North Bank of
the Arno and one on the South.

Guelfs who had suffered in the cause, but later on the Party absorbed the whole. No wonder that the well-meaning efforts of Pope Gregory X. towards reconciliation ended in ludicrous fiasco [1273], and that the more serious attempt of Cardinal Latino in 1279 was only very partially successful.

The influence of the *Parte Guelfa* was also significant in promoting that cleavage between *Grandi* and *Popolani* which brought about so many disasters at the end of the century. For it gave to the Guelf nobles who had been partially excluded from the reformed government a new outlet for their energies, and they used the wealth and influence which the new society gave them in pursuing a militarist and ultra-Guelf policy towards the outside world, and in trying to ride rough-shod over the *popolani* at home. Both Dino Compagni and Villani note how the victory of Campaldino over the Ghibellines of Arezzo in 1289 intensified the arrogance and insubordination of the nobles, and their outrages against the *popolani* increased so much in the next two years that early in 1292 the Priors, instigated by one Giano della Bella, passed the famous *Ordinances of Justice*, by which the bias of the State against the nobles was enormously strengthened. By this extraordinary law the nobles were definitely excluded from the Priorate, and each member of a noble family was held answerable for any crime against a *popolano* committed by the others, while the evidence of two *popolani* bearing witness to 'public fame' should be held sufficient proof of such a crime. To enforce the Ordinances a new official was created, named the Gonfalonier of Justice, whose special business it was to bear the Standard of the People (a red cross on a white ground) against the palace of any offending family, and see it razed to the ground. 'And I Dino Compagni,' writes the chronicler, 'being appointed Gonfalonier of Justice in 1293, went to the houses of the Galigai (one of whom had murdered the son of a *popolano* in France) and of their relatives, and caused them to be pulled down according to the laws.'

Naturally the nobles did not submit with a good grace to such measures, and in 1294 they succeeded in banishing Giano della Bella, though the ordinances remained. Party feeling had never run so high in Florence; and when in 1300 a private feud—between the White and Black branches of the Cancellieri family—was imported from Pistoia into Florence, the leaders on both sides fell naturally into the new divisions. The Grandi, under their proud leader Messer Corso Donati, of an ancient house of Guelf nobles, sided with the Blacks, while the rich bourgeoisie and all who envied the power of the *Parte Guelfa* called themselves *Whites*. At first nothing was further from the minds of Messer Viero di Cerchi and the other *White* leaders than to identify themselves with the Ghibelline remnant, but the Blacks adroitly fastened the suspicion of Ghibellinism upon them, and requested the intervention of Pope Boniface VIII. in the interests of the Guelf cause. Boniface, who was at that moment struggling with revolted Sicily, fell in with the idea, and the result of his deliberations with Corso Donati, who haunted his Court, was that in September, 1301, Charles, Count of Valois, brother of King Philip the Fair, entered Italy with the double commission of reconquering Sicily for the Angevins and of restoring peace in Tuscany. On November 1, 1301, he entered Florence in peace, having cajoled the leaders of the Whites (at that moment the dominant party) into believing that he came in good faith, but no sooner had the 'lordship' of the city been conferred on him by the too trustful Priors than the French knights appeared in arms in the streets, Corso Donati entered the town with an armed band, and the Whites perceived too late that their Papal Peacemaker had come but to sell them to their enemies. The Blacks seized the magistracy, and after an abortive attempt at reconciliation under Papal auspices, the French prince agreed in March, 1302, to have done with half-measures. A document was produced showing that the White leaders were plotting to subvert the rule of the Count of Valois; they were summoned to appear before the Signory, but fled in dismay to Pisa, Arezzo, and Pistoia, and this seeming alliance with the traditional enemies of Florence gave some colour of justice to the wholesale expulsion of the Whites that followed. During the year 1302 over six hundred sentences of confiscation and exile were pronounced against individual Whites, and in that long roll—among those condemned to death by burning if ever they should fall into the hands of the Republic—occurs the name of Dante Alighieri.

The exiles were naturally driven into the arms of the Ghibellines of Tuscany, and with their help made several attempts at a forcible return, but always without success. At last, however, a new crisis arose which put a severe strain upon the resources of the State, and an amnesty was extended to such of the exiles as were known to have Guelf sympathies—but not to reputed Ghibellines such as Dante. Henry of Luxemburg, Emperor-elect, had descended into Italy, and though, like Otto III., he came with the dream of peace and justice in his heart, though he was hailed by Dante as the 'Bridegroom of Italy and Solace of the World,' his passage only blew the flames of discord into a blaze, and his failure proved once for all that the power of the Mediæval Empire was broken and gone.

Florence from the first took up an attitude of uncompromising hostility towards Henry, allied herself with King Robert of Naples, son of Charles II., and stirred the Guelf cities of Lombardy to revolt against him. Brescia again made a heroic defence against the Germans, as in the days of Frederick II.; Cremona, now Guelf under a popular government, was besieged and sacked without mercy, and Henry found himself forced more and more out of his impartial attitude and obliged to take sides with the Visconti and their allies in Lombardy, and with the enemies of Florence and King Robert in Tuscany and Rome. Pisa welcomed him with joy on his way to Rome and furnished him with 60,000 florins, and in Rome itself it was the Ghibelline populace that forced the Cardinal Legates to crown him in the Lateran, in the face of the Neapolitan forces that held Sant' Angelo and the Vatican. But the Pope had already declared against him from his stronghold at Avignon, and Florence and the Guelf League of Tuscany barred his way northward. Reluctantly he undertook the siege of Florence on his return, but his scanty forces were quite inadequate to the task, and the German troops, by plundering friend and foe alike, brought down the hatred of the countryside upon the Emperor. In March, 1313, Henry was back at Pisa, sick and penniless, but with gallant perseverance he set himself to prepare for an invasion of Naples, and had soon collected a sufficient force to make the attempt. In the heat of August he started south, but was struck down by fever at the little town of Buonconvento, south of Siena, and died with startling suddenness. Once more the hopes of the Ghibellines were dashed to the ground, as at the news of Benevento and of Tagliacozzo, and once more that dream of ordered government, so nobly dreamed by Theodoric, by Dante and even by the Second Frederick, faded into air before the vigour and the passions of Italy.

CHAPTER XII

Rome and the Papacy
during the Fourteenth Century

THE tragic ending of Henry of Luxemburg afforded intense relief
and satisfaction to the occupant of the Throne of the Apostles in
distant Avignon. Though the Ghibellines still kept the upper hand
in Lombardy, where Matteo Visconti and Can Grande della Scala
divided the Valley of the Po between them,[1] Pope Clement V. was
now enabled to help on his ally and vassal, King Robert of Naples,
grandson of Charles of Anjou, and to appoint him successively
Senator of Rome and Vicar-Imperial of Italy [1313—1314]. The
Eternal City accepted the Papal Senator with a good grace, but his
power was nominal, and indeed the city of Rome had fallen into
ever-increasing anarchy after the departure of the Papacy. A
Council of *Boni Viri* elected by the guilds of the thirteen *Regions*
maintained itself side by side with the Senator, but the perpetual
clash of arms between the rival families of the lawless nobility
made all government impossible; robbery and violence flourished
unchecked, the population dwindled to some 20,000; buildings and
churches fell to decay. The street-fighting at the coronation of
Henry VII. had ruined many fortresses and towers, which lay in
heaps with none to rebuild them; twice the basilica of the Lateran
was half destroyed; once by fire and once by earthquake [1308,
1348] and silently all the while the buildings of antiquity crumbled
to ruin, stripped of their marble shells, a mere quarry for all to
plunder from. The Romans attributed their misfortunes to the
absence of the Pope, and on Clement's death in 1314 the Italian
Cardinals fought hard for a return to the Lateran, but after a long
vacancy the French party prevailed, and a Gascon Cardinal—
Jacques Duèse of Cahors—was elected in 1316 as John XXII.

The new Pope was determined to abate no jot of the pretensions
of his predecessors to control this world's affairs. A disputed Im-

---

[1] Matteo Visconti ruled over Milan, Como, Bergamo, Lodi, Cremona, Pavia,
Piacenza and Alessandria, while Can Grande, the friend and patron of
Dante, extended his rule from Verona and Vicenza over Padua, Feltre and
Treviso. The House of Este, expelled from Ferrara in 1308 by the Pope and
the Venetians, returned in 1317 and joined the Ghibelline party.

perial election gave him his opportunity; refusing to recognize
either candidate—Louis the Bavarian or Frederick of Austria—he
claimed the Imperial rights for himself during the vacancy, and
summoned the Vicars appointed by Henry VII. in Upper Italy to
lay down their offices. This encroachment was followed by a bitter
quarrel with Louis, the more Ghibelline of the two Emperors, who
at length succeeded in crushing his rival and was recognized as
Emperor by the whole of Germany, by Visconti, Scala, and Este and
by the rising and ambitious Tyrant of Lucca, Castruccio Castracane.
John excommunicated and deposed the Emperor by a Bull issued
in 1324, and it seemed as though the quarrel of Innocent IV. and
Frederick II. was merely to be repeated in a less heroic form. But
the eighty years that had passed since the Council of Lyons had
produced a profound change in the intellectual aspect of Western
Europe. Not only had those years brought about an ever-deepening
corruption of the Papal Curia, combined with such a rise in the
Papal pretensions as not even that age could accept with equani-
mity, but something very like an organized public opinion in the
intellectual world had appeared with the growth of the University
of Paris, while the leaven of Franciscan teaching had continued to
work in the poorer classes, producing those various ascetic or
heretical bodies known as Poor Brothers, Spiritualists or Fraticelli.
Indeed the Franciscan Order, and through it the whole Church, had
been convulsed for the last fifty years by the controversy concerning the Poverty of Christ and the Apostles, which involved the
whole question of the endowments of the Order. Two Papal decisions in favour of the stricter interpretation of the Rule[1] had failed
to satisfy the extremists, who were still in a state of secession from
the Order and troubled the Church with their clamours against her
worldliness and corruption. The General of the Franciscans,
Michael of Cesena, was at first inclined to proceed severely against
these malcontents, and four of them were burnt alive at Marseilles
in 1318 at his instance. But the Order still jealously adhered to its
theoretic defence of the Poverty of Christ, and when Pope John—
who during his eighteen years' Pontificate amassed a treasure of
25,000,000 golden florins[2]—supported the decision of a Dominican
Inquisitor that the Doctrine of Poverty was heretical, the whole
Franciscan Order rose in revolt. The decision was repudiated in a
General Council of the Order held at Perugia in 1322; and when the
quarrel between Pope John and the Emperor blazed forth two years

[1] The Bulls of Nicholas III., *Exiit qui seminat*, and of Clement V., *Exivi
de Paradiso*.
[2] According to G. Villani, Bk. viii., ch. 36.

later, the Court of Louis was thronged with eager Franciscans, and in his protest against the Bull of Deposition he roundly accused Pope John of heresy.

At the same time there emerged from the University of Paris a man and a book which, combined with the Franciscan revolt, lent an altogether new interest and importance to this secular quarrel. Marsiglio of Padua, for many years a Doctor of Theology and Philosophy at the University, wrote in 1325 his celebrated *Defensor Pacis*, a treatise on the relations between Church and State which in its bold survey of Papal encroachments anticipated most of the doctrines of later Protestantism, and in its theory of the foundations of sovereignty foreshadowed those of modern political philosophers.[1] Marsiglio dedicated his book to the Emperor Louis and sought his protection at the Court of Nürnberg, and throughout the Bavarian's Italian journey the learned Doctor stood at his right hand and encouraged him to go to all lengths against the Pope.

For in 1327 the Ghibellines of Italy, hard pressed by the Guelf League of Florence, Naples, and the Papal Vicars, assembled at Trent and invited Louis IV. to enter his Italian Kingdom and receive the two crowns at Milan and at Rome. Louis descended the Alps frankly as a partisan, and as a partisan he at first swept all before him. Can Grande and Visconti opened the gates of Lombardy to him, Castruccio Castracane escorted him to Rome; in Rome itself a popular rising had just driven out King Robert's Vicars and installed the veteran Ghibelline, Sciarra Colonna, as Captain of the People on the Capitol. Sciarra welcomed the Emperor into Rome on January 7, 1328, and as the gates closed on that unholy alliance the Pope's Legate laid the Interdict upon the city. But the people, summoned to a Parliament on the Capitol, acclaimed their Emperor with enthusiasm, and on the following Sunday, Sciarra Colonna, as representative of the Roman People, set the crown upon his head in St. Peter's. Villani, the Guelf chronicler, breaks out into scandalized exclamations as he records the event. 'What presumption in this accursed Bavarian!' he cries, 'Nowhere in all history will you find that any Christian Emperor ever allowed himself to be crowned by anyone but the Pope or his Legate, however hostile he may have been to Holy Church—none but this Barvarian!'[2] Worse, however, was to follow. Marsiglio of Padua, appointed Spiritual Vicar of the city, dexterously inflamed public opinion against Pope John by posting long recitals of his misdeeds on the

---

[1] See Riezler's admirable summary, *Die literarischen Widersacher der Päpste*, etc. Pt. II., §77.
[2] Giovanni Villani, Bk. x., 55.

doors of the principal churches, and finally, on April 18, 1328, the Emperor held another Parliament before the steps of St. Peter's and declared the priest 'Jacques of Cahors' to be a heretic and Anti-Christ, and deposed him from all his offices. Three weeks later a Franciscan monk was elected Pope by popular acclamation under the name of Nicholas V., and Louis himself crowned him in St. Peter's. But the nine days' wonder was drawing to a close. Military operations against King Robert of Naples could no longer be delayed, and in these the Emperor was continuously unsuccessful. By the end of July he reappeared in Rome with a mutinous and beaten army, only to find the temper of the populace completely changed; and amid cries of 'Down with the heretics!' he and his Anti-Pope evacuated the city in August and betook themselves to Pisa. Thence after another year of humiliating adventures Louis IV. retired across the Alps [December, 1329], while the Anti-Pope made an abject submission to John XXII., and died a prisoner in Avignon.

The condition of Rome during the next twenty years remained as wretched as ever. At Pope John's death, in 1334, an embassy from the Romans implored his successor, Benedict XII., to return to the afflicted city, but though the Pope was willing, the French King was inexorable. And indeed there was small inducement now for a migration from the comfort and security of Avignon to the utter barbarism of the capital. The incessant fighting between the two great families of Colonna and Orsini kept Rome in a state of anarchy and terror; famine was added to bloodshed, owing to the insecurity of the country round, and though truces from sheer exhaustion were frequently arranged, they were as frequently broken. Yet at this lowest ebb of Roman civilization two men of genius arose whose whole being was imbued with the spirit of ancient Rome, Francesco Petrarca, the *protégé* of Popes and friend of the Colonna, whose soul yet yearned for liberty and the Republic, and Cola di Rienzi, the 'Tribune of Justice, of Liberty and Peace.' The two men must first have met on that strange occasion when, amid the ruins of Rome, Petrarch received the poet's laurel crown upon the Capitol [1341], but their enthusiastic friendship dates from the time when, two years later, Rienzi was sent on a special embassy to Avignon by the Council of *Boni Viri*, and there found a kindred spirit in the voluntary exile to whom the love of Italy was yet a passion and a faith. 'Ah me,' writes Petrarch after his first intoxicating interviews with the young visionary, 'if indeed these things might come to pass in our time! If indeed Heaven willed that I might take part in an enterprise so great and so glorious!'

Its fulfilment was nearer than he thought. Rienzi returned to Rome in 1344, as a 'Notary to the Civic Camera,'[1] to pursue a relentless campaign against the nobles, by whom his young brother had already been murdered. He roamed the city haranguing the people on the meaning of ancient buildings and inscriptions. He inflamed their imagination by exhibiting allegorical pictures on the walls of the Capitol, representing the misery of Rome under her savage masters. He held secret meetings on the Aventine with members of the burgher class, and at length, taking advantage of a temporary absence of the Colonna, he seized his opportunity [May 19, 1347]. Summoning the Roman people to assemble on the Capitol, he appeared before them clad in full armour, but with bared head, and addressed them in words of passionate eloquence. The *Signoria* was bestowed on him by acclamation (though for form's sake he associated the Papal Legate with himself); he assumed the title of Tribune, and an edict was read aloud announcing measures for the restoration of peace and order. And for a time peace and order did indeed return to the distracted city. A regular militia of a hundred and twenty-five men was raised from each of the thirteen *Regions*, with a body-guard of a hundred youths for the Tribune himself; wherever possible the nobles were banished from their city fortresses, the finances purified and reorganized, the strictest justice enforced on high and low. The nobles themselves were cowed into submission, and came to do homage on the Capitol. Petrarch wrote in ecstasy from Avignon to congratulate the Tribune on his marvellous successes.[2] But the aims of Cola went much further than the mere reform of the administration. To him the city of Rome was indeed the *Caput Mundi* and her people the fount of all authority; he dreamed of setting her at the head of an Italian brotherhood whence peace and righteousness should once more radiate over the whole world. With this end in view he sent messengers bearing silver wands to all the cities and princes of 'Sacred Italy,' summoning them to a National Parliament to be held on the Capitol on August 1st. Twenty-five cities, including Florence, accepted his invitation. One the eve of the festival, when Cola was to take the vows of knighthood, the Tribune bathed in the porphyry bath of Constantine and spent the night in vigil in the Lateran Baptistery. Next day, before the assembled parliament, he issued an edict bestowing the Roman citizenship on all the cities of Italy, and boldly announced his scheme for

[1] The *Civic Camera* was an office for the administration of the city, with power over taxation, public order, etc.
[2] *Letter varie*, No. 48.

the election of a national Emperor. All princes and dignitaries who laid claim to any elective rights were cited to appear for that purpose in the Lateran at the following Whitsuntide. A few weeks later he dispatched a formal embassy to the cities and rulers of Upper Italy, inviting their adherence to this proposal.

But if Cola di Rienzi was the Mazzini of the fourteenth century, neither a soldier nor a statesman had yet appeared to give form to his visions. The fratricidal jealousy of the Italian Communes was still their strongest passion, and five hundred years were yet to pass before the dream of unity could be realized. Meanwhile the Tribune's proceedings naturally caused a growing uneasiness and disgust at the Papal court, where Clement VI. had at first been inclined to patronize his efforts at reform. The news of a theatrical seizure of the persons of the principal barons completed the Pope's dismay, and in October he sent a legate to Rome with power to depose the audacious demagogue. But Cola was already engaged in a bloody war with the Orsini and Colonna, and had no leisure to give to the Pope's remonstrances. He succeeded in defeating the barons with great slaughter at the Gate of San Lorenzo on November 20, but it was his last triumph. Success had turned the Tribune's head, and Petrarch on his way to Italy in November heard sad rumours of his degeneracy from his earlier ideals. He began to tremble at the Pope's threats, and lost the favour of the Romans by offering to yield too much to their distant over-lord, while his increased exactions caused bitter discontent. An accidental riot led to his abdication; thinking himself betrayed he laid his wreath and sceptre on the altar of the Aracœli and departed in secret to the Abruzzi. There for two years he led a hermit's life among the small community of *Fraticelli*, until his restless spirit drove him once more into the vortex of affairs.

The news of Rienzi's fall had hardly spread through Italy before a calamity of unprecedented horror descended on the unhappy land. This was the Black Death, an epidemic imported from the Crimea in Genoese vessels, which crept over the whole country like a blight and during the year 1348 destroyed, according to all contemporary estimates, at least one third of the population. When at length it passed away it left behind a profound confusion and unrest, and the superstitious terror of the people was shown in the vast crowds of pilgrims who flocked to Rome for the Jubilee of 1350, even though no Pope was there to welcome them from the Loggia of the Lateran.

Meanwhile Cola di Rienzi in his mountain solitude had been inspired by the prophecies of a wandering *Fraticello* to visit the

Court of the newly elected Emperor, Charles IV. of Bohemia (grandson of Henry VII.), and there exhort him to deliver widowed Rome. Cola arrived at Prague in July, 1350, but Charles IV., a prince of unromantic though not illiberal temperament, turned a deaf ear to his appeals and kept him prisoner in the fortress of Raudnitz, until the demands of the Pope for his surrender became so importunate that Charles sent him under guard to Avignon [1352], there to abide his trial as a heretic. At Avignon it would have gone hard with the ex-Tribune if, as Petrarch describes in a long and celebrated letter,[1] the rumour had not suddenly arisen that the prisoner wrote verses, an accomplishment dear to the hearts of the Pope's Provençal subjects. The trial hung fire, and during the respite Pope Clement died. His successor Innocent VI., perhaps the best of the Avignonese popes, was faced with a disastrous situation in Italy, where nearly the whole of the State of the Church had revolted under various tyrants. He saw that Rienzi might be useful in recovering Rome for the Pope, and accordingly in September, 1353, sent him to Italy in the suite of his great Legate, the Cardinal d'Albornoz, whose mission was to reconquer and reconstitute the Papal states. Decked with the title of Senator, Rienzi made his triumphal entry into Rome on August 1, 1354, and at first his old ascendancy seemed fully regained. But the enthusiastic visionary of former days, grown fat and worldly, seemed now to have lost his magic touch. In Villani's words 'he set up a harsh and rigid despotism,' while the Colonna defied him from Palestrina, and his lack of money drove him to all kinds of desperate shifts. One after another the chief citizens were seized and put to ransom; a robber captain named Fra Monreale was executed on the Capitol, nominally for his misdeeds, really for the sake of his treasure. At last, barely ten weeks after his return, a tumult broke out against him in the regions controlled by the Savelli and Colonna, and a savage mob, crying 'Death to the traitor! Death to him who taxed our salt!' advanced upon the Capitol. Cola emerged on the balcony, clad in full armour, the banner of Rome in his hand, and endeavoured to address the people; but he was met by yells of hatred and a shower of missiles, and an arrow struck him in the hand. At that the Senator lost heart, and while the mob was battering in the doors below he pulled off his armour, smeared his face, and wrapped himself in a ragged cloak, hoping so to mingle with the throng and escape. 'For,' as the anonymous author of the *Life of Cola* remarks, 'he was a man like all the rest of us, and he feared to die.' But his

[1] *Delle Cose Familiari*, xiii., 6.

gold bracelets glimmered through his rags; he was seized, recognized, and dragged to the steps of the Palace of the Senators, where, after a moment of silence, when awe fell upon the people and none dared lay hands on him, one Cecco del Vecchio stabbed him through the body. The mob leapt on their prey, and soon nothing was left of Cola di Rienzi but a torn and headless corpse.

But to a certain extent his work survived him, for the power of the nobles never again rose to such fantastic heights as before his advent. The statesman Albornoz, following in the wake of the dreamer, excluded the nobility from all civic offices by his great *Statute* of 1363—a codification of the laws of Rome which lets in a flood of light on the manners and customs of that rude age.[1] At the same time the Romans saw to their own defence by forming a Guild of Archers, whose four chiefs, or *Banderesi*, formed with a popular Council of Seven (afterwards called the Conservators) the supreme executive of the State. A Papal Senator was indeed accepted, with all his retinue of judges, notaries, and men-at-arms, but so long as the popes were weak or absent the political predominance lay with the civic magistrates. This settlement produced such unusual tranquillity in Rome that in 1367 Pope Urban V. ventured on a tentative return to the deserted city. The great Albornoz, whose activity in subjugating Romagna, Tuscany, and Umbria had alone made such an enterprise possible, received him at Corneto; Rome welcomed him with transports of joy. But although no untoward events occurred during his sojourn in the capital, where on the contrary he received visits of peace from the Emperors of East and West (John Palæologus and Charles IV.), Urban V. longed in his soul for his native France. His French cardinals constantly urged him to return, and in spite of the impassioned warnings of St. Bridget of Sweden, who prophesied his speedy death should he desert so sacred a post, the weary Pope journeyed back after three years to Avignon [1370]. Albornoz was already dead, and Urban followed him to the grave within a few weeks of his arrival in Provence.

The final return of the Papacy to Rome was made in 1377, for very different reasons from those which had moved Urban V. Urban had come to take peaceful possession of the States conquered by Albornoz; Gregory XI. came in order to save the Papal rule from total disappearance. For in the interval a swarm of rapacious French legates had descended on the unfortunate territories of the Church, undoing all the good effects of Albornoz's

[1] See Segré, *Studi Petrarcheschi*. (Il Giubileo del 1350.)

orderly administration and arousing the hatred of the inhabitants by their cruelty, greed and licentiousness. The evil was increased by the terrible Free Companies—those organized bands of free-booters, the offscourings of the wars of France, England, Germany, and Hungary, who sold themselves to the highest bidder, lived riotously on the blackmail levied under threat of massacre, and harassed with impartial ferocity the lands of Signor, Church and Republic. The most famous of these bands was the English Company under Sir John Hawkwood, which was brought into Italy by the Count of Monferrat in 1361 and was freely used by the Papal legates in their wars with Bernabò Visconti. In 1375, during a truce with Bernabò, it was sent by the Legate of Bologna, who vaguely desired to extend his dominion over Tuscany, to burn the harvests in Florentine territory, and this act of piracy against an ally provoked a storm which all but wrecked the temporal power of the Church. Florence, the former champion of the Church and the Guelf cause, flew to arms in an outburst of nationalist and anti-clerical fury; the clergy were forced to contribute the sinews of war, and a Committee of Eight was formed to direct operations and administer the confiscated funds. These 'Eight Saints,' as the people jocularly called them, designed a red banner with the word *Libertas* inscribed on it in silver letters, and sent it through the cities of Tuscany, Umbria, the Marches, and Romagna, calling them to arms; before the year was out eighty cities had driven out the Papal garrisons, pulled down the fortresses built by Albornoz, and reverted either to republicanism or to the rule of native despots. In March, 1376, Bologna followed the general example, and Hawkwood in revenge stormed Faenza, massacred 4,000 of its inhabitants, and drove the rest forth to seek refuge in more fortunate cities.

But it was not by massacre alone that the Pope sought to win back his revolted territories. The conduct of the Florentines had so exasperated Gregory that he resolved to make of them an example before the whole of Christendom. On hearing the news of the rising of Bologna he pronounced against them a sentence not merely of excommunication and interdict, but of outlawry, commanding all princes and rulers to show their zeal for the Church by seizing the goods of Florentine merchants and selling their persons into slavery. From Avignon alone a community of six hundred persons was expelled, and the Kings of England and France did not scruple to enforce the Pope's commands. Since even this did not suffice to bring the Florentines to their knees, Gregory at last made up his mind to return in person to Italy.

The holy maiden, Catherine of Siena, besought him to return un-armed, with the Cross raised in blessing, but his answer was to dispatch a new and still more brutal band of mercenaries, the Breton Company, under Cardinal Robert of Geneva, to attack Bologna and Florence, while he himself set forth in September and reached Corneto by sea on December 5. All now depended on the attitude of the Romans. As early as January the Florentines had implored the Banderesi to join the national League of Liberty, and now again they sent eloquent letters to 'our honoured brothers, the Bannerets of the City of Rome,' warning them to see in the return of the Pope nothing but the 'imminent ruin of their liberty.' But, rebellious as the Romans were towards their Papal suzerain, they could not refuse him entrance to their city. The pride as well as the cupidity of the burghers was bound up with the presence of the Papal Court, and Gregory was received in state at the Church of St. Paul Without the Walls on January 17, 1377. In the north the war still continued, and the Bretons and English to-gether deluged Cesena with blood on February 1st, while their savage leader, the Cardinal of Geneva, urged them on with cries of 'Kill all! Kill all!' But both sides in reality desired peace, and at last a conference was convened at Sarzana between Florence, Bernabò Visconti, and the Papal envoys. The Republic, finding Bernabò against her, was on the point of submitting to pay a very heavy indemnity for the war, when the news arrived that Pope Gregory had died in Rome [March 27, 1378]. The conference broke up, and all eyes were turned on the momentous drama un-folding itself round the conclave in the Vatican.

For the Roman people, now at last in possession of the dead body of their Bishop, had no intention of losing their hold on the living person of his successor. The cardinals entered the Hall of Conclave on April 7, and all night the clamour of the mob was heard without, crying 'Romano lo volemo, o almeno Italiano!' Terrified and bewildered, the French cardinals, who were not even united amongst themselves,[1] agreed on a compromise with the Italians and hastily elected a Neapolitan named Bartolommeo Prignano, Archbishop of Bari, as Pope. Never was an election more bitterly repented. Prignano, who took the name of Urban VI., professed himself full of zeal for the reform of the Church, but his zeal took the form of unbounded insolence towards the French cardinals, who had never in their lives been treated in such

---

[1] Eleven of the sixteen cardinals were French, but six of these belonged to the *Limousin* faction (*i.e.*, creations of the last two Popes), and as such were bitterly disliked by the other five.

fashion, and of a general self-assertiveness which led his astonished contemporaries to believe that his sudden elevation had
turned his brain. Coarse and violent in language, Urban even
alienated his natural ally Queen Joanna of Naples by insulting
her husband, Otto of Brunswick, who remarked that the new Pope
should have been named *Turbanus* instead of Urbanus. At the end
of May the French cardinals withdrew to Anagni, summoned the
Bretons to their defence, and in August issued an encyclical declaring the election of Urban null and void, seeing that it had been
made under pressure of violence from the Roman mob. Urban
replied by creating twenty-eight fresh cardinals at one stroke, and
the Ultramontanes immediately proceeded to the election of an
Anti-Pope, thus completing the schism. Robert of Geneva, the
butcher of Cesena, was consecrated as Clement VII., and received
the allegiance of France, Naples, Savoy, and Scotland, while Urban
was supported by Rome and Northern Italy, by England, Hungary,
and the Empire. Clement withdrew to Avignon, where he reigned
in peace, while Urban threw all the force of his vindictive nature
into a war of vengeance on Queen Joanna for her desertion of his
cause.

The Kingdom of Naples, during the long reign of Joanna I. [1343
—1381], had been the unhappy scene of an endless series of
dynastic quarrels. The Angevin family had come into close connection with the royal House of Hungary by the marriage of
Charles II. with a daughter of that house, and Charles's eldest son
took the throne of Hungary, while the second, Robert, reigned at
Naples. Now the granddaughter of Robert, Queen Joanna, had
drawn upon herself the mortal enmity of the Hungarian branch
by her supposed connivance at the murder of her first husband,
her cousin Andrew of Hungary, and Urban VI. adroitly sought to
profit by that enmity. He summoned the heir-presumptive to the
Neapolitan crown, Charles of Durazzo, who had been brought up
at the Hungarian court, to take the kingdom from the obnoxious
Queen, and the King of Hungary was not sorry to be rid of one
who might also claim the Hungarian succession. 'Carlo della Pace'
therefore (as he was called in Italy) entered Rome in November,
1380, but found himself obliged, before he could proceed, to sign
a compact with the Pope whereby all the fairest portions of the
kingdom—Capua, Caserta, and the Peninsula of Sorrento—were to
be surrendered to Urban's worthless nephew, Francesco Prignano.
At last, however, Charles entered the kingdom, defeated Joanna's
husband Otto and besieged the Queen herself in the Castel Nuovo

K

at Naples, where she was soon obliged to capitulate. Her life would probably have been spared in the hope that she would adopt Charles as her heir, had not Pope Clement of Avignon raised up another pretender to the throne in the person of Louis Count of Anjou, and sent him with men and money to rescue the Queen. His approach, on the contrary, sealed her fate; by Charles's order she was strangled with a silken cord at the castle of Muro, on May 12, 1382.

The invasion of the Angevin prince caused little trouble to King Charles, for Louis's army melted away from sickness and starvation; but the arrival of Pope Urban himself at Naples in November, 1383, was a different matter. Charles had no wish to be dictated to by his turbulent patron. Urban's sole object in coming was to promote the interests of his nephew, who had not yet been put in possession of his fiefs; but when he found the King intractable he retired in wrath to the castle of Nocera near Salerno, dragging his unfortunate cardinals along with him. Hearing that some of them were conspiring to convene a General Council in Rome [Jan., 1385], he caused six of their number to be seized and thrown into a disused cistern full of noisome reptiles, where he allowed his nephew to torture them with fiendish energy while he himself walked up and down outside their prison, reading his Breviary aloud and listening with delight to their shrieks.[1] When at last he was driven out of Nocera by the royal army he took the cardinals with him, and when the horse of one of them went lame he ordered its rider to be killed, and left his body to lie by the roadside. After many vicissitudes he reached a safe refuge at last in Genoa [Sept., 1385], where he still kept the remaining cardinals in close captivity until, weary of maintaining them for so long, he ordered all of them save one (an Englishman) to be strangled in their dungeons. This done he departed on further wanderings, for the news of the murder of Carlo della Pace in Hungary [1386], whither he had gone to claim the succession, opened new visions in Urban's mind of securing the crown of Naples for his hopeful nephew. Charles had left a young son Ladislaus, while Otto of Brunswick rallied the remnants of the French-Angevin faction, and Urban hoped to snatch his own advantage from the turmoil. But his mercenary troops refused to follow him beyond Ferentino, and with disgust at his heart he was obliged to return to Rome. There after a year's sojourn he died on October 15, 1389, an object of universal execration, but his Pontificate had not taught the

[1] An account of these proceedings has been left by the chronicler Dietrich of Niem, an eye-witness.

Romans to renounce their claims on the Papacy. A new Pope was elected by Urban's fourteen cardinals, and the schism prolonged until the sense of Christendom at length rebelled against the unseemly spectacle. With the Councils of Pisa and of Constance the Papal house was once more set in order, until the growth and ferment of another hundred years prepared a mightier revolt.

CHAPTER XIII

Northern Italy
during the Fourteenth Century

WHILE in Rome and the south the fourteenth century ran out in shoals and shallows—the kingdom of Naples distraught with civil war, the Papacy reduced by Urban to the lowest degradation—that same period in the north showed more perhaps than any other the intense vitality of the Italian people. Never for a moment does the whirl of wars, alliances, intrigues, and outside interference cease; the old animosities of Guelf and Ghibelline, far from being quenched by the brief passage of Henry VII., blaze up afresh round his tomb; the Transalpine Pope rallies the Guelfs round the grandson of Charles of Anjou, King Robert of Naples, while the Ghibelline traditions gather about the great prince-despots of Lombardy and Tuscany—Can Grande della Scala of Verona, Visconti of Milan, Uguccione of Pisa, and Castruccio Castracane of Lucca. The conditions of the struggle, however, have largely changed since the period of the earlier despots described in a previous chapter; now the successful tyrants, having consolidated their power at home, devote all their energies to a policy of expansion and conquest. To acquire the Signoria of as many cities as possible is the object of a Visconti or a Scala, for the Signoria brings wealth, and wealth brings the power of hiring so many thousand men-at-arms for further wars, or actually of buying the Signoria of yet other cities. Hence the tendency of the fourteenth century is all towards the formation of larger states, at the expense of the lesser tyrants who sprang up in such numbers during the latter half of the previous century; and with the larger states goes a haughtier tone towards the outside world, for though a Visconti may be quite willing to use an Emperor-elect against the Guelfs, he will be ready to turn against him too as soon as he has got all that he wants out of his puppet.

A brilliant example of a successful tyranny may be seen in the career of Castruccio Castracane, Lord of Lucca, who for eight years held the Republic of Florence in a state of perpetual alarm. In 1316 he rose to power in Lucca after the revolt of that city against the domination of Pisa, or rather of Pisa's tyrant Uguccione della Faggiuola, who had attempted to unite the two cities under his sway. Castruccio was the hero of the revolt, and was at once named Captain of the People by the Lucchesi, in which capacity he quietly spent the next four years in organizing a fighting force. Then in 1320, when the situation in the north gave him a pretext—for a Guelf league formed by the Pope had attacked his allies the Visconti—he crossed the Florentine border and commenced hostilities in the usual way by ravaging the plain of the Arno. The Florentine army, slow-moving and badly led, was no match for this born strategist, and Castruccio was able with part of his force to establish himself on the Genoese Riviera and to give aid to the Ghibelline army besieging Genoa, while at the same time amply holding his own towards the side of Florence. In 1323 he made a sudden attack on Prato, and such was the consternation in Florence that the Priors offered an amnesty to all exiles who should return to fight against the common enemy, in response to which the banished 'Whites' and Ghibellines gathered to the number of four thousand in the Florentine camp. Even so, however, they were not readmitted, for the rumour ran that the nobles were making common cause with them to overturn the Signory, and Florence remained divided while Castruccio raided at will. In 1325 he seized Pistoia and beat the Florentine army in a pitched battle at Altopascio, a disaster which drove the Republic into the arms of King Robert of Naples, whose son Charles of Calabria she agreed to receive as her Prince in return for the King's protection. But hardly had the rapacious Neapolitan fastened himself upon the Republic than news arrived of the approach of the Ghibelline champion, Louis the Bavarian, and Castruccio hastened to welcome so opportune an ally. With his eye on the sovereignty of Pisa he accepted the title of Duke from his new patron, and after detaining the Bavarian in Tuscany long enough to secure his own position there he accompanied him on his strange journey to Rome. Thence, however, he was suddenly recalled to Tuscany by the news of the capture, in February, 1328, of Pistoia by the Florentines, and the unbounded energy which he threw into the siege of the lost city proved fatal to the victor. On August 3 the town capitulated; on September 3 Castruccio died at Lucca of malarial fever. His duchy died with him, for his young sons, still in their teens, were too weak to seize the sovereignty, and Louis himself dispossessed them on his return from Rome. Fortunately for Florence, Charles of Calabria died in the same year, so that she was delivered at one and the same moment from her open enemy and her too dangerous protector.

More fortunate than Castruccio in one vital respect, the veteran
Ghibelline Matteo Visconti, who had finally expelled the Della
Torre from Milan at the coming of Henry VII., left behind him a
brood of able sons to carry on his dominion. Galeazzo, Marco, and
Luchino took part in all the wars stirred up in Lombardy by Pope
John XXII., and opposed a vigorous resistance to his reputed son,
the Legate Bertrand du Poïet, who appeared on the scene in 1319
and kept the north in a constant state of ferment for the next
fifteen years. But the chief vortex of the struggle during Matteo's
closing years was the civil war between the Guelfs and Ghibellines of Genoa, which followed on the expulsion of the Ghibelline
families of Doria and Spinola by their Guelf rivals, the Grimaldi
and Fieschi [1317]. The Ghibelline exiles laid regular siege to the
town [1319], and here Marco Visconti performed great deeds of
arms, but even after the siege was raised the civil war still went
on, and in the farthest colonies of the Levant the Genoese pursued
each other with unsleeping hatred, until at length a reconciliation
was imposed on the exhausted city by King Robert in 1331.

Meanwhile Matteo Visconti, who earned from his contemporaries the epithet 'Il Grande,' died in 1322, much troubled in his
soul by the curses heaped on him by Holy Church. His eldest son
Galeazzo, after a sharp struggle first against mutinous subjects at
home and then against a Papal army at his gates, succeeded him
in the Signoria, and held it until the advent of Louis the Bavarian
in 1327. The Bavarian, however, probably with a view to his ransom, treacherously seized the Lord of Milan, and imprisoned him
in the dungeons of Monza, whence he was only released some
months later at the intercession of Castruccio. He died in Castruccio's camp before the walls of Pistoia [1328]. But his son Azzo
reigned unchallenged, after ridding himself by assassination of
Marco, his too popular uncle, and became an actor in one of the
strangest episodes of the fourteenth century.

The great power built up in Eastern Lombardy by Can Grande
della Scala, the patron and host of Dante and of many other exiled
Ghibellines, was still strong and threatening under his nephew
Mastino II., who succeeded to the Signoria in 1329. In 1330 Mastino seemed on the point of absorbing Brescia, by the aid of the
Ghibelline exiles cast out from that city, when news came to the
anxious Guelfs within the walls of a possible deliverer, and in
December, 1330, messengers were sent in all haste to Trent to
seek out King John of Bohemia and to confer the sovereignty of
the town upon him on condition that he would rescue it from its
impending fate. John was the son of the ill-fated Emperor Henry

VII., and a man of extraordinary personal attractions; he had practically resigned the charge of his nominal kingdom, and spent his time in travelling from court to court—an unofficial peacemaker in the affairs of Europe. The friend and champion of Louis the Bavarian, he was yet a welcome guest at Avignon or in Paris, and his life of knight-errantry ended at last on the field of Crécy. The invitation of the Brescians reached him in the nick of time; it would open a vast new field to his talents, and he accepted it without more ado. His proceedings in Brescia were signally successful, for not only did he persuade Mastino to retire without a blow, but in January, 1331, he even effected a reconciliation between the hostile parties. The news of it spread through Lombardy with astonishing rapidity, and within a few weeks John found himself the master of an engirdling zone of territories stretching like a vast ellipse round Milan and Verona. All the cities that still dreaded their absorption in the larger centres, or those in which despotism had not yet succeeded in imposing internal peace, opened their gates and their hearts to John, and to all he dictated the same conditions—the recall of exiled partisans. After Brescia—Bergamo, Como, Novara, Vercelli, Pavia, Cremona, Parma, Reggio, and Modena received him as their Signor, and the ellipse was closed at its eastern end by an understanding into which he entered with the Legate Bertrand du Poïet, at a secret interview near Bologna on April 16, 1331. This ill-omened alliance, however, seemed to arouse the real masters of Italy from their torpor; Florence and King Robert of Naples first declared openly against him, and in the following summer the Ghibelline lords of Lombardy—Azzo Visconti, Mastino della Scala, Gonzaga of Mantua, and the Estensi of Ferrara—joined their ancient enemies in a league against Legate and King together. One by one the northern towns surrendered again to Azzo; then in 1333 Romagna revolted against the Legate, under Este's lead, and when John reached Bologna after a few months' absence in France he found his empire on the verge of disappearance. His last effort was to sell his few remaining towns to individual despots for as much as they would fetch; then in October, 1333, he departed across the Alps, and Italy saw him no more.

After this violent disturbance, the currents of Italian politics resumed their more normal course, and with the dismemberment of the Scala dominions in 1338, after a war which gave to Venice her first serious footing on the mainland, the preponderance throughout the whole of Upper Italy went over still more decidedly to the Viscontean dynasty. Luchino [1339—49] absorbed the last remaining Angevin possessions in Piedmont, and even acquired Parma, but his brother and successor, the famous Archbishop John (last of Matteo's sons), lifted the power of his house to a still higher eminence. His first act was to acquire Bologna by a secret bargain with the discredited tyrant of the city, Giovanni Pepoli, and his two nephews Galeazzo and Bernabò rode through the streets at the head of their cavalry before the Bolognese had time to concentrate, or to do more than grumble at the way they were thus bought and sold. But at Avignon the news spread consternation, for Bertrand du Poïet had made Bologna the headquarters of the Papal power in the north, and a Legate was sent to Milan to demand that Visconti should not only restore the town, but lay down his temporal authority as well. A Milanese historian writing about 150 years later[1] gives the following account of what ensued:

Giovanni replied that he would give his answer on the following Sunday in the great church of Milan, and on the appointed day, when everyone was there, Giovanni celebrated Mass with unusual solemnity, after which, according to his intructions, the Legate repeated his message from the Pope before all the people. Then the great-hearted Archbishop unsheathed a shining sword which he had at his side, and taking a Cross in his left hand cried out: 'This is my spiritual power, and this sword shall be my temporal power for the defence of all my authority!'

The Interdict was duly laid upon Milan, but less than a year afterwards the Archbishop had succeeded so well in scattering his gold among the *entourage* of Clement VI. (not forgetting the Countess of Turenne, 'the Pope's director in temporal affairs'[2]) that all censures were removed and John was confirmed in the possession of Bologna for twelve years.

But a still more remarkable feat of the Archbishop's was his acquisition of the ancient republic of Genoa, which gave itself to him in 1353 after suffering a disastrous naval defeat off the Sardinian coast at the hands of the Venetians and Aragonese. Visconti accepted the prize with alacrity, and sent the illustrious Petrarch to urge peace on the Doge of Venice, but the fury of the combatants was not to be allayed by the poet's Latin oration, and at the great battle of Sapienza off the Morea in 1354 the Genoese fully retrieved their defeat of the previous year. Then at last Bernabò Visconti (for the Archbishop had died a month before the victory of the Genoese) was able to negotiate a peace, but so

---

[1] Bernardino Corio, *Istorie Milanesi*, Bk. iii.

[2] So the cotemporary Guelf historian, Matteo Villani, Bk. iii., cap. 2.

many were the causes of quarrel between the two republics in the Levant that at this stage no peace could be anything more than a temporary truce. One result of it, however, was that Genoa soon rose against her imported masters, and a popular tumult drove out the Milanese governor and installed the veteran noble Simon Boccanegra[1] as Doge of the Republic.

While Bernabò Visconti and his brother Galeazzo divided the inheritance of the Archbishop, and Bernabò, the more vigorous and bloodthirsty of the two, spent his long reign in conducting endless wars of aggression or defence against his neighbours (including the great Cardinal Albornoz[2]), Venice, with a new mainland frontier to defend, was drifting towards another and greater struggle with Genoa. Her nearest neighbour on the mainland was the ancient university town of Padua, which at the partition of the Scala dominions in 1338 had fallen to the Carrara family, while Treviso and its surrounding territory had been assigned to Venice. The Carraresi bore no goodwill towards their powerful neighbour, though they were usually too weak to attack her openly, but in 1373 they obtained the assistance of the Angevin King of Hungary, Louis I., who had already once gone to war with the Republic and forced her to cede Dalmatia to him. This time, however, the Venetians were victorious even on land, and Carrara was obliged to submit to a humiliating peace. When therefore, five years later, the inevitable struggle broke out between Venice and Genoa, in the form of a dispute for the island of Tenedos, Genoa found willing allies in Francesco Carrara and the King of Hungary, while Venice could only obtain the lukewarm support of Bernabò Visconti.

The war which followed was the severest test through which the Lagoon people had passed since the half-mythical days of Pepin's blockade. After a few successes, Vettor Pisani, the idol of the sailors, was beaten in May, 1379, in a great battle off Pola at the southern extremity of the Istrian peninsula, and only succeeded in reaching Venice with six galleys out of all his fleet. Though the fight had been forced on him against his better judgment by the Senate's representatives, he was held responsible for the disaster, and was condemned to six months' imprisonment. Meanwhile Carlo Zeno, with the only other Venetian fleet, was far away in the Levant, and Pietro Doria, the Genoese admiral, sailed through the southern openings in the Lido, seized Pellestrina, and presently laid siege to Chioggia. A Paduan army occupied the mainland,

---

[1] Boccanegra had already been proclaimed Doge in 1339, when Genoa first adopted this form of government.
[2] See previous Chapter, p. 142.

while 'Carlo della Pace'[1] with the Hungarians was besieging Treviso. On August 16th Chioggia fell. The Doge in despair sent three ambassadors to ask for terms, but for all answer Doria replied that he had come 'to lay bridles on those unbitted horses of yours that stand on the porch of your Evangelist St. Mark!' Nevertheless the Genoese remained inactive at Chioggia, though the way to Venice lay open before them, and the Venetians by superhuman exertions fitted out a fleet of thirty-four galleys, ran up a palisade across the channel from the Lido to S. Spirito, and harassed the enemy with their fleet of small boats. But the sailors clamoured for their beloved admiral Pisani, and the Senate wisely released him from prison and gave him the supreme command, while messengers were sent in all haste to the east to recall Carlo Zeno. Still the Genoese clung to their base at Chioggia, hoping to reduce their enemy by blockade rather than by assault, but Pisani bore down upon them there and by a brilliant operation succeeded in blocking the only two exits from Chioggia and Brondolo to the sea, while he himself took up his position outside the barrier, thereby completing his blockade of the blockaders [Dec., 1379].[2] To crown his success, Carlo Zeno arrived from the east on January 1, 1380, just at the moment when Pisani's crews were threatening mutiny at their exposed position, and the combined forces pressed the Genoese hard, occupied Brondolo, cut off the supplies sent by Carrara, repulsed all attempts at escape, and finally after six months' fighting reduced the enemy to surrender at discretion on June 24, 1380. Four thousand Genoese prisoners were taken to Venice, and honourably treated by the Republic. But Treviso was still suffering bombardment by Carrara's cannon (for Charles of Hungary had by now moved on in quest of the crown of Naples), and Venice was only able to save it from him by handing it over to a more distant foe, Duke Leopold of Austria. At length, however, all parties agreed to the mediation of the Count of Savoy, and by the Peace of Turin in 1381 the situation resulting from the war was recognized, while the Count of Savoy received Tenedos, the original cause of so much bloodshed. Venice had amply vindicated her position as mistress of the seas, and Genoa never again attained to the position of a first-class naval power. Her internal disorders grew apace, and in 1396 her Doge, Antoniotto Adorno, tired of his

---

[1] See previous Chapter, p. 145.

[2] The chief authority for the War of Chioggia is the 'Cronaca della guerra di Chiozza' of Daniele Chinazzo, who was in Venice at the time (printed in Muratori, *Rer. Italic. Script.*, vol. xv.).

hopeless position, invited the suzerainty of the King of France (Charles VI.), and admitted French troops into the town.

The year of the outbreak of the War of Chioggia [1378] was a very memorable one for Italy. In that year the Roman mob forced the election of Urban VI. to the Papal Chair, and the Great Schism began; in that year the Republic of Florence, after waging her victorious 'War of Liberty' against the Papal legates, fell a prey to a social revolution of great violence, known as the 'Tumult of the Ciompi,'[1] and only emerged four years later under the narrow oligarchy of the Albizzi; in that year the death of Galeazzo Visconti (brother of Bernabò) left the field clear for the emergence of his son Gian Galeazzo, greatest and most formidable of the Visconti race.

At the time of his father's death, Gian Galeazzo was a young man of twenty-five, successor to a precarious sovereignty over Pavia and certain towns of Piedmont, already coveted by his uncle Bernabò. Having good reason to fear his ferocious kinsman, whose chief claim to immortality lies in his famous edict of the *Quaresima*, by which 'conspirators against the State' were condemned to death by a series of tortures spread over a period of forty days, Gian Galeazzo led a modest and retired life within the castle of Pavia for seven years, known only for his personal timidity, his studious tastes, and his remarkable devotion to the Virgin. When therefore, in May, 1385, he informed his uncle that he was starting on a pilgrimage to the Madonna del Monte at Varese, and craved the pleasure of seeing him as he passed the walls of Milan, Bernabò fell blindly into the snare, rode forth with his two sons to meet his nephew, and found himself seized, overpowered, and bound by Gian Galeazzo's German body-guard before his half-scornful salutations were out of his mouth. Gian Galeazzo rode straight into Milan, deposited his uncle and cousins in the dungeons of the Castello,[2] and received the hearty acclamations of the Milanese, well pleased to be so cheaply quit of their terrible despot. Bernabò was successfully poisoned at the third attempt, in the castle of Trezzo, seven months after his capture. His nephew, secure in Milan, hastened to fortify his position throughout Bernabò's dominions by lowering some of the latter's most op-

[1] The *Ciompi* were the lowest class of artisans in Florence, not enrolled in any Guild. They were mostly wool-carders and other hangers-on of the great Guild of Wool.

[2] This was the old 'Castello di Porta Giovia,' which stood on part of the site of the present building.

pressive taxes, and by circulating an indictment against him in which he roundly summed him up as *vir diabolicus;* then, with his mind already set on expansion, he took stock of the external situation.

The feeble descendants of Can Grande della Scala still maintained their rule in Verona and Vicenza, while Francesco Carrara occupied Padua and Treviso[1]; but Venice had never forgiven the Paduan for his share in the War of Chioggia, and was ever on the watch for an opportunity to destroy him. This seemed to occur in 1385, when Carrara intervened in a dispute at Udine between Patriarch and people; Venice persuaded Antonio della Scala to attack him in the rear, and promised money for the war. But, contrary to all expectation, Carrara's mercenaries proved superior to his opponent's, and Scala was on the point of calling in the assistance of Gian Galeazzo when Carrara outbid him with the offer of a partition of the Scala territories: Verona was to go to Visconti and Vicenza to Carrara. This offer was accepted; Antonio della Scala was driven ignominiously out of Verona, the last of the Scaliger dynasty; but when Carrara claimed his share of the bargain it was found that the Vicentines had given themselves spontaneously to Gian Galeazzo's wife, who as a daughter of a Scala princess[2] possessed some shadowy claim over the town. Too late Carrara saw what manner of whirlwind he had raised, and in despair he sought the protection of Venice; but Venice instead joined with Visconti to complete the spoliation of her detested enemy. Carrara and his son Francesco Novello were forced to surrender to Visconti's troops, and the banner of the Viper[3] floated within sight of the lagoons. But for once Gian Galeazzo had reckoned without the force of local sentiment, for when after two years of incredible wanderings and adventures Francesco Novello re-entered Padua with a handful of followers, the population rose, drove out the Milanese garrison, and welcomed him with joy. All the force of Visconti could not dislodge him; he was reserved instead for a more implacable foe.

Notwithstanding the loss of Padua, Gian Galeazzo might well congratulate himself on the results of his first few years' achievements. Like the spider at the centre of his web, he had directed all from his palace at Pavia, sending out in every direction his spies,

---

[1] Carrara had bought Treviso back from the Duke of Austria.

[2] Gian Galeazzo had married his first cousin Caterina Visconti, daughter of Bernabò and of Regina della Scala.

[3] Italian *Biscione*, the famous crest of the Visconti—a serpent swallowing a man.

his agents, his *condottieri*, and even his assassins. For the Lord of Milan was by no means averse from the use of so time-honoured a weapon as murder, when occasion served; he was not bloodthirsty by nature, but no scruples of this sort were ever allowed to stand between him and a matter of high policy.[1] Besides his conquests in Lombardy he had already stretched out feelers into the heart of Tuscany, and had alarmed the Florentines by establishing relations with the Ghibellines of Siena. By one of his 'indirect assassinations' he had in 1392 installed a creature of his own, Jacopo d'Appiano, as Tyrant of Pisa. He could afford now to wait until the fruits of his diplomacy dropped into his mouth. He busied himself with the construction of buildings more splendid than any yet seen in Italy—the Duomo of Milan, the Certosa of Pavia; he rebuilt and reanimated the University of Pavia; he enlarged the Castello of Milan; he made the great canal between Pavia and Milan, known as the Naviglio. And, with that hankering after legitimacy which so often beset the bourgeois princes of Italy, he bought the title of Duke of Milan from the besotted Emperor Wenceslaus [1395], and arranged a solemn ceremony of investiture in the Piazza of Sant' Ambrogio.

Towards the end of the century Gian Galeazzo once more resumed his silent and irresistible march towards the absorption of the North and Centre. The three petty tyrannies of Gonzaga, Este, and Carrara were attacked and seriously weakened by his troops in 1397, though their existence was saved by the intervention of Venice. But the cities of Tuscany and Umbria fell an easier prey. Early in 1399 Pisa was ignominiously sold to him by Gherardo d'Appiano, son of Jacopo, and in the same year Perugia and Siena voluntarily accepted his authority. His generals marched down the long Umbrian valley from Perugia to Spoleto, and the city of St. Francis acknowledged the *Biscione*. Florence, in serious alarm, could appeal to no ally save the distant Emperor, Rupert of Bavaria, but though she actually financed his descent with a feudal army, the Duke of Milan's *condottieri* easily repulsed him, and forced him to retire with scanty glory [April, 1402]. Still Bologna stood as a screen between Florence and the advancing Viper, but after the Emperor's retreat Gian Galeazzo concentrated his whole force upon it, and in spite of the efforts of the Florentines his general Alberigo da Barbiano entered it in June, 1402. Then the Republic turned in despair to Urban's successor in the Roman

[1] For a catalogue of Gian Galeazzo's assasssinations and other crimes, see Symonds, *Age of the Despots*, pp. 114 fol.

Papacy, Boniface IX., while Gian Galeazzo ordered the regalia to be prepared for his coronation in Florence as King of Italy. But the plague appeared in Pavia, and towards the end of July the Duke judged it wise to retire to his castle of Marignano on the Lambro, where he received ambassadors from his new acquisition, Bologna. Suddenly on the 13th of August he was seized with fever; his physicians and astrologers were summoned, but though he lingered for twenty-one days the fever mastered him, and he died on September 3, 1402. He was forty-nine years old.

Naturally enough, the death of Gian Galeazzo altered the whole aspect of affairs. Held together by no bond save that of his own genius for administration, his vast dominions fell asunder at one stroke. Indeed it was found that he had deliberately prepared the way for this by dividing them in his will between his two sons, Giovanni and Filippo, and these two being still mere boys their mother Caterina was obliged to assume the Regency on their behalf. In many of the subject cities native tyrants sprang up once more; the army of Florence and the Pope approached Bologna, and the Duchess found herself compelled to purchase peace by restoring Umbria and Bologna to the Church. In the east too the storm broke. Francesco Carrara advanced on Verona in 1404, installed a Scaliger pretender there, occupied the fortress, and then marched on to Vicenza, where, however, he was met by the news that the Duchess had won Venice to her side by the offer of all the Visconti territories east of the Adige. The Republic of St. Mark had Carrara in her grip at last. Verona, ably defended by Francesco's son Giacomo, was first reduced, and the young Carrara sent a prisoner to Venice. Then the Venetian forces were concentrated against Padua, where Francesco was holding out to the last—now in the hope of Florentine assistance, now playing the more desperate game of fomenting a conspiracy within Venice itself. But the Paduans were tired of the long siege, and at length one of the gates was opened from within and the Venetians admitted. Francesco and his younger son were dragged captive to Venice, and all three set upon their trial before the Council of Ten [1405]. Evidence of a vast plot was said to have been discovered, and the Carraresi were condemned to be strangled in their prison. The sentence was carried out upon the father first, then upon the sons. So fell the Carrara dynasty, following closely on the Scaliger, and on the ruins of both there arose the mainland state of Venice, firm and well-compacted, bounded by the Adige, the Alps, and the Piave; no longer the sport of individual despots, but proudly subject only to the Lion of St. Mark.

CHAPTER XIV

The Age of the Councils: the Rise of Medici and Sforza

Then of their session ended they bid cry
With trumpet's regal sound the great result. MILTON, *Par. Lost*, Bk. ii.

WHEN Gian Galeazzo Visconti was solicited for his support by either of the two Popes who at that time divided Christendom, he was accustomed to reply that he could not conscientiously decide between their claims; what value could the opinion of a mere secular prince like himself have in so exalted a controversy? By this sagacious course he secured practical immunity from Papal interference throughout his territories, and incidentally showed to what miserable straits the Great Schism had reduced the Roman Papacy. The successor of Urban VI., a Neapolitan who took the name of Boniface IX. [1389—1404], found himself obliged to devote his whole energies to the restoration of the Papal authority in Rome and the state of the Church, and of some portion of its influence in Naples. To this end he hastened to recognize Ladislaus, the young son of Carlo della Pace, as rightful King of Naples, and much of the Pope's wealth[1] was devoted to upholding his cause against the Angevin pretender Louis, who drew his support from France and from the Pope of Avignon. After long wars between the rival parties Ladislaus finally entered Naples in 1399 and drove his opponent back to Provence, and this victory greatly strengthened Boniface's hands in suppressing the rebellious nobles who still surrounded Rome with hostile territories. But the most notable triumph of Boniface IX. was that which he won over the republicans of Rome herself; for in the year 1398 he succeeded in abolishing the free government of the *Banderesi* and the *Conservators* and in re-establishing the rule of a Senator, nominated by himself and imported from without. Although the Conservators afterwards reappeared, the Constitution of Boniface IX. marked a considerable step in the destruction of that republican independence which dated through so many vicissitudes from the days of Arnold of Brescia.

Meanwhile a strong party in France, headed by the University of Paris, was taking active steps to end the Schism, and had even

[1] Boniface IX. had a reputation for avarice remarkable even among the princes of that period. See esp. Dietrich of Niem, *De Schismate*.

attempted to prevent the election of a successor to Pope Clement VII. But the inherent vice of the situation was that on the death of either Pope his cardinals were never willing to forgo the tactical advantage of electing a successor, and that however much they might try to hedge in the new Pope with vows to end the Schism, they reckoned in so doing without the Pope's nephews, if not without the Pope himself. Hence to Boniface IX. succeeded Innocent VII. and Gregory XII., and to Clement of Avignon Benedict XIII. As far as Italy was concerned, moreover, the influence of Naples was thrown heavily against reunion, for the young king Ladislaus was too astute not to perceive that a new Pope elected by a mixed Council would have French influence behind him, and would therefore support the Angevin claim to Naples. Ladislaus therefore schemed incessantly to make himself master of Rome, in order to dominate the situation, and he at length accomplished his desire in 1408, when the aged Pope Gregory XII. had left the city in order to take some reluctant and half-hearted steps towards meeting his rival Benedict at Savona. Rome willingly surrendered to the ambitious Ladislaus, and with Rome secure behind him the King pushed on into Tuscany, intending to prevent the threatened Council, or, if it assembled, to carry matters there with a high hand. His approach gave Gregory—who had advanced as far as Lucca—a pretext for abandoning his insincere negotiations, and after quarrelling with his cardinals he retired to seek the protection of the Lord of Rimini, Carlo Malatesta. At the same time Benedict XIII. fled in the opposite direction, from Porto Venere to Perpignan, and at this ludicrous termination of the efforts of both parties to work through their respective Popes, the cardinals took matters into their own hands and summoned a General Council to meet at Pisa in May, 1409.

The choice of Pisa as the scene of this first great Council in a century of Councils was prompted partly no doubt by its convenience and accessibility, but partly also by the fact that its recent conquest by Florence had reduced it to a state of death-like peace and security. For Gian Galeazzo's acquisition of the harbour-town had in the end been the means of handing it over to his arch-enemies the Florentines. His bastard son Gabriele, to whom he had bequeathed this outlying portion of his dominions, found himself unable to maintain his authority there, and in the year 1405 sold the citadel, together with his rights over the town, to his father's ancient but wealthy enemies. But the Pisans would not submit without a long struggle to this ignoble bargain, and it was not until

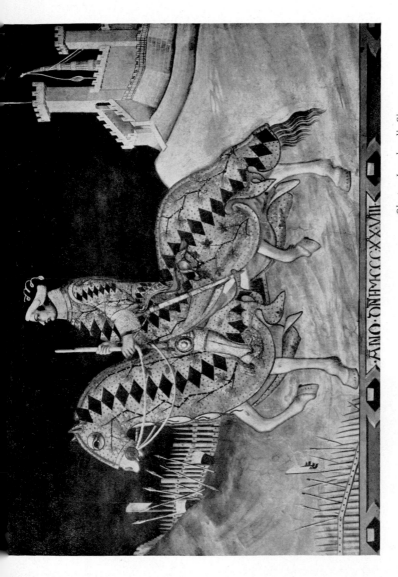

A CONDOTTIERE—FOURTEENTH CENTURY

From a fresco by Simone Martini in the Palazzo Pubblico of Siena

they had endured a siege of five months against the best *condottieri* of the day that they at last succumbed—and even then it was only by the treachery of their native tyrant Gambacorti that the gates were finally opened. Now, however, all was quiet in the conquered town; her nobles had either emigrated to seek service under various *condottieri* or been compelled to remove themselves to Florence, and the Fathers of the Church gathered in the dim Cathedral as though to the obsequies of a fallen state.

The proceedings of the Council of Pisa were short and summary. After declaring itself an Œcumenical Council it deposed both Popes, and the twenty-three cardinals present, led by Baldassare Cossa, Legate of Bologna, then proceeded to elect the aged Cardinal of Milan, Peter Philargi, as Alexander V. But Gregory and Benedict were at the same time holding rival councils at Cividale and Perpignan, and could still count on a number of their old supporters. Alexander lived only a few months, and at his death his adherents elected Cardinal Cossa as John XXIII. Christendom was thus again divided between three Popes. John XXIII. had the soul of a *condottiere* and inspired an extraordinary distrust and hatred among his contemporaries; but at first he was able to make head against his principal enemy, King Ladislaus, by calling in an Angevin pretender to dispute the kingdom with him. This struggle was made memorable by the appearance in it of the two great mercenary leaders of the day, Sforza Attendolo and Braccio da Montone, who established rival schools of warfare and contributed so much to that remarkable Italian product, the *condottiere* system. They had both been trained under the first Italian commander of note, Alberigo da Barbiano, and in the first quarter of the fifteenth century it was rare to find any of the greater cities carrying on a campaign without the assistance of one or other of these professional bloodsuckers. With their aid Pope John succeeded in defeating Ladislaus, but the victory was not a lasting one, and the ambitious king was soon attacking Rome once more and driving the Pope to take refuge in Lombardy [1413]. There he fell in with the Emperor Sigismund, who obliged him to sign the writs of summons to a new Council to be held at Constance, a city of the Empire. John did so with a heavy heart, but before the Council actually met he had the satisfaction of hearing that an untimely death had cut short the career of his presumptuous foe. Ladislaus, after his second conquest of Rome, had overrun the Papal State and was approaching Florence, when a mortal disease struck him down, and he was carried back to die at Naples [1414]. With him perished the hope or danger of a unification under one sceptre of the south and centre,

L

for his crown passed to his feeble sister Joanna II., during whose reign chaos descended once more on the unfortunate Kingdom of Naples.

As he had foreseen, Pope John XXIII. fared ill at Constance. He soon found that the Council had determined on the simultaneous resignation of all three Popes as the only means of securing peace for the Church, and when he prevaricated, delayed, and finally fled from Constance, the Council instituted proceedings against him, and at length, in May, 1415, deposed him as a 'notorious simoniac. . . . causing scandal to the Church of God and Christian people by his detestable and unseemly life and manners.' Gregory XII. made a voluntary abdication, Benedict XIII. was once more deposed, and after a vacancy of over two years the cardinals and the 'four nations' together elected as Universal Pope Cardinal Oddo Colonna, a man well qualified by birth and position to unite all parties [1417]. But that the new Pope (Martin V.) was essentially of the same breed as his recent predecessors is shown by an incident of his journey to Italy related by the representative of the Teutonic Order at the Papal Court:[1]

I had a very fine white horse here, larger than any in the whole court; but one day the Holy Father sent me a message asking me to lend it him for the journey, because he had not enough white horses. I have often been offered two hundred florins for him! But now if the Pope gets hold of him I shall certainly never get him back again, so I had better make it a gift. Please therefore send me another, but let it be a black or a brown one!

The same witness, when Pope Martin at length reached Rome, is never tired of enumerating all the gifts and bribes that he is obliged to dispense, from the Pope himself to the humblest door-keeper, in order to get his wants attended to:

At Easter I gave the Pope a jewel worth thirty-six ducats (would that I could have kept it!), but the reason I did so and the reason I must do so again at Whitsuntide you will easily perceive from the foregoing (a detailed account of the system of 'benevolences' at all the great Feasts). I cannot do anything here without money—all my friends go to sleep if I do not come to them with gifts.[2]

Politically, however, Pope Martin V. might congratulate himself

[1] Johannes Voigt, 'Stimmen aus Rom über den päpstlichen Hof im fünfzehnten Jahrhundert,' in Von Raumer's *Historisches Taschenbuch*, vol. iv., p. 120.

[2] *Historisches Taschenbuch*, vol. iv., p. 109.

on the success of his Pontificate. Rome was obedient, the Colonna family enriched with many new fiefs in Latium and Campania, and the Papal policy in Naples not unsuccessful. Martin had indeed been greatly alarmed by Joanna's adoption, in 1421, of Alfonso King of Aragon as her heir, in opposition to the Papal claimant, Louis II. of Anjou; but the fickle Queen soon quarrelled with Alfonso, adopted Louis instead, and by the help of Sforza forced Alfonso to retire. The two great *condottieri*, Sforza and Braccio, took opposite sides in this quarrel, and died within a few weeks of each other in 1424—Sforza by drowning, and Braccio in battle against Joanna's forces. In the masterless condition of Italy both chiefs had risen to extraordinary power and influence. When Pope Martin was in Florence in 1419 Braccio came to visit him there, and the street-boys sang under the Pope's very windows:

> Braccio valente
> Vince ogni gente;
> Il Papa Martino
> Non vale un quattrino.[1]

But at his death the principality which he had built up in Umbria lapsed without a struggle to the Pope, and Martin V. died in 1431 leaving the Papal State once more a compact and solid reality.

While the dynastic troubles of the Neapolitan Kingdom had absorbed the energies of the elder Sforza and his rival, the North became in the third decade of the fifteenth century the scene of the highest development of the *condottiere* system. There the state of chaos which had continued throughout the nominal reign of Gian Galeazzo's eldest son, Giovanni Maria Visconti, was at length brought to an end by the murder of that impossible prince[2] and the triumphant entry into Milan of his brother Filippo Maria. At the age of twenty this youth had already shown his astuteness by marrying the elderly widow of his father's general, Facino Cane, and thus securing Facino's troops and treasure. For the next five and thirty years this last representative of the Visconti line—so hideous in person and so cowardly in temperament that he rarely

---

[1] Braccio the brave
Makes everyone his slave;
Poor Pope Martin
He isn't worth a farthin'.

[2] Giovanni Maria's favourite amusement was to look on while the victims of his insane bloodthirstiness were torn to pieces by a pack of hounds trained specially for the purpose.

dared to show himself outside the walls of the Castello—held in his hands the threads of Italian politics, for he had inherited his father's subtle brain, and he was master of the wealth of Milan. By the aid of a young *condottiere* whom he raised to power, Francesco Carmagnola, he had reconquered all Central and Western Lombardy by the year 1422, and had even acquired Genoa, whose ungovernable internal factions led her at last to this fate. Then he plunged into the affairs of Romagna, provoked a breach with Florence, and acquired Imola and Forlì by means of the bloodless victories which critics of the *condottieri* system derided as typical.[1] By an offer of higher pay he detached the most promising of the Florentine generals, Niccolo Piccinino, and sent him raiding into Tuscany, and Florence was soon reduced to such straits as to be obliged to implore the assistance of Venice.

It was a turning-point in the history of the Lagoon-republic. The old Doge Tommaso Mocenigo, who died in 1423, viewed with profound distrust the growing strength of the party of mainland expansion led by his younger rival Francesco Foscari. He had been willing enough to expand towards the north, and had actually pushed the borders of the republic from the Piave to the Isonzo, but a collision with Visconti he had ever studiously avoided, and he had opposed with the whole weight of his influence the project of the Florentine alliance. Now, however, the forward party had succeeded in electing Francesco Foscari to the Dogeship, and the desertion of Carmagnola from the Duke of Milan's service to that of the Republic precipitated a breach with Milan [1425]. The Florentine alliance was accepted, and Carmagnola placed in supreme command of the army of the League. Filippo on his side enlisted Francesco Sforza and Niccolo Piccinino, and thus the three ablest tacticians of the period were all engaged in the same war. At first the enormous expenses of the Venetians and Florentines seemed to achieve some solid results; Brescia was taken by Carmagnola, the Venetian fleet sailed up the Po as far as Casalmaggiore, and the Viscontean mercenaries were at length defeated in a pitched battle at Maclovìo in October, 1427. But from this time onwards Carmagnola, with the true half-heartedness of the *condottiere*, refused to press his opponents hard. His inaction at length exasperated his employers, and in 1431 the Senate believed that they held proofs of his treacherous correspondence with the Duke. The

---

[1] At the battle of Zagonara [1424], between the Florentine and Milanese mercenaries, 'none were killed except Lodovico degli Obizzi, and he, with two of his men, was thrown from his horse and suffocated in the mud.' Machiavelli, *Istorie Fiorentine*, Bk. iv.

Council of Ten took the matter in hand, and, in March, 1432, sent an urgent summons to Carmagnola to repair to Venice in order to concert arrangements for the coming campaign. Their victim obeyed, apparently without suspicion. But once within the Ducal Palace he was arrested and conveyed to the dungeons below, and there, under the torture of the strappado and of hot irons to his feet, he confessed his guilt. Sentence of death was passed upon him, and by the execution of Carmagnola, between the two columns of the Piazzetta, the republic asserted her might over the faithless race of *condottieri*.

But Venice by this war had pushed her land frontier to the river Adda, and by an Imperial charter which she secured in 1437 she was given the right, if she had the might, to hold all territories east of that line.

The huge expenditure incurred by the two allied republics in the conduct of this war produced at Venice the first signs of fiscal embarrassment, and at Florence a domestic crisis of the highest importance. The government of the city had since the suppression of the populace or 'Ciompi' in 1381 been in the hands of the magnates of the Greater Guilds—the merchant aristocracy of the town, which had arisen on the ruins of the older feudal aristrocracy. It had been a time of great glory and prosperity for Florence, for after her deliverance from the weight of Gian Galeazzo's ambition in 1402 the city seemed to take a bound forward along the path of civilization and culture. Ghiberti worked, with an enthusiasm felt only by the pioneers in a great art, at the bronze doors of the Baptistery; Masaccio gave new life to painting by his frescoes in the Carmine church; Brunelleschi reared the vast dome which had baffled the powers of all earlier architects. Two wealthy citizens, Palla Strozzi and Giovanni de' Medici, vied with each other in the collection of Greek manuscripts from the East, and Strozzi reanimated the University of Florence by bringing from Byzantium the learned Emanuel Chrysologas to preside over its teaching. But with all this the lower classes—the workers represented by the *Arti Minori* or lesser guilds, and the populace not organized at all —were ground down by an oppressive and irregular poll-tax, and by a system of government which concentrated all power in the hands of the rich merchants; and as the war-taxes grew heavier the murmurs of the people against the ruling clan of the Albizzi grew louder. At this juncture Giovanni de' Medici, the founder of his house, came forward in 1426 as the champion of the poorer classes by proposing an equitable tax on property, known as the *catasto*, instead of the poll-tax, and 'this system of taxation,' says

Machiavelli, 'in some degree checked the tyranny of the upper classes, because they were not able to browbeat the plebeians and with threats make them be silent at the Council, as they formerly did.' But the incident embittered the opposition between the Medici and the Albizzi, and soon afterwards, in 1428, Giovanni died and was succeeded by his still abler son Cosimo. An unjust and unsuccessful war against Lucca, promoted by the headstrong Rinaldo degli Albizzi, precipitated events [1432]; it was hardly over before the Albizzi, feeling themselves discredited before the people, struck savagely at the wealthy merchant whose popularity and open-handedness constituted in their eyes a mortal danger to the State. A *Signoria* favourable to their party was elected in September, 1433, and Cosimo de' Medici was cited to appear before it. He came, and was at once thrown into a cell in the tower of the Palace, where he remained for three days in imminent peril of his life. But he found means to send a handsome bribe to the Gonfalonier of Justice, and Rinaldo's urgent plea for his death was rejected in favour of a decree of banishment. Cosimo departed to Venice, where he lived in princely style until the inevitable turn of the tide summoned him back to his native city. A year had hardly passed before a *Signoria* favourable to him was elected [September, 1434], and Rinaldo urged his friends to another *coup d'état* as their only means of salvation. When he in his turn was cited before the Priors he appeared in arms, at the head of his men, in the Piazza San Pallinari, and there waited for Messer Palla Strozzi to join him. But Strozzi, being a man of peace, rode out unarmed to speak with him, and refused to join in the insurrection. With rage at his heart Rinaldo accepted the offer of Pope Eugenius IV., who happened just then to be in Florence, to mediate between the parties, but his mediation resulted simply in the recall of Cosimo and the banishment of Rinaldo, Strozzi, and some hundreds of their adherents. The long rule of the aristocrats, lineal descendants of the Blacks and the *Parte Guelfa*, was at an end, and on October 6, 1434, Cosimo returned to inaugurate that subtle and indirect personal rule which was the form of despotism best suited to Florence.

The presence of Pope Eugenius IV. in the Tuscan capital at this critical moment was due to events far beyond the control of any of the warring states of Italy. The Council of Basel, summoned unwillingly by his predecessor Martin, had met on July 23, 1431, in the first year of his Pontificate, and Eugenius, deeply mistrusting the spirit of reform with which it was animated, had almost immediately issued a Bull of Dissolution against it [December 18, 1431]. But the Council had shown no intention of submitting to this decree, and a long wrangle began between the Pope and the Council which culminated in the election of an Anti-Pope in 1439. Meanwhile the Pope's enemies in Italy eagerly took up the quarrel; Sforza, encouraged by the Duke of Milan, invaded the Marches [1433], and a *condottiere* named Fortebraccio, calling himself the Executor of the Holy Council, occupied Tivoli and continually harassed Rome. At length the Pope resolved on flight, for he had learnt that the Romans were about to seize him and hand him over as a prisoner to the Council. On June 4, 1434, he escaped in disguise down the Tiber to Ostia, hotly pursued by the populace, and arrived safely at Florence, as we have seen, on the eve of Rinaldo's insurrection. At Florence he remained for the next nine years, while his ferocious Legate Vitelleschi reconquered Rome, put down the rebellious Colonna, destroyed Palestrina afresh, and ruled with an iron hand till his own murder in 1440. Eugenius busied himself with his opposition to the Council of Basel, with the dynastic affairs of the Kingdom of Naples, with ineffectual attempts to dislodge Francesco Sforza from the Marches; but of all his activities only one has survived the deadening hand of time, and that for reasons undreamt of by Eugenius. In 1439, as a counterblast to the Council of Basel, he held a Council in Florence to unite the Greek and Latin Churches,—for the Emperor John Palæologus, hard pressed by the Turks, saw no other method than this of securing help from the West. The Emperor himself with many a gorgeous attendant journeyed to Florence and was lodged in the Peruzzi palaces; the Patriarch of Constantinople in the Casa Vernaccia; and Cosimo de' Medici, whose new-built palace in the Via Larga was nearing completion, determined there to raise an undying memorial to these strange guests of the republic. The hand of Benozzo Gozzoli was set to the task, and so it is that the traveller of today may yet behold them, in all the splendour of eastern raiment, winding in procession across the dim walls of Cosimo's chapel.

Eugenius' attempts to control the affairs of Naples were for a long time singularly unsuccessful. The wretched Queen Joanna II. died childless in 1435, naming as her heir René of Provence, brother of the last Angevin claimant Louis. Eugenius hesitated whether to espouse his cause, but meanwhile Alfonso of Aragon, on the strength of his earlier adoption by Joanna, put forth his whole force to seize the kingdom. He was, however, taken prisoner at the sea-battle of Ponza by the Genoese [1435], whose suzerain, Duke Filippo of Milan, flattered their national pride by thus encouraging them to fight their old enemies the Catalans. The King of Aragon was brought captive to Milan, but there the soundness of his arguments convinced the Duke of the folly of an alliance between Milan and the French, and the Milanese were astonished to see a complete change of sides on the part of the inscrutable Filippo. Alfonso was released without ransom and furnished with supplies for the war, but the Genoese, in fury at this betrayal, rose against the Duke's government, drove out the Milanese garrison and re-established their independence under a native doge [December, 1435].

The Pope now also plunged into the war on the Angevin side, and sent Vitelleschi to attack Alfonso, but fortunately for the Kingdom the Aragonese at length prevailed, after six years of war, and under the long reign of Alfonso the Magnanimous some light of peace and civilization returned to the exhausted country. Eugenius bowed to the accomplished fact, and in 1443 deserted his friends the Florentines for a close alliance with Alfonso and the Duke of Milan—an alliance which incidentally opened to him the path to Rome. He returned to the Lateran amid the acclamations of the very people who had cast him out nine years before, and he spent the last four years of his long Pontificate partly in struggling with Sforza for the possession of the Marches, partly in arranging a Concordat with the Emperor Frederick III. [1446] by which the reforms of the Council of Basel were reduced to insignificance. The Pope and the Curia triumphed once more, and the three great Councils of the fifteenth century left the Papacy securely entrenched for another seventy years behind its old abuses.

Meanwhile the fortunes of Francesco Sforza were slowly rising towards that eminence which his ambition had long coveted. In the early days of his career Duke Filippo had once rashly promised him his only daughter Bianca in marriage, but for long years afterwards the Duke's timid jealousy of his own creature had prevented him from carrying out the bargain. In 1434 Sforza had deserted the Duke's service for that of the Florentine-Venetian league, and by building up an independent power in the Marches he had opposed a solid barrier to Filippo's restless schemes for the absorption of Romagna. But Filippo never renounced the idea of using him again should occasion serve, and when his own leader Piccinino, Sforza's life-long rival, threatened to grow too powerful, he twice betrayed him in favour of Francesco, who would otherwise have been brought to the brink of ruin. On the first of these occasions

Filippo carried out the long-promised marriage-treaty with Sforza and added the town of Cremona as his daughter's dowry. Even this bargain, however, did not permanently detach Francesco from the service of the two republics, though it gave him a strong inducement not to permit the dismemberment of his father-in-law's dominions. Thus when in the course of his endless mutations Filippo formed a league with the Pope and the King of Naples to drive Francesco from the Marches [1445], the latter could count on the support of Florence and Venice, and the Venetian mercenaries were in truth soon driving the Milanese before them across the Adda [1446], and advancing almost to the walls of Milan [1447]. Then in his panic the old 'Viper' turned once more to his son-in-law, and Francesco was actually advancing to his aid when, on August 13, 1447, he was met by the news of the Duke's death. Instantly the situation underwent a profound change. Filippo, cynical to the last, had on the day before his death named Alfonso of Naples as his successor, and a body of Aragonese troops had been admitted into the Castello. But not so easily were the traditions of the ancient republic to be set aside. Though the Venetian army still hovered near, though Sforza was only waiting, at his birthplace of Cotignola, the right moment for a descent on Milan, though French troops were at Asti, eager to assert the claim of Orleans to the Visconti inheritance,[1] Milan would have none of them, and on the morning after the Duke's death she proclaimed the Golden Ambrosian Republic.

The movement was inspired and led by certain Ghibelline nobles imbued with the study of the Classics, of whom Giorgio Lampugnano was the chief, and for a time it seemed as though the dreamer's experiment might succeed. But the days of the *Carroccio* were gone by. Milan had no citizen army now, though the few troops on the spot had sufficed to expel the Aragonese, and with the subject-towns revolting on all hands, and Venice contemptuously rejecting the advances of her sister republic, the 'Captains and Defenders of Liberty' had no choice but to call in the professional, and to engage Francesco Sforza. A regular treaty was made with him on August 30, 1447, by which he agreed to keep none of his conquests, save only Brescia, should he succeed in winning it from the Venetians; and for a whole year Sforza loyally kept his engagements, and succeeded in driving the Venetians from the Milanese. But the arrangement had no real element of stability, for

[1] The Duke of Orleans was the son of Gian Galeazzo's daughter Valentina, whom the first Duke of Milan had married to the French King's brother in 1391.

the Republic feared and mistrusted its too powerful captain and was continually mortifying him by its jealous interference, so that when in October, 1448, the Venetians approached him with an offer of the partition of the Milanese between himself and them, he was only too ready to change sides.

Slowly he pressed back towards the devoted capital, while within the walls the old faction strife of Guelf and Ghibelline broke out anew and distracted the counsels of the rulers. Lampugnano was entrapped and beheaded by his Guelf enemies; Carlo Gonzaga, the 'Captain of the People,' deserted his post and rode out to offer Sforza the surrender of Crema and Lodi [September, 1449]. Then at last the Republic of Venice took alarm and gave a tardy hearing to the proposals of the Ambrosians; but the league which was proclaimed between the two republics on September 24 came too late to save Milan from her fate. Sforza had already occupied the fertile districts whence her corn-supply was drawn, and, as the winter drew on, starvation and anarchy increased apace within the walls. At length, in February, 1450, the Ambrosian and Venetian armies had joined hands in Sforza's rear and were about to march upon him, but the patience of the Milanese was already exhausted. A popular tumult against the Venetian alliance broke out on February 24, and the next day, in the church of Sta. Maria della Scala, it was decided to send ambassadors to Sforza. They found him in his camp at Vimercate, and on the 26th of February he rode in triumph into the town by the Porta Nuova, rode through the very doors of the Duomo, and heard himself hailed as Duke by a multitude blind with enthusiasm. The prize had fallen into his hands at last, and Milan, in her long evolution from the city of St. Ambrose to the spoil of the Austrian, had found the prince and the government that perhaps pleased her best.

CHAPTER XV

The Balance of Power between the Five Great States of Italy

WITH the entry of Francesco Sforza into Milan the last step was taken in the transformation of the Italian city-state into the territorial principality. The Ambrosian Republic, noble as were its ideals, could not survive against the inexorable tendency of the age, for only by the concentration of power in the hands of a single popular ruler could that fatal weakness be avoided which was shown in the revolt of the subject-towns from the ill-fated Republic. Pavia, Lodi, Como, and the rest felt nothing but ill-will towards their ancient enemy and oppressor, left to herself, but all bowed with alacrity under the yoke of so famous a conqueror. The ancient forms of liberty were left to them—the Councils, the Podestà, the Captain of the People—but the Tribute was collected by Francesco's own officials, and with the Tribute went the true substance of power. Never throughout his reign did the proud cities of the Milanese give their new master any trouble.

Beyond the limits of the Duchy, however, the enemies of Sforza were still many, and he soon found himself confronted by a league between Venice, Naples, Savoy, and Monferrat [1451], which might have overwhelmed him but for the constant support he drew, both in money and good advice, from Cosimo de' Medici at Florence. That far-sighted politician, whose friendship for Francesco was genuine and lasting, was engaged in the delicate task of weaning the Florentines from their traditional alliance with Venice, and transferring it to Milan, and it taxed the resources of his power to the utmost to effect the change. But once effected, the new alliance proved an undoubted blessing to the peace of Italy, for by the leverage which it brought to bear against Venice, the Republic was at length induced to agree to the Peace of Lodi [1454], and the long war between Venice and Milan was thus brought to an end. The sole result to the Venetians of their huge expenditure was the town of Crema, which passed to the Republic; otherwise Sforza was confirmed in the possession of the whole of the Visconti territories. But no peace could be complete without Alfonso of Naples, who detested Sforza as the former champion of the Angevin cause, and it needed all the persuasiveness of the humanist Pope, Nicholas V., to bring him at last into the League. It is said that he was finally won over by the gift of the priceless manuscript of Livy, which Cosimo de' Medici dispatched to the romantic scholar-king.

So, with the four strongest powers of Italy at peace with one another, and with the Papacy exerting itself to the utmost to rouse not only Italy but Europe against the Turk, we have reached the brief age of relative stability, of the Balance of Power before the foreign invasions. It is an age full of charm to the student of Italy, for at a time when England and France were still in the grip of blind dynastic struggles and given up to barbarous forms of civil war, Italy had evolved a more settled polity which, if its ideals fell short of those of the Lombard League, yet admitted of a type of life infinitely more civilized, infinitely more gracious, than that of the surrounding countries. Even during the endless wars provoked by Filippo Visconti, the towns of Lombardy and Romagna were sufficiently secure to foster a vigorous intellectual life within their walls, and the repulsive Duke of Milan himself encouraged Human-ism in the person of his most pugnacious of scholars, Francesco Filelfo. At Ferrara, the Marquis Lionello d'Este [1441—1450] pre-sided over the Classical Renaissance at its freshest and purest, and though he wrote Latin epistles which were extolled as worthy of Cicero, he was not above patronizing vernacular poetry also. In the hill-fortress of Urbino the famous Duke Federigo [1422—1482], invincible *condottiere* as he was, gathered together a library of classical books worth thirty thousand ducats. Long before the fall of Constantinople in 1453, a regular intercourse had sprung up between Italy and Byzantium for purposes of pure scholarship, and the hunt for Greek and Latin manuscripts was carried on throughout the East by the agents of the great trading firms of Florence and Venice.

As, however, the stir of the Renaissance had first been felt in the Tuscan capital, so it was there that the revival of classical learning took its fullest form. The Council held in Florence by Eugenius IV. [1438] had filled the town with Greek scholars and scribes, who gave a powerful impulse to the nascent study of Greek, and one among them especially, the aged Gemistus Plethon, launched upon the Florentine world the philosophy of Plato. Cosimo de' Medici and his circle seized upon the new learning with avidity, and Cosimo founded that 'Platonic Academy' for the discussion of the master's teaching which attained to so much fame under his grandson Lorenzo. Cosimo's position as a patron of letters was, indeed, the distinguishing feature of the Florentine revival, and forms his best claim to the proud title of *Pater Patriæ* which his countrymen bestowed on him after his death. But even in that position, as in the ascendancy he gained in political affairs, his record is not wholly admirable. Though his munificence to his own *protégés* was inexhaustible, he could be harsh and ungenerous to political opponents, however brilliant their scholarship; the illustrious Palla Strozzi was never allowed to return from his exile, while the orator Giannozzo Manetti, who preserved some independence from the Medicean influence, was gradually ruined by extortionate taxation until he fled penniless to take refuge with the Pope. So in the domain of politics, though Cosimo's autocracy procured peace for Florence by means of the alliance with Sforza, it was maintained at the expense of the grossest injustice towards his opponents, as well as by artful manipulation of the institutions of a free city. Instead of the bi-monthly choice of the Priors or Signory by lot, according to the time-honoured law of 1282, Cosimo obtained a *Balía*, or committee authorized by popular acclamation to scrutinize the eligible names; and from time to time, as faction raised its head, this *Balía* was renewed, and with it the authority to nominate to all appointments, or at any rate to choose by lot from an extremely limited list. In practice the Signory simply nominated its own successors. Thus Cosimo and his party kept a tight hold on the political machine, and disabled their opponents with crushing taxes[1]; but the common people, being lightly taxed, loved his rule, gloried in their bourgeois prince, whose wealth and liberality became a legend throughout Italy, and were ever ready to fill the Piazza with shouts of '*Palle! Palle!*' (the balls on the Medici shield) when a new *Balía* was needed to prolong his power.

Nowhere was the better side of the Medicean influence more strongly felt than in the Pontificate of Nicholas V., the first true Pope of the Renaissance. Tommaso da Sarzana, as he was called from the place of his up-bringing, was a poor scholar of Bologna University who first strayed to Florence in 1417, to earn a living by his wits, and became tutor to the children first of Rinaldo degli

---

[1] The *Catasto* or property-tax was still the basis of all taxation in Florence, but the power of assessing it was given to a small committee of Cosimo's friends known as 'Sgravatori,' who used their power in arbitrarily increasing the assessments of their enemies and lowering those of their friends. Many of the disaffected were driven to live in the country, beyond the limit of the urban taxation, but even there they were followed by troops of armed tax-gatherers, who frequently sacked their houses. Cavalcanti, *Seconda Storia*, vol. ii., ch. xxviii.

Albizzi and then of Palla Strozzi. Subsequently, when Eugenius IV. had transferred his court to Florence, Tommaso returned thither in the train of the Archbishop of Bologna, and immediately joined the circle of literary enthusiasts who gathered under Cosimo's roof or carried on their eager discussions 'by the side of the Palazzo Pubblico.'[1] Eugenius made him a cardinal in 1446, and a few months later he was raised to the Papacy by a conclave distraught as usual between Colonna and Orsini, and driven to compromise upon the little vivacious scholar who offended no one. So at the mid-century the Papacy was brought within the full stream of Humanism, and the court of Nicholas V. became thronged with scholars from all parts of Italy, whom he set to the laborious task of translating the Greek classics into Latin. The revenues of the Church were freely devoted to this purpose, for Nicholas was a lavish paymaster, and thus the germ of the Vatican Library was formed, with a collection of five thousand manuscripts. In architecture, too, the new Pope showed his towering spirit, for he conceived nothing less than a plan for the rebuilding of Rome, with wider streets and colonnaded *piazze;* but his special efforts were spent upon the Leonine City, where he reared the Vatican Palace, strengthened the Bridge and Castle of Sant' Angelo and laid the foundations for a new St. Peter's. The Papacy was to be secured from the attacks of Roman populace or marauding *condottieri* and from a regenerated and glorious Rome was to scatter light and learning upon the Christian world.

But in these dreams the ardent Pope had reckoned without one force, the spirit of republican independence that still slumbered in Rome. It found its leader now in the Knight Stefano Porcaro, whose restless mind was imbued with a medley of classical ideals, hatred of priests, and visionary beliefs that he was himself the saviour of Rome foretold by Petrarch; and though the generous Pope sought to conciliate the firebrand by bestowing high offices in the Papal States upon him, he could not wean him from his passionate desire to liberate Rome. Banished at last to Bologna, the knight contrived to escape thence and to return to Rome, where he had many confederates. Three hundred mercenaries were secretly collected, and a plan agreed upon for setting fire to the Vatican stables on the Feast of the Epiphany [January 6, 1453], seizing the Pope and cardinals in the confusion and raiding the hoards of gold that they knew to be collected in the Borgo quarter. But the plot was discovered or betrayed, and on the day before

---

[1] So the good bookseller Vespasiano, who describes such a scene in his *Vite di Uomini Illustri.*

the Epiphany, Porcaro's house was surrounded and searched, and the knight himself found hiding in the house of his sister. He was dragged to Sant' Angelo, tried and hanged, and nine of his accomplices suffered the same fate on the Capitol. 'Such,' remarks Machiavelli drily, 'was the end of the dreams of Messer Stefano Porcaro. Although some shadow of glory may appear to cling to such enterprises, the dangers that attend their execution are very real.'

The affair was a bitter disillusionment to Nicholas, and when a few months later the news arrived of the fall of Constantinople, his cup of humiliation seemed filled to overflowing. But he was not the man to inspire Europe with the crusading spirit. His efforts to pacify Italy were well meaning but fruitless, and the Peace of Lodi was arranged altogether without his help [1454]. He had a considerable share, however, in inducing Alfonso to join the League of the northern powers, and as he lay on his death-bed in March, 1455, he had the satisfaction of seeing Italy at peace.

The reign of his successor, Calixtus III. [1455—1458], was remarkable chiefly for the fact that he introduced the name of Borgia into the Papal annals. An old man himself, he placed all power in the hands of his three Spanish nephews, one of whom, Rodrigo, was to become infamous later on as Alexander VI. Calixtus had risen to power in the service of his compatriot Alfonso of Aragon, but when he found that the King had no intention of prosecuting the war against the Turks, but was turning his crusading fleet against the Genoese instead, the Pope lost patience with his former patron, and refused to recognize the right of his bastard son Ferrante to the succession in Naples. When, therefore, Alfonso the Magnanimous died in June, 1458, the unfortunate kingdom was once more face to face with a disputed succession. Nor had the reign of this remarkable prince materially improved the condition of his people, or placed the country in a position to resist the vicissitudes of dynastic strife. Far from being able to improve upon the policy of Frederick II. towards the feudal barons, Alfonso had increased their privileges at the expense of his own, and had no counterbalancing middle class. A knight of romance himself, he was ardently beloved by some people in Naples, and made himself famous by his patronage of letters; but his constant wars were a sore tax upon his backward kingdom, and his implacable hatred of the Genoese brought the Angevin danger perceptibly nearer by driving those formidable mariners into the arms of France.[1] John of Anjou,

[1] The Genoese had enjoyed a stormy independence ever since, in 1435, they had shaken off the Milanese yoke after the sea-battle of Ponza, when Duke Filippo had provoked them by joining sides with their prisoner Alfonso. See p. 168.

son of old King René, entered Genoa as suzerain in 1458, and the next year started on his expedition to reconquer Naples for the Angevins. But the time was not yet ripe, and after five years of war he was finally expelled by Ferrante, who thus secured the succession of the kingdom to himself.

On the death of Calixtus in August, 1458, the Conclave elected a remarkable man who had already played a varied part in the affairs of Europe. Æneas Sylvius Piccolomini, a descendant of a noble family exiled from Siena, was an adventurer delightfully characteristic of that age—clever, restless, ambitious, endowed with a facile pen and a persuasive tongue, a libertine in youth, a martyr in old age, and withal a poet crowned with laurel by the Emperor. Nearly half his life had been spent in Germany, whither he had first gone in the train of the Papal Legate to the Council of Basel; and when the quarrel broke out between Eugenius and the Council, Æneas was to be found hotly on the side of the Council —defending it in a series of Dialogues, and at length accepting the post of secretary to the Anti-Pope Felix. But he soon began to have doubts as to whether he were truly on the winning side, managed to ingratiate himself with the Emperor Frederick III., who had proclaimed his neutrality in the quarrel, and deserted the Anti-Pope's service for the Emperor's. In the capacity of imperial secretary, he began to drift to the side of Eugenius IV., and it was under his auspices that the ignoble bargain was struck, in 1446, between Pope and Emperor, by which Frederick deserted the cause of reform for the sum of 220,000 ducats and the right to nominate to a certain number of bishoprics during his lifetime. Æneas meanwhile had been busily looking out for ecclesiastical preferment, but it was not until the reign of his fellow-humanist Nicholas V., that he was given the bishoprics first of Trieste and then of Siena. Calixtus made him a cardinal, though in Æneas's own words 'he had to use battering-rams and every kind of warlike engine to force the door' of the Sacred College.

When at length, in 1458, he reached the pinnacle of his ambition he took the name of Pius II., in graceful allusion to Virgil's Pius Æneas. Only for six years was he destined to occupy the Papal throne, but his immense versatility and practical vigour filled the time to overflowing with all manner of undertakings, from the rousing of Europe against the Turk to the creation of his city of Pienza on the site of the little Tuscan village which had given him birth. Within two months of his election he was issuing a summons to all Christian princes to attend a Congress at Mantua

ÆNEAS SYLVIUS VISITING THE KING OF SCOTLAND
From a fresco by Pinturicchio in the Cathedral of Siena

in the following summer, in order to launch a crusade against the Turk, but while labouring indefatigably in this unpopular cause he did not neglect the affairs of Italy, and astonished and offended the French-Angevin interest by taking the side of Ferrante of Aragon against the Angevin claimant to the Neapolitan crown. Pius was guided in this decision by the advice of Francesco Sforza, for whose judgment in such matters he felt a profound respect, and Ferrante's victory after a long and doubtful war justified his policy. Though Ferrante's rule proved cruel and tyrannical, the attitude of Pius in the Neapolitan affair was inspired by the highest motives, and resulted in the postponement of the age of the foreign invasions for another thirty years.

But in his greatest enterprise, the preaching of the crusade, Pius was doomed to many bitter disappointments. The scanty attendance of princes at the Congress of Mantua convinced him that the Age of Faith had passed away, and he was obliged to rest content with a barren declaration of war against the Turk. Before the Congress dispersed, however, he used the opportunity it gave him of recording his altered opinions on the relations of Council to Pope in his remarkable Bull *Execrabilis* [1460], which threatened with excommunication any who should go about to appeal to future Councils against a Pope's decision. So the straitness of Pius atoned for the laxity of Æneas.

In his government of the Papal States this most human of Popes showed perhaps his most attractive side. Pius II. was never so happy as when he was effecting some solemn reconciliation between contending factions, to the singing of psalms and the scattering of flowers, and his constant journeys for purposes of business or pleasure gave him a far better insight than his predecessors possessed into the life and needs of the people. He was fortunate in commanding the services of the one trustworthy *condottiere* of the day, Federigo of Montefeltro, Duke of Urbino, in the disciplinary measures which were necessary against refractory vassals, such as the Lord of Rimini, Sigismondo Malatesta. But neither had he any scruples in promoting his own nephews and relatives to lucrative and important posts, and by the benefits which he showered on the Piccolomini Pius may be said to have set the example for the Papal nepotism of later days. But posterity forgives him this and all other shortcomings for the keenness of his delight in the things of the mind, for his joy in antiquities and buildings, for his intense appreciation of what was beautiful. Yet his own life ended after all on an austerer note than this. With incredible perseverance he had at

M

length effected a working alliance with Hungary and Venice against the Turk, and in 1463 he announced to his astonished cardinals that he intended to lead the crusade in person. Crippled with gout, he started in the heat of summer, 1464, for the rendezvous at Ancona, and was borne in a litter up the long Umbrian valley to Assisi and so over the Apennines to the Adriatic seaport. But the hand of death was already upon him, and he lived only to behold, from the high-placed Episcopal Palace beside the Cathedral, the stately approach of the Venetian fleet, and to receive the homage of the Doge. He died two days after its arrival, and the crusade died with him.

But the Venetian Republic, alone of the Italian powers, carried on the war against the Turk in her own way. She had left it, however, till too late. During the ten years that had elapsed since the conquest of Constantinople, the Sultan, Mohammed II., had been building ships, and in 1469 a Venetian sea-captain reported that he had sighted a Turkish armada of four hundred sail. Venice on the contrary had allowed her fleet to decline during the long period of her expansion on land; her finances were in disorder, and the sudden destruction of her eastern commerce made it impossible for her to raise the sums required. The result was that her fleet failed to relieve the important town of Negropont, the capital of Euboea, which in 1470 fell before the Turks, that Turkish irregulars were presently overrunning Friuli, and that Loredano's heroic defence of Scutari in two successive sieges was unavailing, because no relieving force appeared. In the face of these disasters, Venice, in 1479, was obliged to make peace on humiliating terms. She surrendered Euboea, Scutari, Lemnos, and part of the Morea, and only regained her right of keeping a consul at Constantinople by the payment of an annual tribute. Having settled accounts with Venice, Mohammed next attacked Southern Italy. In 1480 his admiral captured Otranto and sawed its Archbishop in two as a warning of what the Pope might expect, should the Turks succeed in reaching Rome. It is probable that only the sudden death of Mohammed in the next year saved Italy from conquest.

The Pope who succeeded Pius II. was a Venetian of stately aspect and imperious will named Pietro Barbo, who took the name of Paul II. [1464—1471]. This time the cardinals had endeavoured to bind tne new Pope in advance by drawing up a series of articles strictly limiting the Papal prerogative, which each swore to observe should he be elected. But Paul II. soon brushed aside these trammels. He drew up another constitution of his own, forced each cardinal to sign it without so much as giving him time to read it through, and then tossed it away to be locked up in a chest and forgotten. He showed equal determination in dealing with the humanists of the Papal Court, by suppressing the so-called College of Abbreviators—the home of all the needy men of letters patronized by Pius and Nicholas V.—and the loud outcry raised by scholars throughout Italy fell upon deaf ears. Indeed he went further still, for in 1468 he suppressed the 'Roman Academy' presided over by one Pomponius Lætus—a remarkable spirit who exercised an extraordinary influence over the minds of the young Romans. It was an influence wholly secular, and his teaching savoured even of classical republicanism, so that in the city of Porcaro and Rienzi the Pope judged it wiser to put a stop to his activities. Pomponius and his friend Platina were imprisoned in Sant' Angelo and the latter put to the torture,[1] but when both had made sufficiently abject apologies to the Pope they were released, and the affair blew over. But though he did not share in the prevailing passion for the classics, Paul outdid all previous Popes in the magnificence of his display; he built the Palazzo Venezia at the upper end of the *Corso*, and from its Loggia was wont to watch the races down the long straight street below, which became so famous a feature of the Roman Carnival. The Romans delighted in their majestic Prince, who left them at least one solid memorial of his reign in his revision of the City Statutes, which had gone untouched since the days of Albornoz.[2]

During the reign of Paul two commanding figures passed away from the Italian stage, Cosimo de' Medici and Francesco Sforza, and left in each case inferior successors. Piero de' Medici would have lost his hold on Florence if the opposition could have produced an able and disinterested leader, but his adversaries lost their chance by embarking on an ill-planned conspiracy resting upon foreign mercenaries, and its failure left Piero unquestioned master of Florence. At Milan, the young Duke Galeazzo Maria exhibited all the worst vices of his Visconti ancestry, and was at length murdered in 1476 as a solemn act of justice by three young nobles who had sworn to rid the state of such a monster. But the

[1] Platina lived to write the life of Paul II. in his famous Vite dei Papi. Sixtus IV. took him into favour, and made him Custodian of the Vatican Library from 1475 till his death in 1481.

[2] The ancient constitution of Senator, Conservators, and Captains of the Regions still continued, and no Roman citizen of lay condition could be brought before an ecclesiastical court.

only result of their action was that Galeazzo's more famous brother, Ludovico *il Moro*, usurped the guardianship of his infant nephew, 'and so,' in Machiavelli's words, 'became the sole ruler of Milan, and the cause of the ruin of Italy.'

Meantime, in Florence, Piero de' Medici's young son, Lorenzo, had peacefully succeeded to the position held by his father and grandfather [1469], and was maintaining the traditional Medicean policy of affability towards the crowd combined with rigorous mastery of the political machine.[1] In the early years of his power, however, he unwisely provoked the hostility of the new Pope, Sixtus IV. (Francesco della Rovere, 1471—1484), by opposing his schemes for the aggrandizement of his nephews, and so brought down upon Florence a tempest from which he barely escaped with his life.

The two nephews upon whom Pope Sixtus principally heaped his favours were Giuliano della Rovere, whom he made a cardinal,[2] and Girolamo Riario, for whom he bought the lordship of Imola, in Romagna. Now Florence had long had designs on Imola, and Lorenzo, using his position as Papal banker, endeavoured to make it impossible for Sixtus to raise the sum required for the purchase. But he was defeated by the rival banking house of the Pazzi, Florentines also, who readily advanced the money to the Pope and thereby ingratiated themselves both with Sixtus and Girolamo. Soon the Pope transferred his business from the Medici to the Pazzi Bank. This deepened the jealousy already existing between the two rich Florentine families, and the profound sensation caused by the murder of the Duke of Milan [1476] set strange schemes floating in the mind of Francesco Pazzi, the manager of the Pazzi Bank in Rome. Whether the idea of the conspiracy was first mooted by him or by his patron Girolamo Riario, who dreaded Lorenzo's power to thwart him in Romagna, will never be certain, but between them the pair elaborated a plan for the simultaneous assassination of Lorenzo de' Medici and his brother Giuliano. They offered the post of murderer to an honest *condottiere* named Montesecco, but in order to silence his scruples it was necessary to obtain the Pope's consent, and this was apparently done at a curious interview between Sixtus and the three conspirators, reported by

[1] In July, 1471, Lorenzo induced the Signory to create a body of five *Accopiatori*, whose business it was to nominate the Priors and the Gonfalonier of Justice, and in November of the same year the number of these *Accopiatori* was increased to ten, Lorenzo accepted a place among them, and their term of office was made unlimited. Perrens, *Hist. de Florence*, vol. i., pp. 362—4.

[2] This was the future Pope Julius II.

Montesecco in his confession to the Signory after the deed.[1] The Archbishop of Pisa, one Francesco Salviati, was also drawn into the plot, and after much hesitation Jacopo de' Pazzi, the head of the family in Florence, gave his consent.

All the conspirators except Riario met in Florence in April, 1478, and Lorenzo entertained them unsuspectingly both at Fiesole and in his palace within the town. But since it was judged essential that both brothers should be murdered together, the occasion finally selected was the celebration of Mass in the Cathedral on Sunday, April 26. Francesco Pazzi undertook to kill Giuliano, but at the last moment the soldier Montesecco refused to add sacrilege to murder by slaying Lorenzo in church, and the deed was entrusted to two priests, who had no such scruples. When Mass had begun it was found that Giuliano had lingered behind, so Francesco Pazzi went back to fetch him, and skilfully ascertained as they walked that he wore no defensive armour. At the elevation of the Host, Pazzi struck Giuliano in the breast, and as he fell stabbed him again and again so savagely that he wounded himself severely in the thigh; but the two priests failed to kill Lorenzo, who at the first attack gathered his cloak round his left arm as a shield, drew his dagger, and sprang away towards the Sacristy. He gained it in safety with a few friends, who barred the door behind them, and as he waited there Florence was filled with murder and wild vengeance. The Archbishop of Pisa, whose part had been to seize the Palazzo Pubblico, was arrested by the Gonfalonier of Justice and hanged from a window of the upper storey as soon as the news of Giuliano's murder reached the Palace. Francesco Pazzi, who had escaped to his house, but whose wound disabled him from mounting a horse, was dragged half naked to the Palazzo and hanged beside the Archbishop. Their followers were massacred without mercy, and the streets strewn with their severed limbs. So the attempt against the Medici was suppressed in blood, and Lorenzo emerged, like so many victims of an unsuccessful outrage, with increased popularity and power. The Pope might fulminate his interdict upon the city for the murder of an Archbishop, but the secular authority compelled the priests to disregard it, and in the war that followed, Florence upheld her 'foremost citizen,' as she loved to call him, with all singleness of heart. The foundations laid by Cosimo were indeed broad and deep, and it needed a mightier hand than that of Pope Sixtus IV. to dislodge the Medici from Florence.

[1] The interview is quoted by Creighton, *Hist. of the Papacy*, vol. iv., p. 85, and by Roscoe, *Life of Lorenzo de' Medici*, Appendix XXVIII.

CHAPTER XVI

Italian Statecraft
and the Invasion of Charles VIII

THE conspiracy of the Pazzi had ended in the personal triumph of Lorenzo de' Medici, but it left the Republic of Florence beset with external dangers. The good relations established between the five great states by the Peace of Lodi had endured for twenty years, but already in 1474 the three northern powers, alarmed by the aggressive nepotism of Sixtus IV., had banded themselves in a defensive league to watch his movements, and the Pope had retaliated by allying himself with Ferrante of Naples. The latter alliance now proved the more effective of the two, for the King of Naples sent his son Alfonso to co-operate with the Papal troops in an advance into the heart of Tuscany, while both Milan and Venice excused themselves from entering into the personal quarrel, as they termed it, of Lorenzo de' Medici. The war therefore—if war it could be called, in which each commander studiously avoided an encounter—went ill for Florence, and in December, 1479, Lorenzo decided on the bold expedient of a visit to Naples, in order to try his powers of reasoning upon the redoubted King. For Ferrante enjoyed a reputation for treachery and barbarity which might well give Lorenzo pause, but he trusted to the appeals he could make to the King's self-interest, and the event proved him right. Ferrante signed a separate treaty with Florence in February, 1480, greatly to the Pope's disgust, and Lorenzo returned to enjoy his triumph. But Alfonso of Calabria[1] lingered on in Siena, lording it over the still independent republic and apparently cherishing designs on the rest of Tuscany, while the alliance of Florence with Naples alienated Venice, which drew closer to the Pope. From this tangle of difficulties Lorenzo was suddenly extricated by the descent of the Turks upon Otranto[2]; Alfonso was recalled to the defence of his father's kingdom, and Sixtus at length consented to absolve the Florentines on condition that they equipped fifteen galleys for the war against the Turks. No wonder that his enemies

[1] The title 'Duke of Calabria' was that usually borne by the eldest son of the King of Naples.
[2] See. p. 178.

openly accused Lorenzo of having incited the Turk to this timely intervention.

Vague talk of a crusade again filled the air, but Sixtus preferred to devote his energies to furthering the interests of his nephew Girolamo. The recent wars against Florence and the Turks had left the Pope angry and dissatisfied with his Neapolitan allies, and also with his vassal Duke Ercole of Ferrara, who had taken the part of Lorenzo de' Medici after the conspiracy of the Pazzi. The brilliant family of the Estensi had by this time been established at Ferrara for nearly three hundred years, for it was in 1208 that the free commune of Ferrara first gave itself to the Guelf Marquis of Este and his heirs for ever. Since then the Estensi had maintained themselves at the head of the second rank of Italian princes, and might now almost be said to have advanced into the first. In 1288 the Marquis Obizzo had added Modena and Reggio to his ancestral territories, which included, besides Ferrara and its surroundings, the district between the Adige and the Po known as the Polesina. All this eastern territory, however, was part of the ancient *Exarchate of Ravenna*, which the Donation of Pippin had handed over to the Pope, and the Papal authority was made a reality in the early part of the fourteenth century, when John XXII. compelled the Estensi of the day to accept investiture for Ferrara and its dependencies at the hands of the Papal Legate. Modena and Reggio, on the other hand, were nominally fiefs of the Empire, and in 1452 the magnificent Borso d'Este bought the title of Duke of these cities from the impecunious Emperor Frederick III., whom he entertained at Ferrara with unheard-of splendour during the Hapsburger's journey to Rome for his coronation. More recently, Borso had acquired the title of Duke of Ferrara from Pope Paul II., while his half-brother and successor, Ercole I., had wedded the daughter of King Ferrante, Leonora of Aragon, with royal pomp [1473]. These irregularly shaped dominions, then, lay as a valuable buffer-state between Milan and Florence on the one hand, and Venice on the other, but causes of friction were continually arising between Ferrara and the Republic of St. Mark, on questions of salt-making or of the navigation of the Po, while, as we have seen, Duke Ercole had earned the ill-will of Sixtus and his nephew by his conduct in the recent war. The result was that in September, 1481, a coalition was formed between Venice and the Pope, directed both against Ferrante of Naples and Ercole of Ferrara. The Duke was thoroughly alarmed, and in his efforts to defend himself all Italy was drawn into the vortex of this personal and local struggle. Lorenzo de' Medici, eager to wipe out his personal score against Riario, helped Ferrara by supporting the smaller tyrants of Umbria and Romagna against the Pope; and Ludovico Sforza, but newly established in Milan, willingly embraced this chance of winning back Bergamo and Brescia from Venice, the traditional enemy. Mantua, Bologna, and Urbino joined in on the same side, but the forces of the League were unable to prevent the Venetians from pressing hard upon Ferrara, which was soon virtually besieged.

The interest of the war, however, was presently centred in the south. There Alfonso of Calabria demanded permission from Sixtus to march his troops to the aid of Ferrara through Papal territory, and when this was refused he advanced as far as Marino in the Alban Hills, and in conjunction with the Colonna and Savelli threatened Rome itself. Sixtus was defended by the Orsini and a few lesser families, for the lawlessness of Riario had encouraged the revival of all the ancient blood-feuds of Rome, and the city had relapsed into the state of barbarism in which Rienzi had found it, a century and a half before. But the Pope was saved by a contingent of Venetian mercenaries, who defeated Alfonso, his Turkish body-guard, and his Colonna allies at a pitched battle in the Pontine Marshes on August 21, 1482, 'a battle,' says Machiavelli, 'which was fought with more valour than had been shown in any engagement in Italy for the last fifty years, for more than a thousand men were killed on one side or the other.'

Such unusual bloodshed, however, was rendered fruitless by diplomatic considerations. Sixtus was weary of the war, which seemed to be turning to the profit of Venice rather than to that of his nephew, and by December he had completely changed sides, was receiving Alfonso and his Turks with all honour in the Vatican, and had written to the Doge forbidding him to wage war any longer on his fief, Ferrara. Venice, however, declined to withdraw, and in spite of Papal anathemas continued to invest Ferrara. Throughout the year 1483 the war continued, while Girolamo Riario and his satellites the Orsini maintained a reign of terror in Rome, and exacted a bloody vengeance on the Colonna for the part they had taken in the recent fighting. When their palaces were demolished in Rome the unconquerable old Ghibelline family took refuge in their fortresses in the Sabine and Abruzzi mountains. Thither Riario followed them, and it was while besieging the castle of Palliano that news reached him of the death of Sixtus IV. in Rome [August 12, 1484]. Peace had at last been concluded in the north, leaving Ferrara despoiled of all her territory beyond the

Po,[1] and it was said that his agitation at the news hastened the end of the turbulent old man.

The Conclave could only be held after a truce had been arranged between Colonna, Orsini, and Riario (who had seized Sant' Angelo), whereby all three parties agreed to evacuate the city, and then the intrigues of Cardinals Rovere and Borgia resulted in the election of an insignificant Genoese named Giovanni Cibò, who took the name of Innocent VIII. Personally the new Pope was only remarkable for the fact that he was the first to acknowledge the possession of an illegitimate family, and to break the custom by which ladies were forbidden to sit at table with the Pope. Politically he was at first wholly under the influence of Cardinal della Rovere (the future Julius II.) who induced him to take up a hostile attitude towards Naples and insist on the payment of the full tribute, which had been commuted by Sixtus to the yearly gift of a white palfrey. This change of policy coincided with the outbreak of a formidable conspiracy among the Neapolitan barons against Ferrante and his detested son Alfonso, and in the war that followed Innocent supported the barons and threatened Ferrante with the latest Angevin pretender, René of Lorraine, while Florence and Milan, from dread of France, supported Naples. Lorenzo de' Medici, indeed, who foresaw better than any other Italian statesman the danger that threatened Italy from 'these Ultramontanes,'[2] strove hard for peace, and Ferrante was glad after a year of war to sign a treaty granting, on paper, all the Pope's demands. But in reality he only wished to free his hands for dealing with his rebel barons. Wiser and more pitiless than his father, he saw that the government of Naples would be impossible so long as the power of the great feudal houses remained unchecked, for not only were the barons absolute lords within their respective territories, but it was among them that the Angevin claimant always found support. But Ferrante's sole idea of dominating them was to have recourse to wholesale murder. Immediately after the peace was proclaimed an instalment of five or six of the principal barons were seized, executed, and their

[1] The peace was negotiated by Ludovico Sforza, who was alarmed by the fact that Venice had invited the Duke of Orleans to make good his claim on Milan. It handed over the Polesina to Venice and did nothing for Girolamo Riario, who had set his heart on winning Ravenna and Cervia.

[2] 'I dislike these Ultramontanes and barbarians beginning to interfere in Italy,' he wrote to his ambassador in Rome in July, 1489. 'We are so disunited and so deceitful that I believe that nothing but shame and loss will be our lot.'

property confiscated, and gradually a much larger number were lured into the net by specious promises and imprisoned in dungeons whence they never issued alive. The Pope dared not remonstrate, though the safety of the rebels had been expressly stipulated in the treaty, and even Lorenzo, disgusted as he was at the King's barbarity, was obliged to cling to his alliance as a lesser evil than a French invasion. It was Italy's greatest misfortune, in this hour of vague fear before the storm, that the rulers of Naples, on whom all depended, were among the basest of mankind.

Humiliated by his treatment at Ferrante's hands,—for the King showed no greater inclination to pay the promised tribute after the treaty than before it,—Innocent forsook the counsel of Cardinal della Rovere for that of Lorenzo de' Medici, and allowed the great Florentine to exercise the fullest influence over him during the last five years of his Pontificate. A family alliance was even arranged between them, in the marriage of the Pope's son to Lorenzo's daughter Maddalena, and in 1489 Lorenzo attained the crown of his ambition in the promise of a cardinal's hat for his second son Giovanni, who was then only fourteen years of age.[1] In Rome itself the violence and lawlessness unchained by Sixtus continued unabated, and the Curia sank into still lower depths of corruption and immorality,[2] but in matters of high policy the pacific influence of Lorenzo was supreme. And never was the need for internal unity more urgent than in these years. The old King René of Provence, whose son John had attempted the conquest of Naples on the death of Alfonso the Magnanimous,[3] had bequeathed his rights upon that realm to the King of France, and the acceptance of the bequest seemed to many a far-seeing Italian only a matter of time and circumstance. Louis XI., too fully occupied at home, had steadily refused the bait, but from the dreams of his feather-brained son Charles any folly might spring. The boy, however, was still a minor, and Italy had her breathing-space.

She used it in an outburst of splendour, of artistic and intellectual genius, such as the world has never seen elsewhere, save in Athens of the Greeks. Not a city of Tuscany or the Lombard Plain but was adorning itself anew with exquisite buildings, decorating its palaces or founding its school of painting during these twenty

---

[1] This son Giovanni was the future Pope Leo X.

[2] Innocent created about 350 new venal offices, of which the most important were the fifty-two *Piombatori* of Apostolic Bulls; these were sold for 2,500 ducats apiece. Under Sixtus there had already been 650 venal offices in the Curia. (Gregorovius, vol. vii. Pt. I, p. 319.)

[3] See p. 175.

years; not a court of petty prince or tyrant but was the scene of
revels on which the touch of perfect art seems to have left an
undying fragrance. The life of Milan during the short years when
Beatrice d'Este held sway there, as the young wife of Ludovic the
Moor, or of Mantua under her still more brilliant sister Isabella,
wife of the Marquis Gonzaga—the gaiety, the youth, the spontan-
eity of this new spirit of revelry and joy—all this has made the
Italy of Lorenzo's day the mistress of our hearts and our imagina-
tions, whatever the darker side of the picture that history may
reveal. A darker side there undoubtedly was—the heaped-up
wickedness, the lust and immorality that were to draw down the
'Sword of the Lord' in the preaching of Savonarola,—but it may
well be doubted whether the wickedness was greater than at the
end of the previous century, or whether it was not rather the
keener self-consciousness of man that had at last become aware of
it. If Italy fell a prey to the stranger for her sins, it was for the
sins of three centuries of civic bloodshed, which had left her at
last exhausted and defenceless before the spoiler—her manhood
sapped by the reaction from endless war, her military system a
mere sham, a cobweb bulwark to be shattered at the first touch
of northern steel.

Until the death of Lorenzo de' Medici in April, 1492, the threads
of Italian statecraft were mostly gathered in his hands. His position at home had been rendered impregnable soon after his return
from Naples in 1480 by a fresh change in the constitution: the
creation of a council of seventy persons, all apparently devoted to
the Medicean interest, who were to hold office for life, and whose
functions were to elect the Executive (the Priors and the Gonfalonier), and to form two committees from among their own number
for the management of foreign affairs and of finance. So comprehensive a programme naturally excluded the two ancient councils
of the Commune and the Podestà from all effective share in the
government, and so long as Lorenzo could dominate the Seventy,
Lorenzo was lord of Florence. But he knew that it was no easy
task; that to maintain his ascendancy it needed constant vigilance,
constant interference in every branch of social life; hence his army
of spies, his strange monopoly of the marriage market, whereby
he prevented any family alliance that might become dangerous to
his interest; his care to keep the people amused by street shows
and entertainments. His most difficult task was to persuade the
Seventy of the wisdom of his alliance with Naples against Pope
Innocent in 1485, for the popular feeling in Florence still ran in

the old Guelf channels—'for Church and Anjou'—against his own more far-sighted statesmanship; and the reaction was to have its way in the fatal days of the French invasion. Yet for his lifetime Florence suffered her bondage gladly; no other prince in Italy could vie with him for magnificence, for culture, for liberality; and his familiar title of 'Magnifico,' though by no means an ambitious one in his own day, is that which still expresses him best to posterity. 'In short,' says Guicciardini, most impartial of historians, 'we must needs conclude that under him the city was not free, but that it would have been impossible to have found a better or more agreeable tyrant; for his natural goodness of disposition produced innumerable benefits, while the fact of his tyranny caused also certain evils, though tempered and limited by the bounds of necessity.' His fine instinct foresaw an enemy in the Dominican friar from Ferrara, Fra Girolamo Savonarola, who was elected Prior of San Marco in 1491, and to whose haughty Puritanism Lorenzo's fine-spun web of policy was contemptible and abhorrent; and it was probably in order to ask the Prior's friendship for his young son Piero that Lorenzo summoned him to his death-bed on that memorable April afternoon in 1492. But the famous story of the three demands, culminating in the stern condition, 'Restore liberty to Florence,' as the price of absolution, crumbles at the touch of historic inquiry; the interview was no confession and ended with no touch of melodrama; its significance lay in the mere contact, at such an hour, between two spirits so great and so opposed as these.[1]

Meanwhile across the Apennines, a statesman whom posterity was to decry as much as it admired Lorenzo, Ludovico il Moro, was seeking to strengthen his precarious hold upon the Duchy of Milan. A man of immense ability, of soaring ambition, and of a subtle understanding, he would be remembered only as a benefactor to the duchy if his lot had been cast in less troublous times, and if above all his title to the ducal throne had been secure. But he could not for an instant forget the nephew whom he had kidnapped from his mother's care a few years after the murder of Duke Galeazzo, and who was now growing up, feeble in mind and body, to be the unwilling centre of opposition to his uncle's usurpation. The youth had been betrothed as a child to Isabella, daughter of Alfonso of Calabria, and when he reached the age of twenty Ludovico had no pretext for prohibiting the marriage [1489]; but the Neapolitan princess introduced a new and dangerous element of discontent into the ducal household. As rightful duchess

[1] See Creighton, *Hist. of the Papacy*, vol. iv., app. 7.

she could not endure the tutelage in which her husband, Gian Galeazzo, was still kept, and when in 1491 Ludovico took to wife the brilliant daughter of the Duke of Ferrara, Beatrice d'Este, the jealousy between the two duchesses[1] greatly embittered the situation. Isabella complained bitterly to her father and grandfather of the slights and humiliations to which she was exposed, and though King Ferrante, old in years and caution, refused to stir in her behalf, the more headstrong Alfonso spoke openly of his hatred for the Moro, and of his longing to reinstate his daughter and her husband in their rights. Should Ferrante die, Ludovico knew that Alfonso would strain every nerve to raise a coalition against him, and the knowledge spurred him to seek an alliance which should outweigh and overawe his Italian neighbours.

The interest of the Court of France in Italian affairs had been exceedingly close throughout the reign of Louis XI., who was so well versed in the intrigues of the Peninsula that in 1463 the Milanese ambassador wrote to his master: 'It seems as though this King had been brought up in Italy, so much does he know of our affairs.' Cosimo de' Medici, in whom Louis recognized a kindred spirit, negotiated an alliance between Francesco Sforza and the King [1463], by which the investiture of Genoa was bestowed by Louis on the Duke of Milan, after the brief submission of that city to John of Anjou[2] in 1458. Francesco's son now sought the same means of attaching the King of France, and since the vision of the Neapolitan adventure was already hovering before the eyes of Charles VIII., both parties saw their advantage in an alliance by which the investiture of Genoa was bestowed on the young Duke, and Ludovico obtained by name the friendship of the King of France. Thus the Moro hoped to have secured his position against the House of Aragon, but he was not guilty, as was long thought on the authority of Philippe de Commines, of suggesting to the French King the idea of the conquest of Naples.[3] Indeed he stood too much in dread of the claims of Orleans upon Milan to wish to see a French army in the Lombard Plain, and it was only when events had marched beyond his control that he decided to embrace the French cause for a while.

[1] Ludovico bore the title of *Duke of Bari* conferred on him by Ferrante in 1479.

[2] See p. 176.

[3] The embassy of March, 1492, which Commines represents as conveying Ludovico's invitation to the King, was really only concerned with the insertion of Ludovico's name in the treaty. Delaborde, *Expéd. de Charles VIII. en Italie*, pp. 238—9.

And in truth there was no need for any suggestion on the part of Italian politicians in order to inflame the young King's mind with this well-worn proposal. Had not the Angevin's claim to Naples had been asserted in arms from French seaports five several times during the preceding century—twice against the legitimate representatives of the Angevin line, Charles III. and his son Ladislaus,[1] and three times against the Aragonese usurpers?[2] King Charles was now the heir of the House of Anjou; he had by a fortunate marriage added the great fief of Brittany to the French crown, by a fortunate bequest obtained Provence and Anjou, and by a fortunate reconciliation won over the Duke of Orleans from his hereditary opposition to the crown. Why should he not use these consolidated forces in the pursuit of a gallant enterprise? His court was moreover beset by Neapolitan exiles, clamouring for vengeance on King Ferrante; the tardy consent of Ludovico in the autumn of 1493 was only decisive as opening the road, not as determining the direction of the King's ambition. By March, 1494, Charles was at Lyons, superintending the assembly of his host, and early in September he crossed the Mont Genèvre and descended into Piedmont.

Meanwhile in the Peninsula all was confusion and alarm. The death of Innocent VIII., in August, 1492, had opened the way for Cardinal Rodrigo Borgia, who ascended the Chair of St. Peter as Alexander VI. At first, having owed his election to Cardinal Sforza,[3] Ludovico's brother, he leaned towards Milan and quarrelled with Ferrante, but when at last the old King of Naples died in January, 1494, full of forebodings for the future, Alexander decided to recognize Alfonso, and sent his Legate to bestow the investiture of Naples upon him. A marriage was even arranged between Alexander's son, Jofré Borgia, and an illegitimate daughter of Alfonso. But at the same time he issued a Bull authorizing Charles VIII. to come to Rome *on his way to the East*, and thus endeavoured to stand well with either party. In Florence, Piero de' Medici, Lorenzo's son, was professing defiance of the French and staunch

---

[1] In 1382—84 and in 1390—99 respectively : see pp. 146 and 159.

[2] Louis III. of Anjou was in Naples from 1420 to 1434, first disputing the succession of Alfonso of Aragon and then reigning for ten years as Duke of Calabria (under Joanna II., see p. 163) ; his brother René, adopted heir of Joanna, fought against Alfonso of Aragon from 1438—42 (see p. 168) ; and finally René's son John of Calabria disputed the kingdom with Ferrante from 1459—63 (see p. 176).

[3] He seems to have promised Sforza his palace with all its contents and the office of vice-chancellor. All the other cardinals except five appear to have been bribed. Greg., vol, vii., Pt. I, p. 322.

adherence to Alfonso's cause, but a strong party among the Seventy were prepared to welcome the invaders as the means of a return to liberty. And above all, the preaching and prophecies of Savonarola, who continually announced an approaching doom which should purge the sins of Italy, stirred men's minds and cast a profound disquiet over the scene.

Ludovico and his wife hastened to meet the French army at Asti, and escorted the King in gorgeous progress to Pavia, where an embarrassing interview took place between Charles and the Duchess Isabella—'still a young and fair lady,' according to Commines—who besought him to have pity on her distress and not to proceed to the dethronement of her father. But Ludovico hurried the King off to Piacenza, where news reached them that the poor young Duke of Milan had breathed his last—whether from poison or from his own evil habits of life, remains a mystery to this day. At any rate, advising the French to march by the Lunigiana Pass into Tuscany, Ludovico hastened back to Milan, and, disregarding Gian Galeazzo's boy, had himself proclaimed Duke with all solemnity. He had prepared the way for this by obtaining the Imperial investiture of the duchy the year before from Maximilian, in exchange for the hand of Bianca Sforza and four hundred thousand ducats.

Three fortresses, garrisoned by the troops of Piero de' Medici, blocked the road of the French into Tuscany—Sarzana, Sarzanello, and Pietrasanta. The army had already been held up for three days before the smallest of these, Sarzanello, when there appeared among them the panic-striken figure of Piero de' Medici, who had left Florence without any authorization from the Priors, in order to throw himself in abject surrender at the feet of Charles VIII. He not only gave up the three fortresses then and there, but also undertook to hand over Pisa and Leghorn to the French for as long as the war should last. A responsible embassy, following in his footsteps, was aghast to find what he had done. Piero returned to Florence as precipitately as he had come, only to find that the news of his treachery had preceded him, and that, as Gino Capponi said, 'the time had come to have done with this baby government.' With the mob at his heels he rode out of Florence, a proclaimed rebel, and did not rest until he had gained the shelter of the Venetian lagoons. Another embassy, headed this time by Girolamo Savonarola, was sent to treat with the King, and found him at Pisa, where the people had risen against the hated Florentine garrison at his entry and treated him as their deliverer. Savonarola solemnly welcomed Charles as the instrument of God's purifying vengeance, but warned him to deal gently with the city of Florence, which was ready to receive him in honour and friendship. So the King passed on, with his lances, his artillery, and his Swiss pikemen, cherishing thoughts of the ransom he would wring from these fat burghers, and on the 17th of November rode into Florence, lance in rest. Lodged in the Medici Palace—which he and his followers stripped of its treasures with shameless effrontery —he haggled with the Signoria, and it was only when Gino Capponi lost patience with his demands and uttered the famous threat, 'Then you can blow your trumpets, and we will sound our bells!' that he reduced his terms. For a sum of 120,000 ducats, to be paid in three instalments, Charles consented to go on his way; the recall of the Medici, which he would have liked to compass, was refused point-blank, and Pisa and the other fortresses were to be restored as soon as he had conquered Naples.

Unopposed, the French army moved on towards Rome, where Alexander VI. awaited it with unconcealed dismay. Cardinal della Rovere, his bitterest enemy, was always at the King's side, urging him to depose the Pope for his simoniacal election, and Savonarola had loudly exhorted him to purge the Augean stables of Rome. Alexander was deeply committed to the cause of Alfonso, yet he dared not fly lest he should be deposed in his absence, and he dared not oppose the French by force of arms. Charles therefore entered Rome with all his force on December 31, and took up his abode in the Palazzo Venezia; but a fortnight's negotiations left Alexander master of the field, for he received from Charles a declaration of the obedience of France, and refused to bestow on him the investiture of Naples. The French marched out of Rome on January 25, 1495, eager to consummate the last act of their glorious enterprise; for the news had just reached them that King Alfonso had abdicated his throne in favour of his son Ferrantino, and had withdrawn to a Sicilian monastery. But the young King, though guiltless of his father's crimes, had no hold on his people's loyalty, and the news of a single massacre perpetrated by the French on their way south was sufficient to turn to flight the Neapolitan army gathered at the pass of San Germano. Capua was surrendered by Alfonso's Milanese general, Trivulzio, who passed into the French service. On February 20 Ferrante II. fled to Ischia, and the next day Charles entered his new capital amid the wild acclamations of the inhabitants.

But as soon as the news reached Milan, Ludovico bestirred himself to conclude a league with Venice, the Pope, the King of Spain and

SIXTUS IV

Pietro and Girolamo Riario, Giuliano and Giovanni della
Rovere, and Platina the librarian. Picture by Melozzo da
Forlì in the Vatican

Maximilian the Emperor-elect, to cut off the retreat of the French. Louis of Orleans had been left behind with French troops at Asti, and had assumed the title of Duke of Milan, which finally determined Ludovico's breach with his former friends. The league was secretly signed in the Doge's bedchamber at Venice on March 31. Ludovico sent troops to besiege Orleans in Asti, and the news of the tempest that was gathering in his rear alarmed King Charles and induced him to bid farewell to the delights of Naples, where he and his soldiers were revelling in debauchery of every kind. On May 20 he marched out of the town, leaving a garrison of Swiss mercenaries to hold the fortresses in his name. On June 13 Louis of Orleans surprised and occupied Novara, and a few days later Charles rode into Pisa, not choosing this time to risk his diminished force within sound of the bells of Florence. But the Pisans overwhelmed him with entreaties not to hand them back to their detested masters, the Florentines, and Charles, obliged to break faith with either Florence or Pisa, chose the easier course, left his own garrisons in the Pisan fortresses and prepared to recross the Apennines by the way that he had come.

But at the northern outlet of the pass the army of the league, under Francesco Gonzaga, Marquis of Mantua, was drawn up to block the passage of the French. The battle of Fornovo, which took place on the 6th of July, is one of the great disappointments of Italian history, for although Gonzaga had twice the numbers of his opponents he failed to use his reserves, and the French escaped along the skirts of the Apennines and reached Asti in safety. No fairer chance could have occurred of crushing the 'barbarians,' but as it was Charles was enabled to negotiate an advantageous treaty with Ludovico, by which the Duke undertook to assist the French in any future attempt to reconquer Naples, while Novara was restored, and Charles renounced the claims of Orleans upon Milan. Ferrante II. was already back in Naples, where the people welcomed him as enthusiastically as they had cheered King Charles, and Ludovico might congratulate himself that he had restored the *status quo*. But as the French army wended its way back across the Alps, its captains cherished the fatal knowledge of Italy's wealth and weakness, and Louis Duke of Orleans exulted in the thought that he had been no party to the renunciation of the Duchy of Milan.

N

CHAPTER XVII

From the Retreat of Charles VIII
to the Spanish Conquest of Naples

A YEAR after the retreat of Charles VIII., the Venetian ambassador indulged in a characteristic outburst against Ludovico il Moro, when writing to his master the Doge:—'His pride and arrogance are beyond description! He boasts that Pope Alexander is his chaplain, the Emperor Maximilian his *condottiere*, the Signory of Venice his treasurers, and the King of France his courier, to come and go as he pleases!' The irritation of the Venetian was due to the ill-success of a great expedition to the support of Pisa against Florence, which Ludovico and the Venetians had planned with the help of Maximilian; the Emperor had indeed been the Duke's *condottiere* for the occasion, and had earned his pay very ill, for he had retired in disgust before the inclemency of the weather, saying that he could not fight against God and man together. The Venetians, who had spent heavily on the fleet that supported him, cursed Ludovico and his Imperial tool, and the ill will of these allies, which contributed so much to the final tragedy of Il Moro, dates from this expedition.

But to all external appearance, the Italian League which had been formed by Ludovico to expel Charles VIII, still subsisted, and it included every power in the Peninsula, except Ferrara and Florence. Florence stood isolated from the rest because, under the inspiration of Savonarola, she had returned to the principles of republican government, and she feared that any compact with the League would inevitably mean the recall of Piero de' Medici, with his Orsini cousins and horsemen. 'The Florentines refuse to enter the League,' said Savonarola to the Milanese ambassador, 'for fear lest the Duke [Ludovico], together with the other powers, should aim at destroying the popular government and playing the despot in Florence.' So they refused the fair offers of Pope Alexander to procure them the submission of Pisa if only they would show themselves to be 'good Italians' by joining the League, and they clung instead to their prophet and to the French alliance, and strove to crush Pisa by their own exertions. But this proved to be a task beyond their strength, and the Pisan War dragged on long after the voice of Savonarola had been choked in death.

The tragedy of the great friar, so often told in many different tongues, is for many reasons the most astonishing episode in all this crowded epoch of Italian life. Foreign as his nature was to some characteristics of the people among whom he lived, terrible as his influence would have been, had it continued longer, in restricting the creative genius of the Florentines, he yet succeeded in rearing for a time something more remarkable than all the artistic 'vanities' that he destroyed—a Puritan Florence, and so in revealing for a moment a new and most strange facet in the ever-shifting life of Iitaly. Savonarola was of the stuff that imperiously calls for martyrdom, and the forces against which he was thrown—the unscrupulous Borgia in Rome, the time-serving magistrates of Florence, and the mob with its ill-varnished instincts of savagery —all conspired to give him what he asked. But for four wonderful years he held the people of Florence in the hollow of his hand, and by his sermons from the Duomo pulpit inspired both their private lives and their public conduct. A fundamental reorganization of the state, he knew, was needed after the long period of Medicean corruption, and to Savonarola was due the creation of the *Great Council*, or assembly of all Florentine citizens over the age of twenty-nine who had either held office themselves or were the sons or descendants of office-holders. This curious limitation automatically reduced the number of citizens eligible for election to between three and four thousand, but Florence was completely satisfied with the new institution, and it became for the next eighteen years the ultimate authority in the state. The Medicean Council of Seventy disappeared, but the older Committee of Eight for the maintenance of public order was preserved, while the Priors and Gonfalonier still formed the supreme executive with the title of 'Magnificent Signory.' There was one institution of the past, however, against which Savonarola resolutely set his face, and that was the *Parlamento*, or tumultuous assembly of the mob on the Piazza, which had always been used by the Medici as an instrument of tyranny. It was formally abolished by a law of August, 1495, and Savonarola denounced the most terrible penalties against whoso should go about to ring the great bell of the Palazzo for the assembling of the populace.

Towards that populace, however, his heart yearned, and he alternately terrified it with prophecies of wrath to come—of 'the armies of the foreign nations that shall trample upon the great men of Italy'—and melted it with appeals for a nobler life. For

two or three years an extraordinary change came over the manners and morals of the Florentines, and the licentious carnivals of
Lorenzo's days were replaced by the solemn 'burning of the vanities' which showed that the women and children no less than the
men were held fast by the friar's spell. A scene from the diary of
the good apothecary Luca Landucci is typical of the change of
atmosphere in Florence; he is speaking of the Carnival of February,
1496:—

And as it pleased the divine grace, such a change had come over us
that instead of playing their usual pranks, the children had been
asking for alms for many days before, and instead of daggers, on
all sides you could see crucifixes in their pure and holy hands.
And about vesper-time they collected in bands in the four quarters
of Florence, and each quarter had its banner. The first was a crucifix, the second an Our Lady, and so with the others; and they came
with the trumpeters and fifers, the mace-bearers and guards of the
Palace, singing lauds and crying out 'Long live Christ and the
Virgin Mary our Queen!' each with a branch of olive in his hand.
And truly the good and sober men amongst us were weeping tears
of joy and saying: 'Truly this change is the work of God. These
are the boys that will enjoy the good things that he [the Friar]
has promised us.' And it seemed as though we were looking on
that crowd in Jerusalem that walked before and after Christ on
Palm Sunday, crying, 'Blessed is he that cometh in the name of the
Lord' . . . .And I have written these things because they are true;
and I saw it myself, and felt the sweetness of it, and some of my
own children were among those blessed and holy bands.

But the bold words of the friar in fulminating against the corruption of the times could not fail to draw down upon him the hatred
of those who sat in high places. Nor was Florence herself united
in support of her prophet. He was far too democratic for the
powerful group of oligarchs who traced their descent from the
Albizzi and the Parte Guelfa, and this party became so bitterly
opposed to him that it was nicknamed the Arrabbiati, or fanatics.
Thus when in May, 1497, a Signory of Arrabbiati came into power,
the Pope used the opportunity to launch an excommunication
against the friar. The Arrabbiati were soon replaced by Savonarolists,[1] but an excommunication once launched was not easily
recalled, and the friar passed the remainder of the year [1497] in
silence. But his heart burned within him. More and more scandalous reports came from Rome of the proceedings of the Borgia
family—of the divorce of Lucrezia from her first husband, of the

[1] The friar's party were called by their opponents Piagnoni, or Snivellers.

murder of the Duke of Gandia, with the dark rumours of his brother's complicity, of the villainous life led by Alexander himself —and at length he resolved to stand forth and to defy the excommunication. On February 11, 1498, he preached once more in the Duomo. In March he expressed his eager desire for a General Council to depose the Pope. The magistrates supported him, but when imperative orders came from Alexander that he should be silenced and sent to Rome they wavered, and caught eagerly at a strange chance of ending the strife which occurred in the last days of March. A Franciscan friar challenged the Savonarolists to go with him through the ordeal of fire to prove whether their master's mission were from God or no. The prophet's disciple, Domenico da Pescia, eagerly took up the gage, and on the 7th of April all Florence crowded to the Piazza to witness this degrading survival from the institutions of the past. But the miserable failure of the spectacle—the long delays, the quibblings of the friars, and finally the drenching thunder-shower that put an end to the proceedings —filled the mob with fury. A violent reaction set in against the so-called prophet, and the next day the mob sacked Savonarola's convent of San Marco and could hardly be prevented from tearing him to pieces as he was conveyed under guard to the Palazzo Pubblico.

His trial for heresy had now become a political necessity; his condemnation a foregone conclusion. The mob had deserted him; Alexander hounded on his judges in briefs from the Vatican. When the Pope complained of delay, the Signory excused themselves by alleging the prisoner's obstinacy: 'Even by long and assiduous examination,' they wrote, 'continued for many days and with the aid of torture, we could barely extort anything from him.' But at length the torture of rope and pulley, combined with the profound disillusionment of failure, induced the friar to set his hand to a 'confession' in which he disclaimed the gift of prophecy and admitted motives of vain-glory in all that he had done for Florence. Largely falsified and garbled, this document was read out before the Great Council on April 19, and caused astonishment and grief to many good Savonarolists among those present. 'My soul was in pain,' writes Landucci once more, 'to see so fair an edifice tumble to earth, because it all rested on the sorry foundation of a lie.' So when a month later two Papal commissioners arrived in Florence to give solemnity to the sentence of death, when the Bargello prison rang once more with the shrieks of tortured men, there was no popular tumult; the friar's disciples awaited with bowed heads the final scene. On May 23, with all the pomp and circumstance of ecclesiastical ceremony, Savonarola and his two faithful followers were led forth to a gallows erected in the centre of the Piazza, and there hanged by the neck while a fire was kindled below to consume their bodies. Not even at the last moment, on that wooden platform, did the prophet lift up his voice to take back his confession.

But, although everything for which Savonarola had striven seemed to lie in ruins about him, though his followers crept back to their homes in dejection deep as that of the Galilæans of old, the leaven of his life and martyrdom worked on in Florence and in Italy. It helped to inspire the glorious resistance of Florence to the Imperial armies a generation later, when the rest of Italy lay crushed under the foreigner's dominion; it penetrated even beyond the Alps, and caused Luther to claim the great friar as the precursor of the Reformation. And in the fulness of time, when the heart of Italy stirred again after the sleep of centuries, it was sometimes to Savonarola that the young men of the Risorgimento turned with faith akin to adoration. His name was ever on their lips; his memory sustained them in defeat and death; exalted them in victory. So, in ways beyond his vision as he stood dumbly surveying that sea of upturned, cruel faces, did he indeed play his small part in bringing deliverance to Italy.

While the three friars were still enduring torture in the Bargello prison, the Pope who had made it his chief complaint against Florence that she would not join the Italian League, was meditating a greater treachery against it than any she could have devised. Charles VIII. of France had died suddenly on April 7, leaving no son, and the crown passed to that very Louis, Duke of Orleans, who had already asserted his claim to Milan during Charles's expedition. At his accession he plainly announced his intentions by styling himself both King of Naples and Duke of Milan. But with Charles's death the fear in which Alexander stood of a French invasion passed away, for while Charles had been making preparations for a Council, and so given point to Savonarola's sermons, Louis stood in need of the Pope's aid, and might therefore be relied on for a substantial *quid pro quo*. He wished to divorce his wife Jeanne, daughter of Louis XI., and to marry the young widow left by Charles, who would bring him Brittany as her dowry. At the same time Alexander was anxious to win a royal bride for his son Cæsar, who had begun life as a cardinal, but who would obviously be better employed as a temporal prince now that death had so mysteriously removed his elder brother. A bargain was therefore arranged between Pope and King, whereby in return for the annulment of his marriage, Louis bestowed the hand of his cousin Charlotte d'Albret upon Cæsar Borgia, together with the Duchy of Valence in Dauphiné, and agreed moreover to support him with French troops in his projected conquest of Romagna, as soon as he himself should become master of the Duchy of Milan.

Meanwhile the Venetians were also approaching the new King with an offer for the partition of the Milanese, and in April, 1499, a treaty was agreed upon by which the republic was to have Cremona and all territory east of the Adda in return for military aid. Ludovico stood without an ally in Italy, for Florence remained neutral, and the King of Naples, though willing enough, could not spare a man from the defence of his own kingdom. In despair he appealed to Maximilian to send him a body of Germans, and invited the Turks to attack Venice in Friuli.

But the Germans did not appear, and worse than that, Ludovico could no longer rely on his own subjects. Since the invasion of Charles his exactions had grown heavier, and Milan no longer enjoyed the same return for its taxes as in the days of the young Duchess Beatrice, who had died in childbirth early in 1497. Leonardo da Vinci, indeed, was still working for the Duke, still modelling the great equestrian statue of Francesco Sforza which was to serve as a target for French archers in the evil days to come, but joy had fled with the Duchess Beatrice, and a dumb feeling grew that Il Moro's luck had turned. So when Alessandria surrendered to the French without a blow [August 29, 1499], and when Ludovico's brother-in-law Gonzaga refused to fight the Venetians, Milan turned against the Duke; his chief tax-collector was murdered in the streets, and he himself decided to abandon it to the enemy. Leaving the Castello amply garrisoned and provisioned, he rode northwards with his remaining treasure to seek his ally Maximilian and to demand from him the promised succours. Behind him the French general, Gian Giacomo Trivulzio, made his victorious entry into Milan on September 6, and a few days later the astounding news was heard that the commandant of the Castello, whom Ludovico had implicitly trusted, had surrendered the impregnable fortress which dominated the city. The priceless treasures which it still contained—pictures, gems, tapestries and manuscripts— were shamelessly divided between himself and Trivulzio.

Thus the way was cleared for King Louis, who entered his new possession on October 6 amid a crowd of parasitic princes, conspicuous among them Cæsar Borgia. But Il Moro was not done with yet. By the month of January [1500] the good will of Maximilian and his own gold had procured him a force of some ten thousand Swiss and Germans, while the old hatred of the French —the same in Lombardy as of old at Palermo—smouldered among his subjects. The result was that by a bold dash he recovered Como, Milan, Pavia, Parma, and some other towns. But the French had only been surprised, not crushed, and as soon as reinforcements arrived they compelled him to take refuge in Novara and besieged him there. Betrayed by the Swiss, who refused to fight against their comrades in the French army, he was obliged to surrender, though the mutineers offered to protect his person by disguising him as one of themselves. But as they marched out, on April 10, a Swiss captain revealed him to the French with the words '*È lo quello,*' and he was instantly arrested.[1] Eight years of captivity in King Louis's fortresses, ending with his death in the dungeon of Loches, repaid the Moro for his too ready welcome of King Charles.

Meanwhile the alliance between King Louis and the Pope had borne fruit in the first efforts of Cæsar Borgia towards the reduction of that constant centre of Papal ambitions, the district of Romagna. At the time of which we are speaking, the cities of Romagna and of the mountainous district to the south of it as far as Perugia and Spoleto, though nominally under the suzerainty of the Church, were in the hands of independent tyrants who styled themselves Papal Vicars, and owed, but never paid, an annual tribute to the Pope. Occasionally some enterprising Pontiff or Papal Legate—a Nicholas III., an Albornoz or a Sixtus IV.—had endeavoured to assert a real authority in these lands of the ancient Exarchate, Marches and Pentapolis, but it was reserved for the colossal egotism of Cæsar Borgia to break the power of the despots to some purpose, and to lay the foundations of the later States of the Church. Cæsar himself was but a transitory phenomenon, for his power crumbled at the death of Alexander, but he led the way where a mightier than he could follow, and Julius II. completed what he had left undone. At this point, however, Cæsar was unable to go beyond Imola and Forlì, the towns which Sixtus IV. had acquired for his nephew Riario, for the brief return of Ludovico necessitated the recall of his French troops. Cæsar returned to Rome early in 1500, and applied himself to collecting the supplies of gold that flowed plentifully into Alexander's coffers during the year of Jubilee.

[1] This Switzer, whose name was Turman, was afterwards executed for his treachery by the cantonal authorities.

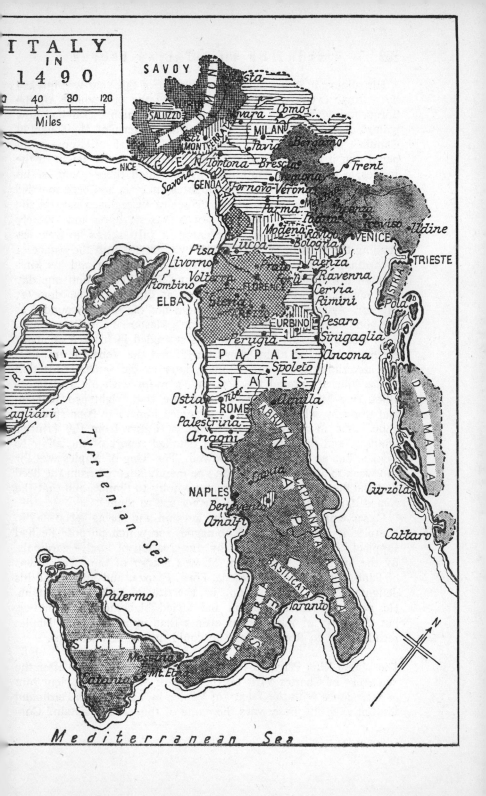

His sojourn in Rome during the summer of this year was marked by a tragic event which aptly illustrates the proceedings of the Borgia family, and the terrible ascendancy which Cæsar had now gained over his father, the Pope. The mystery of the Duke of Gandia's murder had never been solved, though all Rome whispered that it had been Cæsar's deed; but now, at the height of the Jubilee, a crime was committed as to which there could be no manner of doubt. Alexander's daughter Lucrezia had been married *en secondes noces* to the young Prince of Bisceglia, a natural son of Alfonso of Naples, and this youth was set upon and severely wounded by assassins on the evening of July 15, as he was descending the steps of St. Peter's. He was carried into the palace of a cardinal, hard by, and there tended by Lucrezia and his kinswoman the Princess of Squillace, but Cæsar visited him one day and remarked: 'What was not done at dinner can be done at supper!' Accordingly, 'since he would not die of his wounds,' as the good German Burchard, the Pope's Master of the Ceremonies, drily remarks in his Diary, 'he was strangled in his bed at about eleven o'clock last night [August 18]'; and the Venetian ambassador, describing the event a month later to the Senate, adds that Cæsar himself entered the sick man's room with his assassin-in-chief, one Michelotto, drove away the two frightened women, and stood by while Michelotto strangled him. The Pope spread it about that an arrow had been shot at Cæsar from the Prince's window, and promised to send a detailed report of the affair to Venice; but no report ever followed. The King of Naples was far too weak to avenge his kinsman ; he merely augured from the deed that the Borgia had sold themselves wholly to France, and that the Neapolitan alliance was of no further use to them.

Cæsar employed the following autumn and spring [1500—1] in completing his conquest of Romagna, for which purpose he had supplied himself with money by the creation of twelve cardinals. By the month of April, 1501, he was master of the seven towns of Fano, Pesaro, Rimini, Cesena, Forlì, Faenza, and Imola, and his delighted father bestowed on him the title of Duke of Romagna. He next threatened Bologna and levied blackmail on Florence, but the news of momentous events that impended over Naples recalled him to Rome before he could mature his schemes.

The young King Ferrante II. had recovered his kingdom after the departure of Charles VIII. by the help of Spanish arms, lent him in accordance with the Treaty of Venice by his kinsman Ferdinand the Catholic. In these wars the name of the 'Great Captain,' Gonsalvo de Cordova, first became famous on Italian soil. But Ferrante had died soon after the expulsion of the last French garrisons, and was now succeeded by his uncle Federigo, a man whose kindly nature and genuine care for the welfare of his kingdom marked him out as a fitting sacrifice for the sins of his dynasty. He knew that he stood in imminent danger from the French, but he hoped for the support of Spain, although the fact that he himself represented the bastard branch of the House of Aragon, while Ferdinand represented the legitimate, had already made him uneasy. In his distress he offered to pay King Louis an annual tribute and to surrender certain fortified towns, and even applied to the Turkish Sultan for help against an invasion which might develop into a crusade. But he did not know that as early as November, 1500, Louis XII. and Ferdinand the Catholic had signed a secret compact for the partition of Naples—the first of those dynastic partition-treaties which for the next three hundred years were to settle and provoke the wars of Europe. The bargain was not published until June, 1501, when the French army had already reached Rome, and Alexander gladly agreed to the spoliation of his neighbour, foreseeing that it would open the way for the spoliation of Federigo's allies, the Colonna. Cæsar Borgia joined the French army on its southward march, and assisted at the horrible sack of Capua, which so appalled the gentle King Federigo that he abandoned his capital and withdrew to Ischia, unwilling to provoke the barbarians to further butcheries. Naples welcomed the French with its usual demonstrations, while Federigo threw himself on Louis's generosity and received from him that very Duchy of Anjou which had so often sent forth a rival to the house of Aragon. In the meantime Gonsalvo de Cordova had overrun Calabria and Apulia, the portions assigned to Spain in the partition treaty, and by capturing Federigo's son at Taranto had completed the conquest of the kingdom. It now only remained for the thieves to fall out amongst themselves.

Alexander also had drawn his expected profit from the ruin of the Neapolitan monarchy. The great House of Colonna, which had long been a thorn in the Pope's side, took the part of the luckless Federigo, and was drawn down in his fall. Four Bulls issued by the Pope in quick succession, on August 20, September 1, and September 17 of this year, give the history of his dealings with the Colonna and their property; in the first he excommunicates the whole family and confiscates their estates without naming a recipient; in the second and third (both dated September 1) he legitimizes a boy of three years old named Giovanni, described in the one document as Cæsar's son and in the other as his own,[1] and in the fourth he bestows thirty-six towns and castles of the Colonna, Gaetani, and Savelli upon this child, with the title of Duke of Nepi, and twenty-eight others upon the son of Lucrezia and the murdered Duke of Bisceglia, with the title of Duke of Sermoneta. Alexander congratulated himself on having made an end of the Colonna, and then, with Cæsar's help, planned the ruin of the Orsini too.

But the overthrow of the Orsini became part of a larger scheme for rooting out the smaller tyrants of Tuscany and the Marches, in which Cæsar was engaged during the year 1502. Many of these lordlings, including several of the Orsini themselves, had taken service with the Duke as the safest way of preserving their own skins, and with an army mainly composed of these *condottieri* and their men, Cæsar set out against the Duchy of Urbino in June, 1502. Urbino was still in the hands of Guidobaldo of Monte-feltro, son of the 'good Duke' Federigo, and a prince whose brilliant court inspired the famous 'Cortegiano' of Baldassare Castiglione. On Cæsar's approach, however, he was obliged to abandon his father's hill fortress and to flee to Manua, and Cæsar Borgia took possession of the palace and the wonderful library collected with so much loving care by Duke Federigo. Thence he set forth to visit King Louis XII., who had just arrived at Asti, summoned by the perilous condition of his affairs in Naples, and won over the King to support his schemes in return for a promise of assistance against Spain. But in the meantime his *condottieri* had decided to turn against him, and at a meeting at Castel Mugione on Lake Trasimene they formed a league to destroy the Duke. Urbino shook off his yoke and welcomed Guidobaldo once more, and Cæsar, who had reached Imola, was only saved by the timely arrival of 450 French lances. But this was sufficient to stem the tide and to sow fear and mutual distrust among the *condottieri*. They began to treat with their inscrutable enemy, whose dark and taciturn nature, whose habit of going masked and of muttering in Spanish with his father, struck terror into his *entourage*. A hollow reconciliation was effected, but Cæsar was watching his oppor-tunity, and under the eye of Niccolò Machiavelli, who was sent

[1] See Gregorovius, *Lucrezia Borgia*, and Pastor, *Histoire des Papes* (French edition), vol. vi., p. 98, note, for the complex motives that actuated Alexander in issuing these two Bulls. They serve amongst other things as part of the evidence on which the theory of Alexander's incest with Lucrezia rests, for they were kept in Lucrezia's Chancery at Modena, and it is known from other sources that she gave birth to an illegitimate son whose age would coincide with this Giovanni's.

as envoy from Florence to observe his proceedings, a singular drama was enacted. The *condottieri* were all gathered round Sinigaglia, which Cæsar had ordered them to besiege, and when news arrived that they had entered the town he marched swiftly along the coast to join them, and having taken measures to separate them from their troops invited them all to accompany him into his house. Three of the Orsini, a Vitelli, and a certain Oliverotto of Fermo fell blindly into the snare; the two latter were strangled that same night [December 31, 1502], while the Orsini were kept in custody until news should come from Rome as to the Pope's movements. Soon it was heard that Alexander had arrested the Cardinal Orsini and thrown him into Sant' Angelo, whereupon Cæsar coolly ordered two of his own victims to be strangled. The Cardinal died in his dungeon a month later, and his palace was immediately ransacked and all his goods seized by the Pope. This was the usual proceeding on the death of any cardinal; benefices were heaped upon him during his lifetime in order that the Pope might reap the harvest at his death. Or, as Giustiniani, the Venetian ambassador, put it: 'Our Lord generally fattens them up before feasting on them.'

A campaign against the Orsini castles was carried on during the month of February, but the heads of the house were under the protection of France, so that Cæsar would not drive them to extremities. He preferred to conclude a truce with them in April. But the influence of France was in reality already on the wane, and as the summer advanced the Borgia were perplexed as to how best to trim their sails between France and Spain. The expected rupture between the two powers in Naples had occurred as early as July, 1502, over possession of the province of Capitanata, and Gonsalvo de Cordova, after being cooped up on the Adriatic coast throughout the winter by a superior force of French, had now emerged with reinforcements, beaten the French in a great battle at Cerignola [April 28, 1503], and entered Naples on May 14. Alexander negotiated with both sides at once, offering to help France if Louis would cede the Kingdom of Naples to Cæsar in exchange for Romagna, and Spain if Cæsar could thereby be helped to the conquest of Tuscany. Meanwhile he created nine new cardinals for a gross sum of 120,000 ducats, and also eighty new venal offices at a price of 760 ducats apiece. On August 1 his nephew Cardinal Giovanni Borgia died suddenly, leaving property to the value of a hundred thousand ducats, and everyone assumed, wrote the Venetian ambassador, 'that he too had been sent the way that all the other well-fattened ones had gone.' But the sands of Alexander himself were running low. Rome became exceedingly hot and unhealthy; on August 13 both the Pope and Cæsar were taken ill with fever, and on the 18th the Pope was dead. Everything was thrown into the wildest confusion. Cæsar from his sick bed was able to secure the bulk of his father's treasure, but could not control the Papal election. 'He told me,' wrote Machiavelli afterwards in *The Prince*, 'that he had thought over everything that might occur at his father's death, and provided against every contingency except that of being himself at the point of death when the event occurred.' The result was that the French, Spanish, and Italian parties among the cardinals compromised on the election of Francesco Piccolomini, nephew of Pius II., who took the name of Pius III. But the inoffensive old man lived only for two months, and at his death Cæsar was obliged to make the best bargain that he could with his great enemy, Giuliano della Rovere, whose election became ever more likely. In return for Cæsar's influence with the Spanish cardinals, della Rovere promised to restore him to his Duchy of Romagna and even to appoint him Gonfalonier of the Church. On October 31, 1503, Julius II. was elected Pope.

The course of Cæsar Borgia was now run, for the new Pope had no intention of fulfilling his pre-election pledges. Italy ceased to take interest in Cæsar, and was absorbed instead in watching the death-struggle between France and Spain in the marshes besides the river Garigliano. For the King of France had concentrated all his forces in a determined attempt to relieve the fortress of Gaëta, into which the remnants of his army had thrown themselves after the defeat of Cerignola. A gallant army comprising all the best chivalry of France marched southwards to the relief of their comrades during August and September [1503], and Gonsalvo de Cordova, with an inferior force of Spaniards, chose the line of the Garigliano at which to oppose their march. Repulsed in two attempts to cross the river, the French distributed themselves in various villages around the ancient marshes of Minturnæ, while the Spaniards on the southern side endured for seven weeks the hardships of an entrenched camp exposed to all the fury of an unusually wet and stormy autumn. At length the arrival of reinforcements from Rome encouraged Gonsalvo to take the offensive, and on the night of December 29 his army crossed the river at two points and fell upon the French. Surprised and disconcerted, they retreated upon Gaëta, and at the point known as Molo di

Gaëta the retreat became a rout.[1] Gaëta itself surrendered the next day [January 1, 1504], with all its artillery and stores, and the road to Rome was soon covered with miserable bands of disarmed fugitives, on whom the peasantry wreaked their ancient hatred of the French. The rout of the Garigliano had decided the fate of the Neapolitan Kingdom, and had fastened the yoke of Spain for long centuries to come upon the heritage of Frederick II.

[1] Three and a half centuries later, the forces of united Italy under Victor Emmanuel here brought the last independent King of Naples to bay.

CHAPTER XVIII

The Pontificate of Julius II

JULIUS II. entered upon the Papal inheritance with the firm determination to enforce the authority of the Church in the territories which of right belonged to her. 'We wish,' he declared to the Venetian ambassador shortly after his election, 'we wish for the honour of recovering what our predecessors have wrongly alienated.'[1] In pursuit of this policy he brought ruin and deliverance by turns to the distracted states of Italy. Against Venice, on whom this native of Savona looked with the immemorial jealousy of the Ligurian, he let loose 'the armies of the foreign nations,' and when the 'barbarians' whom he had invoked for the destruction of Venice ventured to cross his wishes in Romagna, he launched against them the 'Holy League' and posed to all posterity as the Saviour of Italy. Having no son, he was obliged to rely on himself for the execution of his schemes, and the high and indomitable energy which he brought to bear on all his undertakings made him the wonder of his own age, and still casts its spell on the imagination of our own.

His first care was to secure the fortresses of Romagna which still held out for Cæsar Borgia, and while the French and Spaniards were yet watching each other along the river Garigliano an intricate drama was played out between the Pope and Cæsar, which ended at last in the surrender of all the Borgia fortresses in return for the bare grant of personal liberty to the former 'Duke of the Romagna.'[2] The duel between the two men was complicated by the presence of a third party, the Republic of Venice, bent on drawing profit from their differences, and in November, 1503, came the news that Venice had laid hands on the two cities of Faenza and Rimini, left without master on the downfall of the Duke. The Pope was furious at this encroachment, and when his

---

[1] Julius to Giustinian, in the collection of the latter's *Dispacci*, vol. ii., p. 289.

[2] Cæsar Borgia went to Naples and threw himself on the protection of the 'Great Captain,' Gonsalvo de Cordova, but King Ferdinand ordered him to be sent a prisoner to Spain. There he was incarcerated for two years, but finally escaped and took refuge with his brother-in-law the King of Navarre. He was killed while besieging an insignificant Pyrenean fortress in March, 1507.

RAPHAEL'S PORTRAIT OF POPE JULIUS II
From a painting in the Uffizi Gallery

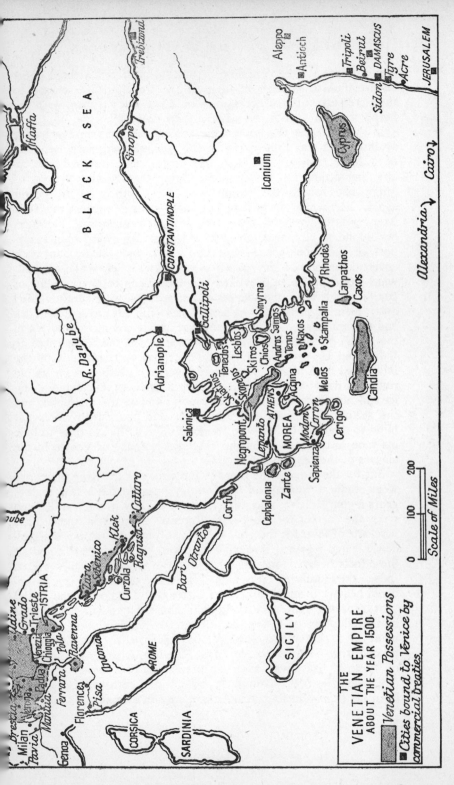

THE
VENETIAN EMPIRE
ABOUT THE YEAR 1500.

Venetian Possessions

Cities bound to Venice by
commercial treaties.

0   100   200
Scale of Miles

remonstrances to the Venetian ambassador remained without effect he declared to Machiavelli that 'if the Venetians persevered in their present course of action he would join with France, with the Emperor, with anyone, to achieve their downfall.'

In this outburst the Pope expressed an old and familiar grudge against what was thought to be the greedy, overgrown Republic of St. Mark. Her gradual expansion on the mainland, and particularly her acquisition of Cremona during the French conquest of Milan had roused the jealousy of every other Italian power against her, while her gallant but losing struggle against the Turk won her little sympathy from a short-sighted generation. Florence, her quondam ally, was embittered against her owing to her support of the rebellious Pisans; Louis XII. and Maximilian both coveted portions of her mainland territories. Yet, while the outward glory of Venice provoked her neighbours to alternate fits of cupidity and dread, the sources of her strength were surely ebbing away before the rise of two new forces—the advance of the Turk and the appearance of the Portuguese as her commercial rivals in the East. In 1498 Vasco da Gama discovered the Cape route to India, and by the year 1504 the lucrative spice-trade with the Indies had been almost completely diverted to Lisbon from its old route via Egypt to Venice. Still, with a declining exchequer, Venice did not abate one jot of her pretensions on the mainland, and the seizure of Faenza and Rimini showed that she was as yet blind to the signs of her own weakness. Julius II. had only to bide his time in order to focus the universal jealousy of Venice in the clauses of the League of Cambrai.

But for the moment neither the Emperor nor the King of France were ready to move, and the country enjoyed for a few uneasy years a comparative immunity from war. Only in the Val d' Arno were the mercenary troops of Florence engaged in their futile blockade of Pisa; for the gallant town still maintained the independence it had regained through the coming of Charles VIII., and all the efforts of the Florentines had not yet availed to subjugate it. Indeed the Florentine republic had, since Savonarola's death, floundered heavily through difficulties internal and external, and in the year 1502 the general discontent of the citizens had borne fruit in the adoption of a new constitutional expedient—the appointment of a permanent Head of the State, or, as the Florentines termed it, a 'Gonfalonier for Life.' Florence, with all her jealousy of 'tyrants,' had never, after all, been without a master since the day when, in 1434, Cosimo de' Medici had returned in triumph from his exile, and four years' experience of Savonarola's constitution, without the friar's guiding hand, had convinced the most democratic that a change was needed. The sheer inconvenience of the Republican forms—the ever-shifting *personnel* of the Signory, changing every two months and so making all responsibility impossible—made itself felt in jealousies and dissensions within and in rebuffs and humiliations without. The Republic cowered before Cæsar Borgia, failed to chastise the Pisans, and clung desperately, almost slavishly, to the French alliance. When therefore the good citizen Piero Soderini was elected by the Great Council, on September 20, 1502, to be Gonfalonier for life, the friends of Florence rejoiced, and the exiled Medici in Rome prepared themselves for a yet longer term of banishment.

Nor was Soderini's reign an unworthy episode in the history of the ancient city for which he stood. The finances were purified, Pisa was at length reconquered and more or less conciliated [1509], and a beginning made, under Machiavelli's influence, with the formation of a citizen army to replace the cowardly and faithless mercenaries who had hitherto devoured the substance of the Republic. But it was above all in the domain of art that the chief glories of these brief years were achieved, for this was the period of Michelangelo's rise to fame, of the *David* and the cartoon of the *Battle of Pisa*, the loss of which is one of the famous tragedies of art. Soderini himself was a generous patron and friend of the mighty sculptor, but he was not able to keep him permanently in Florence, for early in 1505 Pope Julius summoned him to Rome to take part in the vast schemes of building and sculpture by which he intended to commemorate his reign. Michelangelo made his stupendous design for the tomb of Julius, and then left Rome in wrath when the Pope delayed to pay for the marble he had brought from Carrara; but although the design was never carried out, and became indeed the burden and curse of Michelangelo's life, its work was already done, for according to Vasari it was made the occasion for that most momentous piece of vandalism— the destruction of the ancient Basilica of St. Peter. A new basilica was to be built, large and majestic enough to form a worthy setting for the master's colossal scheme, and in spite of the protests and pleadings of his cardinals, Julius ordered the work of demolition to begin in the summer of 1505. Bramante, the Papal architect, pushed it on with barbarous haste; columns were shattered, mosaics destroyed, the tessellated pavement dim with the footsteps of uncounted millions of pilgrims torn up and dispersed; tombs huddled into the Crypt or removed to minor churches. Rome looked on aghast as the Mother Church of Christendom was gradually reduced to a heap of ruins, but Julius never faltered. On the 18th of April, 1506, he descended by a ladder to the bottom of a deep shaft sunk to receive a pier of the new apse, and there laid the foundation stone of St. Peter's Church as we know it today. The indomitable old man was not afraid to disturb the ashes of so many of his predecessors, and his further acts were to show that he had as little fear for the living as for the dead.

He was in fact already laying his plans for the recovery of such of the Papal dominions as were not overshadowed by the Lion of St. Mark, and in the summer of 1506 he set forth, with an immense train of cardinals and ecclesiastics, to assert his authority over the 'tyrants' of Perugia and Bologna. The former city was at this time in the possession of the Baglioni family—pre-eminent even in the Italy of that day for its record of fratricidal crimes—and the head of the clan, Gian Paolo, had not only made himself master of Perugia by a process of extermination, but was also one of the most redoubted *condottieri* of his day. In Pope Julius, however, he had met his match. Baglione came to meet the Pope at Orvieto and there made his submission, but in entering Perugia Julius imprudently outstripped his escort and might have fallen an easy prey to Baglione's men. The tyrant, however, greatly to Machiavelli's astonishment, had not the courage to 'rid himself at one blow of his enemy and enrich himself with booty.' 'It was not goodness or conscience that restrained him,' continues Machiavelli, 'for he was incestuous and a parricide, but he did not dare to do a deed which would have left an eternal memory. He might have been the first to show the priests how little a man is esteemed who lives and rules as they do.'[1] But the priest in this case showed the tyrant that he was his master, and having regulated the affairs of Perugia, he passed on to the still more difficult and important conquest of Bologna. In this also fortune favoured him, for his boldness induced the Venetians to stand neutral and the French governor of Milan to send troops to his support. The tyrant of Bologna, Giovanni Bentivoglio, fled for refuge to the French camp and gave up his city to the Pope [November, 1506]. To celebrate his triumph, Julius summoned Michelangelo from Florence and ordered him to cast a colossal bronze statue of himself for the porch of San Petronio; but four years later, when the Bolognese rose against their clerical masters, the statue was hurled from its place and cast into a cannon by the Duke of Ferrara, who named it in derision 'La Giulia.'

These two successful enterprises enormously enhanced the pres-

[1] *Discorsi sulla Prima Deca di Tito Livio*, bk. i., ch. xxvii.

tige of Julius II. among the Italian powers, but here for the present he was obliged to halt. In January, 1507, King Louis XII. crossed the Alps with a powerful army to enforce his authority in Genoa, which had thrown off the French yoke a few months before, and Julius, who was well aware of the ill will borne him by the King's powerful minister, the Cardinal d'Amboise,[1] prudently retired to Rome before his advance. Louis quelled the Genoese rising with horrible barbarity, and then increased the anxieties of Julius by arranging a conference at Savona, between himself and his old enemy Ferdinand of Aragon, who was also embittered against the Pope on many grounds. Rumours soon ran through Italy that the two kings were planning a General Council for the reform of the Church, and at the same time the incalculable Maximilian, King of the Romans,[2] was holding a great Diet of the Empire at Constance to gather men and money for his projected coronation journey to Rome. Julius felt that he was beset with dangers, but he threw himself with untiring energy into the furtherance of his own peculiar counter-scheme—namely the formation of an alliance between Maximilian and Louis, sworn enemies though they were, for the spoliation of Venice. His ambassador, Carvajal, was sent to Innsbruck in the autumn of 1507, and worked to such good purpose that by February, 1508, a draft agreement had been reached between Maximilian, the French governor of Milan (Chaumont), the Spanish envoy, and the Papal Legate, by which all parties were to recover the territories 'usurped' from them by Venice. This document was sent to Bourges for the French King's ratification, and was there stolen and copied by the Venetian ambassador[3]; but Louis withheld his consent for the moment, for in the meantime Maximilian had entered Italy and attempted to force a passage through Venetia on his road to Rome. The Venetians, however, hurled him back, with the lukewarm assistance of a few French companies from Milan, and after making important conquests in Friuli concluded an advantageous truce with him in June, 1508. But the Republic's very conquests proved her ruin. At

---

[1] Georges d'Amboise, Cardinal of Rouen, had striven hard for the Tiara at the elections both of Pius III. and of Julius II., and was now thought to be intriguing for the deposition of Julius. (See Brosch, *Papst Julius II.*, p. 136.)

[2] 'King of the Romans' was the title borne by the emperors previous to their coronation in Rome, but in February, 1508, Maximilian solemnly assumed that of 'Emperor-elect' in the Church of Trent, and the new title was recognized by the Pope.

[3] See Brosch, *Papst Julius II.*, pp. 155, 338. Brosch discovered the document in the Venetian archives.

once the slumbering animosity against her broke forth anew; King Louis complained that she had neglected his interests in negotiating the truce, and now hesitated no longer when the Pope redoubled his efforts to bring him into the League. On December 10, at the little French town of Cambrai, the representatives of France and the Empire signed the fatal compact for the destruction of Venice —not forgetting, with a final touch of irony, to proclaim the true object of the League to be 'the war against the infidel.' But the most minute arrangements were made in the treaty for the partition of the Venetian territories between the Pope, France, Spain, and the Empire, while even the Dukes of Mantua, Ferrara, and Savoy were to have their share.

The French armies began their march across the Alps in April, 1509, and on the 27th of the same month the Pope launched a Bull of excommunication against Venice. The Venetians treated the Bull with contempt, and prepared to resist the French, but their army suffered from divided counsels, and at its first encounter with the French, at Agnadello near the Adda, it was completely routed. Panic seized upon the Senate, as one after another the cities of the mainland surrendered to the French, and the cities of Romagna to the Pope; indeed, within a month after the battle of Agnadello, the partition clauses of Cambrai were fulfilled to the letter. But then, slowly, the tide turned. Treviso held firm for the republic, and in July Padua was recovered from the Imperialists by a sudden stroke. More important still, Julius II. was said to be far from contented with the sudden aggrandizement of his allies, and the Venetians determined to detach him at all costs from the League. After long and tedious negotiations, in which the domineering Pope humbled the Venetian envoys to the dust, Venice was absolved from the ban, though at the cost of all her ancient ecclesiastical immunities, as well as of the four cities, Faenza, Rimini, Cervia, and Ravenna.

The Pope's sentiments towards France had gradually passed from anxiety to alarm, and from alarm to open hostility, ever since Louis had established himself with preponderating force in Northern Italy; his reconciliation with Venice was intended, as the French cardinals put it, to plunge a dagger in the French King's heart. On May 14, 1510, the anniversary of the battle of Agnadello, he declared to the Venetian ambassador: 'These French have taken away my sleep and appetite; last night I spent in pacing my room, because I could not sleep. But my heart bids me be of good cheer. . . . for it is the will of God to chastise the Duke of Ferrara and deliver Italy from the hands of the French.' His plans, indeed, were already laid. Alfonso, Duke of Ferrara, had reaped an enormous profit from the war against Venice, and now refused to desist from it, or to withdraw from his alliance with France, at the bidding of his feudal suzerain the Pope. Moreover he had set up salt-pans at his lagoon city of Comacchio, greatly to the detriment of the Papal salt industry at Cervia. For all these reasons Alfonso was excommunicated as a son of iniquity and a root of perdition in August, 1510, and in September the Pope moved northwards to Bologna to superintend the war against his vassal. He had made an agreement with the Swiss to advance simultaneously against the French in Milan, but the mountaineers played him false, and Julius suddenly found himself in imminent danger of capture by the French commander, who advanced unchecked upon Bologna. The Bolognese were already bitterly discontented with the misrule of the Pope's Legate, Cardinal Alidosi, and plots for the restoration of Bentivoglio were rife; but Marshal Chaumont failed to press his advantage, and Venetian troops arrived in time to save the Pope. When the danger was over, Julius determined to pursue his attack on Ferrara, but not having the strength to besiege the city itself he went in person, in the depth of winter, to the assault of the fortress of Mirandola, which the Countess of that name was holding for the French. Here, sharing the camp life of his men, the Pope was in his element; he joked and swore with the soldiers, accepted rough compliments from the Venetian troops, and threatened the place with pillage if it did not surrender immediately; finally, when it capitulated, he rode in in triumph through a breach in the walls.

But the capture of Mirandola brought him no nearer to his ultimate goal, the destruction of the French power in Italy. Negotiations for peace were opened in April, 1511, but when Julius rejected the League's terms the French army under Trivulzio, father of the Countess of Mirandola, marched once more upon Bologna, and this time the General was detained by no scruples from pressing home his attack. Julius fled in panic to Ravenna, followed by his favourite Alidosi and by his nephew and Captain-General, the Duke of Urbino, on whom Julius laid all the blame of his defeat. Stung to madness, the Duke murdered Alidosi in the streets of Ravenna, almost before the Pope's eyes, while behind them the French made their triumphal entry into Bologna, and the streets rang once more with shouts of 'Bentivoglio!' The plans of Julius seemed to lie shattered in the dust.

Even in the ecclesiastical domain his enemies raised their heads, and five discontented cardinals issued a summons to a Council to be held at Pisa on September 1, to consider the reform of the Church. Julius, however, took the wind from their sails by issuing a counter-summons to a Council to be held at the Lateran in January, and the Council of Pisa, though patronized by France, served only to embarrass the unfortunate Gonfalonier Soderini, whom Julius never forgave for having permitted it to assemble on Florentine territory. Meanwhile more urgent matters were engaging the attention of the Pope, who had returned to Rome after his flight from Bologna; he succeeded during the summer in detaching Ferdinand of Spain from the League of Cambrai, and on October 5 a new league was published in Rome between the Pope, the King of Spain and the Republic of Venice, for the defence of the Church and the recovery of her territories. This was the celebrated 'Holy League.'

The army of the League was placed under the command of Raimond de Cardona, the Spanish viceroy of Naples, and its chief strength lay in its formidable contingent of Spanish infantry, trained under the 'Great Captain' in the Neapolitan Wars. These Spaniards had never yet appeared on the soil of Northern Italy; their introduction to these unhappy lands, where their name was so soon to become a by-word for cruelty and lust, was the work of the patriot Pope who was said to have coined the famous phrase, 'Fuori i Barbari.' If the French had chastised Italy with whips, the Spaniards were soon to show that they could chastise her with scorpions. The objective of the army was in the first instance Bologna, which it hoped to recover for the Holy See, but the French were now commanded by a young leader of genius, Gaston de Foix, whose rapid movements earned him the title of 'Thunderbolt of Italy.' Gaston threw himself into Bologna in time to overawe Cardona, and then recrossed the Lombard plain with unheard-of swiftness to punish the rebellion of Brescia, which had opened its gates to the Venetians. The sack of Brescia by the troops under Gaston, Bayard, and all the best chivalry of France surpassed in horror anything that the French had yet perpetrated on Italian soil. Then the young general gathered his forces for a decisive campaign against Cardona, followed him as he retreated towards Ravenna, and found him at last in the marshes beside the river Ronco. There the French chivalry drove the Papal troops before it, but broke in vain against the iron wall of Spanish infantry, and when the day was ended the army of the League was indeed in full retreat and the French stood masters of the field, but Gaston de Foix lay dead, and consternation reigned in the French camp.

In Rome too all was confusion, for the French had loudly announced their intention of marching on Rome and recovering Naples
for their sovereign. But the death of Gaston paralysed their action;
they wasted their time in Romagna, waiting for orders from Louis,
and by so doing gave Julius time to repair the fortunes of the
League. He succeeded in winning over Maximilian, and by the
efforts of a remarkable Switzer named Matthäus Schinner, Bishop
of Sitten, the Swiss were at last prevailed upon to enter heartily
into the Papal cause. A fine body of twenty thousand pikemen
appeared at Verona in May to co-operate with the Venetians, many
of them acting as volunteers in this war against their old pay-
masters the French. They espoused the cause of young Massimiliano Sforza, son of Il Moro, and advanced upon Milan proclaiming
their intention to restore the rightful Duke. The French were in
no condition to resist them, but fell back steadily through a hostile
country 'like mist before the wind,' as a contemporary Florentine
described it,[1] until their commander saw that all was lost and
withdrew with his men across the Alps. Only the Castello of
Milan and the Casteletto of Genoa remained in French hands, of
all the wide territories conquered by Louis XII.

It now only remained for the Holy League to divide the spoils,
and for this purpose a congress met at Mantua in August, 1512.
No difficulties were made about the restoration of the Sforza dynasty at Milan, for the Milanese were clamouring for their 'Italian
lord' and the Swiss had taken his part; Massimiliano accordingly
entered his duchy amid pathetic popular rejoicings on December
29. A weak youth of twenty, brought up in Germany and un-
versed in Italian affairs, he was ill-fitted for the heavy task of
reorganization that confronted him, but for the present the Milanese saw no spots in their sun, and the Swiss, being well paid, remained faithful.

The question of Florence, however, presented greater difficulties.
Soderini had provoked the ill-will of the League by his obstinate
persistence in a policy of neutrality, tinged with subservience to
France, and the exiled Medici were determined to seize their
opportunity. Even at this eleventh hour Soderini and the Signory
might have saved the Republic if they had been free enough with
their money, but they trusted to divisions among their enemies,
and their envoy at the congress had no authority to bribe. The
Medici, on the other hand, paid ten thousand ducats down to the
Spanish commander, with promises of much more should he bring
them to their own again, and Cardona accordingly set forth from

[1] F. Vettori, *Somm. della Storia d'Italia dal 1511 al 1527.*

Bologna towards the end of August to march on Florence with his Spaniards. Soderini and his friend and adviser Machiavelli trusted blindly to the militia which the latter had organized, and four thousand of these men were sent to garrison Prato, while negotiations were opened with Cardona. The Spaniard, with Cardinal Medici at his side, announced that he came to depose Soderini and restore the Medici as private citizens, and asked for one hundred thousand ducats for his army. These terms were put before the Great Council by Soderini in an eloquent speech, at the end of which the citizens declared unanimously against them, and vowed that they would stand by the Gonfalonier to the last. Preparations for defence were pushed on, and meanwhile Cardona descended, with a starving and ill-paid army, into the plain before Prato. His first attack failed for want of artillery, and he then sent a second message to the Signory, offering to withdraw if they would merely receive the Medici and send him three thousand ducats and one hundred cartloads of bread. Soderini hesitated and lost time, and meanwhile the attack on Prato was renewed with desperate vigour. A breach was at last made in the wall, the militia fled incontinent, and the Spaniards hurled themselves on their prey. For twenty-one days, from August 29 to September 19, they killed, tortured, and ravished without stint, and the sack of Prato takes its rank for sheer horror beside the sack of Haarlem or the 'Spanish Fury' of Antwerp. 'The victory was not won,' wrote Cardinal Medici to the Pope, 'without a certain amount of cruelty and killing. . . . But the capture of Prato, though the violence of it displeases me, will have an excellent effect in serving as an example and inspiring terror.'

The effect was indeed magical. Pistoja sent to offer its keys to Cardona, and in Florence the Medicean party suddenly raised its head. Two days after the sack, while embassies were still coming and going between Florence and Prato, a band of young men of the old noble families invaded the palace, laid hands on the Gonfalonier, and ordered him to lay down his office. No *coup d'état* was ever more easily accomplished. Soderini rode away under escort to Siena, his ten years of decent government all forgotten in the ten days of mismanagement at their close. Florence could not forgive him for the sack of Prato, and he goes down to history, poor, honest man, as the 'silly soul' of Machiavelli's epigram.[1]

---

[1] 'La notte che morì Pier Soderini
   L'alma n'andò dell'Inferno alla bocca,
   Gridò Pluto: Che Inferno? Anima sciocca,
   Va su nel limbo fragli altri bambini!'

Giuliano de' Medici, the Cardinal's brother, entered Florence next day, and though his good nature would have left things nearly as they were, the Cardinal did not trust him, but followed shortly himself with an armed force to reorganize the government. The the time-honoured expedient of a *Balìa*, or committee of government chosen by acclamation on the Piazza, was resorted to, and naturally every member of this Balìa had been selected by the Cardinal. The institutions dating from before 1494 were allowed to subsist, but all nominations to office were in the hands of the Balìa, and the Balìa itself merely reflected the will of Cardinal Medici. 'In this way,' says Guicciardini, himself a Medicean writer, 'the liberty of Florence was crushed by force.'[2]

Julius II., in the winter of 1512—13, could survey his work with satisfaction. The French had been driven out, Florence compelled to enter the Holy League, the schismatic cardinals and their council hunted across the Alps to Lyons; above all, Parma and Piacenza, Modena and Reggio had been added by the arms of the League to the dominions of the Holy See. The Lateran Council was holding its sessions with pomp and splendour, encouraged by the formal adhesion of the Emperor; the fabric of St. Peter's was rising; the vault of the Sistine Chapel had been covered with marvellous paintings by the hand of Michelangelo. Julius passed away on February 20, 1513, at the height of his reputation and glory. The Romans mourned him as they had mourned no Pope for centuries; after the bestialities of Alexander VI. they had felt the grandeur of ambitions that were at least personally disinterested. But for us, who know the sequel, the germ of the sack of Rome lies hid in the Holy League, and Julius, whose unmeasured violence made Italy the marching ground of the foreign armies, becomes a towering figure in the tragedy of Italy's enslavement.

[2] *Storia d'Italia*, vol. iv., p. 167.

CHAPTER XIX

Leo X and the Struggle for
Lombardy: the Battle of Pavia

LORENZO the Magnificent had been wont to say, looking at his three boys: 'I have three sons, one foolish, one good, and one clever.' These three were Piero, Giuliano, and Giovanni, and the last-named of these, for whom his father had procured a cardinal's hat at the age of fourteen, was now to fill the Italian stage. He was elected Pope after the death of Julius and took the name of Leo X. But he had nothing of the leonine temper, and the cardinals had indeed elected him in order to escape from the rule of *Papi terribili*[1] such as Julius and Alexander. Nor was he to disappoint their expectations. His first remark to his brother Giuliano after the Conclave was said to have been: 'Let us enjoy the Papacy, since God has given it to us,' and his reign embodied the crowning attempt of an Italian Pope and a true son of the Renaissance to live up to this ideal. For 'enjoyment' to a Medici brought up at Lorenzo's court, where the human mind made such a prodigious advance into the realms of enlightenment, meant more than the mere delight in banquets, pageants, and carnivals, which dazzled the visitor to Leo's court. It meant the raising of Rome to a position of pre-eminence in the literary and artistic world, such as Florence had enjoyed under Lorenzo and his circle; the lavish patronage of scholarship and of the nascent art of printing; the acquisition of an undisputed title to be hailed the Mæcenas of the age. In the lean days to come, when Catholic Reaction triumphed, the humanists of Rome looked sadly back to the golden age of Leo, when Raphael walked King of the Vatican, when masques and comedies were performed in the Pope's presence, when no boon was refused to the poor bard who came with his copy of verses to Leo's feet. Music too was one of the Pope's chief delights, and many thousand ducats went in the purchase of a new and wonderful organ from Master Lorenzo of Pavia, as well as of viols and other instruments. Leo's enjoyment of the Papacy coincided indeed with the florescence of Italian art and civilization, and the welcome which he gave to these

[1] The phrase is used by Francesco Vettori, in his *Sommario della Storia d'Italia dal 1511 al 1527*.

represents his high and sufficient claim to the immortality he coveted.

But, being human, he also had his very mundane schemes for the aggrandizement of his family and of the Papal States. He was set on carving a principality for his brother Giuliano out of the ancient territories of Milan and Ferrara, and when this plan was frustrated by the power of France he coolly dispossessed the Duke of Urbino, his predecessor's nephew, by force of arms and bestowed his estates on his own nephew Lorenzo, son of the 'foolish' Piero [1517]. Giuliano, the 'good' brother, who died in 1516, besought the Pope on his death-bed not to proceed against the Duke, who had shown kindness to the Medici in their days of exile, but Leo would make no promise, and a few months afterwards carried out his design. The injured nobleman was afterwards pacified, in characteristic fashion, by the permission to take with him into exile his artillery, and also the priceless collection of manuscripts, bound in red velvet and clasped with silver, made long ago at the castle of Urbino by the 'Good Duke' Federigo.

If Leo could have had a clear field in Italian politics, he might well have won at the game of statecraft in which he had been reared from childhood up. His misfortune was that he was caught in the clash of the mightiest antagonism of the age, the struggle between France and the Empire, in which he could only turn and twist in endless equivocations. The duplicity of his negotiations became a byword in Italy.[1] Nor, if we are in search of the ironies of Fate, need we go further than the spectacle of the smiling, open-handed Pope presiding over the 'humanities' of Rome, while far away in the rugged North gather the forces of conscience and rebellion that were to shake his throne to its foundations.

At the beginning of Leo's reign the diplomatic situation in Italy had shifted once more from the position in which we left it in the latter months of 1512. Venice, mortified at being unable to obtain the restitution of Verona and Vicenza from her patrons of the Holy

---

[1] When Francis I. was preparing to invade Italy, Leo was paid out in his own coin by the Doge of Genoa, Fregoso, who secretly deserted the Pope's side for the King's and then justified himself in the following passage of a letter to the Pope: 'My defence would be more difficult if I were writing to a private person or to a prince who measured affairs of state by private standard; but since I am writing to a prince whose sagacity is unsurpassed in this age, and who therefore knows that I could not save my position in any other way, it is superfluous to excuse myself before one who well knows what it is permitted or at least customary for princes to do, not only when they are reduced to such extremities, but also when they are striving to improve or enlarge their states.'

League, was drifting towards France, and actually concluded an alliance with Louis XII. in March, 1513, for the expulsion of Sforza from Milan. Once more intrigue was concentrated on the fate of Lombardy. Leo had decided to continue the anti-French policy of Julius, for only with a weak native Duke at Milan could he hope to retain possession of Parma and Piacenza; he therefore rejoiced when the Swiss troops in the pay of Sforza routed the French army of invasion at the battle of Novara [June 6, 1513], and so redeemed in the service of Massimiliano the honour they had lost in the betrayal of Il Moro. This victory of the Swiss, won without the aid of artillery against superior numbers, raised their reputation throughout Europe to fantastic heights, and Duke Massimiliano felt himself at last secure upon his throne. But his Duchy was drained dry to provide the cruel exactions needed to pay his Swiss and Spanish troops, and the personal extravagance of the Duke added the last touch to the burdens of his subjects. The far-famed prosperity that Milan had enjoyed in the previous century sank and vanished; the revenues were forestalled two years in advance; the inhabitants had no security against plunder and outrage from the foreign soldiery. No wonder that the good historian Prato, after giving a woeful catalogue of the huge sums disbursed to the Duke's favourites and mercenaries, breaks out in the words of Solomon, 'Woe unto the land whose king is a child!'

But the old civic spirit of the Milanese, which had produced the *carroccio*, the Lombard League, and the Ambrosian Republic, still lived on, and at this crisis won its last victory over misgovernment and oppression. Francis I. succeeded to the throne of France in January, 1515, and immediately announced his intention of asserting his claim to the Duchy of Milan. Massimiliano thereupon demanded a fresh subsidy of three hundred thousands ducats from the town, to be paid within three days, and the Milanese rose in revolt. The banner of St. Ambrose was raised, and the Duke was forced to treat. As the result of negotiations between his ministers and the principal citizens, a constitution was agreed upon by which the Milanese bought back from the Duke the right of electing to all municipal offices, and thereby went far towards recovering the power of the purse. If time had been granted for the development of the scheme, Massimiliano might even have been reduced to the position of constitutional monarch. But time was the one thing lacking: Francis I. was at the gates.

The young King of France, in the first flush of his martial ardour, entered upon the conquest of Italy in the spirit of a paladin of romance. Round him were gathered many of the veterans who had fought at Ravenna and Novara—Trivulzio, Lautrec, Bayard, the Constable of Bourbon—and they commanded the finest army that had ever set forth under the banner of France. The rumour of their approach struck chill into the hearts not only of the Duke of Milan but of his so-called allies of the Holy League, whose army under Cardona lingered near Verona on the pretext of keeping the Venetians in check. Leo ordered his own troops to defend Parma and Piacenza, but to go no further. Only the Milanese under Prospero Colonna and the formidable Swiss were ready to take the offensive. They expected the French to debouch from the Mont Cenis or the Mont Genèvre, and had therefore concentrated at Susa, but Trivulzio conveyed his army by the little-known pass of the Col d'Argentière, far to the south, and appeared in Piedmont unopposed on August 14, 1515. The Swiss fell back to cover Milan, and the usual doubts distracted their ranks as to whether to fight against the King of France or no. But by the exertions of their warlike Legate, Cardinal Schinner, they were induced to take the field, and on September 14 they marched out of Milan by the highroad to attack the position which the King had taken up at Marignano, about ten miles south-east of the town. The battle began in the late afternoon, continued by moonlight, and was resumed again at dawn, the Swiss fighting by sheer strength of pike and weight of numbers, without the aid of cavalry or guns. Cardona and Lorenzo de' Medici[1], far away at Piacenza, were vainly urging each other to go to their assistance. Finally the arrival of a Venetian corps to the assistance of the French decided the long-fought day, and the Swiss broke and fled towards Milan. As they straggled into the town, wounded, drenched to the waist from having fought in the ditches and flooded fields, 'the men of Milan,' says the chronicler Burigozzo, 'seeing so much misery, stood at their doors or at their shops, some with bread, and some with wine, to lighten the hearts of these poor men; and this they did for the honour of God.'

So the invincible Swiss were defeated, and Massimiliano Sforza, to save his skin, handed over his duchy to the King and retired to France on a pension. Francis I. entered Milan in state on October 11. The constitutional reforms were cut down to a minimum, and the city was committed to the tender mercies of the Constable of Bourbon and then of the Sieur de Lautrec, under whose harsh rule the Milanese groaned for the next six years. But Massimiliano's brother Francesco, of tougher fibre than the Duke, had es-

[1] Grandson of Lorenzo the Magnificent.

caped to Trent, and there awaited in poverty the return of better days.

The news of the battle of Marignano came as a thunderbolt to Pope Leo and his court in the Vatican. When the Venetian ambassador announced the Franco-Venetian victory to His Holiness, Leo wrung his hands and exclaimed, 'What will become of us?' But he immediately added, 'We will place ourselves in the hands of the Most Christian King, and will implore his mercy.' Within a month after the battle he had already made an agreement with Francis, whereby in exchange for the surrender of Parma and Piacenza to the King, Leo obtained an assurance of French support for the Medici rule in Florence—a considerable stroke, for the Republicans of Florence had been accustomed hitherto to look to France for their salvation. Leo followed up this advance by journeying to Bologna in December to meet the King, and there a bargain was struck between them at the expense of the liberties of the Gallican Church, which Pope and King combined to despoil for their own advantage.

Meanwhile the Venetians, not having yet obtained the objects for which they fought, still carried on the war against the Emperor for the recovery of Brescia and Verona. Since the battle of Agnadello the Republic had shown marvellous recuperative power, but her daring commander Alviano, renowned among friends and foes for the dash and swiftness of his movements, died before he could add the capture of these two cities to his laurels. At this point, however, the politics of Europe took a turn favourable to Venice, and rendered further fighting unnecessary. The old King Ferdinand of Spain died in January, 1516, leaving his vast dominions of Spain, Naples, Sicily, and the Netherlands to his grandson Charles of Austria; and this cautious stripling, who was also grandson on his father's side of Maximilian, deemed it to be his first necessity to live on terms of amity with his powerful neighbour, France. A treaty was therefore signed at Noyon [1516] between Charles and Francis, which included, though it did not consult, the Venetians and Maximilian. Charles undertook to induce his grandfather to restore Verona to Venice on payment of two hundred thousand ducats, and this bargain was actually carried out in February, 1517. Venice thus emerged from the long wars of the League of Cambrai with territory intact, though with finances woefully depleted; henceforward she withdrew herself as much as possible from the wars of the mainland, and shrouded her activities in the devious paths of diplomacy. She was still the strongest Italian power in the Peninsula, but she knew that her strength was as nothing com-

RAPHAEL'S PORTRAIT OF POPE LEO X, PITTI GALLERY

pared with that of the Transalpine nations, and that only in a skilful system of alliances could safety lie. The glorious period of her expansion was over, but at least she had escaped the fate of Milan and of Naples.

Leo X. was soon called upon to face a political situation still more perplexing to his interests than that which arose after the battle of Marignano. Early in 1519 the old Emperor Maximilian died, and the inevitable rivalry of Francis I. and Charles of Spain, stilled for a moment by the Treaty of Noyon, burst into flame on the question of the succession to the Empire. Each of these monarchs already had enormous interests in Italy—Francis as the ruler of Milan and the upholder of the ancient Angevin claim to Naples, Charles as the actual ruler of the Neapolitan Kingdom. The accession of strength which the Imperial crown would give to either must therefore be a matter of serious concern to Leo, but he certainly dreaded the election of Charles the more, for ever since the days of Frederick II. it had been a Papal maxim that the Empire and the Kingship of Naples must not be combined in the same person. He tried secretly to promote the election of a third candidate, preferably one of the seven Electors themselves, but national feeling in Germany was rousing itself in favour of Charles of Austria, even though he were also Charles of Spain, and Leo's ambassadors, with their supposed French proclivities, found themselves in danger of their lives from the mob of Frankfort. At the last moment Leo was obliged to withdraw his opposition to Charles's election, and to enter into an agreement with him on the subject of Naples. On June 28, 1519, Charles of Austria, Spain, Naples, the Netherlands, and the New World, was duly proclaimed King of the Romans and Emperor-elect.

This was a decided check to Leo's policy, but his busy brain set to work at once to derive whatever advantage was possible from the accomplished fact. Leo was troubled during the years 1519 and 1520 by the attitude of defiance to Papal authority taken up by a certain Augustinian monk in the University of Wittenberg, by name Martin Luther; the aid of the new Emperor would be useful in suppressing him. A Bull of excommunication was issued against the obnoxious monk in June, 1520; but as once the King of France in his struggle with Boniface VIII., so now the humble preacher dared to make a public bonfire of the document. To the mind of Charles V., however, both the act of rebellion and the national enthusiasm which it aroused in Germany were alike distasteful, and the proceedings against Luther at the Diet of

P

Worms [April, 1521] drew the Emperor closer to the Pope. In Italy also it began to appear that the interests of both lay in a combination against France, for Charles was ready to hand over Parma, Piacenza, and even Ferrara to the Pope, whereas Francis thought that he had done enough for Leo in giving him the hand of a French princess for his nephew Lorenzo.[1] To Charles, again, the financial resources of the Papacy would be of the highest service in any war for the recovery of Lombardy. An alliance was therefore signed between Pope and Emperor in May, 1521, by which Charles engaged to set up Francesco Sforza as Duke of Milan, as well as to bestow the aforementioned territories on the Pope. Nor did Leo omit to obtain the revenues of a Spanish archbishopric for his cousin Giulio de' Medici, and an estate in Naples worth ten thousand ducats a year for Lorenzo's bastard Alessandro.

Hostilities with France began in the summer of 1521, with an abortive attempt on the part of a band of Milanese exiles to surprise an entry into the town; but it was not until the autumn that the Papal-Imperial army under Prospero Colonna advanced in earnest upon Milan. The iniquitous rule of Lautrec had already roused the hostility of the whole population against him, while the intrigues of Cardinal Schinner had deprived him of the bulk of his Swiss mercenaries, so that when the advance-guard of the allied army broke in by one of the gates of Milan on the night of November 19, Lautrec and his men lost heart and fled in hot haste into Venetian territory. Once more the French power crumbled, as after the battle of Ravenna, and within a few days of the fall of Milan, only a few fortresses throughout the duchy remained in the hands of French garrisons. The success of the League was overwhelming.

Leo X. was at his villa of Magliana, on the lower Tiber, when the news of his triumph reached him, but he returned at once to Rome to share in the popular rejoicings. His own delight knew no bounds. He declared to the Imperial ambassador that the capture of Milan gave him greater joy than his election to the Papacy. But he soon complained of fever, and retired to bed; his illness, however, seemed slight, and Rome was completely taken by surprise when it was announced on the morning of December 2 that the Pope had expired in the night. He had just lived to hear the news of the surrender of the two much-coveted cities, Parma and Piacenza, to the Papal troops.

A characteristic account of the conclave following the death

---

[1] The offspring of this marriage was the celebrated Catherine de' Medici, afterwards the wife of Henry II. of France.

of Leo X., which resulted in the election of an alien and a 'barbarian,' Adrian VI., has been left in a letter of Cardinal Gonzaga to his kinswoman Isabella d'Este, the famous Marchioness of Mantua.

Today these excellent cardinals and myself have at length come out of the Conclave [writes Gonzaga], where we have spent a fortnight in the greatest discomfort and fatigue, both of body and mind, owing to our endless quarrels. And after all this we have—no doubt according to the will of God, since all is ordered by Him—elected a Pope who is, as people say, a holy man. I, for one, have never seen him. As for my own disappointment, I did my best, and cannot complain that any of these cardinals deceived me. Only this unexpected event, which was never dreamt of by me or any one else, has shattered my hopes. Just when I felt sure of reaching the desired goal, the greater part of the cardinals went and gave their votes to this man, simply throwing them away, without knowing what the others were doing, and when all the votes were read out, he was found to have no less than fifteen![1]

When the result was announced [January 9, 1522], the Roman mob cursed and howled, and Adrian himself—a Fleming by birth, but at the time of his election Charles V.'s Viceroy and Inquisitor-General in Spain—showed no desire to come and take up the burden of his office. Not until eight months after his election did he arrive at length in Rome, and then his attitude of severity and disapproval dismayed the cardinals, while his foreign habits and speech set all Rome against him. Charles V. expected at least that the new Pope, who owed his advancement to the fact that he had been the Emperor's tutor, would take his side in the quarrel with France, but Adrian soon showed that he intended to maintain a strict neutrality in the wars of Christian princes, and that his sole care would be to mediate between them in order to unite their forces against the Turk. One of his first acts was to order Cardinal Giulio de' Medici to proceed with two galleys to the relief of Rhodes—a task which the Cardinal on various pretexts firmly declined.

While the pedantic Fleming endeavoured to cope single-handed with the corruption of Rome, and to deal with the German revolt by a mere barren appeal to coercion, events in upper Italy moved on their course independently of his desires and of his efforts at mediation. After the victory of the League, Milan had been handed over to the young Duke Francesco Sforza, Massimiliano's younger

---

[1] Letter quoted in *Isabella d'Este, Marchioness of Mantua*, by Julia Cartwright, vol ii., p. 197.

brother, and he and his able minister, Girolamo Morone, endeavoured loyally to restore some sort of order and prosperity to the ill-fated duchy. But Lautrec was still at large, and had gathered reinforcements from the Swiss cantons during the winter, so that it was not until he was finally defeated at the battle of the Bicocca in April, 1522, that Sforza could feel himself secure. The Duke had led the Milanese contingent to battle in this fight, and the Duomo was hung with banners taken from the French. But the maintenance of the Imperial army had become so crushing a burden on the exhausted Milanese that its General, the Marquis of Pescara, decided to quarter it mainly upon Papal territory, and to levy a regular monthly tax for its support on all the independent states of Italy; even republics as remote as Siena and Lucca were forced to pay their contributions.[1] To such a pass had the necessity for defending their liberty against the French reduced the Italian states.

The position of Francesco Sforza was strengthened in 1523 by the adhesion of Venice to the general league against France, and the consequent removal of any danger that might threaten him on the east. Morone was busy organizing an efficient city militia, and Milan seemed in a fair way to recover some portion of its ancient prosperity. But the apparently solid front presented by the Italians did not deter the King of France from making preparations on a colossal scale for the recovery of Milan, and in the autumn of 1523 a fresh army under the Admiral Bonnivet descended into Lombardy. Milan bravely endured an eight weeks' siege, and the still more burdensome presence within her walls of a large Imperial army, But Bonnivet was soon compelled to retire into winter quarters beyond the Ticino. An incompetent general, he allowed himself to be beaten at all points in the spring, and the campaign was mainly remarkable for the exploits of the Italian 'Black Bands' of Giovanni de' Medici[2] on the side of the League, and for the death of the Chevalier Bayard in a rear-guard action. When the French finally retreated beyond the Alps, they were followed into Provence by the Imperialists, and the siege of Marseilles relieved the plains of Lombardy for awhile from the presence of both friend and foe.

But the high-spirited King of France resented these continual reverses as intolerable to the prestige of his crown and arms. Francis I. determined to win back in person the honour which

---

[1] Guicc., *Storia d'Italia*, Bk. xv., ch. i.
[2] Giovanne de' Medici was descended from Lorenzo, brother of Cosimo *Pater Patriæ*, and became the progenitor of the Grand Dukes of Tuscany.

Lautrec and Bonnivet had thrown away. The unhappy Milanese, to whom Bonnivet's invasion had brought nothing but a legacy of plague, learnt in September, 1524, that the King was descending the Alps at the head of a fine army, while the Imperialists were yet too far off to defend them. Francesco Sforza decided to evacuate the town, and on October 24, Francis I. took peaceful possession of the capital of Lombardy. But the Imperialists were hard at his heels, and concentrated their troops in Lodi and Pavia, in order to await reinforcements before attacking the French in earnest. Francis laid siege to Pavia, and so great was the expectation of his success that the new Pope, Clement VII.,[1] nominally the faithful ally of the Emperor, made a secret treaty with him in order to insure himself against a French victory. Nevertheless Pavia stubbornly held out, the citizens joining heartily with the German mercenaries in defence of the walls, and the situation of the French began to show signs of peril. Behind the line of the Adda, Pescara and Lannoy, the two Imperialist commanders, were organizing a formidable army of German *Landsknechts*, Spanish infantry and harquebusiers, and Italian horse; by the beginning of February, 1525, it was ready to move to the relief of Pavia. Unpaid and ill-fed, the Imperial troops must stake all on a decisive battle, while Francis, entrenched in the Park of Mirabello before Pavia, stood to gain by a policy of inaction. But the decision was not left to him, for at dawn on February 24, the Emperor's birthday, the whole force of the Imperialists was hurled against his camp in furious attack. At first the French chivalry repulsed the onslaught of Spaniards and Germans, and drove back the charge of Italian horse, but the Imperialists rallied again and again, the garrison of Pavia poured out on the rear of the French, and in a last desperate charge to retrieve the day Francis himself was unhorsed and taken prisoner. In that terrific contest the power of France beyond the Alps went down, never to be fully restored until a certain Corsican adventurer, of Italian name and parentage, should lead a ragged army into the Lombard plain for the overturning of Popes, Emperors, and princes. Until that day should dawn, Italy lay at the mercy of Spaniard and Austrian, victors on the field of Pavia in the strange name of Italian liberty.

---

[1] Adrian VI. had died in September, 1523, and been succeeded by Cardinal Giulio de' Medici, son of that Giuliano who had been murdered in the conspiracy of the Pazzi (see p. 181).

CHAPTER XX

The Sack of Rome—the Pacification and Enslavement of Italy—the Siege and Fall of Florence

For us, and for our tragedy,
Here stooping to your clemency,
We beg your hearing patiently.   *Hamlet*

THE news of the battle of Pavia, and of the terrible completeness of the Imperial victory, spread gloom and apprehension among the anxious people. Guicciardini the historian, at this time Papal Governor of Romagna, wrote bitterly to a friend that he saw no prospect of creating an efficient Italian army,[1] and yet that 'to make terms with such conquerors as these is but to establish our servitude.' Pope Clement in the Vatican Palace trembled lest his secret dealings with Francis I. should be discovered and resented by the Emperor, and, refusing to join a league for the defence of Italy proposed to him by Venice and Ferrara, yielded to the winning side and made a treaty with Charles instead [April, 1525]. His principal motives in so doing were to secure the interests of his family in Florence and to regain two towns (Reggio and Rubiera) which the Duke of Ferrara had won back from the Church two years before; these seemed to him far more important ends than the freeing of Italy from the Spaniard. But Clement VII., who as Cardinal Giulio de' Medici had enjoyed a high reputation for statesmanship under his cousin Leo, was doomed as Pope to be the sport of forces mightier than himself, and to grope for ever after petty ends while the fate of Italy hung in the balance. A faithful estimate of his position at the beginning of his reign has been left to us by the acute Florentine Francesco Vettori, who lived in Rome during all these terrible years.

No doubt [writes Vettori[2]] he entered on the Papal office when it

[1] 'I for one cannot persuade myself that with the forces that remain to Italy it would be possible to put together a fighting army. It might be numerous enough, but not brave like that of the enemy, because it lacks both good captains and good infantry. For although our Italian infantry does contain a few good men, it is full of cowardly rascals who have no stomach for a fight, and care not for their own or their country's honour.' *Op. inedite*, vol. viii., letter of March 25, 1525.

[2] 'Storia d'Italia dal 1511 al 1527,' in *Arch. stor. Ital.*, Appendix, vol. vi., 1848.

was already ruined by Leo's wars and extravagance, and when Adrian had been unable to effect any improvement, owing to the shortness of his reign and to the fact that, being new to the Curia and to Rome, everyone cheated him. More than this, Clement was under heavy obligations to the fifteen cardinals who had stood by him in the Conclave. He found Italy filled with soldiery, Christendom weakened by the loss of Rhodes and the preparations which the Turks were making against Hungary, the Church in the lowest possible repute because of the continual advance of the Lutheran sect. But human ambition is so formed that it always presses on towards the highest goal. Giulio de' Medici knew very well whither he was going; he talked and thought of nothing else; yet he exerted himself to the utmost to exchange the position of a great and influential cardinal for that of a miserable, despised Pope.

Clement in fact soon found that his treaty with the Emperor had brought him no advantage. The two Ferrarese towns were not surrendered to him, the Papal territory near Milan was ravaged to the bone by the Imperial troops, and Clement began to favour a remarkable scheme put forward by the Milanese Chancellor, Girolamo Morone, for the emancipation of Italy from the foreigner. This man, who had served his apprenticeship in the service of Milan during the French domination following on Il Moro's fall, had changed sides with the coming of Massimiliano Sforza [1512], and when the battle of Marignano had once more brought in the French had followed Francesco Sforza into exile and finally returned with him in 1521. His vigour and capacity had infused something like order into the new administration, though no government was ever more cruelly handicapped than Francesco's by the systematic robbery to which it was subjected by its insolent allies. After the battle of Pavia the tyranny of the Imperial generals and their incessant demands for money became more and more intolerable, and Morone entered into a secret alliance with Venice, the Pope, and the Queen-Regent of France for the purpose of freeing Italy from the Imperialists. But he made the mistake of attempting to suborn the Marquis of Pescara, a Neapolitan to whose brilliant leadership the victory of Pavia had been mainly due, from his allegiance to the Emperor; Pescara merely waited until the threads of the plot were in his hands, and then arrested the chief conspirator. Morone was eventually allowed to buy his release, took service with his enemies, and ended his days as Commissary-General to the very army that sacked Rome and quenched the liberties of Florence.

The immediate result of the conspiracy was that Pescara advanced upon Milan, forced the citizens to take an oath of allegiance to the Emperor, and demanded the surrender of the citadels of Milan and Cremona. Francesco Sforza replied with some spirit that he held these fortresses as the loyal vassal of the Emperor, and would yield them to no living man, whereupon Pescara occupied the town with Spanish troops and laid formal siege to the Castello. Once more the luckless Milanese were exposed to all the brutalities of the most inhuman soldiery in Europe, while the Duke, with eight hundred men, held out month after month in the vain hope of succour from the Pope or the Venetians. In the spring of 1526, he was cheered by the news that a league for the defence of Italy had been concluded at Cognac between Francis I., now released from prison, the Pope, Venice, and his own envoys, and throughout Italy hope rose high that at length the Imperialists would be expelled. Even the Pope, whose constitutional indecision of character amounted almost to a disease,[1] espoused the national cause with ardour, and his representative in Lombardy, the renowned Guicciardini, sought to inspire the military leaders with his own enthusiasm for this 'holy war.'   But even now the huckstering spirit of the Medici intervened to prevent success. Clement refused to conciliate the Duke of Ferrara by renouncing his claim to Reggio and Rubiera, and not only were the resources of a rich and powerful state thus lost to the League, but Alfonso was thrown into the arms of Charles V., and when calamity drew near decided by his action the fate of Clement and of Rome.

The Duke of Milan, cooped up in the Castello, now confidently expected the approach of a relieving army, but the supreme command of the forces of the League had by ill luck been given to Francesco della Rovere, Duke of Urbino, a sluggish and cowardly commander who enjoyed an inexplicable reputation among his

[1] Guicciardini's famous character of Pope Clement (*Storia d'Italia*, Bk. xvi., ch. v.) runs as follows: 'For although he was exceedingly intelligent and had a marvellous knowledge of all manner of things, nevertheless his qualities of resolution and of action were far inferior, because he was hampered not only by his natural timidity (which in him was not small) and by his dislike of spending money, but especially by a certain irresolution and perplexity which was habitual with him. Thus he always remained undecided and of two minds, when the moment for decision came, on matters which he had long foreseen, often considered, and practically resolved upon. Both in discussion and in carrying out what had been discussed, every minute consideration that occurred to him again, every insignificant hindrance that might arise, seemed to be enough to throw him back into the original confusions from which he had suffered before the discussion, so that after deciding on one course of action it always seemed to him that the rejected course would have been the best.'

contemporaries for military ability. While he delayed to attack the Spaniards with his superior forces, the sands of the defence ran out, and Francesco Sforza, ill and haggard, rode out of the Castello with the honours of war, on July 24, 1526, and joined the camp of his allies at Lodi. The Spanish domination was riveted more firmly than ever upon Milan. At the same time an extraordinary attack of the Colonna clan—Ghibelline by tradition and now violently Imperialist—upon the Vatican Palace [September 20] so frightened Pope Clement that he agreed to withdraw his troops from the League. True to the traditions of Boniface VIII., however, he used the troops recalled from Lombardy to burn and lay waste the Colonna villages. On such enterprises were the forces of Christendom spent, while on the bloody field of Mohacz, far in the Hungarian plain, Christendom itself lay broken before the Turk.

While the commanders of the League let slip every opportunity for striking a decisive blow, a fresh storm-cloud was gathering in the north. Twelve thousand Lutheran *Landsknechts*—stout fellows who would have done good service against the Turk— were enlisted in the Tyrolese valleys by their leader Georg von Frundsberg, and started in November to reinforce the Imperialists in Italy. They marched without pay, as did all the Italian armies of Charles V., but with 'arrears' piling up as they marched, to be wrung with interest from the conquered land. Nor was this force without its own especial object. 'The Pope,' said Frundsberg, 'is the Emperor's worst enemy and has begun the war. For the honour of God he must be hanged, though I were to do it with my own hand.' In this spirit they debouched into the Lombard plain, opposed only by the 'Black Bands' of Giovanni de' Medici,[1] crossed the Po in the friendly territory of Ferrara, and marched as far west as Piacenza to effect its junction with the main Imperial army under Bourbon. The latter wrote to the Emperor in January, 1527, that he had now 'sucked the blood of Milan dry,'[2] yet he could only prevail on his mutinous troops to leave the town by the prospect of more glorious pillage elsewhere. In February, 1527, the combined army began its march Romewards past Bologna and

---

[1] Giovanni himself was killed in an insignificant skirmish with the *Landsknechts* at Governolo on the Mincio.

[2] The chronicler Burigozzo, describing the state of Milan in this year, says: 'Fortunate was he who could fly, whether in the guise of a peasant or by some means or other, and indeed there were more houses deserted than inhabited. . . . And when the Spaniards who were quartered in such a house saw that the master had fled they set to work to ruin it, and did all manner of evil.'

through the Duchy of Ferrara, while the Duke of Urbino hung a day's march in its rear and seemed to the terrified onlookers to be actually pushing it on towards Rome. Indeed, Francesco della Rovere was not the man to bestir himself to save a Medici Pope, for he had never forgotten the days when Leo's troops had driven him from his duchy to provide an appanage for a Papal nephew.[1] Alfonso of Ferrara, too, paid off old scores by sending money to quell a mutiny of the *Landsknechts* when they lay, half starving, a few miles from his capital.

Undeterred by a messenger from Lannoy, Viceroy of Naples, who announced that he had just made a truce with the Pope and ordered the army to return, Bourbon and his mutinous horde pushed on across the Apennines and threatened Florence. Urbino, however, had crossed on the inner line and covered it effectually, so that no road but the Roman was open to the advancing host. Lannoy himself came to meet and stop it, but since he brought no money he was brushed aside, and on April 26 the army broke up its camp at Montevarchi and made straight for Rome. In ten days it was at the gates. Clement had lulled himself with the false hope that it would pass Rome by and make for Naples, and the preparations for defence were of the slenderest. Yet the first assault on the Leonine walls, in the foggy dawn of May 6, was repulsed, and Bourbon saw that there was danger of a rout. Calling to his men, he mounted a ladder near the Torrioni gate,[2] but immediately fell, struck down by a musket-ball.[3] His death stung the troops to fury, and it was not long before they had found an opening in the wall through some buildings and were pouring into the Borgo. Clement VII., praying in the Vatican chapel, had barely time to escape along the corridor made by Alexander VI. to the Castle of Sant' Angelo, and thither streamed in uncontrollable panic soldiers, priests, Vatican officials, and the indiscriminate population of the Borgo, till the whole space between the castle and the Tiber was blocked with a seething mass of fugitives. About three thousand, including the sculptor Benvenuto Cellini, pressed their way into the castle before the rusty portcullis could be lowered, but even then two cardinals were left outside and had to be hoisted in, one through a window and one by a basket to the battlements. Meanwhile the enemy were swarming in unopposed, slaying all whom they met, and by

[1] See p. 221.
[2] Now *Cavallegieri*.
[3] It is well known that Benvenuto Cellini claims to have been the man that fired the shot, having come out to see the fight from the walls 'near the Campo Santo.'

two o'clock were in full possession of the Borgo. The cannon from Sant' Angelo, however, kept them at a respectful distance from the fortress itself. Renzo da Ceri, the Papal commander, hurried to the Capitol and advised the magistrates to blow up the three bridges which gave access from the Borgo to the town, but the Conservators declared it to be a pity to destroy such beautiful bridges, and besides, they would trust the Colonna to protect them. 'And so,' says the eyewitness Paolo Giovio,[1] 'having taken the Ponte Sisto with very little trouble, put the defenders to flight, and made an immense slaughter of the fugitives, cutting to pieces seven thousand men, there entered into Rome forty thousand of the enemy.' What little authority their leaders had exercised so far was now thrown off, and the forty thousand fell upon the defenceless city, hot with the primæval passions of hunger, blood-thirst, and lust.

Never did Romans or foreigners [says Giovio again] behold a thing more terrible or full of lamentation than that night, because in all parts of the city there were innumerable murders of persons who had not deserved such things; both young and old of the noblest families were given up to excruciating tortures; everywhere the honour of matrons and maids was violated, and nuns were put to shame in the churches. With so much fury did they assault the houses of cardinals and princes that not even the ambassadors of kings were spared, and at length all those who had tried to save themselves from slaughter by hiding were tracked down, and could only buy their lives and liberty by giving up the whole of their possessions.

The fury raged unchecked for at least eight days, after which the Germans were satiated, though the Spaniards and Italians still pursued their search for treasure by the aid of horrible tortures; and slowly a certain number of *Landsknechts* dribbled back to their posts for the assault on the Castle of Sant' Angelo. The trembling Pope within was sending frantic appeals for help to the Duke of Urbino, who had followed by leisurely stages in the track of the Imperial army; but though the Duke advanced to within sight of Rome, he declared the Pope's rescue to be an impossible task without enormous reinforcements. Neither the explicit orders of the Venetian Senate nor the disgust of his own subordinates availed to bring him to a sense of his duty, and at the beginning of June he broke up his camp and retreated towards Umbria. No other course was now open to the Pope than to surrender the fortress,

[1] *Vita del Cardinale Pompeo Colonna.*

which was not provisioned for a siege, and on June 7 his own garrison marched out and he himself became a prisoner in the hands of a mixed force of Germans and Spaniards. He also pledged himself to pay four hundred thousand ducats, and to hand over to the conquerors Ostia, Civitavecchia, Modena, Parma and Piacenza.

But the financial resources of the Papacy seemed to be absolutely exhausted. Indeed, Clement's chief source of supply in previous years, the wealth of Florence, was now cut off, for at the news of the fall of Rome the weak Medicean government there had been overthrown, and the Republic of Savonarola re-established. Not a ducat was sent from Florence to swell the Pope's ransom. As the summer wore on and the plague descended upon Rome, the Pope and his captors wrangled endlessly as to the payment of the ransom; jewels were melted down, money borrowed at enormous interest, and still the *Landsknechts* were not satisfied. The Papal States, moreover, seemed to be crumbling into their original fragments; the Duke of Ferrara seized Modena, Venice took back Ravenna and Cervia, Perugia reverted to the Baglioni. No one heeded the commands of a captive Pope. At length the Germans, who had retired to Narni to escape the ravages of plague and famine,[1] swooped back upon the city in September and subjected it to a second sack almost as terrible as the first. Some idea of the destruction which they had wrought by this time may be gathered from the diary of a German eyewitness, who says: 'The troops had destroyed and burnt down the city; two thirds of the houses were in ruins. Doors, windows, and every bit of woodwork even to the roof-beams were consumed by fire. Most of the inhabitants, especially all the women, had taken flight.'[2] But at length, in the autumn, Clement found means to raise the preliminary instalment of his ransom, and on December 6 the Spanish garrison evacuated Sant' Angelo. The Pope, disguised as a merchant, mounted a horse at a postern in the Vatican wall and rode with a small escort towards Orvieto. Behind him as he rode, on that winter evening, the Rome of Leo, of Julius, of Nicholas V., lay in ruins. Did Clement dimly feel in his bruised soul that all had not been well with his shepherding of Christ's flock? Nothing in the sequel was to show it, yet as the news of the great destruction penetrated to the four corners of the earth, men shuddered at the tale, and echoed, in their different tongues, the words of an honest Spaniard who beheld the sack: 'In Rome all sins were openly committeed—sodomy,

---

[1] By the end of July, 2,500 Germans had died of plague, and the mortality in the city reached 500 to 700 a day. *Sanuto* xlv., xlvi.

[2] Cornelius de Fine, in *Pastor*, vol. x. (Eng.), p. 13

simony, idolatry, hypocrisy, fraud. Surely then, what has come to pass has not been by chance, but by the Judgment of God.'

In Florence, as we have seen, the news of the sack of Rome had led to a rising against the unpopular government of Clement's representative, Cardinal Passerini, and to the re-establishment of Savonarola's 'Great Council' and of the republican forms evolved in Soderini's time. Events had long been leading up to some such revolution. The Medicean rule, though fairly popular while Leo and Cardinal Giulio gave it their personal attention, had always meant a heavy drain on the financial resources of Florence, for both Popes had acted in the spirit of the advice once given them by Charles V.—'Make the Florentines pay!' Moreover, aspirations towards a return to freedom had never died among the cultured classes, and were especially rife among the brilliant clique who formed the so-called 'Society of the Rucellai Gardens.' Here, in this peaceful haunt of the 'intellectuals' of Florence, a note of strenuous patriotism began to invade their literary discussions, as the genius of Machiavelli gradually dominated the scene. The great cynic, who during these years wrote his *Prince*, and dedicated it to the younger Lorenzo de' Medici, shows his real mind in the *Discourse on Florentine Government*, which he dedicated to his host of the Gardens, and in the *Art of War*, the scene of which is laid among its groves. In these patriotic tracts, read aloud chapter by chapter to a sensitive and admiring audience, there glows the real enthusiasm of Machiavelli for liberty, his constant faith in the policy of arming the people. Small wonder that when Cardinal Giulio came to govern Florence during the Pontificate of Adrian VI., some of these youths formed a plot against his life—a plot for which they paid with the forfeit of their own. The Cardinal, however, ruled with moderation and success on the accustomed Medicean lines, and it was only when, on his own elevation to the Papacy, he sent to Florence two illegitimate offshoots of his house —Ippolito, son of the 'good' Giuliano, and Alessandro, reputed son of the younger Lorenzo by a mulatto slave—that discontent in the city began to gather weight. The two boys were under the charge of Cardinal Passerini, a 'gross, fat man' who had not the skill to steer his way amid the restless party-life of Florence; and so when the news of the sack of Rome and of Clement's imprisonment reached the town all parties rose against the Cardinal, and by a bloodless revolution the Medici were expelled once more and the Republic recalled into being. Niccolo Capponi, son of that Capponi who had threatened King Charles with the bells of Florence, was elected Gonfalonier, and the Republic entered upon the last and most glorious episode of her many-coloured life.

Meanwhile Pope Clement, safe in the dilapidated episcopal palace of Orvieto, found himself assailed with entreaties that he should rejoin the League, and so lend support to those who would avenge him on the destroyers of Rome. And in the year 1528 this was by no means an unreasonable demand, for King Francis had once more bestirred himself in the affairs of Italy, and had sent the veteran Lautrec to attempt the reconquest of Naples. In February this old campaigner crossed the boundary of the kingdom, and the mutinous *Landsknechts* were at length induced to evacuate Rome and march south to the defence of Naples. By the end of April the Imperial fleet was destroyed off Salerno by the French under their Genoese Admiral Doria, and the fall of Naples before Lautrec's attack seemed but a matter of days. Clement was torn between his natural desire for vengeance on the Imperialists, and certain older and still more deep-rooted prejudices which deterred him from joining their opponents. For had not his enemy Alfonso of Ferrara joined the League, and had not King Francis promised to protect revolted Florence? To all entreaties therefore Clement returned the same unvarying answer: Alfonso must first surrender Modena and Reggio; Venice must first restore Ravenna and Cervia. Like all weak men, Clement had certain obsessions to which he clung with inflexible obstinacy, and one of these was his feeling with regard to these four towns. When therefore the news arrived that the scale of war had been turned in the South during July—August, 1528, by the defection of Andrea Doria from the French to the Imperial side, and by the death of Lautrec in the plague-stricken camp before Naples, Clement rejoiced that he had maintained his neutrality. Nor was it long before the turn of events in Florence decided him finally to throw in his lot with the Emperor. In April, 1529, Niccolo Capponi, the 'moderate' Gonfalonier, who leaned towards a reconciliation with the Medici while maintaining a free Republic, was deposed from office by the extremer Democrats, and a bitterly anti-Medicean partisan was elected in his place. Charles V. had always offered Clement as the price of his alliance that he would restore the Medici to Florence. Clement now closed with the offer. In July, 1529, the Treaty of Barcelona was signed between Pope and Emperor; on the one hand Clement bound himself to crown the Emperor and invest him with the Kingdom of Naples; on the other Charles undertook to restore the Pope's family to Florence, to reinstate him in the possession of the four towns and to declare the Duke of Ferrara forfeited of his duchy. Thus the Emperor outbid the League. A few weeks later the King of France betrayed his Italian allies in a separate peace with the Emperor concluded at Cambrai [August 5, 1529], by which, in return for the surrender of his two captive sons, he renounced his claims to Milan and to Naples. The League, shorn of its strongest member, was left defenceless before Charles.

The Emperor had already announced his intention of coming to Italy in person to assume the two crowns of Charlemagne, and early in August he set sail from Barcelona. He was received with great pomp at Genoa, where Doria's change of sides had brought about the city's emancipation from the power of France, and produced a condition of comparative dignity and internal peace. The Dogeship was revived, but Doria refused the ducal cap and preferred to follow his career as an Admiral in Charles's service— one of the most notable in this century of seamen. His native city owed much to him, for his desertion of France for the Empire had been due to no personal motives, but solely to the French King's arrogant contempt for the liberties of Genoa.

Clement, meanwhile, was summoned to meet the Emperor at Bologna, since pressing dangers in Germany prevented Charles from travelling as far as Rome. Here, on Friday, November 5, 1529, Clement sat enthroned outside the porch of San Petronio and received in state the man in whose name he had suffered such intolerable wrong. Hither, too, flocked in crowds the princes and rulers of Italy, jostling one another to obtain the Imperial favour and support. Venice obtained her peace by ceding the disputed towns, Ravenna and Cervia, to the Pope, and by paying a war indemnity; Mantua became a duchy; the Duke of Urbino was confirmed in the possession of his lands. But all interest really centred on the fate of Milan, Ferrara, and Florence, and here an intricate game of *quid pro quo* was played between Charles and the Pope. Charles had passed through Reggio on his way to Bologna and had there been won over by Alfonso to the Duke's view of the case; in his own mind he was determined to oppose the Pope's claim to the Emilian towns. On the other hand Clement urged the recognition of Francesco Sforza as Duke of Milan, and in spite of the heavy cloud which had rested on the Duke ever since the conspiracy of Morone, Charles consented to restore him to his duchy in return for an enormous payment to be wrung from the exhausted Milanese. The last of the Sforza did indeed live for six years more to enjoy the sad privilege of reigning over the ghost of Milan, but on his death without heirs, in 1535, he bequeathed his

duchy to the Emperor, by whom it was treated as a private possession of the Hapsburg family. The affairs of Ferrara were settled,
after the Emperor's coronation, in favour of the Duke, much to
Clement's mortification, but in the point above all others on which
the Pope's heart was set he found the Emperor as complaisant as
he could wish. Florence must be taught by force of arms to receive
back her masters.

An expedition against the contumacious Republic had been
decided upon as early as August, 1529, and Clement had entrusted
the task to Filibert, Prince of Orange, who had succeeded to the
command of the Spaniards and Landsknechts after Bourbon's
death. Cardinals were not wanting who implored the Pope not
to turn against his native city the very men who had made Rome
a wilderness, but Clement was inflexible. By the middle of October the Prince of Orange had taken up his quarters at Piano di
Ripoli, two miles south of Florence, his army swollen by the troops
brought over from Spain by the Emperor; and two months later
20,000 men, drawn from the Lombard garrisons, arrived to complete the investment of the city from the north.

But within the walls the spirit of the citizens had risen to meet
the danger with whole-hearted enthusiasm. The remnants of Savonarola's followers went about the streets preaching to an excited
population, promising that Christ would not desert the city that
had chosen Him for King, crying out that they saw the Archangels
guarding it with flaming swords. Even before the change of government in the spring, when Niccolo Capponi had been deposed for
carrying on a secret correspondence with the Pope, preparations
for war had been pushed forward with the utmost energy. Though
Machiavelli did not live to see it,[1] his idea of a popular militia was
now adopted by all parties, although with the characteristic distrust of the governors for the governed, the artisan class was not
armed until the siege had run its course for six months, and then
very imperfectly. But three thousand young men, sons or descendants of citizens eligible for the Great Council, were formed into
a City Guard and trained by officers from the Black Bands of Giovanni de' Medici; and beside this élite a militia of about thirteen
thousand men was raised from the peasants of the countryside.
The Signory felt the need of stiffening this citizen army with a
leaven of professionals, and therefore took the step, so obvious
at the time, so baneful in its result, of engaging as Captain-General
the Lord of Perugia, Malatesta Baglioni, with five thousand foot.

[1] He died in poverty shortly after the proclamation of the Republic in
1527.

THE EMPEROR CHARLES V, BY TITIAN
From the painting in the Prado Gallery, Madrid

A personal enemy of Clement VII., son of a Baglioni who had been decoyed to Rome and put to death by Leo X., surely, they reasoned, his fidelity would be above suspicion. Other notable *condottieri* also found their way to Florence, and were taken into the Republic's pay. Meanwhile the strengthening of the walls and the construction of new fortifications had been carried on during the whole year, and by a memorable decree of April 6, 1529, Michelangelo Buonarotti was appointed Procurator-general of the city walls. His special task was to fortify the hill and church of San Miniato, and so effective were his devices that the guns of the Imperialists could make no impression on this important outwork.

The Prince of Orange, after making one attempt to escalade the walls [November 11], settled down to blockade the town, and the siege became an affair of sorties on the part of the besieged rather than of attacks on the part of the besiegers. The City Guard showed both spirit and discipline in these frequent skirmishes, but in the light of after events it was observed that even in December, Baglioni had prevented one of these sorties from developing into a decisive victory by sounding the retreat too soon. He was in truth pre-occupied with the fate of Perugia, and, distrusting the ultimate victory of Florence, wished to make his retreat secure with his overlord the Pope. But outside in the *Contado*—the all-important countryside to the west whence Florence still drew her supplies—matters were in the hands of no mercenary captain, but of a native leader of genius whose exploits have invested the Siege of Florence with a sort of legendary glory. Francesco Ferrucci, just returned from serving against Naples with the Black Bands, was appointed commissary of the small towns in the Val d'Arno, and there succeeded in organizing a fighting force which for months held its own against the flying columns of the Imperial army. Constantly harassing them with ambuscades and the interception of convoys, Ferrucci even succeeded in introducing regular supplies into Florence from Empoli, which he fortified strongly and converted into an important magazine for stores. But in April, 1530, he was called away to win back the town of Volterra, the inhabitants of which had made common cause with the Imperialists and were besieging a Florentine garrison in the citadel.[1] Ferrucci made a forced march from Empoli, attacked the Spaniards the same evening and drove them from the town, but was then obliged to stand a siege himself against strong reinforcements of

[1] The revolt of some of the subject-towns was a not unexpected feature of the siege; thus Arezzo received the Prince of Orange with alacrity in September, 1529, and declared herself once more an independent republic.

the enemy. All through the months of May and June, he held the Cyclopean walls of Volterra against heavy guns, heedless of wounds and of fever, but in his absence Empoli had been surprised and taken, and its great accumulation of stores was lost to Florence. Famine began to make great strides in the beleaguered town, and when Ferrucci had beaten off the Imperialists from Volterra at the end of June he received orders from the Signory to use any and every means in his power to bring relief to the capital. All hopes rested on him. His efforts would be seconded by a sortie in force from the walls, should he succeed in reaching the enemy's lines.

In response to this desperate appeal, Ferrucci marched in search of reinforcements to Pisa, and there lost thirteen days of precious time by a violent attack of fever. But on July 30 he started with three thousand men to make a circuitous march through the Lucchese mountains, intending to surprise Pistoja and thence make his way into Florence. But the Prince of Orange, now thoroughly alarmed, determined to stop the guerilla leader at all costs, and having made a secret arrangement with Baglioni that the garrison should not attack his camp in his absence, he started on the evening of August 1, with two thousand picked men, to intercept Ferrucci. Already three other columns of the enemy were converging on the devoted band of Florentines, and in the little town of Gavinana, perched in the hills above Pistoja, they met their end. The Prince of Orange himself was killed in the cavalry fight outside the walls, but in the little Piazza Ferrucci, overwhelmed by numbers, fell after three hours' fighting, and was dispatched in cold blood by a Neapolitan captain.

So perished the last hope of Florence. Baglioni meanwhile had disobeyed the repeated and impassioned orders of the Signory to march against the enemy, and when summoned to lay down his command he replied by turning the guns of his bastion upon the city. In vain the Gonfalonier ordered the City Guard to march against the traitor; discouragement pervaded their ranks, and throughout the town the Mediceans, or Palleschi,[1] raised their heads and clamoured for an agreement. On the 11th of August, 1530, the Signory consented to treat, and on the 12th the capitulation was signed. The Medici were to be received back, but some liberties were to be preserved; an amnesty was to be granted for all past offences, and the distant figure of the Emperor was invoked to decide on the future constitution of Florence. Vain and hypocritical promises! Though Florence escaped the last outrage of a

[1] So-called from the *palle*, or balls on the Medici shield.

sack, Pope Clement showed without delay that he meant to be master there, and under the reign of terror of his emissary, Baccio Valori, the Florentines learnt the true value of the engagements of their conqueror. When the ground had been sufficiently prepared by executions, imprisonments, confiscations, and decrees of exile, the bastard mulatto Alessandro de' Medici was sent with all pomp into the town, to bear rule at his good pleasure there in place of the Republic of Florence, deceased.

CHAPTER XXI

Italy in the Sixteenth Century

THE political settlement of Italy achieved by Pope and Emperor at Bologna, and confirmed by the fall of Florence, endured in all its main features until, after the wars of Louis XIV., the Spanish hegemony in the peninsula was transferred to Austria. The predominance of Spain was assured by the actual possession of Milan, Naples, and Sicily, and by the armed protection which it exercised over Florence, while the occasional strivings of the smaller duchies, or even of some recalcitrant Pope, were easily suppressed by the Spanish garrisons, lodged in the new-built fortresses which gradually arose to overawe the people. A deadly exhaustion crept over the ruined country, in literature and art as well as in political feeling; prosperity and wealth seemed to decline, perhaps in part owing to the adoption by the richer classes of the idle manners of a Spanish aristocracy; and in the soil thus impoverished the weeds of despotism and reaction grew unchecked. Following on the establishment of princely or Imperial absolutism at the different courts, the Inquisition was imported from Spain, and the Society of Jesus fastened itself upon the Papal system, to wage war against the forces of intellectual freedom. The exuberant life of the Renaissance, with all its vigour and audacity, its wealth of individual genius, dwindled and died, and in its place we have the vague sweetness of Torquato Tasso, and the ever-increasing formalism of painting. Michelangelo indeed lived on, a solitary Titan, to break his great heart upon the tombs of the Medici and the dome of St. Peter's, but he had fallen upon evil days, and lived to see the nude figures of his *Last Judgment* 'draped' by order of the persecuting Pope, Paul IV.

Towards the vast religious conflict which divided the rest of Europe, Italy, tired out by thirty years of devastating war, made its only contribution in producing the nimble-witted politicians who steered the Council of Trent to a successful conclusion. But the rude shocks delivered by the Lutherans of the North against the Papal system stimulated a movement which had already begun for reforming the Church from within, and as early as the reign of Paul III. she produced a band of true idealists, headed by the Venetian Contarini, who not only strove to carry peace to the

German rebels, but provided the spiritual impulse towards the Counter-Reformation itself. Too soon, however, their movement was drowned in the rising flood; Contarini failed to unite the irreconcilables at the Diet of Ratisbon in 1541, and from that moment the narrow reactionary party in the Church prevailed over the 'Modernist.' Ignatius Loyola had already received the approval of the Pope for the foundation of his Jesuit Order [1540]. The Inquisition was established at Rome in 1542, and from the Inquisition developed in due course the famous 'Congregation of the Index,' which lay like a dead weight upon the literary life of the country, ruined the book-trade of Florence and Venice, and employed a host of ignorant censors to garble and deface even the works of Classical antiquity.

It was no wonder that under such pressure the astute Italians learnt the lesson of conformity to the type required, and that Rome under Paul IV. assumed the air of a 'well-behaved religious community.'[1] But in reality they had but added the sin of hypocrisy to their former sins of violence and dissolute living,[2] and beneath the pious aspect of Rome the corruption of morals and of all ordinary standards of integrity was as profound as ever. In Rome, more than in any other Italian state, the venality of justice became part of the recognized financial system; all but the very highest Judgeships were bought and sold like any other venal office at the Curia,[3] and the Judges subsisted on the 'compositions' they extorted from innocent and guilty alike.[4] The people, whether high or low, seldom voluntarily resorted to the courts of justice, but continued to carry on their private feuds and assassinations in their own fashion—the nobles by hiring professional murderers, or 'bravi,' to whom they gave the protection of their

[1] See Mocenigo's *Report to the Venetian Senate*, 1560, in Alberi, series ii., vol. 4.

[2] 'If any one sinned, they did it as quietly and secretly as possible, whereas in old days everything went on licentiously and without the smallest restraint even amongst bishops and cardinals.' *Ibid.,* p. 48.

[3] *Ibid.,* pp. 29—30.

[4] See Brosch, *Kirchenstaat*, p. 232. Mocenigo, p. 30: 'In criminal affairs, though with poor folk justice is rigorous and prompt, with rich persons or such as have the means of raising money it seems that the procedure is so bad that I do not think it could possibly be worse. For by order of the Popes and under public authority they compound with larger or smaller sums of money as the case may be for all the crimes, however monstrous (always excepting capital offences), that are committed in Rome or in the States of the Church; and these sums, which are called compositions, are entered in the accounts as ordinary revenue: all of which seems to me to be the strangest proceeding that could ever be seen or heard of.'

palaces, the peasants by organizing themselves in roving bands of brigands who terrorized and levied blackmail over the whole countryside. The usual method of proceeding against these outlaws was by offering a price for their murder, so that every bravo's hand was turned against his fellow, but crimes of violence continued to increase in spite of this device, and even the barbarity of the criminal law—the torture of witnesses, the death by prolonged tortures of the criminal himself—was insufficient to act as a deterrent. The Papal and princely methods of taxation also prevented any amelioration in the condition of the people, and sometimes drove the peasants from their homes to swell the ranks of the banditti; hearth-taxes, often levied three times in the year, salt-taxes always on the increase, taxes on all forms of produce entering Rome, kept down the peasants of the Patrimony to the level of wild beasts, while in Ferrara the system of game-laws introduced by Alfonso II. made a wilderness of the vast fertile region round the town, and destroyed, more effectively than any other of his extortions, the ancient loyalty of the people towards the *Casa d' Este.*

But Italy, in spite of the dead weight under which she laboured of foreign and domestic tyranny, could not even yet abdicate her position of supremacy in the things of the mind. The particular form which the struggle for liberty took beyond the Alps—the rugged Puritanism, the sheer revolt from Rome—was not for her, but in subtler though none the less effective ways she kept alight the lamp of truth through evil days. Venice still stood, proud in her contempt for Inquisitors and Popes, safe amid her inviolable lagoons, and at her University of Padua maintained an atmosphere of freedom which, at the end of the century, was to attract the mighty spirit of Galileo. At Florence and Ferrara learning was still protected in the traditional manner by Medici and Este dukes, though here the shadow of the Inquisition lay heavy on the gay courts of former days. But above all, at a moment when in painting and sculpture the impulse of the Renaissance seemed to be exhausted, Italy took over leadership in a new art to comfort a tired world, and by their contribution to modern music Palestrina and others laid posterity under their debt.

Nor was she behind the rest of Europe in the field of political construction. Though this epoch saw the final extinction of some of the most glorious of the mediæval republics—Perugia, Ancona, and Siena—it also saw the rise of the centralized modern state in the two duchies of Tuscany and Savoy. In the former, Cosimo de' Medici, while ruthlessly suppressing the old Republican forms of Florence and quenching the liberties of Siena, yet acted the part of the 'Impartial Podestà' and imposed a sound administration on the whole of Tuscany. In the latter, Emanuel Filibert, returning from long exile, drove out the foreign garrisons from Piedmont and created in that rugged corner of north-western Italy, an autocratic and yet an intensely vital state. Many and great as were the evils bequeathed to modern Italy by the sixteenth century, she yet secured from it this one great boon—a national dynasty, which, when the time was ripe, stood ready to speak and strike for the whole country, and to make Italy at last a nation.

In 1534 the unhappy Pope Clement VII. died, and was succeeded by Cardinal Alessandro Farnese, a relic of the creations of Alexander VI.[1] The new Pope, who took the name of Paul III., summed up in his own person all the characteristics of this age of transition and of contradictions. A prince of the Renaissance at heart, he had a son and grandsons to provide for, and loved to regale the Romans with pageants and displays in semi-Pagan style; but the exigencies of the time were shown in his serious preoccupation with the problem of Church reform, and in his consenting to summon, at the Emperor's repeated demand, the famous Council of Trent. There was a touch of grandeur, too, in his appointment, a few months after his own election, of six of the most distinguished men in Italy, headed by Contarini, to the College of Cardinals, in order to push forward the work of reformation. But though the memorable report which they produced— the *Consilium de Emendandâ Ecclesiâ*—became the foundation for some future reforms, in Paul's own day the vested interests concerned in the maintenance of Curial corruption proved too strong an obstacle even for the zeal of Contarini and his friend, Caraffa. The question of reform was moreover intimately bound up with that of the Council, and it was observed that whenever an understanding seemed imminent between the King of France and the Emperor in the matter of the Council, the Pope urged on the work of reform with feverish energy, in order that that much dreaded body should not have an excuse for too severe a purgation.

But when a small body of Spanish and Italian bishops did at length meet at Trent, in December, 1545, it was not the Pope but the Emperor who soon began to protest indignantly against their

[1] Guicciardini says of him: 'The use he made of the cardinalate was better than his manner of acquiring it, for it is certain that Pope Alexander had granted that dignity not to him, but to Madonna Giulia his sister, a maiden of great excellence of form.' *Storia d'Italia*, last book.

proceedings. Charles had expected that the Council would at once proceed to reform the Church in head and members, and that by that means he would be able to win back his revolted Lutheran subjects. Paul on the other hand had determined to use the assembly in order to draw up a final definition of Catholic dogma, and the result of this was to make the breach impassable between Church and heretics. His subservient Italian majority on the Council gave his Legates complete control over its proceedings, and Charles was soon breaking out into fierce protests to the Papal Nuncio as he saw his schemes for conciliating the Protestant princes thwarted by the obstinacy of the assembled Fathers. In March, 1547, Paul even removed the Council to Bologna, in spite of the Emperor's peremptory orders to the contrary, and in 1548 he suspended its useless sittings. At the same time he drew more definitely towards France, where he found sympathy and support for his schemes of dynastic aggrandizement in Italy.

For Pope Paul III. was the father of a pushing and unscrupulous son, by name Pier-Luigi Farnese, for whom it was imperative that a fitting appanage should be found. He had been made Gonfalonier of the Church in 1537, and in 1540 was employed in suppressing the rebellion of Perugia against an increased salt-tax—a task which he performed so thoroughly that Perugia emerged with the loss of all her ancient liberties, and with the sad necessity of seeing a citadel built within her walls—'ad coercendam Perusinorum audaciam.'[1] But as yet he was only Duke of Castro and Nepi, and in 1545 Paul took advantage of the bestowal of Milan on Don Philip of Spain[2] to bestow on his own son a fief better worthy of his acceptance—the cities of Parma and Piacenza, with the title of Duke of Parma. These two towns had been taken from the Duchy of Milan by Julius II. in 1512, and their transference had never been recognized by the Empire, but Charles now accepted the arrangement with a good grace, though his Governor at Milan, Gonzaga, warned him that Farnese would be the centre for all that was pro-French and anti-Imperialist in the scattered elements of the north and centre. This indeed proved to be the case, but in the end it was more for his virtues than his sins, which were many, that Pier-Luigi fell. He attempted to depress the ancient Ghibelline nobility of the two towns and to encourage the Guelf middle class, and in revenge for his disciplinary measures he was murdered at Piacenza by three young nobles in December,

---

[1] So ran the inscription above the gate. The citadel remained standing until 1860, when it was destroyed by the Piedmontese.
[2] See p. 268.

1547, before his new dukedom was three years old. Gonzaga at Milan knew and approved of the plot, and moved Imperial troops into Piacenza, but though this act still further embittered the relations between Pope and Emperor in the last two years of Paul's life, the Farnesi were a tenacious race, and Pier-Luigi's son Ottavio succeeded in winning back Piacenza in the reign of Paul's successor. The Duchy of Parma in fact was the most permanent of all the Papal appanages, for the Farnesi held it until they became extinct in 1731, and after many vicissitudes it passed at length into the hands of Napoleon's wife, Marie-Louise, to whom the Holy Alliance granted this little spot of earth in compensation for the loss of Europe.

The Pontificate of Julius III., who succeeded to Paul in January, 1550, remains memorable chiefly for the building of the 'Villa di Papa Giulio' outside the Porta del Popolo, with which this easy-going Pontiff busied himself when he, too, had suspended the sittings of the too troublesome Council of Trent. But in 1555 the Cardinals elected, to their own amazement and horror,[1] the most violent of all the reforming party—Gian Pietro Caraffa, who as Pope Paul IV. [1555—1559] was to present to the world the very embodiment of the spirit of persecution. The Venetian ambassador Navagero has left us a vivid picture of this man's tempestuous personality: 'His temperament is choleric and hasty,' he writes; 'he walks as though he hardly touched the ground; he is all sinew and little flesh; in his eyes and in all the movements of his body there is a vigour that greatly exceeds his age.'[2] And the Venetian proceeds to describe his vehemence in discussion, his intolerance of interruption and contempt for all his councillors; his devotion to the Inquisition, the weekly meetings of which he never missed, and his hatred of Charles V. and his son Philip as being traffickers with heretics. He would inveigh against them and the whole Spanish nation during the endless meals at which he drank Neapolitan wine and ate through twenty-five courses; for Paul IV. could never forget that he was a Neapolitan noble, and as such the hatred of Spain was the passion uppermost in his soul.

[1] Mocenigo's *Report*, pp. 46—7: 'He was elected Pope against everyone's expectation, including his own, and he told me himself shortly before he died that he had never made himself agreeable to any one, and that if ever a cardinal had asked him a favour he had always answered roughly and never done what was asked, so that, as he said to me, "I do not know why they elected me Pope, and I am bound to conclude that it is not the Cardinals but God who makes the Popes."'

[2] Navagero's report, in Alberi, *Relazioni degli Amb. Veneti.*, series ii., vol. 3., p. 379.

To the astonishment of his *entourage*, who had expected to see him turn all his energies to the work of Church reform, Paul entered on a bloody war with the Colonna—allies of Spain—in the first year of his Pontificate, and used it in order to push the fortunes of a brood of nephews whose doings soon reminded Rome of the days of the Borgia. The youngest, Carlo Caraffa, a soldier of fortune whose morals were of the loosest, was made a cardinal; the two elder were enriched with fiefs and castles torn from the Colonna. The Romans could not endure the sight of these upstart Neapolitans, and their insolence added greatly to the unpopularity which gathered round the Pope. And soon the headstrong violence of Pope and nephews brought Rome to the brink of such another catastrophe as that of 1527. The war with the Colonna, combined with other provocations against Charles and Philip, led directly to a war with Spain. The Duke of Alva, at this time Viceroy of Naples, gathered his forces for an advance on Rome, and the direst panic seized on the wretched inhabitants, but just emerging from the ruin of the Sack. Paul sought to appeal to Italian patriotism in the manner of Julius II., but he could not conduct the war without the aid of a foreign power, and as Julius had called in the Spaniards, so Paul called in the French. Henry II. of France gladly took up the quarrel, and sent the Duke of Guise to Rome in March, 1557; but Guise was no match for Alva in the campaign that followed, and the sacking of the small towns in the Sabine hills was the only result of his attempt to invade Naples. His forces were soon in full retreat, and Alva advancing unchecked upon Rome. But the Spanish Viceroy had no desire to repeat the rôle of the Constable of Bourbon. After advancing to within shot of the Porta Maggiore he retired to Palliano, and Paul, whose Lutheran and Gascon mercenaries were on the point of mutiny, had no choice but to send three cardinals to seek him there and sue for peace. Though by its terms his Sabine towns were restored to him, he knew well that all was over with his dreams for dislodging the Spanish power from Italy. When Alva came to Rome, a stately penitent, and kissed the Pope's foot with every token of humility [September 19, 1557], Paul knew that the parts were indeed reversed, and that the Spanish heel was planted more firmly than ever on his unhappy country.

Sore and humiliated, the Pope turned with renewed fury to the work from which he had been diverted by the war—that of stamping out heresy and of putting an end to the abuses in Church and Curia. The Council of Trent was not renewed during his Pontificate, because Paul deemed that he could carry out its work single-handed, and indeed scarcely a day passed but some reforming decree was put forth, which afterwards served as a model for the decrees of Trent. Bishops were forced to reside in their sees, the religious orders were strictly purged, and the sale of benefices so sternly reduced that the Dataria, or Board of Appointments, brought in not more than a quarter of the revenue that it had enjoyed under other Popes. The Inquisition was spurred on to ever greater activity. The use of torture for the discovery of accomplices was formally authorized, and the Roman people presented with the spectacle of the burning of heretics in the Campo de' Fiori. The first Papal Index of Prohibited Books was drawn up and published [1559], and the full force of the Inquisition let loose upon those who owned, bought, or sold such volumes. Nor were the Jews spared. All the privileges which they had gradually acquired under former Popes were revoked, and the badge of servitude which they had evaded in gentler reigns—the yellow cap—was reimposed on them under severest penalties. In the midst of these pursuits the Pope became aware, almost by accident, of the delinquencies of his nephews, and after waiting in a fever of agitation for ten days he summoned the Consistory and declared before God that he had known nothing of the vileness of their lives; then he banished them from his sight for ever, and hunted their adherents from the Court.[1] But not even this startling act of justice could win him back the love of the Roman people, and when a few months later the old man lay on his death-bed a fierce insurrection broke out in the streets, the palace of the Inquisition was sacked and its papers burnt, and the arms of the Caraffa torn down wherever they were found. Finally the mob made a rush for the Capitol and threw down a newly-erected statue of the Pope, dressed the head in the yellow cap of a Jew and after dragging it through the streets for hours hurled it into the Tiber. To such an accompaniment the soul of the first Inquisitor Pope passed from the earth that it had troubled.

The reign of the next Pope, Pius IV. [1559—1565], a man in all respects the opposite of Paul, was mainly occupied with the successful winding-up of the Council of Trent. But the manner in which this shrewd, middle-class lawyer from Milan managed the affairs of the Council, so that it was said that 'the Holy Ghost reached Trent in the dispatch-bags of the Pope,' belongs rather to the history of the Church than to that of Italy. Pius had been elected by the influence of a remarkable Italian prince, Cosimo de'

---

[1] The next Pope, Pius IV., had the cardinal strangled in St. Angelo and the eldest brother with two other relatives beheaded. [1560.]

Medici the Younger, and it is time that we followed the fortunes of this successful adventurer, and those of the state which he created.

Cosimo, second Duke of Florence and first Grand Duke of Tuscany, was the only son of the famous Giovanni delle Bande Nere, and as such was gladly accepted by the subservient Senate of Florence when, in 1537, the murder of Duke Alessandro by the hand of a cousin[1] set the whole city in a ferment. The chance for a return to liberty was let slip, not only because the leaders of the Republican movement were in exile and unprepared, but because the newly-built Citadel was in the hands of Imperial troops, who prevented any popular demonstration. Cosimo was received with acclamation by a populace which knew little of his character, but his new subjects were not long in learning that they had given themselves a master. His first task was to suppress the rising of the Republican exiles, led by the ill-starred Filippo Strozzi, and this was accomplished a few months after his accession at the skirmish of Montemurlo, where, by a lucky stroke, all the rebel leaders fell into his hands. They were executed in batches of four a day until the loud murmurs of the crowd induced the new Duke to immure them instead in the dungeons of Volterra and Pisa; and Strozzi, after enduring torture, perished either by his own or an assassin's hand in the Citadel itself.

From the day of Montemurlo, Cosimo de' Medici felt himself secure in the saddle. He was only eighteen years of age, but his long reign of thirty-seven years was to leave an indelible mark on the character of the state he had come to rule. Harsh, able, and self-willed, he had all the qualities necessary for dragging Florence through this period of painful transition, and when he associated his son in the government in 1564 he made over to him a self-dependent state, orderly and obedient, emancipated from all foreign control, defended by a national army, and enlarged by the acquisition of the ancient Republic of Siena and her territory. It was a labour fit for the 'Prince' of Machiavelli's dreams, and indeed the career of Cosimo was the best embodiment of these dreams that Italy had yet beheld. He disfranchised the people, but he ruled them well according to the lights of his age; gave them clean-handed justice and a strong police; trusted them by raising from amongst them an efficient militia on Machiavelli's

[1] Lorenzino de' Medici, a descendant of Cosimo the Elder's brother Lorenzo. He was in his turn murdered by bravoes of Duke Cosimo's at Venice in 1546. See Symonds, *Renaiss. in Italy*, vi.

model. He nursed back Pisa to prosperity by encouraging her seaborne trade and by establishing a university there [1543]; he did much to revive the silk and woollen trades of Florence. His taxation was oppressive, especially during the War of Siena, but at least it was not barbed with political vindictiveness, like Cosimo the Elder's, and his forced loans bore interest and were repayable. Political vindictiveness, however, there certainly was in full measure, for Cosimo's spies were everywhere, and it was seventeen years before even a modified amnesty was granted to the rebels of Strozzi's faction. They requited his hatred to the uttermost, and it was a son of Filippo Strozzi who inspired the last desperate resistance of Siena to his arms.

The Republic of Siena, most turbulent, factious, and passionately religious of all the great republics of Italy, had from time immemorial maintained a bitter rivalry with Florence, whose burgher army she never forgot that she had routed at Montaperti, in the days of Farinata and King Manfred. Her territory stretched from Val di Chiana to the sea, and from Poggibonsi to Monte Amiata; her school of painting, her Duomo and great Palace, her Saints[1] and her Pope[2] had spread her fame far beyond the bounds of Italy. Intensely Ghibelline by tradition, even as Florence was Guelf, she had been a bulwark of the first importance to the mediæval Emperors, in their periodic incursions into Italy, and now since the sack of Rome she had taken the Imperial side and admitted a small Spanish garrison within her walls. But the Spanish Governors agreed ill with the democratic and restless republic, and when in 1550 Don Diego Mendoza announced that he had orders from his master to build a citadel, the Sienese determined that rather than submit to such bondage they would throw themselves into the arms of France. So it came to pass that in the last death-struggle between Siena and Florence the ancient parts stood reversed, and while Cosimo de' Medici victualled and paid the Imperialist besiegers, Henri II. sent Piero Strozzi, now a marshal of France, to organize the defence. It was the coming of this brave adventurer that gave Cosimo his pretext for declaring war, since by a treaty of 1553 Siena had undertaken—as in that old war of Montaperti— not to shelter Florentine exiles.

In the Commentaries of Blaise de Montluc, Strozzi's valiant French lieutenant, and in the diary of Alessandro Sozzini, the Sienese captain, the heartrending story of this siege of fifteen

---

[1] St. Catherine, 1347–1380, and San Bernardino.
[2] Pius II. (Æneas Sylvius Piccolomini), who though born at Corsignano was educated at Siena and always accounted himself a Sienese.

months may yet be read. In these day-by-day recitals we see the light-hearted gallantry of the first months changing to steadfast heroism when Strozzi, with the pick of the garrison, had been defeated in the open field by the Marquis of Marignano,[1] his opponent; we read of the wholesale devastation of the countryside the hanging of peasants, the grim tragedy of the 'useless mouths,' and we cannot wonder when the brave Montluc at length exclaims, 'God will need to be merciful indeed towards us, who wreak so much evil!' When at length the long agony was over, and Siena capitulated to the Most Catholic King, Philip II. of Spain, her inhabitants were reduced from forty thousand to little more than ten thousand,[2] and the Tuscan maremma was depopulated. Philip ceded the town to his faithful ally, the Duke of Florence, two years later, and so it happens that above the great door of the Palazzo the Medici shield hangs to this day, in place of the black and white of the Republic.

Cosimo's relations with the Church had usually been of the best. A typical son of the Counter-Reformation, he invited the Jesuits to Florence, and chose Loyola's successor in the Generalship as his Confessor; in 1566 he gave up his protégé Pietro Carnesecchi—a former official of the Papal Camera, but too deeply tinged with reformist heresy— to the second Inquisitor-Pope, Pius V., and heard of his hanging a year later without a protest. His complaisance in this matter stood him in good stead, for Pius rewarded him with the title of Grand-Duke of Tuscany, thereby putting an end to the vexatious quarrel for precedence between Florence and Ferrara. Cosimo died, an old man though only at the age of fifty-five, in 1574, and his son Francesco entered unopposed into the fruits of his gigantic labours.

An autocrat of a different stamp performed, for Savoy and Piedmont, a similar task to that which Cosimo had achieved for Tuscany. Emanuel Filibert, son of Duke Charles III., had seen as a boy his father's territories invaded and occupied by the French in 1535—6, and his family driven to take refuge in Nice, the only port belonging to the duchy. Piedmont became for the next twenty years a mere battle-ground between French and Spaniards, and its prosperity disappeared as completely as that of Lombardy in the earlier wars; but the young prince determined to devote his whole career to the recovery of his inheritance. With a mixture of astuteness and romance, he took military service with the Em-

[1] Gian-Giacomo Medici (of Milan), brother of Pope Pius IV.
[2] Mocenigo's Report, p. 58.

peror at the age of seventeen, convinced that this would be 'the true opening for the restoration of your possessions,' as he wrote to his father in 1546. Created Captain-General of the Imperial forces in Flanders at the age of twenty-five, he beat the French at the decisive battle of St. Quentin in 1557, and at the Peace of Câteau-Cambrésis which followed it, secured at any rate the partial fulfilment of his hopes. Savoy and Piedmont were restored to him, with the exception of five towns (including Turin) retained for three years by the French, and of two others retained by the Spaniards until the French evacuation should have taken place.

This treaty was the foundation of Savoy as a modern state. Though the counts of Savoy emerge into history early in the eleventh century, with the acquisition of Turin, their position was merely that of feudal lords outside the main stream of Italian politics until the French invasions gave them importance as the door-keepers of the Alps. Much entangled with Swiss politics owing to their claims on Geneva, they had no leisure to set their faces definitely towards Italy until this restoration of Emanuel Filibert. But when he and his French wife, the cultivated daughter of Francis I., made their state entry into Turin in 1562, it seemed almost as though this were a new Italian capital. An enormous work of reconstruction lay before them. The Duchess made Turin an intellectual centre; the Duke had to create, from the ruin around him, an army, a navy, a centralized administration, and a system of finance. His subjects were forced to be prosperous almost against their will, that the Duke might draw revenues from their prosperity. He was troubled by the unorthodoxy of the Waldensian sectaries, but after an expedition against the heretics he was fain to allow them liberty of worship in certain places, for he had not the means to crush the mountaineers. The Nuncio sent by Pope Pius IV. was aghast at his free-handedness. Taking advantage of the weakness of France during the Wars of Religion, he obtained the tardy withdrawal of all the French garrisons in 1580, and left to his son Charles Emanuel [1580—1630], a free and sovereign state. That son even acquired Saluzzo [1601], the last fortress owned by France on the Italian side of the Alps. Thus after a hundred years of conflict the stable-door was closed again when the horse of liberty was stolen, and the sentinel Savoyards kept watch for better days.

Meanwhile the Popes of the Counter-Reformation moved on their stately course, setting their own house in order with the Decrees of the Council of Trent, seeking to reimpose the doctrines of the Church by blood and fire on a section of the world that had outgrown them. Pius V. [1566—1572], who had been Grand Inquisitor of Rome before his accession, sent the consecrated hat and sword to Alva in the Netherlands ; Gregory XIII. [1572—1585] rejoiced at the news of St. Bartholomew. But far more memorable for Italy than the reigns of these two Popes was that of their successor Sixtus V. [1585—1590], for this extraordinary man attempted to accomplish for the Papal States the work of reorganization that had just been carried out in Tuscany and Savoy. The state of misery and disorder in which he found them at his accession was incredible; all the old feuds of Guelf and Ghibelline had sprung up again in the Umbrian towns, and the country was swept by organized bands of brigands, resembling the Free Companies of the fourteenth century and estimated at about twenty-seven thousand men. Sixtus set the whole force of an implacable will to the task of exterminating them, and by dint of energetic military measures, of negotiations with neighbouring Powers, and of an appeal to lynch law amongst the bandits themselves, succeeded within two years in more or less clearing his territories of the pest. But since his measures amounted merely to repression, while his exactions imposed still heavier burdens on the peasants, they had no element of permanence, and at his death the very Conclave was terrorized by a band of freebooters who had been lording it in the Campagna.[1]

The restless energy of Sixtus was by no means confined to this one task. He had found the finances also in woeful disorder, but before he died had deposited a treasure of four and a half million *scudi* in the cellars of St. Angelo. Solemnly he bound himself to use this treasure only for the Church's glory—the extirpation of heresy, the war against the Turk. But the increase of taxation which the accumulation of such a sum involved drew down on him the curses of his subjects, who saw themselves squeezed at every pore to exalt the reputation of their master. Yet some at least of the objects to which his money was devoted went far to redeem him in their eyes. He aspired to restore Rome to splendour, and especially that higher part of Rome about the Viminal, Esquiline, and Quirinal hills which had never recovered from the destruction wrought by Robert Guiscard and his Saracens.[2] Thousands of workmen laboured at the laying out of his streets,[3] the

[1] Other bands were on foot round Spoleto, Terni, Ascoli, and Ostia. Brosch, *Kirchenstaat*, p. 277.

[2] See page 75.

[3] Two of the best known of these are the Via Sistina and the Via Venti Settembre, down which the army of United Italy marched from the Porta Pia in 1870.

construction of his new aqueduct, the building of his palace on the Quirinal, and meanwhile the work on Michelangelo's dome was pressed forward, and the great obelisk from the Circus Neronis removed and set up in the square fronting St. Peter's. The hand of Sixtus can in fact be traced in every quarter of Rome as we see it today, and for the love which, according to his lights, he bore the Eternal City, posterity may well forgive him his vandalism towards the ancient buildings,—his destruction of the Septizonium, his crowning of the columns of Hadrian and Trajan with figures of St. Peter and St. Paul. His monument stands in the splendid but forbidding chapel which he added to the Church of Sta. Maria Maggiore, and opposite to him lies his predecessor Pius V., the Grand Inquisitor. Both men were accounted great, yet in these two monuments, the one to the Autocrat, the other to the Persecutor, lies summed up, for those who mourn over the subjection of the human intellect, the full tragedy of Italy during the sixteenth century.

CHAPTER XXII

The Glory and Decline of Venice

THE Age of the Foreign Invasions had, as we have seen, ended with the subjection of the greater part of Italy under the rule of Spain, or at best with the appearance, in Tuscany and Savoy, of autocratic native dynasties. It had in fact ushered in a period of change and violent convulsion which had cut short the normal development of the country on native lines, and imposed on it the habits and organization of an alien race. If the duchies of Ferrara, Mantua, and Urbino still survived, their initiative was gone, for all were bound by the strictest ties of alliance with the Spanish overlord. But it was otherwise with Venice. Weakened but not destroyed by the shock of Europe's attack upon her in 1509, the ancient Republic still maintained herself in the north-east, and was to show the world, long after the Pacification of Bologna, how brilliant and how long-sustained her development could be. The history of Venice becomes doubly valuable, therefore, after the subjugation of the rest of Italy, not only for its intrinsic fascination, but because, with the extinction of Florence and of Milan, only here can we trace the unimpeded after-life of an Italian state.

The days of Venetian expansion, whether in the East or on the mainland, were of course gone by, and her whole existence was now conditioned by the presence of two hostile neighbours—the Turk in the Levant and the Spaniard in the heart of Lombardy. On land, indeed, Venetian territory was almost completely surrounded by the possessions of the House of Hapsburg, and this fact, combined with the inefficiency of the native militia, produced a continual state of nervous tension in the mind of the government, and led to that extraordinary vigilance on the part of the Council of Ten which made for it a name of terror among the secret tribunals of Europe. The Council of Ten, with its adjunct the Three Inquisitors of State, became indeed the arm and hand of Venice, and in the absence of a military force comparable with that of Spain, secured respect for the Republic by an imposing display of personal integrity, executive ability, and unflinching harshness in the punishment of treason. The older institutions of the State—the Great Council, the Senate, and the Doge—continued

to exist and to provide for the ordinary needs of government,[1]
but the Council of Ten was the supreme executive, and in all
matters of urgency it had authority to act without reference to
the other bodies. In 1529 it strengthened itself by the addition of
a *Giunta*, or body of fifteen members chosen from the other councils; in 1539 it made permanent the institution of the Three Inquisitors of State. Thus the Venetian constitution, so long the
admiration and despair of its Italian neighbours, partly succeeded
in adapting itself to the changed conditions of the world, and by
the sleepless activity of its executive inspired a peculiar sense of
awe even in the great monarchies of modern Europe.

But this respect would not have endured for a day if the Republic had not possessed a solid foundation of wealth and power with
which to back up her pretensions. In spite of her loss of trade
with the East, owing to the discovery of the Cape route, her sources
of wealth were still many and great, and if the conquest of India
was reserved for another and a younger sea-power, Venice was
still the door of communication between the rich south-German
towns and all the varied products of the Mediterranean. The
stately *Fondaco dei Tedeschi* on the Grand Canal,[2] with its fading
remains of frescoes by Giorgione and his young disciple Titian,
bears witness even now to the importance of this traffic. But the
patrician families did gradually lose their interest in trade during
the sixteenth century, and preferred to invest their wealth instead
either in banking or in large landed possessions in the mainland
provinces; round Padua, for instance, about one third of the land
was in the hands of rich Venetian citizens after the middle of the
century. Many of these wealthy families were outside the ranks
of the hereditary Great Councillors, and the extent of their resources was seen when, in the course of the War of Candia (1645
—69), the government decided to admit seventy new heads of
families to the ruling body on payment of 100,000 ducats apiece.
The ducats were raised and paid with astonishing ease.

Yet in spite of this abundant wealth, the public finances of
Venice were constantly in a precarious state, and any unwonted
strain on her resources was apt to produce extraordinary embarrassments, from which she would extricate herself by such

---

[1] This was done partly by the creation of standing committees from
among the members of the Great Council, for the management of the
navy, the army, the finances, etc., and partly by the appointment of
numerous special commissioners or *Provveditori* to deal with urgent matters
as they arose. All these committees and commissioners reported to the
Senate.

[2] Now converted into the Central Post Office.

shifts as the above. This was no doubt partly due to the small understanding of the principles of governmental finance possessed by her rulers, but also largely to the extreme leniency with which Venice treated her mainland possessions. From the capital itself she derived an annual revenue of about 1,000,000 ducats, and from the whole of the *Terrafirma*, including such flourishing cities as Verona, Vicenza, Brescia, and Padua, only 1,200,000 more. The reason for this was that Venice followed the principle of leaving to her subject territories as much of their old local autonomy as possible, merely sending to the towns her Podestà or Rector, her Treasurer and *Capitano*, and to the country districts her Lieutenant. The taxes were decreed from Venice, but only the surplus sent to the capital after local expenses had been paid. Her policy of leniency was indeed carried so far that in the more backward districts of Friuli and Belluno all the old conditions of feudalism still survived, each petty baron possessing rights of absolute jurisdiction, and the result was the oppression of the peasants and a constant drain of emigration to more favoured districts. Venice in fact never modernized her state, never introduced a centralized system of administration, but she was repaid for her neglect by the steady loyalty of her provinces, who valued their local liberties more highly than the best conceivable system that might have been forced on them from above. They had only to look across the frontier at the enslaved condition of the Milanese, to congratulate themselves on the good fortune which had placed them under the mild yoke of the Republic.

But whether, as some maintain, the sources of Venetian strength were already sapped in the sixteenth century, it is certain that never before or since was Venice so filled with the consciousness of glory, and never did that consciousness receive such magnificent expression. Long after the schools of Rome and Upper Italy had ceased to produce anything but third-rate work, the painters of Venice were astonishing the world by the vigour of their conceptions, the brilliance of their colour, the wealth of their production; and the constant theme around which they wove their masterpieces was that of the conquests and the grandeur of Venice. When the older paintings in the Ducal Palace were destroyed by fire in 1577, the government commissioned the younger group of artists—Tintoretto, Paul Veronese, Paris Bordone and their friends—to decorate the walls with pageant-scenes from the life of the Republic, and so it is that in these halls may yet be seen the highest achievement of Italians in recording the sheer splendour and delight of life. And when from the Ducal Palace we follow the genius of Tintoretto where it assumes its profounder and more terrible aspects, the conviction is forced upon us that a society which produced such a man and could appreciate his work was far indeed from the decadence that had overtaken the less fortunate states of conquered Italy.

In the region of ecclesiastical affairs, Venice also displayed a noteworthy spirit of independence. She had always resented Papal interference with her sovereign rights in these matters, and prior to the enforced submission to Julius II.,[1] she had enjoyed large powers of taxing the clergy and of trying criminous clerics in lay courts. Above all, the Senate and clergy had always elected the Venetian bishops, though Rome retained a formal right of approval. After the submission to Julius the State gradually resumed a good deal of its ancient authority,[2] but the rise of Protestantism altered the lines of the struggle, and made it chiefly one for the maintenance of toleration to foreigners as a necessity of the Republic's commerce. Complaints of Venetian laxity were constantly made by Popes Pius IV. and V., and sometimes enforced by the fear of the Spanish neighbour at Milan. Yet to a modern eye the precautions of the Republic against heresy seem stringent enough. As early as 1547 a tribunal of the Inquisition was established in Venice, though with characteristic jealousy the Senate insisted on appointing three nobles as 'Lay Assessors' to the Court, in order to guard against injustice. No doubt this provision acted as a partial safeguard, but cases of extradition to Rome were fairly frequent, and in the famous case of Giordano Bruno, who died at the stake in Rome in 1600, it was seen how easily the Venetian Inquisition could take alarm at any dangerous development of the Copernican theory of the universe. It was well for Galileo, who flourished at Padua shortly after the trial of Bruno, that his securer position as a distinguished teacher of mathematics shielded him from such attacks as were fatal to the poor wandering, unfrocked Dominican.

The Venetians were, in fact, and always remained 'good Catholics,' in spite of their disagreements with the Curia, and nowhere was this conservative tendency more clearly shown than in their conduct with regard to the censorship of books. The printing and bookselling trades were among the chief glories of Venice, yet the Government gradually developed an exceedingly elaborate

---

[1] After the war of the League of Cambrai. See p. 214.
[2] Clement VII. and Paul III. had acknowledged the authority of the State over ecclesiastics accused of serious crimes.

system of censorship, by which a new book had to pass the scrutiny
of a board of censors (including an Inquisitor) appointed by the
University of Padua, of the Governors of the University
themselves, and finally of the Council of Ten, before it
could be 'registered' and published. The resulting trouble and
delay was naturally a considerable discouragement to authors.
Still more was this the case when the Index of the Council of
Trent was accepted by the Signory, and thirty years of slowly
dwindling prosperity followed for the bookselling trade. The final
blow, however, was struck by the Index of Clement VIII., published
in 1598. The vastly increased stringency of this Index caused the
Government to protest in good set terms, and a Concordat was
agreed upon by which Venice was practically authorized to revert
to her former system. So devout, however, were the Venetians,
and so much influenced by the Jesuit confessors who directed
them, that the Papal Index obtained currency in spite of the Concordat, and the number of printing-presses in the town sank
within a year from 125 to 40. The great days of the Venetian
printing-trade were over.

But when, in the early years of the seventeenth century, a
quarrel arose with Pope Paul V. on questions vitally affecting the
temporal jurisdiction of the State, all the old fires awoke in
Venice, and under the guidance of a man of genius, Fra Paolo
Sarpi, she asserted her ancient prerogatives and won a decisive
victory over Pope and Spain together. In 1605 Cardinal Camillo
Borghese, a Sienese, was elected Pope, and being imbued with all
the absolutist doctrines fostered by the Tridentine decrees, he inaugurated his reign by a series of successful interferences with the
domestic affairs of Naples, Savoy, and Genoa. But when he attempted similar proceedings in Venice, the Pope found that he had
stumbled on an unsuspected spirit of resistance. The Senate had
recently renewed two ancient laws, the one forbidding the erection of further churches or religious houses on the soil of Venice
without permission of the Government, and the other prohibiting
the alienation of real property to the Church. Paul V. took offence
at both these measures, and when, in addition the Venetian Government arrested a Canon and an Abbot accused of atrocious
crimes, a violent dispute broke out between Curia and Republic.
The Pope demanded the surrender of the two ecclesiastics, and
the abrogation of the two laws. The Senate absolutely declined
to part with what they considered to be the 'temporal rights of
princes.' The Pope threatened his censures; the Senate, with a true
instinct, called to its aid a Servite monk, Fra Paolo Sarpi, whose

outspoken criticisms on Jesuitry and the new doctrines of Papal absolutism had already brought him into collision with the Holy Office. The figure of Sarpi is one which has always appealed to the sympathy of English readers. A scholar and a man of science by disposition, his discoveries in optics and in physiology might have ranked him beside Galileo if he had been at the pains to publish his experiments; and his passionate feeling for the State and of the duty of every good citizen to work for it links him still more with our island temperament. He had at this time made for himself a distinguished place in the intellectual society of Venice, and was a personal friend of the Doge Donato, who came to the throne at the crisis of the controversy with Rome. Sarpi was immediately appointed Theologian and Canonist to the Republic. When the Pope fulfilled his threats and laid Venice and the Venetian territories under an Interdict [April, 1606], not only did the clergy obey the Senate's commands to disregard it, but Sarpi entered the lists with a complete statement of the claim of the State to temporal jurisdiction in his *Treatise on the Interdict*. The spectacle of the whole-hearted resistance of Venice to the Papal censures (for only the Jesuits and Theatines had preferred expulsion to disobedience) at length aroused the interest of all Europe; and while Spain prepared to assist the Pope by force of arms, the Venetian cause was espoused by France, united at last under her 'bon roi Henri.' The mediation of the French Cardinal de Joyeuse was finally agreed to by both parties, and on April 21, 1607, the two criminous clerics were formally handed over to the French Ambassador, 'without prejudice to the authority of the State to judge ecclesiastics,'[1] and by him transferred to the Cardinal de Joyeuse, who ordered a priest to take them in charge. The Cardinal then announced to the Ducal College that the censures were removed, and without sound of bells or formal absolution, Venice returned quietly within the Papal fold. The Senate had totally declined either to revoke the two disputed laws or to recall the Jesuits to Venice.[2]

So ended the famous episode of the Venetian Interdict, but the animosity of the Roman faction had not spent itself. On October 25, 1607, Paolo Sarpi was attacked by *bravi* in the streets of Venice, stabbed in the face and left for dead, while the assassins fled to the palace of the Papal Nuncio and thence into safe refuge in the Papal States. Sarpi recovered; lived to write his famous History of

[1] These were the words of the Secretary to the Senate who superintended the transfer.
[2] The Jesuits were not re-admitted until 1657.

the Council of Trent; and the state which he had championed honoured him as its most precious servant. His service had indeed been timely, for at the very height of the Counter-Reformation, when the Protestant movement had been checked and flung back, a Catholic state had dared to maintain her independence of Rome, and by Sarpi's aid had maintained it successfully. Never again was Venice so much disturbed in her jurisdiction over her own ecclesiastics.

Meanwhile, all through the sixteenth and seventeenth centuries, it was the function of Venice to trade with, to humour, and occasionally to fight the Turk. At Constantinople she still maintained her representative or *bailo*, who acted partly as ambassador and partly as chief magistrate for the whole of the foreign colony at Pera. The difficulties and dangers which beset the path of this hapless functionary are admirably set forth in Mr. H. F. Brown's study, 'Venetian Diplomacy at the Sublime Porte.'[1] It was to the interest of Venice to maintain peace, if war could by any reasonable means be avoided, and the firmness and sagacity of her envoys stood her in good stead in her dealings with the half barbaric court of the Sultans. Frequently chidden by the Popes for her laxity in fighting the Infidel, Venice knew that she was no longer a match single-handed for the Ottoman sea power; and when she did turn to Europe for assistance in the War of Cyprus, the results were still more disastrous than in the days when she had relied on her own strength alone. Already in 1537 she had made an alliance with the navy organized by Charles V., against the combination of Francis I. with Sultan Suleiman, but the lack of trust and co-operation between Venetians and Spaniards had led to their complete ineffectiveness at sea. At the peace of 1540 Venice had been compelled to give up her last two possessions in the Morea, Nauplia and Malvasia. The same result, but on a larger and more tragic scale, was witnessed in the campaigns of the War of Cyprus, in 1570—71. Sultan Selim (the Drunkard) had demanded the cession of Cyprus as being a stronghold of Christian pirates, and the Venetian Senate, with heavy hearts, prepared to defend the island,— which, with Candia, constituted the last considerable remnant of their Levantine empire. The long and heroic defence of Famagosta by the Venetian garrison, under their brave commander Bragadin, was worthy of the grandest traditions of the Republic, but the fleet which should have gone to its relief found itself hampered at every turn by its forced co-operation with a Spanish contingent,

[1] *Studies in Venetian History*, vol ii., by Horatio Brown, 1907.

whose Genoese commander Doria would accept no orders from the Venetian Senate. The season of 1570 was wasted in incessant delays at Zara, at Candia, and on the coast of Asia Minor, and when Doria finally drew off with all his galleys, alleging that the season was too far advanced, he left the Venetian fleet so seriously weakened by dilapidation and disease that it could attempt no rescue on its own account. The Senate, blind to the lesson of the year, spent the winter in redoubled efforts to organize a grand alliance with Spain and the Pope (Pius V.) for the ensuing spring, but the very success of their efforts sealed the fate of Famagosta. The coalition was formed, and the command of the allied fleets accepted by Don John of Austria, Charles V.'s gifted bastard; but the object of so vast an armament could no longer be the mere relief of a Venetian colony; it must be the destruction of the Turkish sea power. So while the fleet waited as Messina through the long weeks of July and August, 1571, for the tardy arrival of its leader, Famagosta starved and capitulated, and the heroic Bragadin was flayed alive in the market-place by the conqueror he had so long kept at bay. Then at length the Christian forces advanced to the barren victory of Lepanto. On October 7, at the entrance to the Gulf of Patras, the combined fleets of Venice, Spain, Tuscany, and the Pope met and destroyed the Turk, and Venice at the news abandoned herself to an exultation long unknown in the lagoons. But the unity of Europe was a mere transitory phenomenon, while the power of the Turk was permanent. By the following year the Ottoman fleet had been virtually replaced, and financial exhaustion had appeared at Venice. In 1573 peace was made with the Sultan, on the basis of the total cession of the island of Cyprus.

Again, seventy years later, Venice was called upon to defend against the ambition of Sultan Ibrahim her last great possession in the Levant, the island of Candia. The Porte picked a quarrel with Venice on the pretext that a piratical ship of the Knights of Malta had taken refuge at Candia with Turkish prisoners on board, and Venice was driven to send what help she could to her threatened dependency. The island had belonged to her ever since the taking of Constantinople in 1204, but since she had never been able to afford any considerable outlay towards the expense of ruling it, its government was mainly in the hands of feudal chieftains either native or Venetian, whose misrule was occasionally tempered by the efforts of the home government to introduce Venetian ideas of justice and finance. Still, the sentiment of the islanders was wholly against the Turks, and with the gallant assistance of the Venetian navy they resisted for twenty-four years [1645—1669] all attempts

of the invaders to reduce them. Once more, in the first year of
the war, the Senate made the fatal mistake of relying on foreign
succours, and the fortress of Canea was lost while the Venetian
fleet lay waiting at Zante for Papal and Neapolitan contingents.
But thenceforward Venice sustained the burden of the war alone,
and the hardihood and resourcefulness of her sailors was never
more brilliantly shown than in the naval war which raged for
eight years in and around the Dardanelles [1649—57], and resulted
in a series of victories for the Venetian fleet. But the obstinacy of
the Turk in the matter of Candia was only equalled by his staying-
power, and in the end all the efforts of both sides were concentrated in the siege and glorious defence of Candia itself [1658—69].
The tale of the Venetian defence so kindled the imagination of
Europe that three several expeditions set sail from France to bring
relief to the fortress, but each time the impetuous sallies of the
French broke in vain against the dull mass of the besieging force,
and the adventurers returned defeated. The failure of the last of
these attempts left the brave Venetian commander, Francesco
Morosini, no hope of relief, and on September 29, 1669, he surrendered the town and island of Candia to the Sultan, though retain-
ing his cannon and all munitions of war. Morosini, however, lived
to revenge himself on the Turk, for in his old age he re-conquered
the Morea for Venice and even occupied Athens—though this
enterprise was made disastrous for all posterity by the chance
shot from one of his batteries which fired the gunpowder stored
in the Temple of the Parthenon. As he gazed on the ruin he had
wrought, the old general had the grace to exclaim, 'Oh, Athens,
mother of the arts, how art thou now reduced!' Morosini was
honoured on his return by the epithet of *Peloponesiacus*, and ranks
as the last hero of the Republic; but his conquests had all returned
to the Turk by the year 1716, and at the Peace of Passarowitz,
two years later, Venice once more acknowledged her loss of the
Morea. Only Corfu, Cephalonia, and Zante, with Istria and the
Dalmatian coast, remained to the Republic of all the vast possessions she had won before the coming of the Turk.

And, side by side with the decline of her empire, Venice shared
in the general decline that overspread the rest of Italy during the
seventeenth and eighteenth centuries. Even Sarpi complained
before his death of the indifference, nay of the 'Papalism' of the
upper classes, though he still loved Venice so well that when he
came to die his thought was all for her, and the words *Esto perpetua*
were on his lips. The Republic endured, indeed, but it was the
endurance of stagnation, not of life, and her apparent insensibility

to change was but the sign of a loss of vitality within the body politic. An aristrocracy so rigid and so artificial could never have taken its place in the modern world; even in the eighteenth century the Venetian constitution was an anachronism; and so when the Corsican Adventurer brought in the realities of the New Age at the point of the bayonet, the ancient fabric crumbled and collapsed, for in its age-long evolution it had met its fate, and found

'The unimaginable touch of time.'

CHAPTER XXIII

The Spanish Provinces of Italy: the Popes of the Seventeenth Century

AT the death without heirs of the last Sforza Duke in 1535, the Duchy of Milan reverted as a lapsed fief to the Empire, and Charles V. bestowed it, after some hollow negotiations with France, upon his son Don Philip [1545]. Thus the famous duchy passed into the direct possession of Spain, and the Castello of Milan became the headquarters for the Army of Occupation which held down the North of Italy, harassed the Dukes of Savoy on the west and overawed the Republic of Venice on the east. The power of Spain was concentrated in the person of the Governor, who was also the military commander of the Spanish forces; but the civic spirit of the Milanese was still so formidable, even after all disasters, that the Spaniard was obliged to reckon with it, and the Senate of Milan retained all through the reign of Philip II. a considerable share of power. Though its members were appointed by the Governor, they held their seats for life, and a certain representative character accrued to it from the fact that most of the ancient subject-cities of the Milanese—Como, Lodi, Pavia, and the rest—obtained the right, under Charles V., of contributing a member to the Senate. Naturally it was the principal business of the Governor to extort sufficient money from the duchy to maintain his troops and fortresses, and to supply the frequent 'donatives' demanded by his master at Madrid; and as the financial resources of Spain became exhausted under the Hapsburg rule, the drain upon the Spanish provinces of Italy became continually heavier. But so long as the Lombard plain was not ravaged by war the natural wealth of the Milanese could support the burden, and in the year 1589 the native historian Leoni gives an attractive picture of the continued wealth and prosperity of the city of Milan.

Milan [he writes],[1] is extremely rich, but her wealth is distributed among many rather than concentrated among few, so that while

[1] Leoni, *Relatione di Milano e suo stato, fatto nel 1589.*

there are only three or four families with incomes of 25 to 30,000 *scudi*, there are an infinite number with incomes of 2, 3, and 4,000.

And again,

the wealth of the non-noble class is due to trade and manufactures, in which this city is exceedingly rich. It has an infinite number of craftsmen, so that it might well be called the home of the manual arts. Above all, Milan is the inventor of the art and splendour of dress, and produces clothes of so much wealth, beauty, and elaboration that in all these matters other cities are content merely to learn from her.

Yet in the great Castello, now the peaceful Sunday promenade of the townsfolk, and in every important city of the Milanese, there stood an alien garrison of Spanish troops, whom the citizens were obliged to feed, clothe, and pay before they could enjoy their wealth. That wealth itself was almost wholly dependent on the turn of peace or war. The fear of the revival of the French ambitions was never far from the mind of the Spanish Governor, though during all the second half of the sixteenth century the Wars of Religion had kept France busy within her own frontiers. But with the advent of the seventeenth century a more complex situation arose. The Dukes of Savoy had risen into prominence on the western borders of Milan, and Duke Charles Emanuel I., restless, ambitious, and shifty, was on the look-out for any occasion to enlarge his territories. The occasion almost came in 1610, when Henry IV. of France made alliance with his Alpine neighbour to sweep the Spanish power out of Lombardy; but the knife of Ravaillac cut short that and many other fair hopes for the deliverance of Europe. Shortly afterwards, in 1614, another chance arose with a war of succession for the territories of the Gonzaga Dukes of Mantua, which had included, ever since the Pacification of Bologna, the outlying Duchy of Monferrat, stretching from the Apennines into the heart of Piedmont. Charles Emanuel coveted these territories, but was unable to secure them against the energetic opposition of the Spaniards at Milan, and in revenge he sided with Venice and the Protestant powers against Spain in the long-drawn struggle for the possession of the Valtelline, which played so important a part in the first half of the Thirty Years' War. The weakness of Venice on land, however, made it impossible for the Duke to wage an effective war against the Spaniards, and the fate of the Valtelline was reserved for the decision of a stronger power than that of Savoy—the rising autocracy of France, concentrated in the person of Richelieu.

Charles Emanuel, however, was soon found on the side of Spain, because a second war for the Mantuan succession brought in a French pretender backed by the arms of Louis XIII., and the Duke of Savoy fought with all his strength, but without his accustomed good fortune, against these invaders. The frontier fortresses, so painfully won back by his father and himself, passed again into French hands, and amid ruin and disaster the old Duke died [1630], leaving to his son, Victor Amadeus I., a heavy task of reconstruction. To this the new Duke proved equal, and by the hard-won Treaty of Cherasco [1631], part of the Duchy of Monferrat was secured to Savoy, though at the cost of the surrender to France of the fortress of Pinerolo, the key to Turin. But his early death in 1637 left the duchy a prey to the calamities of a long minority and of a civil war between the French and Spanish parties in the Ducal family. The luckless territories of Monferrat were fought over, ravaged and parcelled out amongst Savoyards, French, and Spaniards in an aimless war of twenty-four years' duration, until the Peace of the Pyrenees between the two principal parties, France and Spain, put an end to the ruinous struggle [1659]. An incident of these futile wars had been the sack of Mantua in 1630 by Austrian *Landsknechts*, in nominal alliance with Savoy—a sack so ruthless and complete that Mantua never recovered from the shock.[1] The ancient Castello of the Gonzagas, with all the exquisite apartments of Isabella d' Este, was pillaged and ransacked by German hordes that had learnt their trade in the unspeakable barbarisms of the Thirty Years' War.

If the rule of the Spaniard in Northern Italy brought to it the curse of war and invasion, as well as that of slavery, his presence in the South was sufficient, without any foreign war, to involve the Kingdom of Naples in a deepening morass of corruption and misery. But for the solitary attempt of Paul IV. to strike at Spain by an invasion of Naples in 1557, the Kingdom was untroubled by foreign foes for more than a century; but during this time the blood-sucking policy of Spain and her Viceroys sapped the prosperity of the towns, encouraged brigandage in the countryside and piracy along the defenceless coast, and so ground down

---

[1] The Gonzaga dynasty preserved itself at Mantua till 1701, when the degenerate Carlo Ferdinando sold his state to Louis XIV. By the Treaty of Utrecht [1713] it was incorporated with the Milanese and passed under Austrian rule.

the inhabitants of Naples itself that the popular despair found vent at last [1647] in that most pathetic of insurrections, the rebellion of Masaniello.

The authority of the Spanish conquerors, both in Naples and Sicily, was vested in the person of the Viceroys, who held their court at Naples in the one case and at Palermo in the other. But while the Sicilians made the Viceroy's task a most difficult and thankless one, owing to the independent spirit of their cities, the pugnacity of their nobles and the strength of their mediæval Parliaments, in Naples it was only necessary for the Viceroy to exert himself in the arts of corruption and of fostering the divisions of his subjects in order to enjoy the fruits of his office in all tranquillity. In Sicily, during the sixteenth and seventeenth centuries, there was hardly a Viceroy whose term of office ended otherwise than in his recall and disgrace; in Naples, on the other hand, the Viceroy ruled with a power even more absolute than that of his colleague the Governor of Milan. The reason for this absolutism lay mainly in the immemorial feuds and rancours that had divided the Neapolitans ever since the days of Charles of Anjou, so that by playing off Angevin against Aragonese amongst the nobles, and nobles against *popolo* in the city of Naples, the Viceroys could forestall any possible opposition and 'preserve the state to themselves,' as the Venetian ambassador put it in a despatch of 1580. The ancient constitution of Naples was a very peculiar one, and lent itself at this juncture to the systematic corruption practised by the Viceroys. Before the days even of the Norman kings, when Naples had been a self-governing republic under the Byzantine Empire, a system of clan-associations had formed themselves which became known as the 'Sessions' or *Seggi*, the members of which kept all public appointments in their own hands. Six of these assemblies survived from the larger original number, five of them composed of nobles and the sixth of *popolo* or commons; but under Frederick II. there was also a Parliament for the whole kingdom, composed of feudal nobles and of burghers from the towns, which met from time to time wherever the King might happen to convene it. Charles of Anjou, however, wishing to concentrate his power in Naples, suppressed the Parliament and amalgamated the feudal nobility of the countryside with two of the noble *Seggi* of Naples, an arrangement which resulted in a triple jealousy between the two feudal *Seggi*, the three of the urban nobility and the one of the *popolo*. Successive kings favoured either the one party or the other, and a constant struggle can be traced on the part of the popular *Seggio* to claim an equal share of patronage with the five noble clans together—a claim, however, which was not often admitted. Now under the Spanish Viceroys the *Seggi* were kept subservient by the simple means of fostering their privileges at the expense of the community; and since it was frequently necessary to bribe them in order to induce them to pass new taxes for the royal 'donatives', it was against both their own and the Viceroy's interest to enlarge their membership. The *Seggi* were and remained a set of close hereditary corporations, and in the rare cases when one or two of them resisted the Viceroy's demands the latter could override them with a decree of his Privy Council,[1] certain that their mutual jealousy would prevent a united protest.

My Lord the Viceroy [wrote the ambassador of the Grand Duke of Tuscany in 1643], had four out of the six *Seggi* that exist in this city on his side in the matter of the approval of the last Donation to His Majesty, involving a fresh tax, but wishing also to obtain the consent of the *Seggio* of Nido, in order to lend a greater authority to the tax, he created various new places and offices, and caused many promises to be made through certain nobles to the nobles of that *Seggio*.

But when the Nido remained incorruptible, 'the Viceroy caused his Privy Council to put forth a decree announcing that the taxes were to be paid even if half the *Seggi* had been against them.'

The lines on which the government of Naples was to be conducted had been laid down once for all by the famous Viceroy, Pedro di Toledo, whom Charles V. had appointed in the year 1532. Possessing many of the qualities of a great administrator, Toledo reformed the courts of justice, made the nobles strictly subject to the laws and frequently promoted non-noble citizens to the judgeships, much to the indignation of the nobles; he also did much to embellish and improve the city, and drove through its filthy alleys the long straight street that bears his name to this day. But Toledo's vision was bounded by the mere necessity of 'preserving the state to his master,' and it was he who took over the system of corrupting the nobles by the giving of titles, which sapped their wealth by the encouragement of pomp and luxury, made them ever more odious to the vassals whom they squeezed and robbed, and ever more subservient to the Government. His policy aimed at dividing nobles from populace, and only once did it miscarry—when, at

[1] The so-called *Consiglio Collaterale*, composed of two Spanish and one Neapolitan judge or regent. This was the Viceroy's supreme executive council.

THE FISHERMAN BRINGING THE RING TO THE DOGE

Paris Bordone (Ducal Palace)

his master's bidding, he endeavoured to introduce the Spanish Inquisition into Naples, and was met by so formidable an uprising of nobles and people combined that the Viceroy and the whole Spanish power were all but swept into the Bay of Naples. Never again did Toledo or any subsequent Viceroy attempt the odious enterprise.[1] His finance consisted merely in taxing some basic necessities of life, so that the poorest classes were the most severely hit, and occasionally some new imposition—on cheese, on salted meat, on fish—stirred the mob to a brief and furious rising. One of his successors, the Marquis of Mondeyar, imposed a new tax on the manufacture of silk, the principal industry of Naples, and at one blow destroyed the flourishing foreign trade that had grown up in this article.[2] Toledo's successors indeed, perpetuated the cynicism and corruption of his régime without any of his compensating virtues, and under the rule of a Mondeyar, a Duke of Ossuna, a Duke of Arcos, there was not an office-holder who had not climbed to his position by the most naked bribery, and was not prepared to recoup himself in his turn. The taxes were almost all farmed, and Genoese contractors came to take advantage of this lucrative trade, settling like a swarm of locusts on the country. The misery of the common people, on whom ultimately the burden of all this corruption fell, was incredible, but it seemed that they had lost both the spirit and the power to resent their wrongs. Then, at one slight additional turn of the machine of tyranny, the whole mass flamed into action, and the rebellion of Masaniello shook the Spanish power still more violently than the insurrection, a century before, against the Inquisition.

It broke out on July 7, 1647, in the market-place of Naples, upon an attempt of the authorities to collect a newly-imposed tax on fruit. Showers of stones and fruit assailed the customs officials, and a young leader of rebellion sprang forth in the person of Masaniello, a fisherman of Amalfi, who had already suffered cruelly in his own person from the extortions of the tax-collectors. The mob poured under his leadership towards the Viceroy's Palace, but found that that functionary, who bore the magnificent name of Don Rodrigo Ponce de Leon, Duke of Arcos, had fled at the first sounds of tumult to the Castel Nuovo. Thence he sent envoy after

---

[1] The *Spanish* Inquisition was never introduced into Naples, but the *Roman* Inquisition was constantly making encroachments on the Bishops' Courts, and prisoners were fairly frequently extradited to Rome for execution. Giannone, *Storia Civile*, vol. v., p. 586 fol.

[2] Report of Girolamo Lando to the Venetian Senate, in Barozzi-Berchet, ii., p. 470.

S

envoy to the market-place, promising everything that the populace demanded. But with a shrewd mistrust of the word of a Spanish Viceroy, Masaniello demanded the Charter of Charles V., and would not be put off with the forged documents sent by Arcos to deceive the mob. He spent the first days of the revolution in arming and organizing his followers, to the number of a hundred thousand, and insisted on keeping within bounds their thirst for vengeance on Genoese tax-farmers and others who had so long trodden them underfoot. But an attempt on his life made by some nobles in Spanish pay [July 10] exasperated the half-savage populace and set it burning the houses of all 'enemies of the people,' as well as all documents bearing records of the hated *gabelles*. So formidable was the revolt that Arcos surrendered at discretion, and agreed to a treaty of peace acknowledging the Charter of Charles V., abolishing all taxes imposed since the Emperor's time and granting equality of power between the one popular and the five aristocratic *Seggi*. At a solemn ceremony in the Carmine church, on July 13, the Viceroy swore to maintain these terms. But the very next day, at a *fête* to celebrate the peace on board the Viceroy's barge—so at least ran the popular legend—Masaniello was poisoned by a decoction that attacked his reason, and by his strange and arrogant conduct during that day and the next puzzled and alienated his followers. Whether the story of the potion be credible to a modern age or not, certain it is that on July 16, the Feast of the Madonna of Carmel, Masaniello was assassinated in the precincts of the Carmelite Cathedral by *bravi* in the Viceroy's pay, and that Spanish troops were moved to points of vantage in the city to hold down the mob.

This characteristic act, however, was not sufficient to quell the revolution. The people still had arms in their hands, and during the month of August the movement of revolt spread to every province of the kingdom. By September Arcos was reduced to signing a still more humiliating compact than that of July with the popular leaders. In response to his appeals for help, an expedition was at length sent from Spain under the King's natural son, a second Don John of Austria, to put down the revolution [October, 1647], but after two days of desparate street-fighting the Spaniards were hurled back to their ships. All but the three massive fortresses of Sant' Elmo, the Castel Nuovo, and the Castel dell' Uovo remained in the hands of the people. Their leaders proclaimed the Neapolitan Republic, but with helpless self-distrust they allowed the ancient Angevin faction to invite a French prince, Henry of Guise, who happened at the time to be in Rome, to assume the command of their forces against Spain. Guise entered the city in triumph on November 15, but having no sympathy with the mob and no understanding of the situation, he played only for his own hand, and after three months of his rule a party among the republicans, weary of his arrogance, began secretly to intrigue with Don John. During a temporary absence of Guise the Spanish troops debouched from the fortresses and appeared unexpectedly in the streets [April 6, 1648], where they were greeted by the weary populace with shouts of *Viva il Re!* Arcos had already resigned the Viceroyalty; Don John had promised an amnesty, and a new Viceroy, the Count of Onate, entered the town to re-establish authority and order. But the amnesty was not observed, and by his executions and confiscations the new Viceroy struck terror into all who still cherished thoughts of liberty. Only one concession remained to the wretched population of all the reforms wrung from the Duke of Arcos : the tax on fruit was not re-imposed.[1]

Thus the seventeenth century brought with it no lightening, but if anything an aggravation of the burdens borne by the Italian people under Spanish rule. How they fared in the vast central tract of territory under the rule of the Papacy may be judged from a glance at the period of the great Nepotist Popes who founded the princely families of modern Rome between the reign of Sixtus V. and the age of Louis XIV. The mere enumeration of the family names of these six Popes, Aldobrandini, Borghese, Ludovisi, Barberini, Pamfili, Chigi—will show that the nepotism which they practised took a form more enduring even than that of the Medici or the Borgia, for it consisted not in the foundation of sovereign houses, but in the accumulation of wealth and position. The stateliest palaces of Rome today, the loveliest villas on the Alban Hills, are those bearing the names of this later series of Nepotist Popes. The three first-named, Clement VIII., Paul V., and Gregory XV., each possessed a single energetic and unscrupulous nephew, on whose head the revenues of the Church were heaped during the lifetime of his uncle; each was made a Cardinal; each wielded the Papal power almost as freely as the Pope himself. To Cardinal Aldobrandini, indeed, fell a lot that distinguished him above all others of his kind, for he received in person the surrender, as a fief of the Church, of the most ancient principality of Northern

[1] Onate made an agreement with the *Seggi* by which a heavy hearth-tax was to be substituted for half the taxes on food; the other half was to be farmed out to contractors as before.

Italy—the Duchy of Ferrara. By a Bull of Pius V. it had been decreed that no fief of the Church should be transmitted to any but the direct male line of the then existing holders, and since the old Duke Alfonso II. died childless in 1597 the terms of the Bull came into operation. In vain the Duke's cousin, Cesare d'Este, strove to make good his claim to the succession; neither he nor the Ferrarese were prepared to maintain it by force of arms. Don Cesare retired to his Imperial fief of Modena, where his family carried on in much diminished glory until the coming of Napoleon; and Ferrara, with its castles, its palaces, and its immortal memories, passed under the direct rule of the Papal overlord.

The same fate befell the Duchy of Urbino on the death of the last Duke of the Rovere line in 1631. The tragedy of Francesco Maria II., who reigned from 1574 to 1625, was to see in his old age the hand of the Church creeping steadily towards his mountain stronghold, for in 1623 his only son Federigo died, and the reversionary right of the Church to this Papal fief[1] was undisputed. So grasping, however, was the spirit in which the newly elected Pope, Urban VIII., entered upon the negotiations for the reversion, so sorely was the old Duke harassed by his continually increasing demands, that he determined at length to make over the government to the Church during his own life-time, and in 1624 charged the Venetian envoy at his court with the task of conveying his abdication to the Vatican. Urban VIII. accepted the offer with alacrity, and early in 1625 appointed a Papal Legate to take possession of the duchy.[2] The native population was naturally not consulted in these high transactions, but the Della Rovere Dukes, like the Montefeltri before them, had been beloved beyond other Italian princes for their mild yoke and the lightness of their taxes. Even before the death of the old Duke, the burden of taxation was cautiously increased, and the loss of independence was not atoned for in his subjects' eyes by the special boon conferred on them by Urban—the establishment of a tribunal of the Inquisition at Gubbio. But if Urbino had lost her ancient liberty, she had among the bare ridges of the Apennines to the north-west a tiny neighbour, the rock-republic of San Marino, which, thanks to an impregnable position on the three peaks of Monte Titano, was to maintain through all vicissitudes her mountain freedom.

[1] Urbino had been a fief of the Church since 1508, when Francesco Maria della Rovere, nephew of Julius II., had succeeded to the duchy by his marriage with the heiress of Guidobaldo, last Duke of the Montefeltro line.
[2] See the Report of Girolamo Corner to the Venetian Senate, Jan., 1625, in Barozzi-Berchet, vol. i., p. 227.

Pope Urban VIII. came of the Florentine family of the Barberini, and brought with him to the Vatican a brother and three nephews, who soon surpassed all previous Papal families in the colossal wealth which they amassed. Everywhere in Rome today the Barberini bees meet the eye, and not only in Rome but on the Sabine and Alban hills the nephews bought up Colonna and Orsini palaces and established themselves as the equals of the oldest families. Three of the Barberini were made Cardinals, and a fourth, Taddeo, Captain-General of the Church; and to this last was entrusted the task of reorganizing the Papal forces—an object that lay very near to Urban's heart. For Urban aspired to play a grandiose part in the affairs of the Peninsula by means of a strong military force that he dreamed of creating; he ordered a vast new fortress to be erected near Bologna, and enlarged those of many other peace-loving towns, while the enormous loans that he was obliged to raise for this purpose seriously embarrassed the Papal finances. He attempted to recruit a native army from among the inhabitants of the Papal States, but the conduct of these levies on the only occasion when they were called upon to fight, in the War of Castro, convinced even Urban of the hopelessness of imposing the military virtues on the subjects of the Church. It was to his militarism, moreover, that was due the incident that provoked Pasquino's famous squib[1]—*Quod non fecerunt barbari, fecerunt Barberini*—for Urban caused the brazen tubes that supported the roof of the Pantheon to be removed and cast into cannon for the fortress of Sant' Angelo.

Urban himself was a man of cultivation and even of some learning, for he wrote indifferent Latin poetry and had studied mathematics; but he lives in history as the Pontiff under whose guidance the Church committed the irreparable blunder of the condemnation of Galileo. The veteran astronomer had run his own head into the noose by disregarding a solemn warning administered to him by the Inquisition in 1616, and had published a *Dialogue* on the Copernican and Ptolemaic systems in which the superiority of the former had been darkly hinted at. Such a breach of discipline could not be tolerated by the Holy Office, and in 1633 Galileo was cited to Rome and forced under threat of torture to 'abjure, curse, and abhor' the opinions of which he stood suspected, viz. 'that the sun was the centre of the world and immovable, and that the earth was not the centre and had movement.' Urban was

[1] Pasquino was the name given to the mutilated statue, unearthed in 1501 and set up at a corner of the Piazza Navona, to which it became the custom to affix squibs and lampoons attacking the Papal government.

believed to have had a personal interest in the humiliation of the old scholar, having discovered, as he thought, an unflattering portrait of himself in the upholder of the Ptolemaic system in the *Dialogue*. To all appearance, then, the Pope and the Inquisition had won an easy victory by the aid of their threat of torture,[1] but posterity delights in the tradition that on rising from his knees after the abjuration, Galileo turned the tables on his persecutors with the muttered words *E pur si muove*.

During the long reign of Urban the conditions of life in Rome became so disorderly as to remind onlookers of the days before the Counter-Reformation; once more the palaces of many Cardinals were filled with *bravi*; once more the retainers of Colonna, Medici, and Este came to armed brawls in the streets. Cardinal Antonio Barberini kept a band of *bravi* commanded by a famous brigand chief from the Abruzzi; but the warlike proceedings of the Barberini went farther than mere street affrays, and in 1642 they kindled an Italian war that combined in a remarkable degree the elements of the *bravo* and of the Stock Exchange. A feud had arisen on questions of precedence between Taddeo Barberini and the Farnese Duke of Parma, who was lord also of the Papal fiefs of Castro and Ronciglione; and the Barberini resolved to ruin the Duke by striking at him first on the financial side. He had raised a loan of which the interest was secured on the revenues of Castro; the Pope prohibited the export of corn from Castro, and the revenue dropped to zero. The bond-holders, defrauded of their interest, sold their shares at a ruinous loss, and found purchasers in the Barberini; but meanwhile for his failure to pay the interest the Duke was excommunicated and declared forfeited of all his possessions. The Papal army, on which Urban had lavished so much treasure and forethought, was ordered to march on Parma, but at this serious menace to Italian equilibrium Tuscany, Venice, and the Duchy of Modena took up the Duke of Parma's cause and formed a league for his protection. The Duke himself gathered three thousand horse, with which he scattered the Papal troops and rode half way to Rome; had he pressed on he would have had Urban at his mercy. But he missed his opportunity, and the

---

[1] The report of the trial of Galileo published by Epinois from the Vatican Archives contains two documents both mentioning the threat of torture, one the decision of the Holy Office, dated June 16, 1633, in which these words occur: 'Sanctissimus decrevit ipsum Galilaeum interrogandum esse super intentione et comminata ei tortura, *et si sustinuerit,*' and the other the report of his actual interrogation on June 21, in which the threat is made. See Karl v. Gebler, Galileo Galilei, Appendix, Document xv. and p. 282. There is no evidence that the threat was actually carried out.

war dragged on in small skirmishes and shameful devastations all through the next year, until France and Venice together put an end to the unseemly spectacle. Peace was concluded in the spring of 1644, on the basis of the *status quo ante*, and the death of Urban, which followed shortly afterwards, was put down by many to the bitterness of his humiliation at this inglorious ending.

Nor was the reputation of the Papacy lifted any higher by the two Popes who followed Urban. Innocent X. (Pamfili) [1644—55] allowed the affairs of state to drift into the hands of his terrible sister-in-law, Donna Olimpia Maidalchini, who lorded it in the Vatican and whose favour had to be sought in hard cash by all aspirants to church dignities ; who was said to have made enormous sums by a corner in wheat during a year of scarcity, and who, for a consideration, granted to prostitutes immunity from police persecution. In Rome Innocent was long remembered as the Pope who revived the practice of taking money compositions for criminal offences[1]; in Europe as the Pope who made a solemn protest against the Peace that ended the Thirty Years' War. His successor Alexander VII. (Chigi) lived to see the Papal dignity dragged still deeper in the mire. At first he appeared to make a stand against the rising flood of nepotism, but within a year there were as many Chigi about the Vatican as there had ever been Barberini.[2] Avowedly adherents of the Spanish and anti-French party, the Chigi light-heartedly encouraged the Pope's Corsican guard to come to blows with the musketeers of the French embassy, and in August, 1662, the Corsicans violently attacked the embassy and even fired at the person of the ambassador. But the Chigi did not yet know with whom they had to deal. The star of Louis XIV. was in the ascendant, and the King replied to the outrage by expelling the Papal Legate from France, seizing Avignon, and demanding an apology in the most abject terms. Long the Curia endeavoured to fence with the King's demands, but his threat of war produced compliance in the end, and Alexander VII. saw himself actually compelled to erect a monument in Rome to commemorate the terms of his humiliation. Never since the days of the 'Babylonish Captivity' had the Papacy been so deeply humbled before a foreign monarch. Though the next Pope, Clem-

---

[1] Report of Giov. Giustinian to the Venetian Senate, in Barozzi-Berchet, vol. ii., p. 91.

[2] Report of Pietro Basadonna to the Venetian Senate, 1664: 'His spirit was too weak to maintain the sacred resolution [of the abolition of nepotism], and there appeared in Rome not *one* brother or nephew but a regular deluge of Chigis.' Barozzi-Berchet, ii., p. 264.

ent IX., obtained leave to pull down the obnoxious monument, the memory of it had sunk deep into the minds of the Romans.

At the same time the domestic affairs of the Papal States were not calculated to compensate in any degree for the rebuffs sustained abroad. The ruinous financial system of the Popes, by which a national debt had been piled up in the form of ever-increasing loans known as *Monti*, had fastened on the population an immense load of taxation for the purpose of meeting the interest on these borrowings. By the end of the seventeenth century the sum annually required was over a million and a quarter *scudi*,[1] while the total revenue did not exceed two million. Moreover the population of the Papal States, according to the careful estimate of the Venetian ambassador Mocenigo in 1676,[2] had declined by one third in forty years, while the taxes had doubled in the same period, so that 'the population is reduced to the extremist misery, and from lack of means the boys are not sent to school and the dowries of the girls dwindle away; nothing is left for the men but to turn priests; the monasteries are filled with monks and the convents with nuns.'[3]

So disastrous, in fact, was the condition of affairs that it provoked at last a serious effort towards amendment under the two reforming Popes, Innocent XI. and Innocent XII., who closed the history of the Papacy during the seventeenth century. The former, although occupied in the eyes of the world almost solely with his great contest against Louis XIV. on the liberties of the Gallican Church, found time to reorganize the finances of the Papal States, and to balance the receipts and expenditure in his annual budget. But in spite of his strict economies he was still obliged to increase the taxes, and though respected for his personal integrity he gained no particular love from his much-harassed subjects. His controversy with Louis over the Four Propositions of the Gallican Church [1682] was followed five years later by a bitter quarrel with the same formidable adversary on the right of sanctuary in the French embassy in Rome. Innocent insisted on its abrogation, and when Louis declined all concessions he refused to see the French ambassador and placed the French church of San Luigi under an interdict. The quarrel simmered on under his successor, the easy-going Venetian Alexander VIII., but under the admirable Innocent XII., the last Pope of the century, an agreement was at length reached

---

[1] Report of Girolamo Lando to the Senate, 1691, in Barozzi-Berchet, ii., 414.

[2] Barozzi-Berchet, ii., 378.

[3] *Ibid*, ii., 379.

by which the Pope undertook that his police should crave permission to enter the embassy, and Louis undertook that such permission should not be refused.

Innocent XII. ranks as the Pope who finally rooted out the curse of nepotism from the Papal system. Not only by a formal Bull against it which passed the Consistory in 1692, but by his own practice and example, Innocent gave the death-blow to this immemorial abuse. Though seventy-six years old when he assumed the tiara, Innocent spent the nine years of his Pontificate in a ceaseless round of reforming activities; reducing the number of venal offices, limiting the revenues of the highest dignitaries, accelerating and amending the judicial procedure. When he died, on the eve of the new century, he left to his successors a swept and garnished chamber; yet nothing could restore to the territories over which he ruled the vitality, the rich and varied life that had been drained by so many centuries of conquest, misrule and plunder. The States of the Church, so long the sport of Papal relatives and place-hunters, slept from exhaustion, and a territory which included cities once so great as Bologna, Ferrara, Ravenna, Rimini, and Urbino, sank to a level of poverty and ruin almost as low as that of the Neapolitan kingdom. Innocent XII. made possible the Respectable Papacy of the eighteenth century, but he could not undo the work of the Borgia, the Medici, and above all of the Nepotist Popes of the century just gone by.

CHAPTER XXIV

The Evolution of Savoy:
the Political Changes of the
Eighteenth Century

SINCE the overthrow of Francis I. and his paladins on the field of Pavia, no serious attempt had been made by the French monarchy to challenge the Spanish hegemony in Italy. Henri Quatre had dreamed of doing so in conjunction with the Duke of Savoy [1610]; Richelieu, when that same Duke in his old age had joined with Spain, sent King Louis XIII. to punish him by asserting a French prince's claim to Mantua [1627]. But since the rise of the duchy of Savoy to a less insignificant rank among Italian states the direct French claim to Milan or to Naples could no longer be asserted as of old; it is the Duke of Savoy who sooner or later will hold the scales, and who must either be won over or beaten down before the French armies can appear in Italy at all. Hence the importance to France of the Treaty of Cherasco in 1631, when Pinerolo and Casale were left in French hands; of the long weakness of Savoy under the regency of the Duchess Christina [1638—1655], herself a French princess, and of the French bias bequeathed by her to the government of her son Charles Emanuel II. By the time that Louis XIV. had reached the zenith of his power it had become customary in France to look upon Savoy almost as a vassal state, and the boy-Duke who succeeded his father Charles Emanuel in 1675 showed for many years no disposition to rebel against this tutelage. Yet it was to Victor Amadeus II. that Savoy in the end owed its emancipation and its advancement to the rank of a kingdom. By a fortunate combination of courage with craft, of constancy with double-dealing, this second founder of Savoy's fortunes knew how to take advantage of each turn in the European struggle against Louis XIV., and by throwing his weight now on one side, now on the other, emerged after each crisis with increased territory, if not with increased reputation.

But the first transactions of Victor Amadeus with his formidable neighbour showed how complete was still the ascendancy of France even in the domestic affairs of the duchy. In 1685 Louis

XIV. revoked his grandfather's edict of toleration, and let loose upon his Huguenot subjects those *Dragonnades* which have for ever blackened his name in history. His governor at Pinerolo simultaneously had orders to convert the heretic *Vaudois* inhabiting the long Alpine valley that debouched on the town, while the French ambassador at Turin was instructed to urge the young Duke to perform his own duty in the neighbouring valleys.

The inhabitants of these homes of refuge from age-long persecution were the descendants of the primitive Christian sects of the eleventh and twelfth centuries—Waldenses, Paterines, Poor Men of Lyons, and so forth—who had fled to these mountain solitudes from the fierce cruelty of the plains on either side. There they had clung with stern simplicity to their ancient worship, though exposed ever and anon to the crusading zeal of dukes and popes, filling the valleys with rapine and slaughter. Occasionally, however, the dukes of Savoy, jealous of too much ecclesiastical interference, had intervened to save their subjects from extermination, and thus the Waldenses of the seventeenth century could point to the Charter granted them by Emanuel Filibert in 1561, by which they were granted liberty of worship in the upper valleys of the Pellice and Chisone.[1] But once beyond these limits they had no protection, and Duke Victor Amadeus I. had carried out in 1633 an expulsion on a grand scale from Saluzzo and all the lower regions of the Pellice.

In the middle of the seventeenth century, however, a persecution of unexampled violence burst upon them, following on the establishment of the powerful *De Propaganda Fide* at Turin. The young Duke Charles Emanuel II. was prevailed on to issue an edict of expulsion from all regions beyond the 'limits' in January, 1655; but rather than face the terrors of a midwinter pilgrimage to the high valleys or to Switzerland, the sectaries sent humble supplications to Turin, and remained at home. But as soon as the snows had melted an overwhelming force was marched against them, and the Waldensian villages were subjected to one of the most prolonged and revolting massacres that even the annals of religious persecution can show. The cry of agony raised by the victims penetrated even to the far shores of England; Cromwell sent money to the martyrs, which enabled them to build a strong dyke across the Pellice valley; Milton called down the vengeance of Heaven on

> The bloody Piedmontese, that rolled
> Mother with infant down the rocks.

[1] See p. 255.

The whole of Protestant Europe sent remonstrances and offers of mediation to the Duchess-Regent Christina, and at length [August 18, 1655] a treaty was agreed upon by the intervention of France, England, and the Protestant Cantons, by which the heretics were once more guaranteed in the possession of a limited territory. But after an uneasy peace of thirty years' duration the wave of persecution penetrated once more into the valleys, this time from France, and at the bidding of Louis XIV. Duke Victor Amadeus II. revoked his predecessor's edict of toleration and plunged the valleys yet again in massacre and ruin.

At this point the vicissitudes of Vaudois history became merged in the quarrel of the whole of Europe. When William of Orange won the throne of England and formed the Grand Alliance against France, the Duke of Savoy began to meditate a rupture with Louis, and the first sign of his revolt was the permission he gave to the Waldensian exiles, in the winter of 1689, to return to their deserted valleys. They rewarded him by faithful service during the wars that followed. In June, 1690, Victor Amadeus dropped the mask and declared himself allied with Spain, England, and the Empire against France. But the war went ill for the Savoyards, who could hardly make head against the French even with the aid of the Duke's cousin, Prince Eugene,[1] a brilliant young general in the service of Austria. By 1694 the idea of a change of sides was already floating before the mind of Victor Amadeus.

Louis XIV. considered it worth his while to bribe his former ally with substantial offers of territory, and in the spring of 1696 a secret treaty was signed between the two, by which on condition of renewing his alliance with France, the Duke was to receive Pinerolo and all other territories held for so long by the French. General Catinat with a fresh army was sent over the Alps to enforce the preliminary condition, and with this spur in his rear Victor Amadeus faced the Imperial generals with a demand for the 'Neutrality of Italy.' When these terms were refused the Duke of Savoy ranged himself openly on the side of France, and the Imperialists, whose forces in Italy were unequal to such a contest, submitted to necessity. In October, 1696, the treaty guaranteeing the 'Neutrality of Italy' was signed at Turin. The armies of France and of the Grand Alliance simultaneously evacuated Italian soil, the Spaniards alone remaining at Milan, and in the following year the Duke's acquisitions of territory were formally ratified at the Peace of Ryswick.

[1] Eugene was a great grandson of Duke Charles Emanuel I. and a second cousin of Victor Amadeus.

Success had vindicated the dangerous game played by Victor Amadeus in this first upheaval of Europe against the preponderance of France. His fresh pact with Louis was even sealed by the marriage of his little daughter Marie-Adelaide with that Duc de Bourgogne, heir to the French crown, whose early death was accounted by Saint-Simon one of the grand tragedies of history. But the War of the Grand Alliance was but child's play compared with the war that broke out in 1701, when it became known that Louis had accepted for his grandson Philip the succession to the Spanish crown beqeathed to him by the last Hapsburg King of Spain. That France should become the virtual mistress of Spain, of the Spanish Netherlands, of the Spanish possessions in Italy, and of the Spanish colonies was not to be tolerated either by the House of Austria or by the Maritime Powers, and the long patience of William III. was rewarded at last by the conclusion in 1701 of a fresh and powerful league against France between Austria, England, Holland, and the bulk of the German states. This time, however, the gate of Italy was not closed to Louis, for the Duke of Savoy chose to abide by his recent treaty, and French and Piedmontese troops passed eastward together to defend the Milanese against Prince Eugene.

But the example of the Duke's change of sides in the last war was not thrown away on the Emperor Leopold, and all through the year 1702 the Imperial agents were busy at Turin endeavouring to detach him from the French alliance. The Duke's terms, however, were so high that it was not until the autumn of 1703 that an accord with the Grand Alliance was finally reached, and in the meantime Louis had got wind of the negotiations and ordered Marshal Vendôme to take energetic measures against his false ally. Victor Amadeus was caught at an unfavourable moment; Savoy was overrun during 1704 by a French army, and while Marlborough was making his famous march across Europe to the field of Blenheim, Vendôme was pressing the Piedmontese back on Turin and laying siege to one strong place after another. But the Duke held out with obstinate courage until, in the spring of 1705, Eugene was at last able to come to his aid; even so his intervention was not decisive, and only served to postpone the final struggle for the possession of Turin.

Towards this object Louis ordered the whole efforts of his Italian army to be bent with the opening of the year 1706. Turin was formally invested by the French under La Feuillade in the month of May, while another army under Vendôme was watching for the appearance of Eugene from the Tyrol. Eugene, however, skilfully outmarched and outmanœuvred his opponent, while Marlborough's victory at Ramillies soon necessitated the recall of Vendôme to the Netherlands. With inferior leaders to oppose his march, Eugene effected his junction with the Duke of Savoy at Villastellone, in the hilly country to the south of Turin, and prepared to attack the besiegers. Meanwhile the garrison left within the town had held out for four months with the greatest obstinacy, and while the relieving army was approaching hurled back two desperate assaults of the French against the Citadel. A few days later, the Duke and Eugene, making a wide circuit round the investing lines, fell upon the French entrenchments in the narrow interval between the Dora and Stura rivers [September 7, 1706]. By dogged pressure on the part of Austrians, Prussians, Brandenburgers, and Saxons,[1] no less than by brilliant leadership on the part of Eugene, they at length forced back the French; Marshal Marsin was killed, the Duke of Orleans severely wounded, and when the garrison broke out of the town upon their rear the French fled headlong for the only bridge over the Dora. Hastening in disorderly march towards the south, Orleans halted to consider his line of retreat; whether to attempt a junction with the French forces still in the Milanese, or to retire on Pinerolo; and when he chose the latter course and the news of his decision reached Eugene, the Prince is said to have exclaimed in ecstasy, 'Then Italy is ours!' Its reconquest was indeed only a matter of weeks. One after another the fortified towns of Piedmont taken by Vendôme surrendered again to Eugene or the Duke; and not only Piedmont but the Milanese went over heart and soul to the Imperialists. On September 24 the two Princes of Savoy rode into Milan. As after the Italian conquests of Louis XII., so now the French forces melted away 'like mist before the wind,' and in March, 1707, the last French generals were reduced to signing a capitulation for the evacuation of Upper Italy. A few months later, Naples followed the example of the North. A small Austrian force was sufficient to overturn the newly-established Bourbon authority there, and by September, 1707, the whole kingdom excepting Sicily recognized the Austrian Archduke Charles as King.

Victor Amadeus had of course drawn his own particular profit from the triumph of his Allies. He entered at once into the possession of Monferrat, Alessandria, and the Lomellina, and when the Treaty of Utrecht ended the long war [1713] he obtained the

---

[1] The Allied army at the battle of Turin consisted almost entirely of Germans, the Piedmontese troops having been detached towards Chieri to attempt to re-victual the fortress from that side. Arneth, *Prinz Eugen*, i., 379.

cession of Sicily, with the title of King, from the Bourbon King of Spain. The long domination of Spain in the Peninsula was shattered, for at the Peace the Austrian conquests were confirmed, and Milan, Sardinia, and Naples passed from the Spanish to the Austrian yoke.

But the Treaty of Utrecht, important as it was in excluding the Spanish Bourbons for a time from the Peninsula, failed to effect more than a momentary settlement of Italian affairs. The junction of Sicily with Piedmont was a highly unstable arrangement, and when in 1717 a Spanish raid on the island provoked another war with Spain, Austria insisted at the Peace of 1720 that the Duke of Savoy should be content to exchange Sicily for Sardinia, while Sicily passed, like Naples, under Austrian rule. Thus it occurred that the Dukes of Savoy became known in the European polity as Kings of Sardinia, a title which they bore until the impulse of *risorgimento* opened to them a wider kingdom. The aspirations of Spain had been contented at the Peace with the promise of the reversion of the Duchies of Tuscany and Parma for Don Carlos, son of Philip V. and his Italian wife, Elizabeth Farnese, and it was this clause in the treaty that opened at last a happier chapter in the long martyrdom of the Neapolitan kingdom.

On the death of the last Farnese Duke of Parma in 1731, Don Carlos of Bourbon, an adventurous youth of sixteen, duly arrived in his adopted Duchy, and had hardly established himself there before the general war broke out once more on the pretext of a disputed Polish Succession. France, Spain, and Savoy combined to attack the Austrian possessions in Italy, and while the Austrians were beaten out of Milan, Don Carlos, at the head of a small Spanish army, set forth on the march to Naples. Like another Charles VIII., he carried all before him. Naples, seeing in him an independent king, welcomed him with transports of joy; the Imperialists retired to the various fortresses, which surrendered one after another, and before the year was out even Sicily had recognized King Charles III.[1] The Great Powers accepted the accomplished fact in the Peace concluded at Vienna in 1735, and though Milan was given back to Austria, and the reversion of Tuscany promised to Francis of Lorraine instead of to Don Carlos, the young adventurer was confirmed in his conquest of the Two Sicilies. After two centuries and more of government by plunder-

---

[1] 'Charles III.' was in reality his later appellation, when he had ascended the throne of Spain.

ing Spanish viceroys, Naples and Sicily had at last acquired an independent dynasty.

The new government was honestly desirous of setting up a decent administration in the conquered kingdom, but the task of reform was so colossal that it was small wonder it did not accomplish everything. It was much that the government itself was well-intentioned ; that the King had picked up on his passage through Tuscany a lawyer, one Bernardo Tanucci, grimly fanatic in his reforming zeal, and that the change of masters coincided at Naples with an intellectual revival closely connected with the movement for reform. It was the Century of Enlightenment, and some of the first apostles of the new age arose in Naples, with the historians Giannone and Vico and the humanitarian reformer Genovesi. Each of these in his different way helped on the impulse of emancipation, and prepared the way for the principal political achievements of Carlo's reign—the reform of justice and finance and the assertion of the supremacy of the State over the Church.

For all their orthodoxy, the Bourbon monarchs were exceedingly jealous of the existence of Church privileges and immunities in the states over which they reigned, and Don Carlos of Naples was no exception to this rule. He found a third of the land in the hands of the Church, and therefore exempt from taxation; one-fortieth of the population were 'religious'; the towns were filled with churches granting the right of asylum to criminals. Charles applied himself with great pertinacity to the task of wresting concessions on all these points from Rome, and from the witty and amiable Benedict XIV. (Lambertini) he obtained a Concordat which remedied the worst of these abuses [1741]. Church lands were to be taxed, and limits set to the jurisdiction of the bishops, to the privileges and numbers of the clergy and to the right of asylum. Whole-hearted reformers like Genovesi were not satisfied, and the perversity of the Neapolitans stultified in many cases the good intentions of the law, but a first step had at least been taken towards the removal of an immemorial abuse. In the domain of justice, Tanucci effected various reforms in the barbarous procedure of the criminal law, and reduced the feudal jurisdiction of the nobles, but his attempt to codify the law remained incomplete, and Naples still lay under eleven different codes inherited from Romans, Byzantines, Lombards, Normans, Hohenstaufen, Angevins, Aragonese, and Popes. In financial affairs the new government showed energy and enlightenment, and certain long overdue reforms were effected which largely increased the revenue. Some of the *gabelles* were bought back from the tax-farmers and

GIAN GASTONE, THE LAST MEDICI GRAND DUKE OF TUSCANY
From a bust in the Uffizi Gallery, Florence

administered directly by the crown; a tax on property known as a *catasto* was imposed, which brought in a regular and more ascertainable revenue (though the noble was still assessed far more lightly than the commoner); and certain timid steps were taken in the encouragement of foreign trade.

But the feudal rights and privileges of those who owned the soil were scarcely touched by the reforms of Tanucci and his master. Although they abolished much of the jurisdiction of the baronial courts and so increased the power of the royal judges, the baronial rights of extortion over the luckless townships and villages of coast and country remained as burdensome as ever. Nowhere in Europe were the feudal dues and tolls so crushing as in the kingdom of Naples; nowhere were they less compensated by the feudal obligation of a paternal master for his men; nowhere was the population more completely enslaved than by these descendants of Norman and Angevin conquerors. And the government of the good-natured 'Re Carlo' was not equal to coping with so deep a canker as this. It was left to fester on—disguised during his reign by other much-needed measures of reform—until under his boorish son the impulse of reform died out and the disease alone remained. What violent process of cure was then at last adopted will be seen hereafter.

Yet, in the dearth of benefactors to the Neapolitan kingdom, King Charles III. has remained enshrined in the affections of his subjects by contrast with Spanish viceroys, Angevin tyrants, and later Bourbon kings. He was an ardent builder and excavator; his palace at Caserta, with the elaborate cascades descending in tiers from the wooded hill in its rear, was extolled as the Versailles of Naples; and the accidental discovery of Roman remains on the site of a royal hunting-lodge led to the excavation of the long-buried Herculaneum. When he was called to the throne of Spain in 1759 by the death of his elder brother, Naples regretted him sorely, but he left Tanucci at the head of a Council of Regency for his young son Ferdinand, and the régime of anti-clericalism and of moderate reform continued. The former indeed culminated in the year 1776 in the refusal to pay the traditional tribute of a white palfrey to the Pope as overlord, and though the gift was restored in the next year at the wish of the young Queen, Maria Carolina of Austria, it was finally abrogated in 1788. Thus the last vestige of the Papal suzerainty accepted by Robert the Norman disappeared after seven centuries.

By the Treaty of Vienna in 1735 the succession to the Grand

T

Duchy of Tuscany, where the last Medici Grand Duke was dragging out his corrupt existence, was made over, in what now appears to us as the cynical fashion that characterized the dynastic treaties of the eighteenth century, to Francis Duke of Lorraine, the prospective husband of Maria-Theresa of Austria. The Tuscan people were naturally not consulted in this buying and selling of their liberty, and it is almost anomalous that mention of the sovereign rights of the Florentine State was made at the Congress of The Hague in 1710, when Cosimo III., foreseeing the extinction of his family, proposed the eventual restoration of the Republic, and obtained the support of England and Holland for the proposal.[1]

In one of the antechambers to the Uffizzi Galleries in Florence there may be seen a complete series of portrait-busts of the Medici rulers of Tuscany, from Cosimo *Pater Patriæ* to Gian Gastone, who died of dropsy and debauchery in 1737. It is an example of progressive degradation surely unsurpassed in all the dynasties of Europe. No refinement of vice, of weakness, or pomposity seems omitted from that line of bronze and marble faces, and the decadence of the Tuscan spirit, that was content to live under such rulers, seems to the idle gazer to have found there its bitterest monument. Yet some even among that latest group were men in whom the old Medicean tradition still lived on. Ferdinand II., whose long reign covered the best part of the seventeenth century, easy-going and genial, sheltered Galileo in his old age, patronized his followers, and made a labour of love of the arrangement of the Uffizzi collections; while his brother Cardinal Leopold, last of the Medicean celebrities, devoted all his influence to the encouragement of science, and gathered from among Galileo's disciples an 'academy' of scientific scholars.[2] But Cosimo III., whose interminable reign endured from 1670 to 1723, allowed the blight of his own morose, pedantic spirit to fall on these last manifestations of the Tuscan genius. Though still nominally a patron of learning and the arts—for no Medici could escape the influence of so potent a tradition—he was a far more effective patron of priests and monks, and in his later years it was said of him that he regarded it as a point of honour to have at least one convent of every religious order in his dominions. A formalist and an inquisitor by nature, he maintained an army of spies to pry into the

---

[1] The project miscarried owing to the opposition of the Imperial envoy Zinzendorf, who regarded Tuscany almost as a vassal state of the Empire.

[2] This was the celebrated 'Accademia del Cimento' ('Academy of Experiment') which flourished from 1657 to 1667, and the proceedings of which are recorded in the interesting report of its Secretary, Lorenzo Magalotti.

morals and manners of his subjects, and made himself much disliked by his petty tyranny in domestic matters. Yet the domestic affairs of his own family hardly offered an edifying example to the state. His wife, Marguerite Louise of Orleans, left him after fourteen years of misery and dissension and retired to France; his eldest son's wife, a Bavarian princess, detested her husband, and the marriage was childless; his younger son, Gian Gastone, married a Bohemian heiress, but once having seen the bridegroom, the lady refused even to accompany him to Italy, and remained in Bohemia. Faced with the extinction of his family, Cosimo then induced his brother, Cardinal Francesco, to unfrock himself and marry, but the selected lady—a Gonzaga princess—refused in her turn to follow her bridegroom home. The days of the Medici were evidently numbered, and when it pleased the Great Powers of Europe to assign the Grand Duchy to Francis of Lorraine, the debauched but amiable Gian Gastone had no choice but to accept their decision.

Thus it occurred that Tuscany was brought in the latter half of the eighteenth century under the influence of a remarkable group of men, the Emperors of the House of Lorraine, who attempted in all their dominions to bring in the reign of light and reason by persevering efforts from above. Francis of Lorraine, crowned Emperor, made over the government of Tuscany to a set of ministers who initiated the first sorely needed reforms, but it was reserved for his second son Leopold, to whom the Grand Duchy was bequeathed at his death, to carry out a still more remarkable experiment in autocratic reform. He found every department of public life choked with corruption, superstition, and the survival of mediæval customs, and Leopold in his twenty-five years' reign set himself to purge them all. The criminal code was revised from top to bottom according to the principles of Beccaria, and torture and even the death-penalty abolished; the feudal jurisdictions were severely limited and the status of the agricultural population vastly improved by the abolition of serfdom and the removal of the internal customs-barriers that had hampered trade. So with the time-honoured abuses of the Church; the Inquisition was suppressed, and ecclesiastical jurisdiction confined to purely spiritual offences, while the religious foundations of Cosimo III. were rigidly reduced in number and reformed in discipline. Foreign trade was encouraged by a reduction of customs, monopolies were abolished, alienated taxes redeemed, and the annual budget published to the world. Leopold was supported in his work by a group of able Tuscan ministers, but the people for whom he toiled seem to have looked with suspicion on his efforts, and to the end distrusted their foreign schoolmaster. When in 1790 he was called to the empire on the death of his brother Joseph he left to his son Ferdinand a model state, skilled in all arts save one, the art of war. But the age of the bayonet was approaching, and Tuscany, for all its virtues, had little chance of survival in the flood that was to sweep away the paternal governments of Europe.

The long-suffering Milanese also, under the enlightened Austrian rule initiated by the Emperor Joseph, brother of Leopold, made great strides in material prosperity, and seemed to breathe more freely after two centuries of Spanish oppression. Long-vanished thoughts of liberty stirred the air, and under the benevolent patronage of the government the ideas of the French encyclopædists invaded the *salons* of Milan and revivified the University of Pavia. But in the neighbouring Piedmont, where the long reign of Charles Emanuel III. carried on the traditions of his father Victor Amadeus, the new light penetrated but slowly and with difficulty; there the Holy Office was still a power, and the *sbirri* of the government kept a heavy hand on all would-be innovators or purveyors of French ideas. The Waldenses, though no longer massacred, remained excluded from civic employment; the peasants remained subject to their feudal lords, while those lords themselves drained the last penny from their villages and spent it in aping the frivolities of Versailles at Turin. But in war and politics the King of Sardinia carried on the successes of his father. In the War of the Austrian Succession, which devastated parts of Italy from 1742 to 1747, his alliance was solicited both by Maria-Theresa and by her Franco-Spanish adversaries, and since the latters' terms were not high enough he joined the Austrians, and received at the Peace of Aix-la-Chapelle all portions of the Milanese lying to the west of the Ticino, including even the beautiful little town and palace of Vigevano, built long ago with loving care by Duke Ludovico and his bride. The war had demonstrated that the Austrian power could not easily be dislodged from Lombardy, but at the Peace the Spanish Bourbons were compensated by the recognition of Don Philip, younger brother of Don Carlos of Naples, as Duke of Parma and Piacenza [1748]. Thus the little Duchy escaped incorporation with any of its larger neighbours, and perhaps was glad to accept a ruler who represented the old Farnese blood.[1] Don Philip's court became a centre of French culture and enlighten-

[1] Don Philip's mother was Elisabeth Farnese, wife of Philip V. of Spain.

ment, and by the stand which it took up against Papal domination became prominently involved in the great European drama that ended in the downfall of the Jesuit Order.

The Papacy of the eighteenth century found itself exposed in ever-increasing measure to the attacks of the European sovereigns upon its ancient privileges and pretensions. Prince after prince demanded his 'Concordat,' securing the abolition of clerical immunity from taxation, of rights of asylum and so forth, and during the reign of Benedict XIV. [1740—1758] the policy of conciliation and concession had made rapid strides. But towards the end of his reign the point of attack had already been shifted from the Papacy itself to its traditional champion, the Society of Jesus, and in Portugal and France strong national movements had arisen which threatened to destroy the Jesuits. Benedict's successor, Clement XIII. [1758—1769], took the part of the Order, and endeavoured by innumerable letters of protest and monition to avert the doom that menaced it, but his complaints went unheeded, and between the years 1758 and 1767 the Jesuits were actually expelled from Portugal, France, Spain, and Naples. Then it was that the Bourbon Duke of Parma put forth a number of decrees abolishing clerical immunities in his dominions, and Clement, exasperated by his ill-success elsewhere, struck heavily at the Duke in a *Monitorium* that threatened him with excommunication. Immediately the three allied Bourbon monarchs of France, Spain, and Naples took up the defence of their kinsman with a demand for the withdrawal of the *Monitorium*, and when this was refused French and Neapolitan troops were sent to occupy Avignon and Benevento respectively, while Carlos of Spain demanded the formal dissolution of the Jesuit Order. The much-harassed Pope died in the midst of these calamities, and the attention of Europe was focussed, in a measure unknown for centuries, on the Conclave that was to elect his successor. The united influence of the Bourbon powers was exerted in favour of a candidate pledged to suppress the Jesuits, but in the end Lorenzo Ganganelli emerged from the Conclave unfettered by any definite pledge, though the fact that he was a Franciscan gave a sufficiently shrewd augury of his intentions. Without letting himself be hurried, the new Pope (Clement XIV.) [1769—1774], first conciliated the Powers with smaller measures and then, after three years' deliberation, issued the celebrated Bull, *Dominus ac Redemptor*, which put an end for the time to the Jesuit organization [July 21, 1773]. The fury with which the Jesuits assailed his memory is shown in the story which they put about, that the Pope was struck down by madness on the night after his signing of the Bull, while their adversaries, with equal bitterness, accused the Jesuits of having poisoned him.

Clement's successor was a man of noble presence and excellent intentions, who dreamed of leaving a name as the benefactor of the Papal States, but whose eyes beheld instead the reign of tribulation and woe. As far as he dared, Pius VI. [1774—1797] favoured the Jesuit remnant, and the far-reaching reforms carried out by the Emperor Joseph at Milan and throughout his dominions caused him acute concern. Finding remonstrance vain, the Pope determined to visit the Emperor in person, and made a pilgrimage to Vienna in 1782—the first visit of supplication made by a Pope to a Transalpine sovereign since the flight of Leo III. to Charles the Frank at Paderborn in 799. Joseph received the Pope with courtesy, but met his demand for the abrogation of his 'Patent of Toleration' with a firm refusal, and Pius returned unsatisfied to Rome. Thither the Emperor followed him in the next year, travelling incognito, and so delighted the mob with his condescensions and his *bonhomie* that he was frequently greeted by the old Ghibelline party-cry, 'Viva il *nostro* Imperatore!' But he yielded nothing to the Pope in his policy of emancipating Lombardy and Austria from the more onerous Papal claims, and if the destinies of Europe had been left in his hands, it is possible that a serious breach with the Papacy might have been provoked by His Apostolic Majesty. But the game was passing to a younger power, and while Pope and Emperor continued their stately moves, the underground forces gathered head beyond the Alps which were to humble the Papacy in the dust, and to sweep away the very name of the Holy Roman Empire.

CHAPTER XXV

Napoleon's First Conquest of Italy

Cannon his name,
Cannon his voice, he came. *(Meredith, Napoléon)*

WHEN the French Revolution broke out in July, 1789, Italy had enjoyed forty years of continuous peace. Since the Treaty of Aix-la-Chapelle in 1748, which had confirmed the Austrian rule at Milan and once more enlarged the territories of Savoy, no foreign attack or domestic quarrel had occurred to disturb the equilibrium of the Italian States. Their prosperity during the Century of Enlightenment had increased by leaps and bounds, and so secure did their rulers feel from outside interference that they had suffered their military forces to dwindle almost to disappearance. Lombardy had ransomed itself from the Austrian conscription by a money payment; Tuscany maintained four thousand men, the Papal States six thousand; Venice relied on her fleet of about fifty sail, with a small body of Slavonian mercenaries and a half-trained militia of thirty thousand peasants[1]; only in Piedmont and Naples was any serious effort made at maintaining a professional army. Charles Emanuel III., indeed, had loved to hear his kingdom called the Prussia of Italy, and the parade-ground at Turin had become famous for the precision of his regiments' evolutions; but the Piedmontese army suffered from the rigid exclusion of the bourgeois class from the commissioned ranks, and Victor Amadeus III., who succeeded his father in 1774, squandered much hard-won treasure in satisfying his mania for designing uniforms. At Naples the indolent King Ferdinand, friend of *lazzaroni* and of every gross indulgence, cared not at all for military glory; but his high-spirited wife, Maria-Carolina of Austria, intended that Naples should play a prominent part in European affairs, and imported an English adventurer named Sir John Acton[2] to reorganize the army and navy. Large sums were spent in building a fleet and in recruiting an army of thirty thousand men from the dregs of the population; but the attempt to instruct them by means of foreign officers

---

[1] Cantù, *Indipendenza Italiana*, vol. i., p. 61.
[2] Acton was descended from an old Shropshire family, but was born at Besançon [1736] and entered the Tuscan naval service, whence he was 'borrowed' by Queen Mary Caroline in 1779. He became successively Minister of Marine, Minister of War, Generalissimo, Minister of Finance, and Prime Minister of Naples. He died at Palermo in 1811.

ITALY
BEFORE THE
FRENCH REVOLUTION

0   40   100
Scale of Miles

N

SWITZERLAND

SAVOY

FRANCE

GERMANY

Aosta

DAUPHINE

PROVENCE

TURIN

Vigevano

MONTFERRAT

MILAN

Bergamo

Pavia

BISHOP OF TREN

NICE

Monaco

STATE OF GENOA

Genoa

DUCHY
OF
PARMA

Parma

Reggio

Brescia

Mantua

Verona

Vicenza

R. Adige

STATE
OF
FRIU

KINGDOM
of SARDINIA

Spezia

DUCHY
OF
MODENA

Mo

Padua

VENICE

Pisa

Livorno

Elba I.

GRAND
DUCHY
OF
TUSCANY

Floren

Ravenna

Rimini

Gulf

CORSICA

Bastia

Ajaccio

Siena

RINO

of Venice or Adriatic Sea

Porto Vecchio

Strait of Bonifacio

Ancona

SARDINIA

Civitavecchia

STATE OF
THE CHURCH

Cagliari

Ostia

ROME

Aquila

Pescara

Tyrrhenian Sea

Gulf of
Gaeta

Gaeta

K
I
N
G
D
O
M

Termoli

I. of Ischia

Capua

A
P
L
E
S

I. of Capri

NAPLES

Benevento

Vieste

Salerno

O
F

N

Marsala

Policastro

Potenza

Bari

Taranto

Palermo

Isles of
Lipari

Brindisi

SICILY

Cefalù

Gulf of
Taranto

Otranto

Messina

Cosenza

St. Eufemia

Catania

Reggio

Mediterranean Sea

proved a failure, and only the artillery and cavalry became in any degree effective. The *lazzaroni* of Naples could always fight when their mob rage was aroused, but it was a different matter to instil into them the discipline and order of the professional soldier.

Such was the meagre preparation with which Italy was called upon to face the greatest outpouring of military power which Europe had known since the decline of the Roman Empire. And along with her military unpreparedness went the divided temper of the people, halting between approval and abhorrence of the Revolution and all that it stood for, so that no unity of action could be organized by the distracted rulers. In every state of the Peninsula the normal development of the eighteenth century had produced 'Liberal' parties, powerful enough to welcome the 'liberating' armies of France when they entered each successive capital, even if not in any sense representative of the whole people. The result was the inevitable subjugation of the non-military by the military nation, and the violent interruption of the normal political development of the Italians. Yet in that strange welter of democracy and tyranny which Napoleon's grenadiers brought in, the foundations of an Italian national consciousness were laid, in spite of all, for with the French equalitarians came the breath of a new age that swept away the abuses of centuries, and made it impossible for men so freed to be treated in the same way again. Not all the plunderings of the French commissaries, or the blood-taxes laid upon Italy by Napoleon in his later years, served to efface the memory of certain tasks accomplished—the Papal misgovernment destroyed, feudalism abolished, the career thrown open to talent. When the flood of reaction again overwhelmed the land these things were remembered, and it remained for Italians to accomplish for themselves what the foreign conqueror, being a child of the Revolution, had imposed on them from without. And, after long years of suffering, Italy fulfilled the task.

The interference of France in the affairs of Italy was determined by the Austrian occupation of Lombardy. Austria, the arch-enemy of the Republic, must be defeated in the plain of the Po as well as on the Rhine. But between the two great Powers lay wedged the kingdom of Sardinia, with its strip of coast line running from Nice to Savona; to secure the goodwill of the House of Savoy was worth some sacrifice on the part of the new Republic. In June, 1792, the reversion of Lombardy was offered to the King, but Victor Amadeus III., too honest and limited a reactionary to follow in the footsteps of his great namesake, chose to ally himself with Austria, and remained faithful to the alliance. His troops were beaten out of Savoy and Nice at the first shock [September, 1792], and by the end of 1795 the French under Scherer held the whole coast as far as Savona, while the Austro-Sardinians held the crest of the Apennines at Ceva and Dego. At this juncture the command of the French Army of Italy was given to a young Corsican general of artillery named Napoleon Bonaparte, who had come to the front in a certain street affair in Paris,[1] and the new leader arrived at Nice to take over the command at the end of March, 1796.

Into the details of Napoleon's Italian Campaign it is impossible to enter within the narrow limits of the present survey. It must suffice to say that in eleven days of mountain fighting he had completely severed the Austrian and Piedmontese armies, beaten both and forced the King of Sardinia to a truce which relieved the French of all anxiety as to their communications. By the Armistice of Cherasco [April 28, 1796], King Victor Amadeus withdrew from the Austrian alliance, gave free passage through his territories to the French armies and placed three fortresses in Bonaparte's hands. The Treaty of Paris, which confirmed these terms a fortnight later [May 15], made no mention whatever of any compensation in Lombardy for the King's losses in Savoy, Nice and elsewhere. Then Bonaparte hastened on to finish with the Austrians; crossed the Po at Piacenza—further east than they expected him, —terrorized the incapable Beaulieu into a premature retreat across the Adda and fell upon his rearguard at the Bridge of Lodi; then turned back to make his triumphal entry into Milan on May 14. Soon, however, he was on the banks of the Mincio, and by an adroit crossing had forced Beaulieu to retire into the Tyrol, leaving the great fortress of Mantua isolated, though amply provisioned for a siege. Around the siege of Mantua, the citadel of Austrian power in Italy, the war now centred for the next six months. Three several attempts were made by the Aulic Council at Vienna to relieve the fortress and to crush the audacious invaders, the first in July under Würmser, the second and third under Alvintzy in November and January respectively. Each time the genius of Napoleon seized the weak spot in his adversaries' dispositions, and at Castiglione, Arcola, and finally at Rivoli he delivered his crushing blows. The last-named was decisive, for on February 2, 1797, Mantua fell, and the last Austrian white-coats were either dispersed or taken captive. But Napoleon did not even rest there, for in

[1] The rising against the Convention on October 4, 1795, known as 'Vendémiaire.'

April, 1797, he carried the war across the Isonzo into Austrian territory, and having penetrated beyond Klagenfurt obtained from the Archduke Charles the Preliminaries of Leoben. By this famous agreement Austria renounced her claims to Lombardy, in exchange for compensation at the expense of Venice. The Venetian *terra firma* was made over to the Austrians.

Bonaparte had thus effected the deliverance of Milan and the Lombard Plain from Austrian rule, and Italy had her first taste of liberty as imposed by the cannon of the French Republicans. Milan had welcomed the French troops after the Battle of Lodi with delight; but it was not many days before the joy-bells gave place to murmurs of indignation and rage as the extortions of the French in money, in requisitions, and in works of art fell upon the city. Pavia and the little town of Binasco rose against the Jacobins, at the news that Bonaparte had laid hands on the sacred treasures of the 'Monti di Pietà,'[1] and parties of French soldiers were murdered by the furious peasantry. Bonaparte himself marched to exact retribution. Binasco was burned to the ground and its male inhabitants massacred; Pavia, which still defied the French column, was entered by storm and given up for twenty-four hours to massacre and pillage. So the reign of liberty was confirmed and established. Throughout the whole period of Napoleon's campaign against Austria, that is until after the Preliminaries of Leoben, Milan was treated like a conquered city and sucked dry by the swarm of French contractors, commissaries, and jobbers of all sorts who followed the army, while a police code of Draconian severity held down the malcontents. It was not long before the ironic wit of the Milanese found vent in rhymes like these:

> Liberté, fraternité, égalité—
> I Frances in carrocia e nun a pee;
> Libertà, indipendenza
> Fin al dazi di Porta Renza![2]

Yet notwithstanding all this, the leaven of liberty worked on in Upper Italy. In June, 1796, after his first expulsion of the Austrians, Bonaparte had time for a flying visit to Bologna, and at once the citizens rose against the Papal government and proclaimed their ancient freedom. Napoleon took advantage of the situation to

---

[1] The Monti di Pietà were equivalent to popular savings-banks, and were specially used for accumulating dowries for the daughters of the family. They took deposits in kind as well as in money.

[2] Michele Rosi, *Storia contemporanea d'Italia*, p. 27.

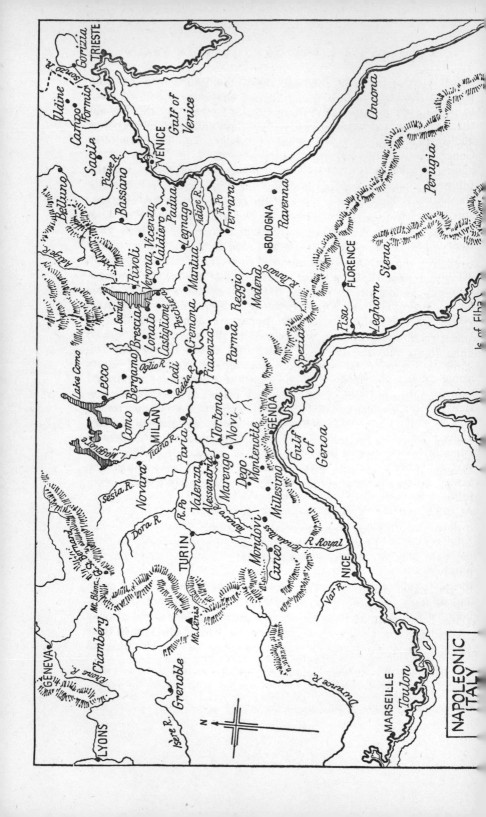

extort a truce from the Pope, by which Pius agreed to close his
ports to the English, to hand over one hundred works of art, and
to pay an indemnity of fifteen million francs. The instructions of
the Directory had been precise that the Temporal Power must be
abolished and the Pope if possible exiled; but for the present the
General prudently halted there. The Bolognese Senate willingly
agreed to take an oath of fidelity to the French Republic. Ferrara
followed suit; in August, Reggio rose against the government of
the Duke of Modena,[1] and the revolt, stiffened by French troops,
spread to Modena itself; by October Bonaparte was able to hold a
Congress there of deputies from the four towns, and to form with
their consent the 'Cispadane Confederation.'

Meanwhile the grievances of the French Government were
accumulating against Pope Pius VI. An agent of the new-born
Republic, Hugo Basseville, flaunting his tricolours along the Corso,
had been murdered by the Roman mob as early as January, 1793,
under circumstances of aggravated cruelty,[2] and since then the
Pope had in a hundred ways proclaimed himself the enemy of the
Republic. More recently he had neglected to carry out the terms
of the Truce of Bologna, and at each reappearance of the Austrian
armies under Würmser or Alvintzy there had been stirrings of
sympathy in the Papal States. Pius had finally borrowed an Austrian general to lead and organize his troops. Now the reckoning
was at hand. No sooner had Mantua fallen than Bonaparte advanced into the Papal States by the Emilian Way, driving the
Papalini before him in headlong rout. By the 9th of February he
was at Ancona, and the road to Rome lay open and undefended
before him. The instructions of the Directory could have been
fulfilled to the letter, but Bonaparte was inclined for moderation.
At the little town of Tolentino he met the deputation sent forward
in haste by the Pope to conclude a truce, and at the price of the
total renunciation of Avignon, the Legations[3] and Romagna, the
payment of thirty millions of francs and the surrender of the one
hundred works of art stipulated for at Bologna, Napoleon suffered
the remnants of the Temporal Power to survive. 'Rome is saved,
and religion also,' wrote the good envoy Mattei to the Pope, but
Bonaparte remarked drily to the Directory that they need not be

---

[1] This was a descendant of the House of Este, expelled from Ferrara in
1597. See p. 276.
[2] He was taken, severely wounded, to the guard-room of the Papal police,
and allowed to die without any medical care or comfort. Romanin, *Stor.
di Venezia*, ix., 499.
[3] This was the name given to the provinces of Bologna, Ravenna, Forlì,
and Ferrara, each governed by a Cardinal Legate.

disappointed, for 'Cette vieille machine se détraquera toute seule.'

The year 1797, having opened thus with the surrender of
Mantua and the humiliation of the Pope, was to witness the destruction of Italy's most ancient Republic, and the foundation of a
brand-new and nominally independent state in the valley of the Po.
Bonaparte's sale of the Republic of Venice to Austria has never
found many defenders even in France, and even in his own day the
government of the Directory had much ado to swallow the transaction. From the moment that he followed Beaulieu across the
Mincio, Bonaparte found himself in contact with this strange
survival from the past—this oligarchy which claimed obedience
from its people on the strength of its thousand years' subsistence;
which denied all share in the government not only to its merchant
class, but even to the nobles of the *terra firma;* which detested
French ideas of equality as the spawn of the devil; which maintained itself by its spies and by the mysterious terror surrounding
its three 'Inquisitors of State'; and which yet gave a greater measure of contentment to the bulk of its population than any other
state in Italy. Only anxious to preserve Venetian neutrality in the
midst of the convulsions around them, the Senate had already
refused the invitations of the King of Sardinia, of the Pope, of
Naples, to form a league for the defence of Italy; they refused
the alliance of Austria; they refused, in July, 1796, the proffered
alliance of France. Yet they failed to take measures to defend
their neutrality by force of arms. The result was that French and
Austrians used Venetian territory as their battleground, and when
the French were left in possession they treated the Venetians as
slaves to be bullied and plundered at will. It is impossible to
doubt that Bonaparte's own feelings towards the Venetian government were inspired by strong personal animosity; he regarded it
as both effete and tyrannical; and when its partisans among the
peasantry replied to the nameless provocations of the French by
a campaign of murder he looked on them with all the contempt
and hatred of the professional soldier for the *franc-tireur.* Matters
were complicated by the existence of a third party composed of
native malcontents only too ready to turn against the government
that denied them political rights, and this class made common
cause with the French and organized risings with their aid in
Bergamo, Brescia, and Crema in March, 1797. Democratic republics were proclaimed in all three towns, and the Venetian officials
driven out. Bonaparte, at that time pursuing his campaign against
the Archduke Charles beyond the Isonzo, received the protests of

the Venetian Senate with politeness, but refused to render up the citadels of Bergamo and Brescia, and demanded a further contribution of six million francs. Already, in fact, the idea of settling his differences with Austria at the expense of Venice had presented itself to his mind. He now sought only to provoke a definite rupture, in order to secure a pretext for declaring war on Venice. He ordered General Kilmaine, left in command at Mantua, to disarm all the Venetian garrisons of the *terra firma* and to set up municipal councils in the towns. This was safely done everywhere save in Verona, where the Senate had concentrated all its available forces. There, on Easter Monday, April 17, a chance affray between Slavonian troops of the government and a body of Cispadane volunteers fired the train of smouldering hatred between Venetians and French. The whole town flew to arms, and all French soldiers found outside the walls of the citadel were massacred without mercy in the course of a week of bloody street fighting. These were the *Pâques Veronaises*, and they gave Napoleon his pretext for revenge. Long before the news reached him he had secretly signed the Preliminaries of Leoben [April 18], bartering away the territories of a neutral and defenceless state, but now he was able to drop the mask and to declare war on the Republic. Gradually the French armies closed in on the Lagoons, and the helpless government was left face to face with a divided population within and a relentless foe without. Incapable of rousing the people to a defence worthy of their history, the Venetian oligarchy took refuge in an ignoble suicide. At the instigation of the French Agent, Villetard, the Doge and Great Council of Venice voted their own abolition on May 14, 1797, as the one sacrifice which might yet appease this second Attila. A provisional government was elected and a garrison of French troops admitted [May 16], conveyed to the capital in Venetian vessels. On the same day Bonaparte at Milan granted a treaty of peace to the new government, the terms of which were not unreasonable[1]; but far other thoughts were in his mind. The definitive treaty with Austria had not yet been concluded, but Bonaparte would be saved from many embarrassments if he could content the Emperor with the offer of Venice herself. Within eleven days of signing the Treaty of Milan, Bonaparte informed the Directory that that offer had already been

---

[1] The hereditary aristocracy was to be abolished and a more democratic government set up; the two Republics were to negotiate as to the *exchange* of certain territories; Venice was to pay 3 million francs in money and 3 million in naval equipment, and to surrender 3 ships of the line, 2 frigates, 20 pictures, and 500 manuscripts.

made. It was embodied in the Treaty of Campo-Formio, signed
on October 17, 1797. Venice was sold to Austria, her ancient
enemy, for the crime of having lived too long. It remained only
for the French garrison, before it evacuated the city, to pillage
and destroy the Arsenal, to burn the *bucentaur* and to carry off the
famous Bronze Horses to adorn the conqueror's Triumphal Arch
on the Place du Carrousel.

If Bonaparte's treatment of Venice still at this latter day
arouses feelings of abhorrence, his conduct towards Lombardy and
towards the ancient oligarchy of Genoa reaches a different plane
both of morality and of political organization. As a Corsican he
had little cause to love the Republic of Genoa, which stood to
every Corsican patriot as the very type of selfish and grinding
despotism; but when a fierce civil affray in which a couple of
French subjects were killed gave him his pretext for intervention
[May 23, 1797], he contented himself with remodelling the constitution of Genoa and leaving her at least a nominal independence.
The Republic took the name of the *Ligurian*, and subsisted un-
easily—as the sole outpost of French power during the reaction
of 1799—until it petitioned for union with France during Napoleon's visit to Italy as Emperor in 1805.

But it was at Milan, during his famous sojourn at the Castle of
Montebello in the months of May—July, 1797, that he made a
more serious essay in constructive statesmanship. It was time that
the Lombards should be organized in a democratic republic, and
Bonaparte, fresh from the destruction of Venetian liberties, employed the best minds of Northern Italy in drafting the constitution
and the laws of the new 'Cisalpine Republic.' Its form was a
replica in miniature of the French Directory, and Bonaparte himself appointed the first group of Directors and even the first members of the two Legislative Councils; but it was readily accepted
by all classes save the pro-Austrian minority, and proved so popular that the smaller and weaker Cispadane Republic petitioned
urgently for union with it [July 15]. This appeal was granted, and
since the Papal territories of Romagna had already been joined to
the Cispadane, and the ancient possessions of Venice west of the
Mincio to the Cisalpine, the boundaries of the new state extended
from the Piedmontese frontier to the Mincio[1] and the Adriatic, and
from the Alps to the borders of Parma, Tuscany, and the Papal
States. Equality and local self-government were the rule through-

[1] At the Treaty of Campo-Formio the eastern boundary was extended to
the Adige.

out this 'liberated' area, but the French military occupation continued even after the departure of Napoleon from Italy in
November, and the Cisalpines found themselves burdened not
only with the maintenance of their own promised contingent of
Lombard troops, but with that of the French army of occupation
as well. No wonder that the Austrian Emperor refused to accredit
an ambassador to the Republic, on the ground that it was not a
sovereign and independent state.

During the two and a half years of Napoleon's absence from
Italy [November, 1797—May, 1800], the unfortunate peoples of
the Peninsula went through every extreme of suffering at the hands
both of Liberators and Reactionaries. In December, 1797, an
outbreak of the clerical populace of Rome against the French
embassy, resulting in the murder of General Duphot, gave the
Directory its pretext for fininshing with the Pope, and General
Berthier was sent to sweep out the Vatican and set up the Roman
Republic on the Capitol. This the General had no difficulty in
doing. He arrived before Rome on February 10, 1798, with a
mixed body of French and Cisalpine troops. The octogenarian
Pope was brusquely informed that he must prepare for exile, and
when he pleaded to be allowed to die in Rome he was told that
'he could die anywhere.' French troops escorted him to the Tuscan frontier, where the Grand Duke Ferdinand received him as
his guest. But after a year of precarious safety in Siena and Florence—a source of equal honour and embarrassment to his host—
the storm struck him once more, and he was carried off into exile
in good earnest by the French. Dragged from place to place by
his relentless gaolers, he succumbed at last at the little town of
Valence in Dauphiné—the first Pope since Clement VII. to have
suffered the worst tribulations of war.

Meanwhile the Roman Republic had been inaugurated with all
the usual ceremonies, and a shadowy executive of seven consuls
employed itself in draining the last penny from an already bank-
rupt state for the benefit of Generals Berthier and Masséna and
the horde of French commissaries who followed the army. Cardinals were plundered, insulted, and exiled, monasteries suppressed,
churches pillaged of their sacred vessels. But help was at hand.
The slow-moving King Ferdinand of Naples, egged on by his Queen
Mary Caroline, by the English favourite Sir John Acton, and by
the English Ambassador Sir William Hamilton, determined at
length to intervene in the cause of religion and the peace of
Europe. In May, 1798, he concluded a secret alliance with Aust-

ria; in August, Nelson sailed triumphantly into the Bay of Naples, fresh from his destruction of the French fleet at Aboukir. Encouraged by his presence, and by the loan of an Austrian General of high repute, the redoubtable Mack, the King decided to take the field in person at the head of the newly created Neapolitan army. He summoned the French—now under the command of Championnet, one of the most gifted of the younger Republican generals—to evacuate Rome and Tuscany on the instant. They did retire some twenty miles to the northward before superior force, and King Ferdinand made his triumphal entry into Rome on November 28, while the populace indulged in a furious outburst of Jew-baiting and Patriot-hunting. But within seventeen days Championnet was back in Rome, having inflicted a whole series of defeats on the astonished Mack, and finally driven him, his King, and his troops through Rome in headlong flight [December 12]. Ferdinand did not rest until he reached Naples, disguised as his own equerry,[1] but finding the capital in a turmoil of panic and rage he decided not even to trust himself there, but to fly to Palermo on board Nelson's ships. The embarkation was secretly carried out under Nelson's supervision, and in spite of the agonized supplications of his people, the King and Queen, with their children, their jewels, and a favoured suite deserted the capital. A month later Championnet entered Naples amid fierce and bloody street fighting, for the Lazzaroni had been armed and fought with desperate courage until Championnet won them over by an adroit act of reverence to San Gennaro.[2] Once master of the town, he proceeded to set up a republic on the usual model, to which he gave the name *Parthenopean;* the bourgeois and educated classes rallied at once to its support, and compromised themselves deeply by their service to the new state. Championnet himself was soon recalled by the Directory, owing to the severity of his proceedings against the plundering French commissaries, and his successor Macdonald was not long able to give his support to the young republic. Storm-clouds had gathered in the north. The Second Coalition against France had been formed during the winter, and the veteran Suvaroff, at the head of a great Russian and Austrian army, had entered Lombardy and driven the French before him at the battle of Cassano [April 28, 1799]. Macdonald was hastily recalled to the north, and his departure sealed the fate of the Parthenopean Republic.

The story of its end must ever remain a painful one for English

[1] Colletta, ii., p. 15.
[2] *Ibid.*, ii., p. 51.

readers. The Republicans, holding out with some success in the two great castles of Nuovo and dell' Uovo against the king's vice-gerent, Cardinal Ruffo, and his savage 'Army of the Holy Faith,' agreed to come to terms with him on the basis of a capitulation signed not only by the Cardinal but by a Russian, a Turkish, and a British naval officer[1] [June 20]. The garrisons were to be allowed to march out with the honours of war, and to be embarked on transports which should convey them to Toulon. The treaty had not yet been executed, when Nelson sailed into the Bay of Naples from Palermo with the whole British squadron [June 24]. Unfortunately for his fame he had the enchantress Emma Hamilton on board, and Emma was but the mouthpiece of the Queen Mary Caroline, whose one absorbing passion was a desire for revenge on her own subjects. Nelson, though highly incensed with Ruffo for granting so generous a capitulation, signified his acceptance of it on June 26 and sent British officers ashore to superintend the embarkation of the rebels; but two days later, on receipt of letters from the King and Queen at Palermo, he informed Ruffo that

in consequence of an order which he has just received from his Sicilian Majesty, who disapproves entirely of the capitulation made with his rebellious subjects in the castles of Uovo and Nuovo, he is about to seize and make sure of those who have left them.

The transports were accordingly anchored under the guns of the British ships, and many of the leaders arrested and distributed through the squadron [June 28]. Nelson could cover himself, though dishonourably, by posing as the mere servant of the King of Naples. Prince Caracciolo, an admiral of the Neapolitan fleet who had gone over to the Republic, was court-martialled and sentenced to death on board Nelson's flagship. He was hung from the yardarm of the *Minerva* (a Neapolitan frigate), and his body cast into the sea.[2]

A frightful persecution of the Republicans followed on these events. Once more the savage *Sanfedisti* broke loose in Naples, murdering, burning, and torturing, and a Bloody Assize, drawn from the dregs of the royal spy-service, was empowered to proceed

[1] Captain Foote, at that time in command of the British vessels in the Bay.
[2] See the detailed account of these transactions in *Nelson and the Neapolitan Jacobins* (Navy Records Society, 1903), and in F. P. Badham's *Nelson at Naples*, 1900.

against all those who had supported the 'infamous Republic.' About a hundred victims of this tribunal were hung in Naples alone, including two women, but throughout the kingdom it is estimated by Botta that at least four thousand persons perished in the Reaction. Finally, to set the seal on the recovery of the royal power, a decree was put forth abolishing the *Seggi*, or ancient Assemblies of Naples.

A similar reaction followed on the victories of the Austro-Russian troops throughout the Peninsula. Macdonald had been defeated by Suvaroff on the Trebbia in June; Moreau and Joubert at Novi in August; only Genoa remained to the French of all Napoleon's conquests. But before the arrival of Suvaroff they had succeeded in dethroning two more of the hapless rulers of Italy: Charles Emanuel IV., King of Sardinia, and Ferdinand III., Grand Duke of Tuscany.

The Republican leaven had spread with alarming rapidity among the educated classes of Piedmont, for the government was thoroughly old-fashioned and reactionary, and feudal abuses survived in plenty. In 1797 it had come to risings, cruelly suppressed, at Asti, Moncalieri, and other places, and the Piedmontese patriots had learnt in the hard school of persecution to cherish their faith. In this favourable soil the French and Cisalpine envoys worked to good purpose during the year 1798, and finally, when Ferdinand of Naples was marching on Rome, the Directory decided to pick a quarrel with the King and expel him from his dominions. General Joubert was instructed to demand the surrender of the arsenal of Turin. Charles Emanuel—a weak and exceedingly religious prince—equivocated and lost heart, and on December 9 signed a capitulation ceding the whole of his mainland possessions to the French, and reserving only to himself the island of Sardinia. Thither, travelling through coldly hostile Cisalpine territories and then through a still friendly Tuscany, the exiled King retired with his wife [February, 1799]—never to be recalled to rule at Turin. His host, the Grand Duke Ferdinand, met a similar fate, a month after Charles Emanuel's departure from Livorno. The Grand Duke's connection with the Austrian court was sufficient ground on which to base a military occupation of Tuscany, as soon as war between Austria and France broke out in March, 1799. The cherished neutrality of Tuscany was rudely swept aside, and on March 26 an aide-de-camp of General Gaultier presented the Grand Duke with a notification that he must quit the country within twenty-four hours. Ferdinand, his wife, and four children took the road to Vienna.

These were the last triumphs of the French, before Suvaroff and his Russians turned the tide of war against them. By the end of the year the whole Peninsula—save Genoa alone—had been cleared of the French armies; the Cisalpine and Roman Republics had been abolished; the white-coats were enthroned at Milan and the Neapolitans in Rome. Yet neither the Grand Duke nor the King of Sardinia were recalled to their states. Austria had other designs, and when Suvaroff pressed for their restoration Baron von Thugut procured his transference to Switzerland, there to waste his strength against both the Alps and Masséna. Italy was once more in the possession of Austria, and the statesmen of Vienna did not intend to let her slip again. The Republicans were everywhere feeling the full weight of Austrian vengeance and of popular fury; in a few months—so augured Vienna—the memory of the French invasion would have disappeared as a dream in the night.

Yet on October 9, 1799, General Bonaparte landed at Fréjus on his return from Egypt; on November 10 the *coup d'état* of Brumaire placed France at his feet, and, emerging from the crisis as First Consul, he cast his eyes once more on Italy.

CHAPTER XXVI

The Napoleonic Era in Italy

NAPOLEON'S second and final conquest of Italy was achieved by the campaign which opened with his famous passage of the great St. Bernard in May, 1800, and ended, less than a month later, with the victory wrung from defeat on the field of Marengo [June 14]. Although Masséna was left to starve in Genoa, where he capitulated on June 6, although the battle of Marengo was lost by Bonaparte before it was won by Désaix and Kellermann, yet the whole campaign had been so surely planned that, the Austrians once defeated, nothing remained for them but to propose an armistice, and to accept the conditions attached to it by the conqueror. The armies which, during the previous year, had overrun Lombardy, Piedmont, Tuscany, and the Papal States, were all to retire behind the Mincio, while the First Consul proposed to the Emperor Francis a return to the Treaty of Campo-Formio. But Austria was not yet convinced of defeat, and it needed the winter campaign of Moreau in Bavaria and of Brune on the Mincio and Adige to supply the decisive arguments. Then the Emperor yielded, and by the treaty signed in Lunéville on February 9, 1801, he accepted terms far more disastrous than those of Campo-Formio. Though Austria still kept Venice, she was forced to recognize once more the Cisalpine Republic and to accept the Adige frontier; France remained in military occupation of Piedmont, whose exiled King, Charles Emanuel IV., retired about this time to Naples and abdicated a year later [1802]; the Duke of Modena—relic of the great Este family—was dispossessed and consoled with the duchy of Breisgau; while Tuscany, deprived of her Grand Duke Ferdinand, was erected into the puppet-kingdom of Etruria and ceded to the Bourbon Duke of Parma. The kingdom of Naples, under Ferdinand and Mary Caroline, was allowed for the time to retain its existence, largely owing to the mediation of the Czar of Russia,[1] but by the Treaty of Florence, concluded in March, 1801, the King was compelled to accept a French garrison in Taranto.

So the map of Italy was refashioned in the interests of France, and the 'patriots' of Milan and of Piedmont emerged once more

---

[1] Paul I., at this time the enthusiastic admirer of Bonaparte and friend of Mary Caroline.

from the prisons and the hiding-places to which they had been driven by Austria. The public floggings which went down to folk memory as the mark of Austrian domination ceased, but in their place the French brought in a *régime* of systematic pillage, under the name of 'Provisional Government.' It was not now a question of works of art, but of unending requisitions for the support of the army, both in money and in kind; of the ruthless stripping of the countryside by French troops; of open trafficking in the revenues of the country by French and Italian peculators. Bonaparte was in no hurry to give a constitution to the Cisalpine Republic, and all that he had done during his residence at Milan to conciliate opinion was to announce his firm support of the Catholic religion, and to attend a solemn Te Deum in the cathedral for the victory of Marengo. This change from the aggressive atheism of the early days was to have far-reaching effects, and even during the worst period of French oppression it served more than all Bonaparte's success in the field to attach to his reign the solid classes and the aristocrats.

After the signature of the Peace of Lunéville—which guaranteed the 'independence' of the Cisalpine Republic—the unhappy Lombards grew restive at the continued delay in the grant of their constitution, and augured the worst from the reports that reached them of Bonaparte's scolding tongue. Yet in the end he served them well. The constructive instinct, in these days of the Consulate, was strong within him, and having demonstrated his omnipotence to the Italians he was not averse from playing the rôle of the enlightened liberator—provided indeed that all real power remained in his hands. Towards the end of 1801, therefore, it was decided to summon a congress of representative 'Cisalpines' to Lyons, and to submit to them a constitution which had been drafted in Paris and approved by the First Consul. The delegates were nominated by the Provisional Government at Milan under the searching eye of Joachim Murat, commanding the army of Italy; they were all 'well-affected,' but even so no freedom of deliberation was allowed them at Lyons. On the question of the choice of President, on which all depended, they were informed that Bonaparte himself must be elected, and when the way had been prepared by the astute Talleyrand, a final session of the Congress was held [January 26, 1802], at which the constitution was passed without debate and the First Consul acclaimed as President of the Republic. In return for this complaisance the name of the Republic was changed from *Cisalpine* to *Italian*, and a native Vice-President was appointed in the person of Count

Melzi, a distinguished Milanese noble. To seal the compact, Melzi and Bonaparte embraced each other before the whole assembly.

Thus was created the Italian Republic, perhaps the most remarkable of Napoleon's attempts at constitution-building outside France itself. Not that the constitution had in it any elements of political liberty, for the different bodies were all nominated by the President and their functions were carefully arranged so as to eliminate from each any power of opposition to the government. But for the first time since the days of Theodoric a uniform administration was given to the whole stretch of territory between the Piedmontese frontier and the Adriatic; the French organization in communes and departments was applied to the Papal Legations as much as to the Venetian provinces of Brescia and Bergamo, to the Milanese proper, and to the fragments of Piedmont attached to the new state; and the spirit of localism which had been the bane of Italian politics since the Middle Ages received its first definite check. A national army was formed under the national flag—the green, white and red[1]—and an official class sprang up which learnt in the administration of such matters as education, public works, and local taxation the first difficult apprenticeship in the art of self-government. The power of the Church was regulated by the Concordat negotiated by Melzi with Pius VII. in 1803, and though more favourable to the hierarchy than the French Concordat of 1801, it was followed up by a decree of 'Organic Articles' which remained a bone of contention between Melzi and the Pope until the end of the former's reign.

For the excellent Vice-President was not allowed to carry on for too long his somewhat thankless task of mediator between the Italian Republic and its real master in Paris. In December, 1804, Napoleon crowned himself Emperor of the French in Notre Dame, and it became clear to all the world that the Imperial title harmonized ill with the Presidental. The Italian Republic must be transformed into a kingdom, and its king must be no other than the 'Liberator' himself. Austria was informed in January, 1805, that Joseph Bonaparte had accepted the crown of Italy; but Joseph had done nothing of the sort, and in March a series of decrees was put forth which disclosed the real intentions of the Emperor. Napoleon assumed the title of King of Italy, though with the proviso that the two crowns should be separated as soon as England abandoned Malta and Russia the Ionian Islands. Since the first of

[1] This was the flag given to the Italian army by Bonaparte, but it had first been used in a rising at Bologna against the Papal government in 1794.

these happy events never took place, Napoleon remained King of Italy.

His installation was effected by the memorable coronation journey to Milan, which occupied the months of May and June, 1805. The Iron Crown of the Lombards—the crown fashioned to include a nail of the True Cross by Queen Theodolinda[1]—was brought with all pomp from Monza, and the Emperor-King placed it upon his own head in the Cathedral of Milan with the words: 'Dio me la diede: guai a chi la tocca!'[2] He appointed his stepson, Eugène Beauharnais, viceroy, and installed him at Milan with a court and a council of state, and when his own presence was removed he continued to direct his steps with the most meticulous instructions, which Eugène endeavoured to carry out with conscientious care. Eugène was, in fact, the 'good boy' of the Imperial family; simple and straightforward by nature, a good soldier and a hard worker, he never disappointed his stepfather,[3] and he even endeared himself to the Italians by his pleasant manner and his attention to detail. The kingdom of Italy made remarkable strides under his administration in material prosperity, in education, in the construction of public works; and the Cathedral of Milan, long left an unfinished hulk, stood forth at last under its amazing incrustation of marble statues. More than this, there was some partial introduction of the career thrown open to talent; the national army served with distinction in the campaigns of Spain, of Wagram, and of Russia, and the Liberal element of the population, distrustful at first, rallied on second thoughts to the government. Of political liberty there was not much, but the times were times of war, and the Austrian and clerical enemies were never far below the surface. Yet Napoleon himself advised Eugène to cut down the expense of the spy-service from seven hundred thousand to two hundred thousand francs a year.[4]

While Napoleon was still in Italy the fate of Genoa—or rather of the Ligurian Republic, as it had been termed since 1797—was settled by its incorporation with the French Empire, so that France ruled directly not only over Piedmont but over what became its natural outlet on the coast. A deputation from the republic—whose Doge and senate had been nominated by Bonaparte since 1802—attended him at Milan and humbly petitioned for union with the empire, and Napoleon, to seal the compact, passed

---

[1] See p. 52.
[2] 'God has given it to me; woe to him that touches it!'
[3] 'Eugene ne m'a jamais causé aucun chagrin.' Napoleon at St. Helena.
[4] Letter of June 12, 1805.

through Genoa on his return to France and witnessed the celebration of the republic's fall in a series of magnificent sea-fêtes. To him it meant the establishment of a strong outpost against British sea-power in the Mediterranean; to Italy the breaking of another link with her glorious but disunited past.

During this brief but productive coronation journey one more territorial arrangement was made which led, four years later, to a further remarkable development of Napoleonic power in Italy. The little republic of Lucca, left relatively untouched by the changes of the eighteenth century, was prompted to express a wish that a member of the Imperial family should be sent to rule it, and Napoleon accordingly conferred the title of 'Princess of Lucca' on his sister Elisa. Elisa was married to an Italian, by name Felix Bacciochi, and together the new Prince and Princess held court in popular fashion at Lucca, while in the neighbouring 'kingdom of Etruria' a singular attempt at clerical reaction was carried out by the Spanish Infanta on whom the government of Tuscany had devolved. The arrangement by which, at the Peace of Lunéville, the Bourbon Duke of Parma had become 'King of Etruria' still held good, but the King had died in 1803, and his young Spanish widow had proclaimed herself regent. Bigoted and incompetent, her reign became a scandal in the eyes of her Gallicized neighbours, and Napoleon himself grew impatient at her reluctance to exclude British goods from the port of Leghorn. His decision was taken in October, 1807; the Bourbon family must be shipped to Spain and indemnified with a portion of Portugal for the loss of Etruria. The kingdom was formally annexed to the French Empire and carved into three departments [March, 1808], but the violent discontent provoked by the French *régime* induced Napoleon to modify it to the extent of giving Tuscany the rank of a grand duchy and conferring it on his sister Elisa [March, 1809]. Florence gave a warm welcome to the new Grand Duchess, who made herself popular with the Tuscans by endeavouring to mitigate for them some of the hardships of the conscription. But her powers were strictly limited, and the peasants of the Val d'Arno and the Maremma found themselves duly marched to the barrack-yard and turned into fodder for the guns of Wellesley, of the Archduke Charles, and of Marshall Kutuzoff.

Ever since the conclusion of peace between Naples and France in 1801, the kingdom of Naples had continued to enjoy a precarious independence, and to present to Europe the spectacle of a survival into the new age of feudal and clerical abuses inherited from its unhappy past. There the normal state of society in the interior was one of brigandage, since a barren soil and a backward social organization made any other life relatively unprofitable; there the coasts lay waste and deserted owing to the slave-raids of Barbary pirates; there the dungeon and the fetter were the ordinary weapons of the government in its contest with the better elements of the population. Ferdinand and Mary Caroline had made their re-entry into Naples in 1802, not without lively apprehensions on the part of those who remembered the butcheries of 1799, but this time the Queen's powers of vengeance were more limited than in the days of Nelson. The royal couple were bullied and spied upon by the French envoy Alquier, and overawed by the French army of occupation which entered Apulia on the rupture of the Treaty of Amiens. When the Third Coalition was brewing against France in 1805 the Queen was for joining it openly, but the King's counsels of prudence prevailed, and a treaty of neutrality which Napoleon offered to the kingdom was accepted and ratified by its rulers [October 4, 1805]. The French troops were to be withdrawn from Apulia, and in return the Neapolitan ports were to be closed against the English. But no sooner had General Saint-Cyr disappeared over the frontier than the Queen denounced the treaty and admitted a force of English from Malta and of Russians from the Ionian Islands to garrison the kingdom [November 19, 1805].

Unfortunately for the Bourbon schemes, Mary Caroline had thus provoked Napoleon at a moment when he was ill-disposed to tolerate such affronts. Austerlitz was fought on December 2; the Czar recalled his troops from Naples, and the King and Queen stood defenceless before the storm they had invoked. It burst upon them in the form of the famous Schönbrunn Proclamation of December 27, 1805, in which Napoleon announced to his army that the dynasty of Naples had 'ceased to reign' and that his brother would lead the soldiers of France to its overthrow. The threat was carried out with complete success. Joseph Bonaparte accepted the proffered crown, and advanced on Naples with Marshal Masséna early in February, 1806. King Ferdinand had already fled to Palermo at the end of January, and the Queen followed him on February 11; four days later the French made their entry unopposed into the capital.

The reign of Joseph Bonaparte at Naples marks one more attempt to enter and cleanse those Augean Stables. Enormous difficulties confronted him: the ancient hostility of the people towards the French invader; the presence across the Straits of Messina of an active and powerful enemy, constantly on the watch for a chance of overturning the new order; the lack of ready money; the lack of a sufficient army to complete the conquest of the kingdom. Yet during the two years of his reign Joseph, assisted by a small group of French and Italian ministers,[1] laid the foundations of reform in every department of the state. A decree abolishing the feudal rights of the Barons was issued in August, 1806; the Code Napoleon, ill-adapted though it was to the peculiar needs of Naples, was introduced to replace the cruel tangle of codes, customs, and prerogatives which had baffled the reforming spirit of Tanucci; roads were made; schools and academies set up; some vestiges of order slowly evolved out of the chaos of the finances. Rejecting the Emperor's advice to mulct the kingdom by a huge war-tax, Joseph raised money by issuing bonds secured on the royal domains, and to this security was presently added that of the confiscated estates of absentee landlords and the vast possessions of the monasteries, the greater part of which were suppressed by the new government. By the end of 1807 a tolerable equilibrium had at last been established in the budget of the Neapolitan state. The sweeping decree on feudalism naturally took time to come into operation. For a year or more it led to no result save that of endless litigation between communes and barons, but in 1808, before his transference to Spain, Joseph established a special court known as the Feudal Commission, which tried and disposed of every case, and, by its colossal labours carried on during the reign of Murat, at least made a start in freeing Naples from the curse of so many centuries.

All this was accomplished in the face of the exceptional difficulties raised against the new government by the Sicilian court. Mary Caroline's method of warfare consisted in using the British fleet to transport *capomassi*, or brigand leaders, with arms and money to the Calabrian coast, thence to raise the 'bands' of the interior, and the ferocity of the guerilla war thus kindled against the French detachments surpasses all description.[2] Once at least the brigands had the assistance of a regular force of British infantry,

---

[1] Of the latter the most remarkable were Zurlo, Minister of the Interior, who carried through the legal abolition of feudalism under Murat; Saliceti, the ubiquitous Corsican, who had been active in the service of France since Napoleon's first invasion (1796), and the Genoese, Maghella, who became Minister of Police under Murat in 1810, patronized and encouraged the loosely-organized secret society of the *Carbonari*, and was one of the earliest Italians to believe in the possibility of unity or at least of independence.

[2] See especially the letters of Paul Louis Courier, lieutenant of artillery in the French army. *Œuvres de P. L. Courier*, vol. iv.

disembarked at the Bay of St. Euphemia; and the superiority of
the British line over the French column was first proved in this
obscure skirmish of Maida, fought in a cause of which the general
himself was almost ashamed. But the advance of Masséna from
the north, where he had just reduced the fortress of Gaëta, turned
the tide against the Anglo-Sicilians, and the supremacy of the
French was established as far as the toe of Italy. The brigands
submitted for the time, but had not been fully crushed, and it
needed the energy of Murat, the *beau sabreur* and brother-in-law
of Napoleon who succeeded Joseph on the throne in 1808, to
'pacify' Calabria effectively. Murat carried on the work of Joseph
in the spirit of a cavalry leader; drove the British out of Capri by a
slashing attack within six weeks of his arrival in Naples; preserved
the kingdom from a formidable Anglo-Sicilian expedition in 1809;
invaded Sicily in 1810, and shortly afterwards sent General Manhès
to suppress and exterminate the Calabrian brigands whom these
alarums had set moving again. With his childish vanity and
bombast, Murat became the darling of the *lazzaroni*, whom he
drilled and clothed in costly uniforms, but his growing ill-will
towards Napoleon attracted towards him a more serious party,
and he became, after 1810, the hope of one small group on whom
the vision of Italian independence had already dawned. Not by
the inn-keeper's son of Cahors, however, was it fated that Italy
should be saved.

By the beginning of the year 1806, all the mainland of Northern and Southern Italy had passed under the sway of Napoleon,
for by the Treaty of Presburg, Austria had been forced to cede
even Venice and the Venetian Provinces (Istria and Dalmatia) to
the kingdom of Italy. Venetia and Friuli were parcelled out into
twelve duchies for Napoleon's marshals, while French and Italian
troops took possession of the whole coast-line of Dalmatia, save
only the Bouches de Cattaro, and were even admitted by the spirited little republic of Ragusa, which had never been subject to the
Venetian Empire. For over a year a bloody war raged along the
coast between French and Italians on the one side and Russians
and Montenegrins on the other, but the peace of Tilsit [July, 1807]
brought the evacuation of Cattaro by its Russian garrison, and
Marshal Marmont substantially ruled the coast—making roads,
founding schools, and trying to establish the reign of 'order and
justice.'[1] After Wagram Napoleon constituted for him the 'Illy-
rian Provinces,' with their capital at Laybach, thus detaching Dal-

[1] *Méms. du Maréchal Duc de Raguse*, bk. ix.

matia from the kingdom of Italy, but the gallant marshal's rule
was equally successful in this larger sphere, and when the Austrian
Emperor Francis visited Dalmatia in 1818 he is said to have exclaimed: 'If only Marshal Marmont could have stayed here two
or three years longer!'[1]

Yet one obstacle to the complete subjection of Italy still remained in the existence of the Papal States, spared by the Treaty
of Tolentino and all subsequent arrangements, but none the less
an offence and an anachronism in the eyes of the impatient conqueror. Moreover the spacious coast lines on both seas possessed
by the Pope gave harbourage to British traders and men-of-war
in a manner wholly inconsistent with the principles of the Conti-
nental Blockade. Napoleon's relations with Pope Pius VII. had
become troubled in 1805, when the Code Napoleon, which permitted divorce, had been introduced into the kingdom of Italy,
and from that moment onwards the causes of quarrel between
the two antagonistic forces had multiplied rapidly. When the
French troops were recalled from Taranto [1805], the Emperor
ordered their commander to leave a garrison in Ancona; Pius protested bitterly, and in reply Napoleon laid down the doctrine that
it was his business to protect the Papal States 'against the English
and Turks'; that he was the successor of Charlemagne, and that
'though your Holiness is the Sovereign of Rome, I am her Emperor' [February 13, 1806]. The Pope did not mend matters by
replying that His Majesty had made a mistake; he had been crowned
as Emperor of the French, not as Emperor of Rome; there was in
fact no such thing as an Emperor of Rome [March 21, 1806]. The
quarrel was aggravated by the question of Naples. Pius revived
the ancient claims of the Holy See to suzerainty over the kingdom,
and refused to recognize Joseph unless these were met; in reply
the Emperor ordered Joseph to occupy Civitavecchia and sent
French troops into Urbino [June, 1806], while he conferred the
Papal *enclave* of Benevento as a princely appanage on his atheis-
tic foreign minister, Talleyrand. The burden of his demands,
however, constantly repeated throughout these altercations, was
that the Pope should regard the enemies of France as his enemies,
that he should expel the envoys of England, Russia, and Sweden,
and that he should close his ports to the English. Pius persisted
in offering a dignified refusal to these proposals. It was not seemly
that the Vicar of Christ, he declared, should take part in the wars
of Christian princes, and he must maintain his right to observe
neutrality. The dispute varied in intensity according to the Em-

[1] *Méms du Maréchal Duc de Raguse*, bk. x.

peror's military fortunes, but after the Peace of Tilsit [July, 1807] he was free to turn the whole force of his impatience against Rome. A final offer of alliance was made to the Pope in the autumn of 1807, and on its rejection Napoleon ordered General Lemarrois to proclaim himself governor of the Papal States [November 1, 1807], and shortly afterwards sent General Miollis to occupy Rome. The French entered the city on February 2, 1808, without opposition, and a few days later the General reviewed the Papal guards and told them that they were thenceforth incorporated in the French army and would no longer 'receive orders from priests or from women.' Pius VII. maintained his attitude of passive resistance to superior force, and all through the year 1808 remained shut up in the Quirinal Palace, while the French troops lorded it in Rome. The Papal States were formally annexed to the kingdom of Italy on April 2,[1] and Napoleon began to revolve his plan for the total abolition of the Temporal Power. The project came to maturity during his victorious advance into Austria in the spring of 1809, and from the palace of Schönbrunn, on May 17, he flung his challenge to the Catholic world. Rome was proclaimed a free Imperial city; the Pope was assured of independence in all spiritual affairs and of the free use of the Papal palaces, together with a revenue of two million francs a year. For all reply, Pius issued the famous Bull of Excommunication, *Quam memoranda*, and had it affixed by night to the doors of the three great basilicas of Rome [June 11]. Only one counter-stroke remained to the Emperor; Pius must be removed from Rome. Miollis and the clever Minister of Police from Naples, Saliceti, took the matter in hand, and, with or without a direct order from the Emperor,[2] arrested and carried off the Pope on the morning of July 6, 1809. He was taken via Florence and Turin to Grenoble, and thence back to Savona, where, lodged in the episcopal palace, deprived of friends, secretaries, and sometimes even of writing materials, he maintained for three years before the eyes of Europe the rôle of the

---

[1] On the ground, as the official proclamation states, that the Pope had 'constantly refused to make war on the English.'

[2] On June 19, Napoleon wrote to Murat: 'Si le pape, contre l'esprit de son état et de l'Evangile, prêche la révolte et veut se servir de l'immunité de sa maison pour faire imprimer des circulaires, on doit l'arrêter. Le temps de ces scènes est passé. Philippe le Bel fit arrêter Boniface et Charles-Quint tint longtemps en prison Clément VII.; et ceux-là avaient fait encore moins'. But when he heard of the arrest he wrote to Fouché, 'Je suis fâché qu'on ait arrêté le Pape: c'est une grande folie. Il fallait arrêter le Cardinal Pacca et laisser le Pape tranquille à Rome.   Mais enfin il n'y a point de remède: ce qui est fait.' *Corr.*, xix., 15, 555.

outraged defender of the Church's liberties. Napoleon's disasters gradually restored the Papal power; Moscow brought about the Concordat of Fontainebleau [January 25, 1813]—which Pius, however, repudiated a few weeks after it was signed; Leipzig the offer to restore the Papal States; finally when Pius refused to negotiate, the advance of the Allies into France induced Napoleon to release him unconditionally [January 18, 1814]. The Pope returned amid popular acclamations to a land distraught by conflicting counsels. The fabric of Napoleon hung tottering, and it was not the Church's part to prevent its fall. Pius VII. entered Rome on May 24, 1814, the forerunner of Reaction.

The break-up of the Napoleonic system in Italy followed hard upon these events; but it was made significant to Europe by the emergence in it of the nascent feeling of Italian freedom—weak and groping as yet, but full of omen for the future. For six years, from 1808 to 1814, the whole Peninsula had been administered under a more or less uniform system, and even in the States of the Church, where the Inquisition had still flourished under Pius VII., the people were taught to live under the Code Napoleon. In Bologna and the other towns of the Romagna, which had lived under French institutions, with one brief interval, for nearly twenty years,[1] there was a middle and professional class which was the most advanced in Italy, and in the kingdom of Italy and the kingdom of Naples too the questions of union and independence began to be agitated, especially among the army officers. In Naples the 'warrior King,' Joachim Murat, was looked to as the leader of a liberating movement, the rather as Joachim's relations with Napoleon were known to be of the coolest. But Murat's primary concern was for the preservation of his throne amid the clash of European forces, and his vacillations during the years 1813—1815 were inspired by no higher motive than the desire to remain 'Re Gioacchino.' He joined Napoleon in the Russian and the German campaigns of 1812 and 1813, and at the Battle of Dresden completed the French victory by his masterly cavalry tactics; but already in the spring of 1813 he had opened negotiations with Austria, and after Leipzig [October, 1813] he deserted the army, sick with Napoleon's policy of endless war. He began to intrigue at once with the Italian patriots, with Austria, and with the masterful Englishman, Lord William Bentinck, who filled the post of British envoy and commander-in-chief at the court of Sicily. He made a last appeal to Napoleon in December to allow him a free hand in Italy and to place all the French troops there

[1] The interval was during the Austro-Russian reconquest of Italy in 1799.

under his command, but when his letter remained unanswered he inclined to Austria, and concluded a treaty of alliance with the Emperor Francis in January, 1814. Bentinck at Palermo, however, would never do more than sign an armistice with Murat. He had carried out a remarkable piece of work in Sicily in 1812, by forcing upon the reluctant King and Queen the adoption of a constitution framed on the British model, and his intention was to improve upon his work by bringing Ferdinand back to Naples as constitutional sovereign. Incidentally, however, Queen Mary Caroline's rage at the Englishman's proceedings had been such that he was forced to expel her from the island, and she left Sicily for Vienna in June, 1813, never to return. She died of apoplexy in the following year, and when King Ferdinand finally returned to his palace at Naples, events had so shaped themselves that he was unencumbered either by his wife or by a constitution.

The defection of Murat from the side of Napoleon had shattered the Emperor's last hope of creating a diversion in the rear of the allied forces. Eugène, instead of marching through Switzerland with Murat in order to fall upon the Allies' communications, was obliged to make head in the plain of the Po against Austria and Murat together. The latter's halting movements reflected indeed the indecision of his mind, but the news of Napoleon's abdication at Fontainebleau [April 11] soon arrived to quench all doubts. Bentinck was at Genoa, re-establishing the ancient government and distributing proclamations that called on the Italians to rise in defence of their liberty, but Austria was also on the spot, and an Austrian army occupied Milan, in defiance of a convention signed with Eugène, on April 26. The fate of Northern and Central Italy was decided by the Allies in Paris, even before the Congress of Vienna met. The first to return from exile was Victor Emanuel I., King of Sardinia, who had carried on a diminished royalty in Sardinia ever since the abdication of his brother Charles Emanuel in 1802; the Czar Alexander had wished that he should be given the whole of Northern Italy, but Austria implacably opposed this scheme, and the only accession of territory which he received was that of the Republic of Genoa. The bitter discontent of the Genoese with this arrangement was to provide a new focus for disaffection in the future against the re-established order. For the rest, Austrian princelings returned in force to the thrones which Napoleon had emptied; Francesco of Austria-Este to Modena, the Grand Duke Ferdinand III. to Tuscany, and Parma was conferred on another Hapsburg princess, Marie Louise, wife of Napoleon. The Pope eventually regained the Legations, but a strip of his territories from Ancona to Rimini remained for a time in the hands of Murat, by virtue of a military convention signed with the Austrian commander.

The fate of Murat and of Naples hung on the decision of the European Congress which met at Vienna on November 1, 1814. Bourbon France loudly demanded the restoration of Ferdinand, but Metternich was disposed to abide by his treaty of alliance with Murat, and England, though hostile to the King, was not prepared to quarrel with Austria on such a point. All through the winter the diplomatic battle raged, while Joachim and his wife held high court at Naples, but in March, 1815, the escape of Napoleon from Elba stirred the old Marshal in Murat's soul, and he took the field once more on the side that perhaps he should never have left. Marching north by Ancona and the old Pentapolis, he issued his famous appeal to Italian patriotism[1] at Rimini on March 30 and entered Bologna amid wild enthusiasm on April 2, to the watchword of 'Italian Independence.' But Austria was now fully aroused, and the Austrian forces soon showed themselves superior in numbers and in quality to the Neapolitan levies of Murat. Beaten at Macerata, the King's army crumbled away by desertion, and Murat himself made his way to the coast and escaped in a French ship to Cannes. Behind him the Austrians entered Naples with Prince Leopold, Ferdinand's second son, at their head, and Ferdinand himself re-entered his capital on June 6. The influence of Austria restrained him from taking vengeance on those who had served Murat, but when the ex-King, after wandering and conspiring in Corsica, landed at Pizzo in Calabria with a handful of companions, in the mad hope of raising Calabria against the Bourbon, Ferdinand's orders were precise, and Murat was shot by a file of soldiers in the courtyard of the little mediæval fortress of Pizzo. With him fell the last hope of the patriots of his day, and the dreams they had cherished during his brief ascendancy, driven underground by the Reaction, found an outlet congenial to the Neapolitan mind in the secret activities of the *Carbonari*.

---

[1] The Proclamation begins: 'Italians! Providence has called you at last to be an independent nation; from the Alps to the Straits of Scilla one universal cry is heard—*Italian Independence!*' See Cantù, *Cronistoria*, vol ii., p. 39.

CHAPTER XXVII

The Years of Reaction
and Repression

*No Italian can hate an Austrian more than I do : unless it be the English,
the Austrians seem to me the most obnoxious race under the sky.*
LORD BYRON, Ravenna, 1820

THE spirit of the Restoration of 1814—15 may be summed up in
the words of the edict issued by Victor Emanuel I. on the day
after his entry into Turin. 'Disregarding all other laws whatsoever,
the public will, from the date of this edict, observe the Royal
Ordinances of 1770, together with all other decrees issued up to
June 23, 1800, by Our Royal Predecessors.'[1] The rulers assembled
in Council at Vienna saw safety only in a return to the conditions
of life prevailing before the deluge, and in the case of Italy they
believed that paternal government by a ring of Austrian and
semi-Austrian princes would be the best guarantee for the peace
and contentment of the populations. But if, owing to the evil
influences to which they had been exposed, the populations concerned failed to take this view of their deliverance; if they showed
any signs of claiming a share in the business of government, or
otherwise displayed their contamination with French ideas, the
princes would know how to deal with them. The police and their
shadows the *sbirri* would act as the sure support of the state in
each of the restored governments; Napoleon's system of conscription would be retained as a convenient method of repressing outbreaks, and behind all native safeguards would stand the Austrian
army of occupation, strong shield and bulwark of the re-established
order. Thus reasoned the Holy Alliance of Sovereigns, which
emerged from the Congress of Vienna as the new disposer of the
destinies of Europe, and the dominating figure of Prince Metternich, Imperial Chancellor of Austria, supplied the persistence, the
brains, and the longevity necessary to carry out such a conception.

The Congress partitioned Italy into eight States: (1) the Austrian
'kingdom of Lombardy-Venetia,' with an archduke as viceroy;
(2) the kingdom of Sardinia with its accession of Genoa and the
Genoese Riviera; (3) the kingdom of the Two Sicilies, as Ferdinand
now chose to rename his dominions[2]; (4) the grand duchy of Tus-

---

[1] Edict of May 21, 1814.
[2] Previously the King had been known as Ferdinand IV. of Naples and
III. of Sicily; now he was Ferdinand I., King of the Two Sicilies.

cany; (5—7) the duchies of Parma, Modena, and Lucca,[1] and finally the States of the Church, restored to the Pope in their entirety by the adroit diplomacy of Cardinal Consalvi. The tendency of some of these arrangements was unifying so far as it went, e.g. the final suppression of the two republics of Venice and Genoa, both of which had nourished hopes that the Congress would restore them to their ancient independence.[2] So also with King Ferdinand's destruction of the autonomy of Sicily [1816], which followed closely on his re-establishment at Naples. With characteristic perfidy he rewarded the islanders for their loyalty during his long exile by depriving them, with a stroke of the royal pen, of the local autonomy which they had cherished all through the centuries of Spanish domination. Lord William Bentinck's constitution was swept away, with hardly a protest from England, and the island was flooded with Neapolitan officials whose misgovernment and corruption soon produced a state of intolerable tension between the two 'united Sicilies.' In the States of the Church the old municipal liberties which had survived from the Middle Ages had already been abolished by Napoleon, and the field was therefore left clear for the erection of a more untrammelled Papal despotism. As long as Pius VII. and his Minister Consalvi lived, the despotism was tempered by the latter's efforts to encourage the employment of laymen in the administration, to keep the provincial Legates and Delegates under check from Rome, and to maintain a sound finance; but with the restoration all the old abuses had in reality returned, and the proud cities of Romagna groaned under a government of priests which had the added odium of being forced anew on a generation that had outgrown it. In Piedmont and the duchy of Modena the Jesuits were re-established and soon had the whole educational system in their hands; no Protestant chapel might be built in Turin; no Waldensian might hold office in the kingdom of Sardinia. If in Lombardy-Venetia the less clerical traditions of Joseph II. were followed in this and other matters, the dead weight of the Austrian occupation made itself felt in a political tyranny which was as ruthless as the ordinary administration was decent, and a sullen hatred of the white-coat and his ways arose among the educated classes.

---

[1] Lucca was made over as a duchy to Maria Luisa, the quondam Queen of Etruria, but in 1847 it was ceded by her son Carlo Luigi to Tuscany and incorporated with the grand duchy.

[2] Genoa bore a special grudge against England for having deserted her at the Congress, after Lord William Bentinck's re-establishment of the old government in April, 1814.

Perhaps it was only in Tuscany that the Restoration was truly welcomed, for there the Grand Duke Ferdinand (son of Leopold I.) and his Minister Fossombroni pursued the principle of letting well alone, and, having no domestic revolutionaries to fear, even extended a mild welcome to political refugees from other states. In Parma the ex-Empress Marie Louise prided herself on maintaining French law, liberty, and justice in spite of an Austrian garrison; but in the neighbouring duchy of Modena the restless, bigoted Duke Francis embodied all the darkest features of reaction pure and simple.

The return of King Ferdinand to Naples had not, as we have seen, been marked by any sanguinary persecution of the Muratists, nor indeed was any violent change carried out in the institutions left by the Napoleonic period. But the feebleness and corruption of the government—which made a new Concordat with the Pope in 1818, which could not master its own brigands and which suffered law and administration to fall once more into the hands of a corrupt police—slowly provoked a gathering opposition. The secret society of the Carbonari—which had existed in Murat's time[1] and professed vague ideals of liberty and the regeneration of mankind—cast its network of lodges over the whole country and drew to its ranks all those who were exasperated by the caprice or petty tyranny of the government. General Pepe, an ardent Liberal who had, strange to say, found favour with Ferdinand's Ministers, led the movement skilfully towards revolution, and on July 2, 1820, a revolt actually broke out by the defection of a squadron of cavalry from the barracks at Nola. No revolution was ever more bloodlessly or smoothly accomplished. Within four days Ferdinand had promised a constitution; within twelve he had sworn, with every solemnity that his religion could devise, to maintain the constitution recently proclaimed in Spain, which was that selected by the Carbonari. Preparations advanced apace for the election of a constituent assembly, and that assembly actually met on October 1st, to the accompaniment of further sonorous oaths from the King. But the course of events at Naples had already produced a profound sensation, not only in the rest of Italy, but in the cabinets of the Holy Alliance. In the mind of Prince Metternich, constitutional government was a 'germ,'[2] which

[1] Mr. Johnston (*Napoleonic Empire in Southern Italy*) believes that the Carbonari were introduced into Naples by a French-Swiss regiment in Murat's service, and were therefore identical with the *Charbonniers* of the Jura; others see in them a branch of the Freemasons.

[2] Report of a conversation between Metternich and the envoy of the Neapolitan government at Vienna, quoted in Bianchi, *Storia della Diplomazia europea in Italia*, vol. ii., p. 19.

must at all costs be prevented from spreading into other countries, and he concentrated every effort, from the end of July onwards, on obtaining the consent of the Powers to the armed intervention of Austria. In October a Congress was held at Troppau between the sovereigns of Prussia, Austria, and Russia, attended by their ministers and the representatives of England and France, with the sole object of considering the measures to be taken to deal with the revolution of Naples. Ferdinand was invited to meet the same family of sovereigns at Laybach in December, and thither the Neapolitan Assembly gave him leave to go—naïvely stipulating that he should undertake to defend the Constitution. Needless to say, Ferdinand accepted the condition. Meanwhile the military defence of the kingdom had been neglected by the new ministers, and the best troops had been locked up in Sicily, where the mob of Palermo had risen against the Neapolitan garrison to the passionate cry of Independence and the *Constitution of 1812*. Therefore when on February 13, 1821, the inevitable news reached the Assembly that Ferdinand had betrayed them and that Austrian troops were on the march, no serious defence was possible, and Pepe alone, with a few thousand militia, attacked an Austrian brigade at Rieti [March 7, 1821]. The result was the scandalous rout of the militiamen, and all resistance immediately collapsed. When Ferdinand returned in the wake of the Austrian army he had the country at his mercy, and by his executions, public floggings, and wholesale imprisonments in the dungeons of the islands he revealed to his subjects the full extent of his Bourbon benevolence. For four more years Ferdinand I. cumbered the soil of Naples, and when at length he quitted the scene of his crimes and his perjuries he left to his people the crowning gift of a like son and a like grandson to succeed him.

The Neapolitan Revolution was scarcely crushed before a military rising broke out in Piedmont, remarkable not for its success, for it lasted barely a month, but because it brought on the scene a new figure in the Italian tragedy—Charles Albert, Prince of Carignano, heir-presumptive to the Sardinian crown. On this young man the hopes of the Piedmontese Liberals were set, for he had been educated in France and at Geneva, and at the age of sixteen had held a commission in Napoleon's dragoons. Moreover since his return to Piedmont he had consorted with Liberals and Carbonari, and had frequently expressed anti-Austrian sentiments. But the traditions of the House of Savoy were not to be lightly cast aside, and in this the first crisis of his career Charles Albert already displayed that fatal vacillation which was to haunt him through life and to earn for him the name of 'Re Tentenna.'[1] The old King Victor Emanuel abdicated rather than swear, like his Neapolitan cousin, to the Constitution, and appointed Charles Albert regent; but he had also a brother, Charles Felix, whose claim to the crown came before Charles Albert's, and this brother immediately called in Austrian troops and ordered the Prince of Carignano away into seclusion in Tuscany. Thither Charles Albert retired, execrated by his Liberal friends for having betrayed the Revolution, frowned upon by the new King, and gravely suspected by Metternich; until in 1823 he obtained permission to accompany the French expedition against the Spanish constitutionalists, and so repaired his damaged orthodoxy. Charles Felix reigned for ten years on the accepted lines of clericalism and repression; an honest but unattractive obscurantist, jealous of his dynastic independence and not too friendly, after the first impulse, towards the Austrian bully across the Ticino.

But the movement of 1820 was not exhausted by the Neapolitan and Piedmontese rebellions. There were stirrings also in Lombardy and Romagna, whence Byron wrote in April in joyous anticipation of a 'row.'[2] But no outbreak occurred in either quarter, for the Austrians were on the watch, and as early as 1819 they made their first wholesale arrests of Carbonari. After the Neapolitan rising a decree was issued threatening with death all members of secret societies, and with imprisonment all those who failed to denounce them. The government employed a clever Italian from Trent, named Salvotti, as *Juge d'Instruction* to conduct these proceedings, and his first victims were the gentle Silvio Pellico and his friend Maroncelli, who were found guilty of endeavouring to found a Carbonaro lodge at Milan and condemned to death. Pellico was probably altogether innocent of the charge. Their sentence was eventually commuted by the Emperor to one of fifteen years of *carcere duro* in the Spielberg. Salvotti's diabolical skill in extorting confessions and lists of accomplices from the accused was next employed in the trial of Count Federico Confalonieri and certain other Milanese nobles, who had been in correspondence with the Piedmontese revolutionaries. Confalonieri and six others were condemned to death, and it was only by the desperate efforts of his wife—whose journey to Vienna and heroic importunities make one of the classic episodes of the Risorgimento—that this sentence also was commuted to one of lifelong imprisonment in the Spiel-

---

[1] King Shilly-Shally. He was also called the 'Italian Hamlet.'
[2] Byron to Murray, Ravenna, April 23, 1820.

berg. In that rock-hewn tomb the first martyrs of Italian liberty dragged out the best years of their lives, chained, starved, deprived of all news of wife or home, the degree of their torture minutely regulated by the Emperor himself. But when, one by one, they emerged again into the world of men, after eight, ten, twelve, and fourteen years, they found that their work was accomplished, for their sufferings had done more than all their conspiracies to convince the Italians that they had a cause.

Meanwhile the misgovernment of the Papal States had acquired a darker hue during the reign of the 'Zealot' Pope, Leo XII. [1823 —29]. Romagna was ravaged by the blood-feuds of Carbonari and Sanfedisti, and all that the government would do when the assassinations grew intolerable was to take the side of the Sanfedists and to send down a Cardinal *a latere* or a special commission with plenary powers to scourge the Liberals. Even Metternich complained that the 'weakness of the Papal Government was so inherent in its very constitution, in its very existence, that it would be difficult if not impossible to find a remedy.'[1] Châteaubriand, Ambassador of Charles X. at Rome in 1829, sent home a scathing analysis, legitimist as he was, of the ineptitude of this same government, and prophesied revolution.[2] The revolution came on the impulse given by the Days of July in Paris (1830),— an upheaval that produced the 'Citizen King,' Louis Philippe, with a bunch of ministers who announced themselves as the defenders of liberties of small nations against the 'principle of intervention' of the Holy Alliance. Relying on such support, the Italian conspirators, who had an active committee in Paris, gave the word for the outbreak in Modena and Bologna, but in the former city their blow was anticipated by the Duke, Francis IV., who had himself dabbled in the conspiracy but who now considered it safer to take the Austrian side. He arrested the Modenese patriot, Ciro Menotti [February 3, 1831], and carried him off, wounded and chained, to Mantua; for Bologna had in the meantime risen, and the news decided the Duke on flight. Modena also joined the insurrection, but within six weeks the wave of Austrian 'intervention' had restored Duke Francis to his throne [March 9]. It was not long before he was able to indulge his capital with the spectacle of the public hanging of Ciro Menotti, a man of noble character who had lived for a time on intimate terms with the Duke, and who had aspired to make him Prince of a free Central

[1] Dispatch of the Piedmontese minister to his government, dated Milan, June 18, 1825, in Bianchi, vol. ii., p. 214.
[2] Hubaine, *Gouvernement Temporel des Papes*, p. 134.

Italy. France had in the interval explained that by the 'principle of non-intervention' she meant that she did not herself intend to intervene.[1]

But in the Papal States the rising had been more formidable, and had spread from Bologna to Ancona and even through the Marches and Umbria to the neighbourhood of Rome. Hardly a hand was raised in defence of the Papal government, and within three weeks an assembly of representatives from all the revolted districts was held at Bologna. They decreed the abolition of the Temporal Power of the Pope, and named themselves the 'Assembly of the Free Provinces of Italy.' But already the newly elected Pope, Gregory XVI.,—whose long reign was to see the States of the Church once more under a repressive government,—had appealed to Austria for aid [February 19] and the Austrian troops had no difficulty in crushing the rebellion. The Papal government once restored, the Powers themselves made serious demands for reform. They presented a Memorandum to the Pope in May, urging the establishment of provincial councils and the admission of laymen to office, and pressed it upon the Papal *entourage* with a persistence that recalls the patient efforts of the Concert of Europe, sixty years later, to press reforms upon the Turk. Their endeavours were hardly as successful as Lord Salisbury's. Some show of concession was made by a *Motuproprio* issued in July, and thereupon the Austrian troops were withdrawn. But Romagna sent its Deputies to Rome to demand valid reforms, and while the Government haggled with them it secretly enlisted Swiss troops and fresh bodies of Sanfedists and announced in December that order would be restored by force of arms. The Papal troops sacked Cesena and Forlì, and Bologna was glad to welcome a second Austrian garrison to protect it from the *Papalini*. In the years that followed, a new force of Papal irregulars, known as the *Centurioni*, arose from the dregs of the Sanfedists and carried on their reign of terror in Romagna under the protection of the Cardinal Legates; and the Powers of Europe, tired of their fruitless efforts, allowed the Pope to govern his subjects in his own peculiar way.

Dispirited by so many failures, the Carbonari seemed to have exhausted the impulse that gave them birth, and to have reached the limit of their capacity for rousing the national spirit. Something, clearly, was lacking from their programme, some word of might which should awaken the masses not only to a passing effervescence, but to the strenuous effort, the willing sacrifice

[1] Speech of the Premier Casimir Périer in the Chamber, March 18, 1831.

required for the freeing of Italian soil from both foreign and domestic oppressors. That word was spoken by the new force that
arose on the ruins of the Revolution of 1831—the force of *Young
Italy*, created by a young and unknown advocate from Genoa
named Giuseppe Mazzini. Born in 1805, Mazzini had joined the
Carbonari in 1827, but soon grew impatient with their mystery-
making and their oaths, their tendency to rely on help from
France, their lack of the one definite and absorbing aim. Arrested
in 1830 on the usual charge of having initiated a new member, he
was imprisoned for six months, awaiting trial, in the fortress of
Savona, and there thought out the principles on which a new
association for the regeneration of his country must be formed.
The Senate of Turin passed sentence of exile upon him, and he
retired to Marseilles, where he soon found himself among a band
of refugees escaping from the vengeance of Pope Gregory and the
Duke of Modena. Among these men—all young like himself—he
established his ascendancy; with their help he founded the new
society. Young Italy—*La Giovane Italia*—had for its motto *God
and the People;* for Mazzini gave it from the very first the religious
basis which he knew was needed to inspire the rising generation.

The religious conception [he wrote in 1835] has created for man
that theory of *duty* which is the parent of sacrifice; which has
inspired and ever will inspire him to high and holy things; the
sublime theory which brings man nearer to God, lends to the
human creature a spark of omnipotence, overleaps every obstacle,
and converts the scaffold of the martyr into a ladder of triumph.[1]

Or again, in 1832:

Do you desire that your citizens should become free? Begin by
giving them a lofty sense of their own dignity, of their own inviol-
ability, of their own power. Do not lower the conception of
liberty to them, but raise them to it: convert it into a mission, and
create them its apostles: say to them that there is a moral law
superior to them, which binds them all, in one bond, to the execution of a great design; to the sacrifice, if necessary, of the individual to society.[2]

So this band of exiled youths threw their challenge in the face
of Metternich and the Holy Alliance, and, working night and day
at their printing-presses and all the manifold toil of propaganda,

[1] *Faith and the Future.*
[2] *From the Pope to the Council.*

they built up a small list of adepts here and there and replaced the Carbonari by a creed that was new, vital, and inspiring. They preached Independence and Union: Independence by means of a guerilla war of the masses against Austria, and Union through the merging of all the separate states into an Italian Republic, one and indivisible.

Yet the first attempt of the new Society was directed towards the winning over of an instrument ready made, as they thought, for the national war—the army of Piedmont; and they reserved a place in their conspiracy for Piedmont's new King, Charles Albert. The accession of the Prince of Carignano to the throne in April, 1831, had inevitably caused a flutter of hope among the Liberals of the North, and even Mazzini had addressed to him from Marseilles a noble letter, calling on him to arise and lead the holy war against the stranger. But no trace of his youthful Liberalism seemed to have remained with Charles Albert. A morbid piety had taken possession of his soul, manifesting itself in fastings and hair-shirts, and if he did nourish, at the bottom of his Italian heart, a conviction that it was his destiny to fight the Austrian, he would not be bidden thereto by a parcel of *canaille* who flouted religion and tried to tamper with his army. Charles Albert maintained in office all the most reactionary Ministers of his predecessor; he gave no amnesty to the exiles of 1821; he showed greater favour to the Jesuits than they had ever won from Charles Felix. Thus when in 1833 his police discovered a vast conspiracy by which *Young Italy* had sought to win over the army, the King inevitably struck back. But scenes of torture, both mental and physical, enacted in his prisons left an indelible stain on his good name, and brought on himself in after years the torments of remorse. Jacopo Ruffini, Mazzini's closest friend, hanged himself in his cell lest in a moment of weakness he might betray his friends, and twelve humble soldiers faced death from the King's firing-parties. But persecution only served to fill up the ranks of the new Society. In the following year an attempt was made to invade Piedmont with a revolutionary band from Savoy, and a certain young sailor of Nice, Giuseppe Garibaldi, entered the royal navy with the deliberate purpose of winning over his ship to the rebellion. The movement was easily stamped out, and Mazzini, who had carried a flag over the border, was driven to take refuge abroad, while Garibaldi, with a price on his head, fled to the freer air of South America. There, in a rough school of warfare, privation, and romance, he forged a weapon without which Mazzini's faith would have been of no avail, *the power to fight*, and kept it bright and tempered against the day when Italy should have need of it.

Meanwhile in the south a brief period of hope had also dawned in 1830, with the accession to the Neopolitan throne of Ferdinand II., grandson of Ferdinand I. His father, Francis I., had reigned for five years, given up to mistresses and Court favourites who made their living out of the sale of offices of state and kept the King, for their own purposes, surrounded by spies and police and in constant dread of assassination. At his accession, the younger Ferdinand swept away his father's unclean crew, gave an amnesty to the offenders of 1820, announced by proclamation that the 'wounds of the State' required healing, and proceeded to devote himself to the re-organization of the army. He and his father had once had a dispute as to the uniforms of the infantry. 'Dress them how you like,' said King Francis, 'they will run away all the same.' But Ferdinand thought otherwise, and his apparent desire to rely on his army and to rid himself of Austrian influence raised hopes among the Liberals that he intended to bid for the crown of Italy. They did not yet know King Ferdinand. Ambitious he was, but only with the ambition of reigning undisturbed, either by Austria or by his own subjects, and his meagre education had corrected none of the baser tendencies of a mind disposed towards cruelty, mendacity, and the grosser forms of superstition. Blind to all the nobler springs of action, he surrounded himself with mediocrities and became an adept in the art of playing on their weaknesses. He had the shrewd wit of the lazzarone, and believed that 'the world liked to be fooled, and a King should know the art of fooling it better than any one else.' His victim of later years, Luigi Settembrini, summed him up in the term 'Re Lazzarone,' and until he earned a blacker title this became him well enough.

At his accession Sicily still smarted under its enforced union with the mainland,[1] and no act of the new King's was more popular than his appointment of his brother Leopold, Count of Syracuse, to the Viceroyalty. The Count was young, artistic, and anxious to play a fine part with the Sicilians, and two years after his arrival he succeeded in obtaining certain concessions for the islanders which raised his popularity to a high pinnacle. But this was enough to provoke the jealousy of his brother. In 1835 the Count of Syracuse was suddenly recalled, and the island subjected once more to the unmitigated misgovernment of the Neapolitan officials.

---

[1] In 1824 the administration of Sicilian affairs had been still further concentrated at Naples.

In this state of smouldering wrath it was stricken in 1837 by the terrible scourge of cholera, which had already ravaged almost every part of Italy and now fell with peculiar virulence upon the south. Twenty-two thousand victims died at Naples; nearly seventy thousand in Sicily. The terror of the population found vent in frenzied massacres of the 'poisoners' whom they accused of spreading the disease in collusion with the Government, but if these outbreaks showed the mediæval barbarism of the Sicilians, the repression showed an equal brutality on the part of their rulers. Ferdinand dispatched a General of Gendarmerie named Del Carretto to bring the island to its senses, and under his shootings, floggings, and the orgies of cruelty that he permitted in the prisons, Sicily lay crushed for another decade. Ferdinand II. had begun to show himself in his true colours.

After the fiasco of the Savoy revolt, Young Italy entered on a period of depression and eclipse. Mazzini still believed with unquenchable faith in his policy of revolution, and by collecting money in London and establishing committees of Young Italy in Malta and Paris he was able to keep alive the secret agitation for revolt. After 1840 the exasperation in the Papal States led to ever more extensive plans of insurrection. But no combined movement was effected, and small isolated outbreaks in Romagna and Calabria [1843 and 1844] only provoked a more savage repression than usual. In the summer of 1844, however, the expedition of the Bandiera brothers—officers in the Austrian navy, who left it in order to immolate themselves for Italy—attracted the attention of a wider public to their cause. They sailed with a band of about twenty youths, devoted like themselves, from Corfu to the Calabrian coast, hoping to rouse the peasants of the interior against the Bourbon. They were betrayed and easily entrapped and taken, and at Cosenza they faced Ferdinand's firing-party with the cry of *Viva l'Italia* on their lips. Mazzini had disapproved of the wild enterprise and had refused to give money for it, but when it was over he was able to prove before an astonished London that the British Government had systematically opened his correspondence while the plot was being hatched, and he accused it of having betrayed the Bandieras to the King of Naples. Long afterwards the accusation has been laid to rest, so far at least as Lord Aberdeen was concerned,[1] but at the time it gave Mazzini the opportunity of pleading his country's cause in the famous 'Letter to

[1] See the letter of Lord Stanmore to the *Times*, August 22, 1907, entitled, 'Lord Aberdeen, Mazzini, and the Bandieras.'

Sir James Graham' with all the mingling of passionate fervour, irony, and invective of which he was master. The claims of the Italian rebels had at last obtained a European hearing.

Yet it was just at this moment that another current of opinion made itself felt in Italy which became the most formidable rival of the Mazzinian propaganda. Industrial inventions could not but produce a wave of material prosperity, even in the reactionary States of Italy, and the construction of the first railways promised to bring about by mechanical means that union of the different populations which the revolutionists looked to attain by insurrection. In 1839 the first stretch of line was built from Naples to Portici, and in the early forties railway construction made great strides in Lombardy-Venetia and in Piedmont. And, simultaneously with these developments, a new school of thought arose in the Subalpine Kingdom. Disgust at the ill-success of the Mazzinian risings, with their apparently barren round of bloodshed and repression, produced a reaction in favour of moderate courses. The exiled Abbé Vincenzo Gioberti published in 1843 his remarkable book, *The Moral and Civil Primacy of the Italians*, in which he declared that 'without shocks and without injustices' Italy could attain once more to the supremacy that belonged to her of right. He looked to Piedmont for the military leadership which should drive out the Austrian; to Rome and the Papacy for the moral leadership of a free Italian Federation. So moderate was Gioberti's appeal, so immaculate his orthodoxy, that the book was allowed to circulate all over Italy, and its disciples —the 'Neo-Guelfs'—were soon to be reckoned in many thousands. The cry was taken up from a slightly different point of view by Cesare Balbo, a sturdy Piedmontese who in his *Speranze d'Italia* pointed to the Savoyard dynasty as the Hope of Italy. And indeed the change in Charles Albert's attitude seemed in these years to justify such hopes. Gradually the cloud of timidity and subservience appeared to lift from the King's mind, and the idea of leading his people in a national war against the foreigner to gather shape instead. He had already shown his desire for good government at home by the publication in 1837—42 of the Albertine Codes— Penal, Civil, Military, and Commercial—and his diminishing distrust of his own subjects by the permission granted them in 1842 to form an Agrarian Association, with the right of free discussion. Now in 1844 his response to the ideas of Gioberti and Balbo came in a sensational manner by the coining of a medal with the motto 'J'attends mon astre' and the device of the Savoyard lion crushing an eagle. Massimo d'Azeglio, the charming Piedmontese noble, turned artist and traveller, betook himself in 1845 to Romagna, there to preach the gospel of 'faith in Piedmont and its King,' and on his return craved the opinion of Charles Albert on his mission. 'Tell those fellows,' replied the King, 'that they must keep quiet for the present, because nothing can yet be done; but they may rest assured that, when the occasion comes, my life, and the life of my sons, my arms, my gold, my troops—nay, my all, will be spent in the cause of Italy.'[1] And a still more famous saying fell from his lips in the following year. He and his Ministers had had a brush with Austria on the subject of the supply of salt to Switzerland, and Charles Albert had stood his ground against the hectoring tone of Vienna. Warned by his more timid Ministers that this might lead to a rupture, he replied, 'Well, if we lose Austria we shall gain Italy, and then—*l'Italia farà da sè.*' But he would not yet appeal for public support, and when the Liberals organized an ovation to welcome his attitude he disappointed their expectations and remained shut up in his palace.

In the midst of these rising agitations, the aged Pope Gregory XVI. died unwept in the Quirinal. Unpopular even in Rome, he had rarely shown himself in public lest petitions should be showered upon him; he had turned a deaf ear to the bitter cry of Romagna for decent government; he had plunged the Papal States ever deeper in debt. He had taught his subjects to say, as loud as they dared, 'Better the Turk than the Pope.' The Conclave which assembled to elect his successor was aware of the terrible need for improvement, and in order to defeat Cardinal Lambruschini, who represented Gregory's system, they united on a recently created Cardinal named Mastai Ferretti, Bishop of Imola and a reputed Liberal. Pius IX. ascended St. Peter's Chair on June 17, 1846: was he to prove the Liberator Pope of Gioberti and the Neo-Guelfs? The events of the next three years were to give the answer.

---

[1] Massimo d'Azeglio, *I miei Ricordi*, vol. i., p. 462.

CHAPTER XXVIII

The Years of Revolution

To sacrifice she prompts her best;
She reaps them as the sower reaps. GEORGE MEREDITH

WHEN Pius IX. ascended the Papal throne, the system of government established in Italy by the Congress of Vienna still stood unchanged in all essentials. Every week, in Tuscany and the Duchies, the several Ministers of State waited upon their prince to present their reports and to submit knotty points for His Highness's decision; every day King Ferdinand of Naples applied himself with zest to the business of guiding his people's steps in the way they should go, while the same monotonous task was carried on in Lombardy-Venetia by methodical German-speaking officials and in the Papal States by the more intangible but still more dreaded army of priests, *centurions*, and *sbirri*. All this the coming of Pio Nono was fated to send toppling to earth, but the work of the informer and the spy had been too effectually done to enable the Italian people, this first time, to take advantage of the cataclysm. Among a people brought up in the midst of terror, hypocrisy, and corruption, how was it possible that a tradition of public virtue should exist, sufficient to carry through so great an enterprise? Individual heroism indeed was not to seek, and the young men of the barricades and of the walls of Rome sleep with the Spartans and the men of Marathon, but the capacity for sustained effort and the ungrudging subordination of the part to the whole were qualities not as yet to be found among Mazzini's 'twenty-six millions of men.' The result was that when the movement for liberty and independence passed into the region of revolution the weaknesses of the Italian character, as it then was, made themselves felt, and the follies and knaveries of the rulers were sufficient to turn aside a whole nation from the path of success. Yet when the turmoils of 1848 were over, the 'two or three immortal lights'— Mazzini, Garibaldi, Daniele Manin—had already emerged who were to give to the year 1849 all the nobility that 1848 had lacked. And under the pressure of disaster other leaders were also brought forth to whom the Italian people, in the ten years of slavery that followed, could look for guidance in the way that led to freedom.

But in the year 1846 the Italians acclaimed as their leader one man only—the reforming Pontiff of stately presence and benevolent aspect who took the name of Pius IX. As Bishop of Imola he

MAZZINI IN EXILE
From a Daguerreotype

had read Gioberti's book and had done what he could to mitigate
the harshness of Gregory's *régime* in Romagna; and now, barely
a month after his accession, he took the dramatic step of granting
an amnesty to the many scores of political prisoners who still lay
rotting in Gregory's dungeons.[1] This act at once evoked great
enthusiasm. Rome was as a city transformed, and the repercussion
of the event throughout the Italian States produced the first symp-
toms of that nationalist feeling which was so soon to sweep
everything before it. 'Viva Pio Nono, and death to the Austrian!'
was a cry now heard for the first time in the piazza of many an
Italian town. In the Papal States themselves all was rejoicing in
the present and eager expectation for the future; a wave of religious feeling swept over the towns, and Pio Nono became the object
of a veritable cult. In the midst of this excited atmosphere the
Pope made some hesitating attempts to reform the administration,
but he spoke only too truly when he exclaimed to the French
Ambassador, Pellegrino Rossi, 'They want to make a Napoleon
of me, who am only a poor priest!' His favourite expedient was
to appoint commissions—on which a few laymen made their appearance—to advise and report on the measures necessary for
reforming this or that branch of the administration; but the inertia
of the official bureaucracy, which was still filled with adherents
of the old régime, was sufficient to shelve many of these attempts
at change. Thus Pius drifted through the winter of 1846—7, still
idolized by the populace of Rome; but in January, 1847, the general
impatience induced him to grant a decree on the Censorship of
the Press which opened the way to many important newspapers.[2]
Soon afterwards came a decree announcing the establishment of a
consultative Council of State, more or less on the lines recommen-
ded by the Memorandum of the Powers of 1831,[3] and next the
appointment of a ministry of a more modern type, though all its
members were ecclesiastics. But the Pope and his timid counsellors
were not to be suffered to guide the advancing flood at their own
gentle pace. The mob of Rome had to be reckoned with, as in the
days of Rienzi, and this time the leader of the people was a certain
burly horsedealer named Angelo Brunetti, surnamed Ciceruacchio
from his gift of speech. This good-natured giant passed sometimes

[1] The number of prisoners was 394, according to Gennarelli, *Documenti
sul Governo Pontificio*, and of exiles 605 (Savelli, *Manuale di Storia.*,
vol. iii., p. 556).
[2] The most celebrated were the weekly *Contemporaneo*, organ of the
democratic party (Rome), and the *Felsineo*, edited by Marco Minghetti
(Bologna). The *Bilancia* was the Clerical organ.
[3] See p. 329.

W

from adulation to clamour, in the cries with which he greeted the Popes carriage,[1] and all through the month of June, 1847, he taught his followers to clamour for a civic guard, to maintain public order against the outrages of the *centurions*. The civic guard was conceded on July 5th; but already Austria had taken alarm. Metternich foresaw only too clearly the disastrous consequences of a reforming Papacy to his system of repression, and he resolved to read the Pope a salutary lesson. On July 17, 1847, on the pretext of maintaining order, 1,500 Austrian troops were sent to occupy the Papal city of Ferrara.

The occupation of Ferrara was the spark that kindled to a blaze the smouldering embers of indignation. The Pope was overwhelmed with offers of assistance, in money and in blood, against the impious invader, and his Secretary of State, Cardinal Ferretti, had much ado to keep pace with the popular rage in the notes that he addressed to the government of Vienna. Yet Pius sincerely shared the general resentment, and the provocations of Austria lent a far greater zest to the negotiations which he now initiated for a Customs Union with Tuscany and Piedmont. Here he came up against the Piedmontese reluctance to play second fiddle. Only in fancy was there to exist that Federation of the Italian States under Pope and King which was to restore the 'primacy of Europe' to the Italians. At the same time all three states were advancing on the road of internal reform, though timidly as yet. In Rome the Council of State actually met in November, counting among its members many names that were to become famous in the Risorgimento story; but the speech in which Pius addressed its opening meeting was remembered afterwards as the first decided sign of his drawing back from the popular path. In Tuscany the Grand Duke Leopold—whose *amour propre* had been severely tried at finding himself outdistanced by the Pope in the race for a liberal reputation—granted a modified liberty of the press in May and a civic guard in September [1847], and the enthusiasm evoked by this latter step silenced for a time the ominous turbulence of Leghorn. In Piedmont the reluctance of Charles Albert to meet the demands of the liberals had at length been partially overcome, and in October his reactionary minister of twelve years' standing, Count della Margherita, was dismissed, and a decree put forth establishing elective provincial councils and giving relative freedom to the press. Immediately the way was

---

[1] On January 2, 1848, he sprang up at the back of the Papal carriage as it was passing along the Corso and unfurled a huge banner with the inscription, 'Santo Padre, fidatevi nel Popolo.' Farini, i., 325.

cleared for the emergence of the future leader. Count Camillo Cavour, aristocrat and friend of England, hated by his own order for his liberalism and nicknamed by the democrats 'Milord Camillo,' founded a daily newspaper to which he gave the prophetic name of *Il Risorgimento*—the Resurrection. As yet, however, the King distrusted Cavour and all his works, and cared only for the quarrel with Austria. Charles Albert had fiercely resented the occupation of Ferrara, and had sent a message to an Agrarian Congress at Casale in October in which he spoke openly of his desire to lead his people in a war of liberation. But the affair of Ferrara was compromised soon afterwards by the withdrawal of the Austrians from the town to the fortress, and for the moment the storm passed away.

It was to break forth with tenfold violence in those states of the Peninsula where there was least hope of any orderly progress towards freedom. In Lombardy and Venetia, held down as they were under the Austrian tyranny, a remarkable agitation had been carried on during the autumn of 1847 on strictly legal lines for the attainment of the liberties guaranteed by Austria to her Italian provinces in 1815. But the Austrian retort had been to arrest and imprison the two fearless leaders of the movement in Venetia, Daniele Manin and Niccolo Tommaseo, on charges of high treason. At Milan the popular hatred took the form of a boycott of tobacco, the government monopoly, and Field Marshal Radetzky used this as a pretext for provoking bloody collisions in the streets between his troops and the passers-by. The famous tobacco riots of January 3 made the breach impassable between the once easy-going Milanese and their alien masters. At the same time a more formidable explosion took place in the south. The long misrule of Ferdinand II. had at last aroused the city of Palermo to an act of revolt as fierce and determined as that of the Sicilian Vespers. Movements at Messina and Reggio in the previous September had been suppressed with the usual brutal massacres and shootings; but in the early days of January, 1848, handbills began to appear in the streets of Palermo calling on the Sicilians to rise on January 12, the King's birthday, and to seize their freedom by force of arms. The revolt was carried out with such persistency, by the aid of armed bands from the countryside,[1] that after fifteen days of desper-

[1] A letter of the Neapolitan Field Marshal de Sauget to the King [Jan. 24] complains of the 'continual communication' between the two British warships *Bull-dog* and *Gladiator* and the insurgents; Nisco (*Ultimi Trentasei Anni del Reame di Napoli*) affirms that the English lent two guns to the rebels (p. 109).

ate street fighting the royal garrison was expelled [January 26] and the 'British' constitution of 1812[1] proclaimed. The whole of Sicily had followed suit by the end of the month, and Ferdinand, terrified by demonstrations in Naples itself, decided to tread in his grand-father's footsteps and to swear to a constitution. The swearing cost him little, and as the months of February and March passed by, a shrewd observer could have seen that Ferdinand II. had but to bide his time until the chances of the situation should roll the ball to his feet once more. The rancours old and new let loose by the Revolution—between Sicily and the mainland, between army and national guard, between liberals and lazzaroni—were such as to deny all stability to the new government.

But long before Ferdinand's turn had come, the impulse given at Palermo had spread to every capital in Italy. In Piedmont Cavour voiced the cry for a constitution in an address which he and other journalists sent to the King, and so universal was the pressure exer-cised on the unfortunate Charles Albert that his torturing doubts at length gave way.[2] On February 8, 1848, the Piedmontese 'Statuto,' which was until yesterday the constitution of all Italy, was an-nounced by royal decree, and the sober Turinese defiled before their King with irrepressible rejoicing. Leopold of Tuscany fol-lowed suit [February 11], and all eyes were turned to Rome, where the well-meaning Pope stood torn by conflicting counsels, unable to dominate the mob and unwilling to compromise his sacred rights by granting full powers to a Parliament. But he had already admitted laymen and liberals to his ministry, and in the last days of February came the news of the fall of Louis Philippe, the citizen-king, before the barricades of Paris. It became clear that Pius must hesitate no longer. Characteristically enough, the preparation of the constitutional decree was not left to the newly made ministry, but to a special commission composed entirely of clerics. When it appeared, on March 14, 1848, it bore stamped in every line the inherent contradiction between the claims of the people to self-government and the claims of the Successors of St. Peter to unlimited authority. The entire field of ecclesiastical and 'mixed' affairs, which included the greater part of the daily lives of the Pope's subjects, was withdrawn from the cognizance of the elected Chamber, and the ultimate decision on all projects of law

---

[1] See p. 321.

[2] In 1824 Charles Albert had given a solemn pledge to the King, Charles Felix, that he would never alter the institutions of the kingdom when he came to the throne. Finally the Bishop of Vercelli absolved him from his oath on February 4, 1848.

was reserved for the secret consistory of cardinals, debating in concert with the Pope. But, such as it was, the constitution evoked the usual frenzy of applause, and mingled with the cries of the piazza there now rang out the persistent note, 'Death to the Jesuit, the friend of Austria,' 'Viva l'Italia,' 'Down with the foreigner.' The tide of national feeling was rising ever higher, and the able men who found themselves in the difficult position of Papal ministers saw that the one thing needful was to prepare the people for the fast-approaching conflict with Austria.

The storm burst finally at Milan, when it became known, on the evening of March 17, that Vienna itself had risen, that Metternich had fallen and fled, and that the Emperor had promised a constitution. The famous Five Days began on the afternoon of March 18 with a confused attack on the palace of the Governor; that night the first barricades made their appearance, and little by little, during the next three days, the Austrians were driven from all their central points of vantage towards the gates and walls, while nearly 1,700 barricades secured the conquered ground. A small council of war took command of the people; palaces and armourers' shops were ransacked for arms; the soldiers were assailed from the roofs with tiles and all manner of missiles, while their ears were deafened by the clashing of bells; and finally on the 22nd a victorious attack, led by the heroic young Luciano Manara, on the Austrian garrison at Porta Tosa opened the way to the succours that were pouring in from the countryside. Marshal Radetzky and fifteen thousand men had been defeated by an unarmed mob, and fearing an attack from the Piedmontese as well he decided to abandon even the Castello and to retreat on the 'Quadrilateral'—the four great fortresses of Mantua, Verona, Peschiera, and the Legnago which secured Austria's debouchment into Italy from the mouth of the Brenner. There the old fox went to earth, while behind him Italy rose in arms and the hour of liberation seemed to have struck in a thousand cities of the plain and Apennine. Venice, too, had shaken herself free, and under the wise guidance of Daniele Manin had turned out the Austrian garrison and proclaimed the Republic of St. Mark, with the loss of only a single life.

All now turned on the promptitude with which the army of Piedmont could be thrown into the scale against Radetzky's veterans. At Milan, even during the Five Days, feeling had run high between republicans and 'Albertists,' and the King, who certainly aimed at the annexation of Lombardy, and who detested the very name of a republic, was disappointed by the final proposal of the provisional government that all questions of future status should be postponed until after the defeat of Austria. Four precious days [March 23—26] were lost in hesitations and in negotiations with a chorus of angry foreign Powers—including England[1]—and when at length the little army of Piedmont crossed the Ticino, Radetzky had been given time to reach the Quadrilateral.

The history of the campaign of 1848 is, on the Italian side, a lamentable record of disunion, incompetence, and bad generalship; on the Austrian, an example of the solidity and recuperative power of a well-trained military machine. In the intoxication of the hour, Rome, Naples, and Tuscany all sent forth their contingents to the Holy War, while the Duchies of Parma and Modena drove out their princelings and voted for union with Piedmont; but Pius was already thoroughly alarmed at his position, and King Ferdinand, as everyone knew, was only waiting for the opportunity of stabbing the Neapolitan patriots in the back. At the end of April the Pope issued an 'Allocution,' in which he declared that a war against Austria was 'wholly abhorrent from our counsels' and that he embraced all princes and peoples in an equal paternal love [April 29, 1848]. The Allocution was received with dismay by liberal Italians, and when it reached the corps of seventeen thousand Papal volunteers who had followed General Durando to the front, they began to melt away by desertion. A little later, Ferdinand of Naples took advantage of a riot occurring at the inauguration of his new Parliament to turn loose his faithful troops upon the people, alter the constitution, and prorogue the Parliament [May 15], while orders were sent to the Neapolitan contingent at Bologna to return immediately. But the Neapolitans were under the command of old General Pepe, the veteran of 1820, and Pepe induced some two thousand of them to defy the King and to follow him across the Venetian frontier. They made their way to Venice, where many of these southern youths bore the long martyrdom of the siege, and died by the lagoons, fighting for the last shreds of Italian liberty.

At first the Piedmontese army obtained some slight advantages against the Austrians. The high-watermark of their success was reached at the end of May, when after the brave resistance of the little Tuscan corps at the battle of Curtatone, the Piedmontese drove back the Austrians at Goito [May 30] and forced Peschiera

---

[1] Palmerston, then Prime Minister, did all he could to restrain the King from declaring war. (*Corresp. resp. the Affairs of Italy, 1848—9,* part ii., nos. 185, 292, 408.)

to surrender. But every opportunity of overwhelming Radetzky while he was still weak had been lost, and even after Goito the inaction of the King enabled his opponent to march on Vicenza, force it to capitulate [June 10], and then reduce the whole of Venetia except Venice herself to submission. Reinforcements had already reached him, and while the King and his advisers, from their dread of republicanism, discouraged the volunteers who would have flocked to a more generous leader, the Austrian forces steadily won back their old superiority. From April to June the Austrian Cabinet was imploring England to mediate on the basis of the cession of Lombardy and the Duchies of Piedmont and the grant of autonomy to Venice, but after June no more such offers were made. Meanwhile the question of union with Piedmont had been decided in Lombardy during May by the holding of a plebiscite, which, in spite of Mazzini's opposition, gave an overwhelming majority in favour of 'Fusion.' After the disasters in Venetia even the Republic of St. Mark followed the same course, and Manin resigned his authority into the hands of Charles Albert's commissioners. But it was all too late. At the end of July, Radetzky heavily defeated the Piedmontese army at Custoza [July 24—25], and in total discouragement the King retreated on Milan. There, amid the howls of the mob, who saw themselves handed back to slavery by the very man who had promised to defend them, Charles Albert passed the bitterest day of his life. The capitulation of Milan was signed on August 5, and the next day the Austrians re-entered the despairing city. A long column of fugitives accompanied the Piedmontese in their sad march to the Sardinian frontier, and found on the King's territory a refuge from persecution. Meanwhile an armistice was signed by the opposing generals, restoring to Austria all her original possessions —save only Venice. For Manin and his islanders would submit to no compromise; they appealed both to France and England to take up the cause of Venice and to mediate with Austria on the basis of her independence.

In despair of that terrible August it was no wonder that a fierce reaction set in against Charles Albert and the 'Royal War,' while the republicans everywhere pointed to the contrast between the glorious Five Days, the people's achievement, and the ignominious capitulation of the royal army. Some of the volunteers refused to accept the armistice, and continued to fight for two or three weeks around Lake Maggiore under a leader whom they had learnt to trust. Giuseppe Garibaldi had returned from South America in June, accompanied by a small band of hardy and devoted followers. Although Charles Albert had refused his help, he had received a commission from the provisional government of Milan, and, after carrying on the war in the Alps till the last moment, he crossed into Switzerland and thence returned to Genoa. A few weeks later the vicissitudes of his fortune led him through Tuscany to the Romagna in search of the ideal recruiting-ground for the 'Legion' which he proposed to form [November, 1848]. While the Papal government was anxiously endeavouring to pass these inconvenient visitors through to Venice an event occurred in Rome which precipitated the last act in the revolutionary drama.

Since Pio Nono's abandonment of the national cause with the famous Allocution,[1] difficulties had thickened around the Pope's constitutional government. The ministry of Count Mamiani had endeavoured to conduct the affairs of state in a liberal and anti-Austrian sense from May to the end of July, but the reactionary party in the Vatican, headed by Cardinal Antonelli, had secured the control of foreign affairs more and more completely behind the backs of the ministers; disorders had increased in the provinces, and in August a crisis had arisen owing to the anarchical condition of Bologna, where the débris of the disbanded armies had drifted together from Lombardy and Venetia. In his straits the Pope had called upon the one strong man in his *entourage*, Pellegrino Rossi, to undertake the government, and Rossi accepted the Ministry of the Interior on September 16, 1848. For two months he bent the whole energies of a hard and autocratic will to the task of restoring order and good government, but his proceedings raised up too many enemies against him, and he was assassinated at the reopening of the Chamber of Deputies on November 15, by Luigi Brunetti, son of Ciceruacchio. Many Romans openly rejoiced at the deed, and the unfortunate Pius, his cup of bitterness filled, began to make secret preparations for flight. France offered him hospitality and placed a gunboat at his disposal, but Antonelli had other views, and on the night of November 22, Pius was secretly and swiftly conveyed to the Neapolitan border and took up his abode at Gaëta under the protection of King Ferdinand. The Neapolitan perjurer had already regained the upper hand in his own dominions, had suspended his Parliament, and taken the first step in the reconquest of Sicily by the long and horrible bombardment of Messina [September 1—7], which earned for him the glorious title of *King Bomba*. Such was the august protection to which the reforming Pope had now committeed his person and his fortunes.

[1] See p. 342.

The winter of 1848—9 was a time of increasing agitation and tension in every part of the Peninsula. The efforts of England and France to procure a settlement on the basis of the abandonment of Lombardy by Austria had proved unavailing, and only the armistice ensured a precarious peace. Radetzky was carrying on a brutal tyranny at Milan. Charles Albert, melancholy and pessimistic, had confided the conduct of affairs to the 'prophet' Gioberti and a democratic ministry, while in Tuscany an attempt was being made by the able but egoistic Guerrazzi to carry on the government in difficult times and to reconcile the Grand Duke with the more extreme element among his subjects. But Tuscany always responded to the lead of Rome, and when the provisional government which had assumed power there after the Pope's flight, announced the convocation of a Roman Constituent Assembly [December], a strong party in Tuscany desired to join forces with Rome and to form a democratic Central Italian State. Leopold at first gave his consent to a law authorizing Tuscany to send representatives to the Roman Assembly, but his reluctance to jeopardize his own crown and to meddle with the Pope's temporal power was obvious, and on February 7, 1849, he fled to a little seaport at the southern border of his territory and there entered into active correspondence with the Pope. The Florentines proclaimed a provisional government and tore down the Grand Ducal arms, and on February 21 Duke Leopold sadly shook off the dust of Tuscany from his velvet slippers and went to swell the family circle assembled at Gaëta.

In the meantime the republic had been proclaimed in Rome [February 9]. Garibaldi and his legion marched south to defend it, and Mazzini, after passing through Florence in order to persuade the Tuscans to cast in their lot with Rome,[1] came also to the city of his desire [March 5]. The Assembly had conferred Roman citizenship upon him, for now in the bankruptcy of Kingship and Papacy the ideas of the exile had come to their own at last, and the factious politicians of Pius' time made way for the true leader. From the moment of his arrival he exercised the decisive influence in the republic's counsels, by right of a sheer moral ascendancy that belonged to him, and throughout the four months of his rule almost no act of crime or persecution stained the action of the Roman State. With the thickening of calamities at the end

---

[1] He spoke to them from Orcagna's Loggia and almost persuaded them to proclaim the republic, but Guerrazzi, who did not wish for union, succeeded in parrying the demand by calling for two thousand volunteers for the war. Only eighty-three presented themselves.

of March the Assembly conferred unlimited authority upon him and his two colleagues, Armellini and Saffi, with the title of Triumvirs.

For in the short and disastrous campaign of Novara, Charles Albert had tried the fortune of war once more; had staked all upon the throw and lost. On the night after the battle, when Radetzky stood between the beaten Piedmontese and Turin, the unhappy king chose the one course that might yet save his country, and abdicated in favour of his son Victor Emanuel. No very severe terms were imposed upon the young King; the occupation of a strip of his territory by Austrian troops, the obligation to withdraw his fleet from the Adriatic, where it had been sheltering Venice, the evacuation of the Duchies, the payment of a war indemnity, and the disbandment of the volunteers who had joined his colours.[1] But France made it clear that she would tolerate no further encroachment on the part of Austria, and, by whatever narrow margin liberal government survived in Piedmont, the new King loyally swore to maintain the constitution which his father had granted. The moral effect of his staunchness was incalculable, and served to rally to the sub-Alpine kingdom the hopes of those who had bitterly renounced all faith in kings and princes.

On the receipt of the news of Novara, Mazzini admitted to his friends that he had little hope for the survival of the Roman Republic. He did not then guess from which quarter the blow would fall. Pius IX. had appealed from Gaëta to all the Catholic Powers—Austria, Spain, Naples, and France—to restore him to his throne,[2] and after Novara it was confidently assumed by Antonelli that Austrian troops would be detached to crush the republicans. But the traditional French jealousy of Austrian aggrandizement in Italy, added to a complex internal situation, induced the government of the French Republic to forestall such a move. Louis Napoleon, who had by this time induced the French democracy to vote him the title of 'Prince President,' had need of clerical support; his ministry was largely composed of clericals, and the attractions of a Roman adventure to restore the Pope loomed large in their sight. General Oudinot, with a force of eight thousand men, was accordingly dispatched to the port of Civitavecchia,

---

[1] This latter clause was responsible for the fact that the fine battalion of Lombard *Bersaglieri* or sharpshooters, under their Colonel Luciano Manara, left Piedmont in order to take part in the defence of Rome. Manara was killed in the Villa Spada on the last day of the assault [June 30].

[2] In a note of February 18, 1849, addressed to the Four Powers.

where he arrived on April 24, 1849, and the misgivings of the
French republicans were lulled by the assurance that the intervention of France was intended to save the Roman people from the
excesses that would otherwise mark a Papal restoration. Unfortunately, however, the revolutionary army could not be induced
to view the advance of French troops against them in this light;
and a vigorous repulse of Oudinot's force on April 30 under the
Janiculan walls showed not only the spirit of the republicans, but
the fine fighting qualities which Garibaldi's presence had infused
into the heterogeneous mass of townsmen, half-trained volunteers,
'legionaries' and converted Papal regiments which composed the
garrison of Rome. Oudinot retreated to Civitavecchia, but the
defeat had roused the military *amour-propre* of France, and Oudinot was heavily reinforced, while the French envoy, Ferdinand
de Lesseps, was disowned at the last moment. On May 31, just
after he had concluded an arrangement with the Triumvirs, the
envoy was curtly recalled, and the next day General Oudinot
announced that he would resume hostilities.

Already the fires of liberty had been quenched to north and
south of the republic. Florence had recalled her Grand Duke, in
the vain hope that so she might avoid an Austrian occupation;
Bologna and the Marches were overrun by the Whitecoats; Sicily,
lectured and abandoned by France and England,[1] succumbed during May to the tender mercies of Ferdinand II. Yet in Rome and
Venice the resistance was still prolonged, far into the summer, and
the valour of Garibaldi and his legionaries, the austere purity of
Mazzini, the steadfastness of Manin and his Venetian children,
showed to an unwilling world that Italy was still unconquered.
Around the Gate of San Pancrazio and on the slope of the Villa
Corsini, the best blood of Romans and Lombards was poured,
during those days of June, that Rome might live, and when at
length the defence was abandoned before overwhelming force
the moral situation of the whole country had been profoundly
changed. Henceforth there could be no capital but Rome, though
the years might be long in bringing its redemption. The bayonets
of the French republicans brought back the Pope, but the Rome
to which he returned was a city that had learnt much during his
months of exile.

Garibaldi and a body of three thousand volunteers disdained to
join in the capitulation, and went forth from Rome on their famous

---

[1] Palmerston's words to Prince Granatelli, envoy of the Sicilian Provisional Government in London, were: 'France has betrayed you, and England
has abandoned you.' June 13, 1849. [*Sicily and England*, Tina Whitaker.]

attempt to reach the dying republic of Venice. Handled with marvellous skill by their wary leader, they escaped from Spaniards and Neapolitans in the south and from three converging columns of Austrians in the north, until they reached, exhausted, the neutral territory of San Marino [July 31]. The Fathers of the little republic gave them shelter and negotiated as best they could with the Austrian forces for the safety of the little army,[1] but Garibaldi and his wife, Ugo Bassi the priest, Ciceruacchio and about two hundred more, still made head for Venice. The flotilla of fishing-boats which they had launched was overhauled and captured by the Austrian patrol, but Garibaldi, his wife, and about a score of others reached the shore in the lagoon district of Comacchio. There, worn out by the hardships of the flight, Anita died in her husband's arms, but Garibaldi himself, concealed by faithful parti-sans, escaped the scattered Whitecoats and after long wanderings reached the Tuscan coast. Ciceruacchio and Ugo Bassi were taken and shot, with many humbler patriots, and thus not one of all that forlorn hope succeeded in bringing help to Venice.

And indeed by the time that the attempt was made the republic was already agonizing. For a whole year Venice had maintained her resistance single-handed against the Austrian Empire, and the hopes which she had entertained of French and British assistance had gradually died away.[2] Neither France nor England were pre-pared to go to war for the sake of Venetian independence, and their mediation, deprived of such a sanction, was powerless against the determination of Vienna. After the battle of Novara Radetzky was free to concentrate his troops against Venice, and a close cordon was drawn round the edge of the lagoon, while the Austrian fleet maintained a strict blockade from the sea. The defending

---

[1] The negotiations dragged on for many weeks, and no definite promise of immunity could be obtained, but gradually most of the men got away to their homes. Some, however, were seized, imprisoned, and cruelly flogged.

[2] Manin had addressed a moving appeal to Palmerston on August 20, 1848. Palmerston's reply, after a delay of nearly two months, ran as follows: 'Sir, I have had the honour to receive your letter of the 20th of August last, adverting to the relations of Venice towards the Austrian Empire, and calling upon Her Majesty's Government to use their endeav-ours in order to prevent that city from again falling under Austrian rule. In reply I have to inform you that it forms no part of the proposals made by the British Government to the government of Austria for the pacifica-tion of Italy, that Venice should cease to be under the Imperial Crown, and that consequently it would be wise for the people of Venice to come to an understanding with the Austrian Government.' *Corresp. resp. the Affairs of Italy*, Pt. III., no. 464, October 16, 1848.

army, numbering some twenty thousand men, was bravely led by old Pepe, but at the end of May their last foothold on the opposite shore, the fort of Malghera, was taken by an overwhelming attack, and this gave the Austrian gunners power to advance their pieces within range of the town itself. Throughout the month of June missiles fell upon the western quarter, while cholera and typhus broke out among the crowded and starving population. Still the Assembly decreed *resistance at all costs*, and the people supported Manin and the army with unwavering fortitude. But the stores of food were running out; the revolt of Hungary, which had promised a gleam of hope, was crushed by the intervention of Russia, and on August 6 Manin asked the Assembly for authority to treat with the enemy. The defence, however, was prolonged for another eighteen days, while Manin handled every emergency alike with the same patient wisdom and courage. It was not until August 24, when only two days' food remained in the magazines, that the capitulation was finally signed. Honourable terms were obtained, insomuch as all persons compromised with the Austrian authorities were allowed free exit in French vessels, and Manin himself, with thirty-nine other civilians, quitted for ever the city he had loved so well. Once more the Austrian black and yellow waved from the three giant flagstaffs before St. Mark's, symbolizing the re-enslavement of Italy. But, as Manin said in his last address to the despairing people: 'We have sown the good seed; it will fructify in good soil.'

CHAPTER XXIX
Cavour and the Making of Italy

And Nobleness walks in our ways again;
And we have come into our heritage. RUPERT BROOKE

ITALY lay once more under the Austrian heel. Whatever had been the character of the Restoration of 1815, that of 1849 was a simple military reconquest, and the restored rulers held their power by virtue of the Austrian armies of occupation which heralded their return to their respective capitals. An Imperial decree appointed Radetzky Governor-General of the Kingdom of Lombardy-Venetia, and Radetzy's method of governing was to enforce obedience by severity, and to subject the towns under his jurisdiction to such a system of war-contributions as would effectually curb their spirit and delay their return to prosperity. In regular taxes alone it was calculated by one not completely reliable authority that Lombardy-Venetia paid 120,000,000 *lire* a year, of which only 50,000,000 remained in the country, while the extraordinary contributions reached 200,000,000 *lire* in the first two years.[1] Martial law was maintained until 1854, the press was gagged, on occasion even women were flogged in public before the Castello of Milan. The little town of Brescia, which had risen with desperate courage against its Austrian garrison simultaneously with the battle of Novara, and had suffered an atrocious repression at the hands of General Haynau, was mulcted again and again in heavy fines, among them being a bill for the powder and shot spent in bombarding it. The liberals nursed their bitter wrongs in secret, but the underground life of conspiracy awoke once more, and from his exile in Switzerland and London Mazzini wove the threads of one brave but hopeless attempt after another to kindle fresh revolt. This was the time of the prophet's highest reputation, for the great deeds of Milan, Venice, and Rome shone clear in the people's memory against the failure of Piedmont, and the prospect of liberty under a monarchy seemed remote indeed. When the Austrian police unearthed a conspiracy in the famous treason trials of Mantua in 1852, the nine victims whom they sentenced to the gallows went to their death in the pure spirit of republican self-sacrifice, dedicating their lives to Italy. Some of the many thousand political refugees from Lombardy and Venetia brought their republican faith with them into Piedmont, where they fre-

[1] Zini. *Storia d'Italia*, I., i., 249—251.

quently embarrassed the government that had given them shelter. But when after the first executions of Mantua Mazzini stirred up another outbreak at Milan [February 6, 1853], followed by the usual harvest of shootings and imprisonments, his influence received a decisive check, and many of his followers turned their eyes instead towards the steadier though less heroic leadership of the Sardinian kingdom.

In Tuscany and the Duchies of Parma and Modena the reaction followed the same lines as in Lombardy-Venetia, for these three were now practically vassal states of Austria, bound by treaty to maintain Austrian contingents and to abolish the last remnants of constitutional rule. Large concessions were made to the Church, which regained by a series of concordats most of the ground lost through the reforms of Joseph and Leopold in the previous century. The Jesuits closed down upon education in the same manner as the police closed down upon public and private life. Leopold of Tuscany was still tolerated by his Florentines, but Charles III. of Parma took a pleasure in lashing his subjects across the face if they failed to greet him as he rode by, and after a career of debauchery and cruelty worthy of a degenerate Visconti he was removed at length by the dagger of an assassin.

After the capitulation of Palermo in May, 1849, the path of King Ferdinand was cleared for that punishment of his rebellious subjects which he had been meditating since the previous summer. He had already dissolved his Parliament [March 13, 1849], and although the constitution was never repealed, the Neapolitans understood well enough that it was from thenceforth a dead letter. Gradually the King's toils closed around all the most distinguished deputies and ex-ministers who had served him during the brief year of freedom; his new minister of justice, an ex-spy named Longobardi, had provided his master with an alphabetical list, running to many thousand names, of all the suspects in the kingdom, with notes of their own or their parents' spoken and unspoken thoughts ever since 1799,[1] and by the end of 1851, 4,462 of these were said to be suffering penalties more or less horrible as political offenders.[2] But it was fated that the trial of the most celebrated group of these unfortunates—Carlo Poerio, Luigi Settembrini, and their friends—should take place under the eye of a certain formidable Englishman travelling for his pleasure in foreign parts, William Ewart Gladstone, and that having witnessed the

[1] Zini, *Storia d'Italia.*, I., i., p. 169.
[2] Tivaroni, *L'Italia degli Italiani*, I., 234.

methods employed in the trial this Englishman should also insist on visiting the prisons where the convicted men were sent to rot in chains. The result of these observations was given to Europe in the burning words of the *Letters to Lord Aberdeen*, which unmasked the character of Bomba's rule in Naples. Thenceforth the Bourbon took his natural place as the outcast of Europe in the eyes of the Western Powers at least, and the way was prepared for that active sympathy with the Italian movement on the part of our countrymen which was to render such effective help in the critical year 1860.

If Mr. Gladstone had proceeded to visit the Papal prisons of Palliano, San Leo, or Ancona he might have had a tale to tell as dreadful as that of his exposure of the famous *Vicaria* of Naples. For Pio Nono had come back to his dominions determined to have no further adventures with liberalism or constitutional government, and while he devoted himself to the study of doctrinal reform, he allowed the conduct of affairs to fall into the hands of that party among the cardinals which represented the pure school of Gregory XVI. Under pressure from France he had put forth a *motu-proprio* from Portici [September 12, 1849], announcing the establishment of a Council of State, a *Consulta* for finance, provincial councils, and an amnesty; but when the amnesty came to be published it was found to consist rather in a general proscription, so many and so large were the classes of those excepted from its operation.[1] Louis Napoleon was gravely disturbed at the falseness of his position, in having handed back the population of the Papal States to a priestly despotism, but the French Chamber did not support him in his protests, and he was obliged to allow his garrison at Rome to become an accomplice in the re-enslavement of the Pope's subjects. The prime mover in the Papal reaction was that same Cardinal Antonelli who had counselled the Pope's flight to Gaëta, and it was this extraordinary man who now took the helm of state and saw to it that even the *motu-proprio* of Portici should remain a dead letter. The son of a peasant of the southern Campagna, Antonelli seems to have had all the instincts of a brigand, combined with the talents of a Wall Street manipulator, and to have used his position to devise so colossal a system of 'graft' that he died with a fortune

---

[1] Those excluded from the amnesty were: (1) All persons amnestied in 1846 who had taken part in the rebellion; (2) all members of the Provisional Government, Constituent Assembly, Triumvirate, and Republican Government; (3) heads of military corps; (4) persons who in addition to political crimes had committed crimes against the common law.

From a photo by Alinari

THE INTERVIEW BETWEEN VICTOR EMANUEL II AND GENERAL RADETZKY

From the painting by Pietro Aldi in the Palazzo della Signoria, Siena

variously estimated at twenty-five to sixty million *lire*. He had himself and his family ennobled, and placed one of his brothers at the head of the *Annona*, or corn distribution of Rome, and another at the head of the *Banca Romana*, so that between them the two could control the rise and fall of prices and (so gossip said) make vast sums from the distresses of the poor. Totally devoid of culture, Antonelli yet had a great power of fascination over women, and the gossip here reached scandalous proportions. His control over the feeble Pope was so remarkable that the Romans could only ascribe it to the evil eye. Such was the spirit that presided over the last twenty years of the decline and fall of the Temporal Power.

Nor might they have been the final years, had there not been saved from the wreck of Italy's fortune one virile state ruled by a man of shrewd common sense and guided by a man of genius. Victor Emanuel and Cavour did for the Sardinian kingdom what only the rarest combination of pluck, foresight, and determination could have done, in the ten years after Novara; they restored her internal prosperity, and at the same time so conducted her affairs that not only to the Italians from farthest Sicily and Venetia, but to the governments of Europe, Piedmont came to speak and stand for Italy. The 'Federal Solution' had still seemed the most promising to many of the moderate politicians after the disasters of the revolution, but when Cavour had had five years to educate the Piedmontese in the uses of freedom and to place the Italian cause before the eyes of Europe, federalism was seen to be inadequate or impossible, and at last in 1860 the whole country rallied to the cry of 'Italy and Victor Emanuel.'

Cavour first took office under the high-minded Massimo d'Azeglio in October, 1850, when the country had barely recovered from the shock of Novara, when the young King was hardly yet in the saddle, and when public opinion was severely agitated by the first open quarrel with Rome on the so-called Siccardi Laws. For the sub-Alpine kingdom was still far behind the greater Catholic states in its relations with the Church; the country swarmed with monastic institutions, and the clergy still claimed the privilege of being tried by their own courts for offences against the common law. Victor Emanuel's government had to begin where Leopold and Joseph II. had begun a hundred years before, but neither side showed much readiness to compromise. Nevertheless all the most fundamental reforms were accomplished between 1850 and 1856, though the King, good Catholic as he was, needed some persuasion

X

to brave the Papal censures. When Pius IX. made a progress through the Papal dominions in 1857, and at Bologna met one of his quondam constitutional ministers, he poured out to him the bitterest complaints of Piedmont, 'where religion is persecuted, and the Church is spared no outrage!'[1] Hard indeed must it have been for the Vicar of Christ to see the heretic Waldenses admitted at last, though only in 1848, to civil and religious liberty.

Cavour's first appointment was to the Ministry of Agriculture and Commerce, for which his long apprenticeship as the administrator of the family property at Leri gave him peculiar qualifications. But his immense capacity for work soon led him to absorb the portfolio of the Navy as well, and presently also that of Finance, while a series of commercial treaties bore witness to his talent for diplomacy. Railway and telegraph systems were laid down, the budget reorganized and heavier taxation imposed in order to meet some of the very heavy increase in state indebtedness. His colleagues soon found that Cavour and no other was master in D'Azeglio's cabinet, and the whimsical premier himself wrote to his nephew: 'Cavour was expressly created to lead affairs and Parliament. But he is as despotic as the devil!' He was, however, obliged to resign for a time when, not content with making an unauthorized alliance with the radical party of the Left Centre, he proceeded to secure the election of its leader, Rattazzi, to the Presidency of the Chamber. This alliance was nicknamed the *connubio*, or *marriage*, and when Cavour returned to power in November, 1852, and formed the memorable 'Great Ministry,' the *connubio* remained the basis of his parliamentary system and showed his resolute determination to advance in a democratic direction.

The work of the *Gran Ministero* came to be watched with ever-increasing anxiety by Austria, with admiration by Cavour's many friends in England, and with growing approval by the crowned schemer who now sat upon the throne of France, Napoleon III. When, after the Mazzinian rising at Milan in February, 1853, the Austrian Government issued a decree of sequestration against the property of all Lombard 'emigrants,' Cavour refused to be cowed by the stroke, broke off diplomatic relations with Austria and won to his side the public opinion of England and France by a masterly memorandum[2] intended to show that the Austrian decree was an open breach of the Treaty of 1849. Though the Western Powers would not take diplomatic action, Austria was taunted with the

---

[1] De Cesare, *Last Days of Papal Rome*, p. 166.
[2] Printed in full in Zini, vol. ii., p. 395.

accusation of robbery. Cavour was anxious to pursue his advantage, and in the next year opportunity came. England and France had decided to go to war with Russia on behalf of the decaying empire of Turkey, although the Russian Government had accepted their terms while the Turkish had declined them, and perhaps the only good result of the Crimean War which posterity can discern was the chance it gave to Cavour of unfurling the Italian flag side by side with those of the Western Powers. The contingent which he sent to the Crimea distinguished itself at the Battle of Tchernaya, and earned for Cavour the right to represent his country at the Congress of Paris in 1856. Although he came back from the Congress 'without the tiniest Duchy in his pocket,' as D'Azeglio ruefully remarked, he had succeeded in getting a special sitting devoted to the condition of Italy, and had heard the British Foreign Minister, Lord Clarendon, denouncing the misgovernment of the Pope and the King of Naples in terms which Cavour himself could hardly have outdone.

Cavour and the King had by this time definitely decided that *le canon* alone could arbitrate between themselves and Austria. Confidence in Piedmont was increasing by leaps and bounds among the Italian patriots, and in the year 1856 a movement was set on foot by Manin, La Farina, a Sicilian, and G. Pallavicino, a Milanese noble of the 'emigration,' for uniting the revolutionaries of every party in the newly formed 'National Society' under the watchword 'Italy and Victor Emanuel.' Cavour gave his assistance secretly to the movement, and used to receive La Farina at six o'clock in the morning, by the private staircase leading to his rooms. Garibaldi, who had returned a second time from America two years earlier and taken up his abode on the island of Caprera, gave in his adhesion in 1857; Daniele Manin, from his exile in Paris, inspired the movement, and the last public act of his life was to sign the society's manifesto. The great Venetian died on September 22, 1857, before his eyes had seen the promised land, but his famous declaration of hope in Piedmont—'Convinced that before everything *Italy must be made*, the republican party says to the House of Savoy, "Make Italy, and I am with you! If not, not" '—brought in many thousands of converts, and marked the dividing line between himself and Mazzini. Irreconcilable as ever, Mazzini brooded and conspired in London, while in Italy the current of action deserted the republican channel and followed instead a leader, Camillo di Cavour, in whose great heart there burnt a passion as clear and terrible as Mazzini's, the passion to *make Italy, or die.*

It was when affairs were in this state of suppressed tension that an event occurred in Paris which all but brought Cavour's carefully reared schemes in ruins to the ground. Felice Orsini, a Mazzinian exile from the Papal States, threw a bomb at the Emperor Napoleon's carriage, and came within an ace of destroying him [Jan. 14, 1858]. The Emperor's anger blazed out in furious recriminations against Piedmont, the harbourer of assassins,[1] but it was met by the King's unflinching dignity, and the storm passed. More curious still, Napoleon was profoundly moved by the noble letter addressed to him by Orsini before his execution; in his own restless youth he had taken part in the Carbonari Revolution of 1831, and in his heart he could respect a good conspirator. Within three months after Orsini's execution he had sent a confidential agent to Turin with a suggestion that Cavour should meet him privately at Plombières during the summer vacation. Thus was brought about the interview at the little health-resort in the Vosges, which changed the face of Italy and sent a hundred thousand French bayonets to their old game of driving out the Austrian from the Lombard plain.

The Pact of Plombières [July, 1858] was a verbal agreement between Napoleon and Cavour for the complete liberation of Italy, as far as the Isonzo, from Austrian rule; the annexation to Piedmont of Lombardy, Venetia, the Duchies and the Legations, and the establishment of a Federation between the newly-enlarged kingdom, the Papal States, Tuscany, and Naples. The price to be paid was the cession to France of Savoy, and possibly of Nice. But it was not easy even for Cavour to shape events towards the fulfilment of the Pact. Napoleon agreed in January, 1859, to a secret treaty binding him to come to the support of Piedmont if she were attacked by Austria, but he hung back when he found, in March, how averse from war were the French clericals and bourgeois, while England, under the Conservative ministry of Lord Derby, did all in her power to prevent an outbreak. But Cavour had already appealed above the heads of France and England to another force, which he believed to be irresistible—the Italian people. Italian youths, at Cavour's secret invitation, flocked into Piedmont by the thousand to join the King's army, and the great Minister even went so far as to commission Garibaldi to organize a corps of three thousand volunteers. Austria took violent offence at these proceedings, as Cavour intended her to do. England in alarm proposed the simultaneous disarmament of all three Powers,

---

[1] In this case the assassin had been harboured in England, not in Piedmont.

and even Napoleon sent a peremptory telegram advising compliance [April 18]. It was a moment of intense anxiety for Cavour, but Austria's bullying saved Italy. Piedmont bowed to the mandate of England and France, on condition that Austria also should disarm. On April 23, however, Austria sent an ultimatum to Turin, demanding disarmament within three days on pain of war, and Cavour was able to claim the French alliance. Napoleon could not escape his pledge, and on April 29 France declared war on Austria.

Fortunately for Italy, the Austrian commander against whom the Piedmontese were pitted in the first critical week before the arrival of the French was not of Radetzky's stamp, and wasted his time in aimless counter-marchings while Turin might have been taken and sacked. General Gyulai never felt himself really at ease outside the Quadrilateral, and when the French had safely poured in by road, railway, and steamer he suffered himself to be beaten at Magenta [June 4] in spite of Napoleon's blunders, while three brigades of his best troops were out-generalled and defeated at Varese and Como by Garibaldi and his three thousand ill-armed volunteers. Sullenly the Austrian retreated beyond the Mincio, and on June 8 Napoleon and Victor Emanuel entered Milan in triumph. It was the final liberation of the great Lombard city. But the Austrian army, heavily reinforced and now commanded by its young Emperor Francis Joseph, had still to be met and destroyed, and on June 24 a desperate struggle took place on the heights of San Martino and Solferino, running southward from the Lake of Garda. French and Piedmontese remained masters of the field, after twelve hours of terrible carnage, and it seemed as though one more advance would fulfil the dreams of Plombières. But that advance was never made. Napoleon, who wished only for a federated, not a united Italy, had taken alarm at the rapid uprising of Tuscany, the Duchies, and Romagna, as soon as the Austrian garrisons were withdrawn; at the prospect of endless difficulties with the Pope, the Empress, and the French clericals if Papal territory were annexed to Piedmont; and, last but not least, at the danger of a Prussian diversion on the Rhine. Without consulting Cavour, he went to meet Francis Joseph at Villafranca [July 9], and there signed away the fruits of his victories. Only Lombardy and, by implication, Parma, were to be united to Piedmont; Tuscany, Modena, and Romagna were to receive back their old masters; Venetia was to remain under Austria. As though in bitter mockery of Cavour, an 'Italian Federation' was to be formed under the presidency of the Pope. Italy never forgave Napoleon III. for the 'betrayal' of Villafranca, thereby displaying small comprehension for the straits of a much-harassed autocrat.

Victor Emanuel saw the necessity of bowing to the inevitable, and signed the treaty *pour ce qui me concerne*. But Cavour reeled from the shock, and after a passionate interview with the King, in which the great Minister in his despair said things which it was hard for a soldier to forgive, he flung down his resignation. Nine days had to elapse, however, before a new ministry could be formed, and during those days Cavour did what in him lay to undo the work of Villafranca. It fell to him to send the orders of recall to the Piedmontese 'Commissioners,' Massimo d'Azeglio and Farini, who had been installed at Bologna and Modena respectively, but he accompanied the orders by private telegrams urging them to remain at their posts. Farini telegraphed back that if the Duke tried to return he would be treated as a public enemy, and Cavour's reply ran: 'The Minister is dead, but the friend applauds your decision.'

It was in fact easier to lay down than to execute the terms of the truce of Villafranca. With the ruling parties in the three states, Tuscany, Modena, and Romagna, determined to work at all costs for annexation to Piedmont, with the French at any rate unwilling to see the old rulers restored by Austrian arms, and with England at last actively on the side of the Italians, a state of deadlock had been reached which endured throughout the six months' retirement of Cavour. Tuscany was in the hands of her own indomitable 'Iron Baron,' Bettino Ricasoli, who had taken office on the departure of the Grand Duke [April 27]; and Ricasoli's faith in United Italy was more robust than Cavour's. England had, by the general election of May, 1859, gone over to the Whigs, and under the leadership of 'Pam,' Lord John Russell, and Gladstone, upheld the doctrine that Italy should be allowed to work out her own salvation. Thus when the inevitable tide brought Cavour back to office in January, 1860, he found the situation ripe for bold decisions. Napoleon was ready to abandon the 'Federal Solution' at a price —the price of the cession of Savoy and Nice—and Cavour took upon himself the responsibility for carrying out the bargain. The 'Annexation of the Centre' was decided by plebiscite on March 12, 1860, and on the same day Cavour signed the treaty which gave to France Nizza, the birthplace of Garibaldi, and Savoy, the cradle of the royal house. The 'Re Galantuomo' made the sacrifice with a heavy heart, but in face of his renewed alliance with France, Austria was fain to let the annexation take its course.

On May 22, 1859, Ferdinand II., tyrant of the Two Sicilies, died in the odour of sanctity at Caserta. He was succeeded by a half idiotic son, Francis II., who was destined to close the long line of Neapolitan kings. Cavour and Victor Emanuel gave him his chance, three several times, of making alliance with them on equal terms in the national cause, but Francis was the tool of reactionary forces, Austrian and Papal, and his ministers were conspiring instead, during the winter of 1859—60, for an armed attack on the liberated provinces.[1] Meanwhile the Sicilians were laying their plans for another insurrection, and as early as September, 1859, they invited Garibaldi to come and take command. He was unable to consider the request seriously until the following spring, but then, with a heart full of bitterness at Cavour's sale of his birthplace, Nice, he agreed to make preparations, on condition that the programme was 'Italy and Victor Emanuel' and that the Sicilians showed their mettle by rising first. This condition they fulfilled by the brave but hopeless outbreak at the Gancia Convent in Palermo on April 4, 1860, and all through that month, amid doubts and perplexities and many changes of plan, Garibaldi proceeded with the enrolment of volunteers at Genoa. Cavour, or at any rate the King, secretly connived at the preparations, though the hostility of Napoleon obliged them to conceal their real thoughts. At length Garibaldi and his Thousand set sail in two old steamers from the little bay of Quarto, on the night of May 5, 1860,—a handful of men flung out against a kingdom.

They succeeded beyond the wildest hopes of the anxious watchers whom they left behind. Landing at Marsala on May 11, under the accidental protection of two British ships of war, the Garibaldini marched inland towards Palermo, met and defeated a greatly superior force of Neapolitans at Calatafimi on the 15th, and advanced by devious routes upon the capital, with its garrison of twenty-four thousand regular troops. On the night of May 27 they plunged fighting into the town, and by a miraculous combination of luck, courage, and bluff they had brought the Neapolitan commander to sue for an armistice by the end of the third day, when Garibaldi's own last cartridge was nearly spent. A capitulation followed the armistice, and during the month of June over twenty thousand Neapolitan soldiers were embarked in the Bay of Palermo, never more to tread the soil of Sicily.

In vain King Francis proclaimed the constitution, in time-honoured Bourbon fashion, and craved the very alliance with Piedmont which he had previously rejected. All that Victor Eman-

[1] See documents quoted in Bianchi's *Cavour*, p. 89.

uel would do, in deference to Napoleon's wishes, was to send an autograph letter to Garibaldi, bidding him halt at the Straits of Messina; but his messenger bore in his pocket a second autograph, to be shown but not given to the general, instructing him on this one occasion to disregard his sovereign's orders. By a device so simple was the making of United Italy assured. Garibaldi, now strongly reinforced, crossed the Straits unhindered on the night of August 18, and after some fighting in the hills about Reggio drove the Neapolitans before him in headlong flight. Then began that amazing march northward which was not to be stayed until the Dictator slept in the Palazzo d'Angri at Naples. Francis and his young Queen, Maria Sophia of Bavaria, fled to Gaëta on September 6; Garibaldi entered the capital amid scenes of frenzied excitement on the following day. He and his Red-shirts had won their kingdom.

While Garibaldi's followers hesitated and quarrelled as to whether or no the 'Annexation of the South' to Victor Emanuel's kingdom should be proclaimed immediately, Cavour and the King took matters into their own hands. They knew that it was Garibaldi's firm intention to march on Rome, where the Papal extremists had gathered together an army of 'Crusaders' from every Catholic state in Europe. And Cavour knew also that this must be prevented at all costs, since Napoleon's garrison still held the shield of France over Pio Nono, in spite of the insults to which it was daily subjected at the hands of his cardinals. Therefore it was necessary for the regular army of Piedmont to invade the Papal States, in order to forestall Garibaldi, to safeguard Rome, and to 'absorb the Revolution.' It was the finest stroke that even Cavour ever played. The consent of Napoleon, who disliked the Papal Crusaders, was easily obtained, and Cavour accepted as inevitable the risk of an Austrian attack. Gaily the King's *Bersaglieri* marched through Umbria and the Marches, and near the shrine of Loreto they completely defeated the Crusaders at the Battle of Castelfidardo [September 18]. Next the fortress of Ancona fell to a combined attack by sea and land [September 29], and at the same time the King started from Turin to overtake his troops and enter the Neapolitan kingdom. At this moment Garibaldi was engaged in his last desperate uphill fight, in the hills overlooking the Volturno, with the reorganized forces of King Francis, but he proved himself as well able in this battle to defeat a regular army in the open as amid the barricades of Palermo [October, 1, 2]. As Victor Emanuel approached, the dispute on the annexation question was decided in favour of an immediate plebiscite, and on October 21 the Neapolitans voted by 1,300,000 to 10,000 for 'Italy one and indivisible, with Victor Emanuel as Constitutional King.' The voting was not secret, and whole districts afterwards proved their Bourbon sympathies by a resort to brigandage, but such as they were the figures served their purpose. Sicily voted *Yes* in still more overwhelming proportion.

Thus was the Kingdom of Italy established by a union between rulers and people fitly symbolized by the familiar picture portraying the meeting between the King and Garibaldi on the damp autumn morning of October 26, on the road outside the little town of Teano. In the far north the three despotic powers, Austria, Russia, and Prussia, were bewailing the work of these two men, while even Napoleon, to please his clericals, joined in the chorus; but to an English ear the sentences of Lord John Russell's famous dispatch to the British Minister at Turin ring true and clear. 'Her Majesty's Government,' wrote Lord John, 'can see no sufficient ground for the severe censure with which Austria, France, Prussia, and Russia have visited the acts of the King of Sardinia. Her Majesty's Government will turn their eyes rather to the gratifying prospect of a people building up the edifice of their liberties, and consolidating the work of their independence.'[1]

---

[1] Lord John Russell to Sir James Hudson, October 27, 1860. *Brit. Parl. Papers*, 'Affairs of Italy,' Part VII.

CHAPTER XXX

The Completion of Italian Unity

THE Kingdom of Italy was made and won, but the difficulties confronting the new government were sufficient to daunt the most obstinate apostles of Unity. To amalgamate the North with the South, to conciliate Sicily, to win over the Church to a *modus vivendi* with its spoliators, to guide the State successfully between republicanism on the one hand and the old despotic tendencies on the other; to keep Garibaldi in check while yet maintaining a firm front towards Napoleon III., to grapple with the universal curse of poverty—these were the tasks which awaited the King's government, and brought it, many a time during the ten years that followed the Liberation, near to foundering. Add to this that the unity of the new State was not yet complete—that the Austrian still ruled in Venetia and the Pope in Rome—and the obstacles in free Italy's path may be dimly conceived.

The first and greatest of these lay in the barbarism of the South. Victor Emanuel had 'stitched the boot,' but the toe and the heel still pinched. Imperative as the winning of Naples had been for the evolution of liberty, it brought with it burdens and perplexities which might well have overset a more mature creation than Cavour's Italian kingdom. The very conquest, by letting loose the nether passions of the population, revealed the terrible heritage left by Bourbon misrule, and for two years and more the whole of the South was tormented by a savage brigandage, fomented by priests and other agents of King Francis, and purporting to be the people's rebellion against the 'foreign' conquest. The best men of the North—Generals Cialdini and La Marmora—were needed to put it down, nor was it finally crushed without drastic methods of repression, magnified by clerical writers into a ruthless war on liberty. Supplied and armed from Rome, the brigand bands were sure of a safe refuge on Papal territory, and it was not until the French Empire was induced to co-operate against them that the tide finally turned in favour of order. Even so, brigandage remained endemic in the soil of the South until a much later date, handicapping its normal development and absorbing energies which should have gone instead to building up the resources of the country.

While his lieutenants were endeavouring to bring order out of chaos in Naples and Sicily, Cavour himself, in the last months of his life, addressed his undimmed powers to a still more vexatious problem, the relations of Italy with the Church. He could not persuade himself that a peaceful solution of the Roman question was beyond his reach, and he devoted long and patient efforts in the winter of 1860—61 to an attempt to win over the Vatican to his conception of a *Free Church in a Free State*. Once abandon the outworn claim to the Temporal Power, he urged, and the Church would acquire an influence never before attained over the spiritual life of the people; he offered to abrogate the many existing rights of the State over the Church *(Exequatur, Placet,* etc.); to grant the Pope every possible freedom in the exercise of his spiritual authority; to guarantee him an ample revenue; if only the Church would recognize the Italian kingdom and abandon its claim to exercise temporal sovereignty over Rome and the surrounding 'Patrimony.' His agents sent him encouraging reports from Rome, where Pius and Antonelli seemed on the point of accepting the inevitable [February, 1861]; but then the conservative forces gained the ascendant once more, and on March 21 Cavour's envoy was suddenly expelled. Still undaunted, Cavour tried another path; obtained a vote from the newly assembled Parliament claiming Rome as capital [March 27], and addressed himself to Napoleon III. with a view to inducing him to withdraw his troops from Rome. The negotiations prospered, for the Emperor was sick and tired of his unnatural position as protector of a Power that continually derided his advice, and in the month of May a promise was obtained that the French troops should be withdrawn on June 20. The promise, however, never came to fulfilment, for the great Minister, on the faith of whose declarations it was made, had rendered by that time his last services to Italy. Cavour, worn out by his incessant labours and overburdened by too many cares, fell ill on May 29, and died eight days later [June 6, 1861]. As he lay dying his thoughts were all preoccupied with the state of the country, especially of the South. 'Poor fellows,' he said of the Neapolitans, 'it is not their fault—they have been so badly governed. It is that rogue Ferdinand.' And again, 'Any one can govern by the "state of siege." I shall govern them by means of liberty, and I shall show what ten years of liberty can do for that fine country.' But at the end one thought alone prevailed—'Italy is made—all is safe.'

At the news of Cavour's death Napoleon immediately withdrew his offer of evacuation, and the Roman Question lingered on unsolved. It remained to overshadow the whole evolution of the new kingdom for the next nine years. Lesser men filled the place of Cavour, and grappled desperately with the overwhelming difficulties of the finances, of railway construction, and of the provision of a uniform system of administration, but all roads led to Rome, even in such everyday affairs, and until Rome was won the State could acquire neither stability nor freedom. Ricasoli, Cavour's immediate successor, made renewed attempts to conciliate the Pope by proposals which he sent to the French Emperor; but so rigid was by this time the attitude of Rome that Napoleon did not even forward them. A petition signed by nine thousand priests fell equally on deaf ears. Then, in the next year, the initiative passed to the 'Party of Action,' who, under the leadership of Garibaldi, trusted to quicker methods to convince the Pope. Ricasoli, whose Puritan ways and unbending temper had led to much friction with the King, fell in February, 1862, leaving the way clear for Urbano Rattazzi, the man of facile temperament and plausible shifts who thought to rule the country by finesse in place of the lost genius of Cavour. Rattazzi and the King first encouraged Garibaldi to make an attempt on the Trentino [May, 1862], then stopped him at the last moment, and sent him in wrath back to Caprera. The hero's own instinct was for Rome, and in July he was back in Sicily, revisiting the scenes of his legendary exploits and rousing a vehement enthusiasm for the 'new Vespers,' *i.e.*, the expulsion of the French from Rome. In the Cathedral of Marsala he gave the Sicilians the watchword 'Rome or death'— *Roma o morte.* The King issued a proclamation, warning his subjects against impatient enterprises, but Garibaldi read it to his troops and informed them that he knew the King's real mind. Again the government hesitated and did not impede the volunteers in their crossing of the Straits, but once on the mainland Rattazzi took alarm at the threatening attitude of France and ordered General Cialdini, the governor of Naples, to stop the movement at all costs. Garibaldi had taken to the hills of Aspromonte above Reggio, and there his small force was found and overpowered by a column of Italian troops, and himself wounded in the heel by an Italian bullet [August 29, 1862]. He had exposed himself in exhorting his own men not to fire. The tragedy of the affair sank deep into the heart of Italy, and though Rattazzi tried to turn it to account by appealing once more to France to abandon Rome, the public could not forgive him for Garibaldi's wound, and he found himself obliged to resign on December 1.

Rattazzi's fall brought to power the moderate men of the Right

Centre, many of whom had borne distinguished parts in the national movement from 1848 onwards; but this Ministry of All the Talents, as it might well have been called, did little during its two years of power to grapple with the urgent problems of the day. A dangerous tendency to mere faction and obstructiveness grew up in the Chamber, while outside it the grinding poverty of the country, the continuance of brigandage, and the discontent of the Party of Action all combined to bring disillusionment to the common people. No Golden Age had followed the attainment of Unity, and Mazzini, from his sad exile in London or Lugano, or during his secret visits to Genoa, still mourned over the triumph of monarchy and still conspired for the republic. The Ministry, however, did at length take in hand the question of Rome, and signed a Convention with France on September 15, 1864, providing for the retirement of the French troops within the next two years. In its main features the Convention followed the lines of the agreement proposed by Cavour; the Italian kingdom was to guarantee the frontiers of the Papal State, or 'Comarca,' against external attack, and to permit the formation of a Papal army. Only if the Romans themselves rose and called in Victor Emanuel was it tacitly understood that Italy might 'go to Rome.' But in the September Convention one addition was made to these conditions: the Italians were to remove their capital from Turin to Florence—a step, as Napoleon said, 'which will allow me to make people think that you have given up Rome.' The Ministry consented, partly because an unworthy jealousy of Piedmont had already arisen among the politicians of the other states, and partly, no doubt, from reasons of geographical convenience. Turin, however, took the change very ill. Fierce riots broke out on September 21, quelled with much bloodshed the next day, and so great was the outcry against the Convention that the Moderate Ministry resigned within a week. But the next government, headed by the brave Piedmontese La Marmora, decided to maintain it, and the capital was duly moved to Florence in June, 1865.

The September Convention earned the just criticism of Italian patriots as an unworthy compromise based on a quibble, and the government's formal renunciation of their right to go to Rome exasperated the Party of Action. At the Vatican, however, the prospect of the withdrawal of the French garrison—the only shield between the Pope and his subjects—was viewed with indignant apprehension, and Pius sent forth his answer to the threat in the form of his Encyclical 'Quanta Cura,' with an attached syllabus of condemned opinions. In this long list of 'errors,' which it was

the duty of all good Catholics to combat, may be found not only
every approach to liberalism or the toleration of other creeds, but
also every attempt to place the civil authority on a level with the
ecclesiastical and above all any denial of the Temporal Power of
the Pope. The spirit of the syllabus is in fact summed up in its
last clause, wherein the doctrine that 'the Roman Pontiff should
or ought to reconcile himself or come to terms with progress,
liberalism, and modern civilization' is anathematized with the rest.
The challenge to the modern world was at least squarely flung
down.

The government of La Marmora, handicapped as it was by
the yawning deficits of the treasury, which led the War Minister
to reduce the army almost to a peace footing in 1865, still found
itself obliged to move forward along the national path. The
chance for the freeing of Venetia arose at last through the jealousies of the Germanic powers themselves, and Bismarck's unscrupulous ambition achieved for Italy what Napoleon's faint-hearted-
ness had left undone. Ever since his accession to power in 1862,
Bismarck had manœuvred for a war of hegemony between Prussia
and Austria, and had shrewdly reckoned upon Italy as a possible
ally. In the bitterness of mood following on the September Convention the eyes of Italian patriots fastened themselves once more
on Venice, since Rome was denied them, and when in the early
spring of 1866 Bismarck made overtures for an Italian alliance
against Austria, La Marmora met him half-way. A treaty was
signed between Prussia and Italy at the end of March. Austria
offered in May to cede Venetia for the price of Italy's neutrality,
but La Marmora stood firm to his engagements, and war was
declared on June 20.
    Unfortunately La Marmora's military ability was not equal to
the honesty of his administration. While Prussia marched to her
astonishing victory at Sadowa [July 3], the Italian armies, victims
of a divided command and of a consequent lack of driving power,
suffered a severe check at Custoza [June 24], and though undefeated
were allowed to waste the ensuing fortnight in a fatal inaction. In
the interval Napoleon III., unwilling to see Austria crushed, proposed an armistice on the basis of the cession of Venetia to himself
and so to Italy [July 5]. But the offer was declined, and at length
the Italians under Cialdini pushed on with energy into Venetia,
while the Austrians fell back to cover Vienna. At the same time
Garibaldi, with a large force of volunteers, invaded the Trentino,
and General Medici, his comrade-in-arms from the days of Rome

onwards, advanced up the Val Sugana and compelled the Austrians to evacuate the southern part of that district. The Italian arms had partly regained the prestige lost at Custoza, when the news of a naval reverse suffered at Lissa [July 20] by the incompetent Admiral Persano sent a thrill of anger and shame through the country. La Marmora accepted a truce [July 25], and although Ricasoli, now once more Prime Minister, struggled hard for peace on the basis of *uti possidetis*, which would have secured the southern Trentino for Italy, neither Prussia nor France supported him, and he was compelled at length to accept the bare province of Venetia, without Trieste, Istria, or Trento, as a 'gift' from Napoleon.

In the first days of the war the difficult question of the dissolution of the monasteries had been settled by a measure, hurriedly passed through the Chamber, providing for the secularization and sale of monastic lands, and the disposal of the funds so acquired. In spite of the cry of robbery which the Act aroused,[1] Ricasoli still pursued his aim of an understanding with the Church on the lines of Cavour's proposals; but every attempt shipwrecked against the refusal of Pius to negotiate on any terms that would have recognized the King's authority in Naples or the Papal provinces. Ricasoli, however, belonged to the earnest school of reformers who believed that the feud between Church and State was fatal to the welfare of the country, and he made one more determined attempt, in his Free Church Bill, to bridge the gulf between the two powers. But neither the Church nor the democrats would have aught to say to his proposals, and after an unsuccessful appeal to the country Ricasoli once more resigned [April, 1867].

Much excitement had been aroused among the Party of Action by these proceedings, and when Ricasoli's fall brought back Rattazzi to power it was felt that a fresh chance had arisen for a

---

[1] When Mr. Gladstone was in Rome in the autumn of 1866 he was filled with apprehensions for the fate of the great monastery of Monte Cassino. 'It has, as you know,' he wrote to Sir James Lacaita, 'been pressed upon me that I should endeavour to make a respectful appeal to the Italian Government on this subject through the medium of a discussion in the House of Commons. But I shrink from taking such a course, as I fear that the general effect might be to present an appearance of intrusive and impertinent interference with the affairs of a foreign country, and that the very country towards which I should least wish to offer the appearance of a slight. I cannot likewise refuse to cherish the hope that the enlightened mind of Baron Ricasoli and his colleagues may lead them either to avert or mitigate the blow.' The blow was happily averted; Monte Cassino was declared a 'National Monument,' and, although destroyed in the Second World War, has been rebuilt since.

move on Rome. The French troops had evacuated the city, in accordance with the September Convention, in December, 1866, and the Garibaldians, smarting from the humiliations of the war of '66 and the abandonment of the Trentino to Austria, turned again to their watchword *Rome or Death*. Two revolutionary committees existed within Rome, the one Mazzinian and the other monarchical; but they lacked the spirit of 1849, and had never succeeded in baffling the Papal police sufficiently to procure a supply of arms. Assistance must therefore be brought to them from outside, and from the month of May, 1867, Garibaldi was collecting volunteers and making his plans for a rush to Rome. Rattazzi was universally supposed to be in favour of such a rush, though fear of France might force him to discountenance it; but the King was more cautious, or more honourable, and his respect for the September Convention, reinforced by his dislike as a Piedmontese for Rome and his shrinking as a Catholic from attacking the Pope, made him at best a lukewarm adherent of the enterprise. In an atmosphere of uncertainty and drift the preparations continued; but the attitude of France was uncompromising; and Rattazzi found it necessary to prove his *bona fides* by having Garibaldi arrested on September 23 and conveyed to Caprera. The Chief's lieutenants, however, continued their preparations with the connivance of the Ministry; on October 13 Napoleon threatened to intervene unless the movement were put down, and six days later Rattazzi, unable to persuade the King to go forward, saved himself by resignation from a coil of difficulties. To such a pass had this second-rate intriguer brought the national affairs. In the midst of the confusion Garibaldi escaped from Caprera [October 20] and joined his men on the Papal border; with about eight thousand volunteers he stormed Monte Rotondo and advanced on Rome. On the 29th he was close to the walls, but no movement occurred within the city, and the General, unlike the Garibaldi of old, gave the order to retire on Monte Rotondo. Meanwhile two French divisions had landed at Civitavecchia, and entered Rome on the 30th. Garibaldi decided to transfer his force, now much thinned by desertion, to Tivoli, but on the march thither he was attacked by Papal troops at Mentana, and finally overborne by the French regiments which came up in reserve [November 3, 1867]. His men broke and fled before the new French rifles, and Garibaldi himself was arrested by Italian regulars at the frontier and conveyed once more to Caprera. The whole affair was a bitter humiliation to the country, and when the French Foreign Minister announced in the Chamber that 'France would *never* allow Italy

GARIBALDI IN HIS "PUNCIO," 1860
From a photograph taken in Naples that autumn

to go to Rome' it was grimly felt that the debt for Magenta and Solferino had been wiped out. Napoleon's infatuation for the Temporal Power prepared the way not only for Italy's abandonment of his cause in 1870, but for the whole trend of feeling which led her at last into the Triple Alliance.

Pius IX. had triumphed at Mentana, by virtue of the French *chassepots*, and his Jesuit advisers were swift to take advantage of the situation so created. While the French troops remained to occupy Civitavecchia and so ensured to the Papal Government a certain immunity from insurrection, the Jesuits evolved the grandiose idea of the summoning of an Œcumenical Council to establish the Pope's authority on a basis unassailable to all futurity. The first intention had been to cause such a Council to proclaim the necessity of the Temporal Power as a dogma, but this was finally abandoned in favour of a more all-embracing proposition—that of the Infallibility of the Pope. The Council assembled in St. Peter's on December 8, 1869, and it was soon apparent that although much opposition to the dogma existed, especially among the French and German Bishops, it was an opposition not to the *truth* but only to the *expediency* of the definition. Still, so formidable was the stand made by the 'Inopportunists,' as they were called, that although unsupported by their governments they succeeded in protracting the sittings of the Council for over six months, and it needed all the pressure which the Vatican knew so well how to apply to bring them at last into something like unanimity. Thus it occurred that in spite of the efforts of the most learned Catholics of the day—Acton, Döllinger, Hefele, Dupanloup—and of the distant rumblings of the Gladstonian thunder,[1] the party of Papal despotism prevailed, and the Decree of Infallibility was proclaimed on July 18, 1870, by 533 votes to 2. Fifty-five prelates absented themselves from the final session, and signed a humble protest.

On the very day after the promulgation of the Vatican Decrees, Napoleon III. declared war upon the King of Prussia. Victor Emanuel would fain have gone to his assistance, remembering the French blood shed for Italy in 1859, but the Roman Question barred the way. Not even to buy a new alliance would the Emperor —and still less the Empress—throw over the Temporal Power, while Italian sentiment, still smarting from Mentana, was openly and angrily on the side of Prussia. The Garibaldians were stirring

---

[1] Mr. Gladstone's famous pamphlet, *The Vatican Decrees in their bearing on Civil Allegiance*, was not published until 1874, but during the whole course of the Council he carried on an active correspondence with Lord Acton.

Y

once more, and the King's two principal ministers, Giovanni Lanza and Quintino Sella, saw that unless the government led the way the Revolution would be in Rome before them. Events came to reinforce their decision. France staggered under the blows of Wörth, Weissenburg, and Gravelotte; her troops were withdrawn from Civitavecchia on August 19 and Napoleon sent his cousin Jerome to plead for military aid at the price of a complete abandonment of the Papal cause. But it was too late. The news of Sedan reached Florence on September 3, and the Italian army marched for Rome, not Paris. The Cabinet informed the governments of England, France, Prussia, and Austria of their intention to occupy the Papal territories, and not a finger was lifted by any of these to save the Infallible Pope. Victor Emanuel made one more attempt to win over Pius to a voluntary surrender, but the old man spurned his offers. Then the order to advance was given, and on September 20, after a few hours' bombardment, the Italian troops entered their capital by the breach at the Porta Pia. To the last the country was disappointed in its hope of a rising within Rome itself.

For a moment it seemed as though Pius would accept the proffered 'Law of Guarantees,' which secured him in all his spiritual privileges and authority. But once more narrower counsels prevailed, and he decided instead to ignore the existence of the Italian State and to adopt the reproachful part of 'Prisoner of the Vatican.' Pius IX. and his Cardinals were seen no more in the streets of Rome, and the Italian people, with their eyes set on new destinies, took their place among the free nations of modern Europe.

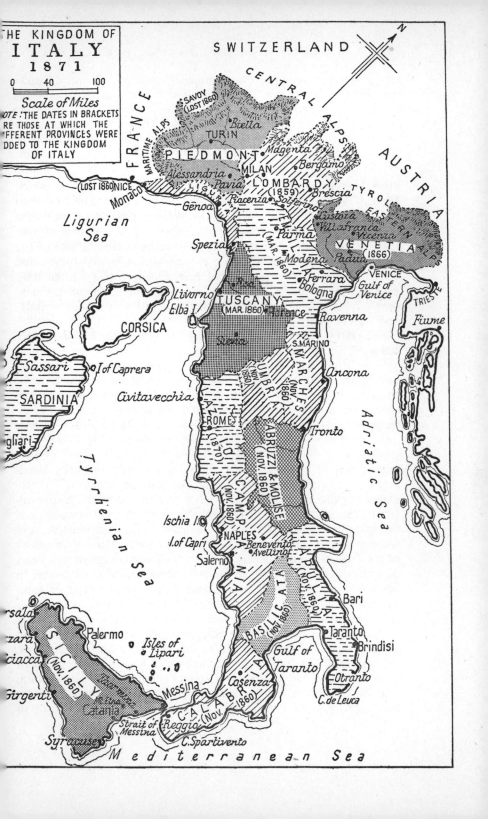

THE KINGDOM OF
ITALY
1871

0   40   100

Scale of Miles

NOTE: THE DATES IN BRACKETS
ARE THOSE AT WHICH THE
DIFFERENT PROVINCES WERE
ADDED TO THE KINGDOM
OF ITALY

SWITZERLAND

N

CENTRAL ALPS

AUSTRIA

SAVOY
(LOST 1860)

FRANCE

MARITIME ALPS

Biella

TURIN

PIEDMONT

Magenta

MILAN

Bergamo

LOMBARDY
(1859)

Brescia

TYROL

EASTERN ALPS

(LOST 1860) NICE

Monaco

LIGURIA

Alessandria

Pavia

Piacenza

Solferino

Genoa

Custoza
Villafranca

Vicenza

VENETIA
(1866)

*Ligurian
Sea*

Spezia

Parma

(MAR. 1860)

Modena

Padua

Ferrara
Bologna

VENICE

*Gulf of
Venice*

TRIESTE

Livorno

Elba I.

TUSCANY
(MAR. 1860)

Florence

Ravenna

Fiume

CORSICA

Siena

S.MARINO

MARCHES

Ancona

Sassari

I. of Caprera

Civitavecchia

UMBRIA
(NOV.
1860)

*Adriatic
Sea*

SARDINIA

Cagliari

ROME
(1870)

Tronto

ABRUZZI
& MOLISE
(NOV. 1860)

Tyrrhenian Sea

CAMPANIA

Ischia I.

I. of Capri

NAPLES

Benevento
Avellino

Salerno

APULIA
(NOV. 1860)

Bari

BASILICATA
(NOV. 1860)

Taranto

Brindisi

*Gulf of
Taranto*

Otranto

Marsala

SICILY
(Nov. 1860)

Palermo

*Isles of
Lipari*

Messina

Cosenza
(1860)

C. de Leuca

Sciacca

Etna

CALABRIA
(Nov.

Girgenti

Catania

Reggio

*Strait of
Messina*

Syracuse

C. Spartivento

Mediterranean Sea

CHAPTER XXXI
United Italy

Per damna, per caedes, ab ipso
Ducit opes animumque ferro. HORACE, *Odes*, Bk. IV.

THUS was created. that third Italy—*la Terza Italia*—for which
Mazzini had toiled and suffered, and to which he had looked to
crown the work already accomplished for the world by the Rome
of the Cæsars and the Rome of the Popes. After the lapse of over
half a century it may be possible to attempt some estimate of the
result achieved, through so many years of battle, conspiracy and
effort, by the mighty impulse of *Risorgimento*. Has United Italy
proved worthy of the giants who fashioned her, and can she now
rebuke Mazzini's bitter cry, 'I thought to call up the soul of Italy,
and I see only its corpse'?

For thirty years after the taking of Rome the Italian people
laboured in the trough of the wave that had carried them to
victory. They looked in vain for the prosperity which the patriots
had promised them, and an age of industrial revolution brought
to the proletariat new sufferings which their earlier simplicity had
spared them. The South remained a cruel drag upon the more
progressive North; taxation was heavy and its incidence unjust;
year after year—save for a brief interval from 1875 to 1881—a
gaping deficit in every Budget swelled the national debt. Capital
expenditure of every kind—in railways, in roads, in public buildings—was forced upon the young kingdom, in order to knit together her diverse populations and to put an end to the mediæval-
ism of the South and Centre. But for many years it seemed as if
the taxpayers' millions were condemned to lie unproductive, and
were powerless to evoke the latent enterprise and inventive genius
of the Italians. Not so easily was the terrible heritage of 350 years
of oppression and misrule to be lived down, and if the labourer in
Lombardy and the South still remained in a chronic state of semi-
starvation; if political corruption fastened on the machine of
government and hampered every effort to develop the national
resources, the cause must be sought in the hard fate which had
given Italy to be exploited for so long by alien and selfish races.
The genius of the Italians had flowered for a time in the group of
great men who had guided their different sections to the common
goal, but the effort itself produced exhaustion. It is small wonder
that when Cavour's generation had all passed away a race of

politicians arose whose only care was to surmount the difficulties of each day, and who were not too fastidious in the means they employed for the purpose. Agostino Depretis, the first Premier after Rattazzi produced by the Left or so-called Progressive parties, held office with two brief interruptions from 1876 to 1887, but although he extended the Parliamentary franchise he also developed the system known as Transformism, which consisted in buying the votes of this or that Parliamentary group by luring its leaders into the Government. The result was that the already indeterminate lines of party division disappeared altogether and the Chamber became the home of an unscrupulous opportunism. Francesco Crispi, who followed Depretis, carried the art of applying Government pressure at the elections to a height never before attempted, and for all his republican antecedents ruled the country with a cynical disregard for its hard-won liberties. The neglect of the politicians of the Left to further the interests of the working-classes during this period produced an unhappy cleavage between Government and people, and a militant Socialist party arose on the ruins of the Mazzinian idealists, pledged to fight for the material welfare of the workers.

In the meantime the attitude of the Papacy towards the Kingdom of Italy had undergone no serious modification, and even at the end of the reign of Leo XIII., the 'Diplomatic Pope,' in 1903, Church and State still seemed divided by an impassable gulf on the Roman Question. The Law of Guarantees had remained a unilateral obligation, never accepted by the Pope; the Black aristocracy of Rome had kept up an attitude of haughty seclusion and held no traffic with the Quirinal, while for a whole generation the Papal Decree of *Non Expedit* had decreed the abstention of Catholic voters from taking part in Parliamentary elections. Victor Emanuel and Pius IX. had both died in 1878, but the new reigns of Umberto and of Leo XIII. respectively brought very little *rapprochement*, though attempts at conciliation were made by one or two eminent clerics during the later 'eighties. These were wrecked principally upon the opposition of the non-Italian Catholic world, which favoured the state of schism as prolonging the weakness of Italy in foreign affairs, and dreaded to see the Papacy sink to the position, in Bismarck's words, of a 'Chaplaincy of the House of Savoy.' Italian anti-clericalism helped to widen the breach, and incidents like the rioting at the translation of the remains of Pius IX. from the Lateran to San Lorenzo in 1881 let loose the bitterest passions. Under the long ascendancy of the Left, from Depretis to the fall of Crispi (1876—96), the Masonic Order, historic emanation of

French revolutionary atheism, established itself at the sources of political power in Rome. Yet in spite of all, common sense and the passage of time served to modify bitterness on both sides, so that although the front door of the Vatican remained closed to the Kingdom of Italy, it was said that the back and side doors were always accessible to her officials. Leo XIII.'s successor, the Venetian Pius X., practically withdrew the *Non Expedit*, in order to combat the increasing strength of the anti-Catholic Socialist party; but he also withdrew his Nuncio from France to mark his disapproval of the visit of President Loubet to Victor Emanuel III. in Rome [1904].

If the internal history of Italy during the last thirty years of the century is so largely the chronicle of an unhappy social struggle, the record of her foreign relations shows the same elements of drift and uncertainty, the same failure to attain to a dignified and solid position. The events of 1866—70 had left her with a legacy of ill-feeling towards France as well as Austria, and after the Franco-Prussian War neither the platonic friendship of England nor the growing patronage of Bismarck availed to redress the balance. At the Congress of Berlin, held to revise the results of the Russo-Turkish War of 1877, Italy failed to secure a revision of the arrangement of 1866, and while Austria received a mandate to occupy Bosnia and Herzegovina, Italy found herself unable to raise the question of her frontiers or to claim any compensating advantage in the Balkans. Her statesmen at this period were of mediocre stamp, and the part played by Cavour at the Congress of Paris was not for them. France on the other hand had received the secret approval of the other Powers for her scheme to occupy Tunis, and in 1881 the occupation became an accomplished fact in despite of Italian public opinion. The deep resentment felt by Italy at this action of her neighbour's found expression in the next year in a definite drawing towards Germany and Austria, and on May 20, 1882, the Government of Depretis signed a secret agreement with the two Empires, which has gone ever since by the name of the Triple Alliance. In its earliest form the Treaty was simply the adhesion of Italy to the defensive alliance formed between Germany and Austria in 1879, but on its renewal in 1887 a further clause was inserted between Italy and Austria which declared the right of either power to compensation if the other made territorial acquisitions in the Balkans (Clause VII.). This was the form in which the Treaty subsisted down to its denunciation by Italy in May, 1915.

Thus was Italy yoked to her two Teutonic neighbours, from

one of whom she had received nothing but injury in the past, while from the other she was to receive that gift of 'economic penetration' which had its political dangers as well as its economic advantages. For a time the alliance gave her a sense of stability and of recognition which made it acceptable to the masses, but this was counterbalanced, especially in the eyes of a growing Nationalist party, by the implied abandonment of the cause of the 'Irredentists' in the Trentino, Trieste, and the little Venetian towns along the Dalmatian coast. The Government of Vienna would brook no encouragement by her ally of the machinations of these disinherited Italians, and the Austrian police frequently requested the assistance of the Italian in hunting out the agitators. Irredentism, which had produced many outbreaks throughout the seventies, and especially in 1879, died down temporarily into a sullen undercurrent, and the Austrian Government pursued with impunity its well-known arts of cultural and political persecution against the Italian remnant. Meanwhile the effects of the Triple Alliance showed themselves in another direction in a dangerous tension between Italy and France, and the disastrous tariff war which followed the denunciation of the commercial treaty between them in 1886 brought widespread ruin to the Italian industries affected.

The rebuff which Italy had sustained in the affair of Tunis led her to seek other opportunities for colonial expansion in more distant parts of Africa. The name of Francesco Crispi—conspirator, demagogue, and at length all-powerful dictator—is inseparably bound up with the tragic adventure of Abyssinia, when a young and untried army, ill-provided for tropical warfare, was lashed on by telegrams from home to find its bloody grave at Adowa [March, 1896]. The horror of that spring in Italy, when the dispatch of reinforcements produced riots in every part of the country, and peasant-women threw themselves in front of the trains that were to bear their conscripts away, sank deep into the minds of all who beheld it. Crispi fell before the universal cry of rage, and his ambitious design of an Abyssinian protectorate dwindled to the more manageable reality of an 'Erythrean Colony.' But the profound unrest produced by the campaign found vent in a growing social agitation, blindly repressed by a reactionary Government, and the Milanese massacres of May, 1898 (the so-called *Fatti di Maggio)*, brought to a head the seething animosity between governors and governed. The party of the Extreme Left took up the popular cause, and by its prolonged and violent struggle in the Chamber against the Ministry's demand for extraordinary powers stemmed the tide of reaction, and produced at length a saner atmosphere. King Humbert, good-natured, but perhaps too much identified with the reactionaries, fell a victim to an anarchist's bullet in July, 1900, and his successor, Victor Emanuel III., realized at once that Italy's only hope lay in a policy of 'Trust the people.' He called the moderate Left once more to power, and with the Ministry of Giovanni Giolitti [February, 1901] began that era of advancing prosperity which continued down to the outbreak of the Great War.

For in spite of high taxation, bad government, and industrial unrest, the patient, hard-working people of the peninsula had contrived even during this period to advance along the path of economic progress. When the introduction of machinery caused the inevitable crisis in the labour-market, a vast movement of emigration set in which sent thousands of Italy's best men to build railways in North America or to develop Brazil and the Argentine Republic, and the mother-country soon benefited from the stream of remittances that flowed back across the Atlantic at a time when her industrial organisation was still unable to absorb her growing man-power. Italy thus lost a large population, too exclusively proletarian to make homogeneous colonies abroad, especially in the United States, but at least she built few Wigans, Bethnal Greens or Poplars. And when under Giolitti's long ascendancy the weight of Government persecution was lifted from the working classes, when labour found itself free to organize and even to strike, and wages rose from one end of the peninsula to the other, prosperity took the long-awaited stride. The budgets of Minister Luzzatti [1903—1906] showed surpluses; the state took over the whole railway system from two incompetent companies [1905], and gradually brought the running up to a higher level of efficiency; while the steady exploitation of Italy's water power produced electric installations which have since bade fair to compensate for the national lack of coal. The intelligence and perseverance of the Italian, struggling against both the forces of nature and the political corruption which so often robbed him of the fruits of his labour, at length carried the country through the most dangerous years. But if Giolitti's sagacity brought peace and comparative prosperity to the nation at large, the cynicism with which he managed the political machine and disposed of Government patronage fatally undermined the public confidence in Parliamentary institutions, and prepared the way for the distant yet sure reaction.

To the foreign observer of Italy's policy it seemed that the same cynicism attended Giolitti's declaration of war on Turkey, in September, 1911, on the question of Tripoli; but to the Italian this appeared merely as the logical outcome of England's establishment in Egypt and of the French and Spanish occupation of Morocco, recently confirmed after the Agadir incident. Italy's special interest in Tripoli and Cyrenaica had been recognized in international agreements. The advent of the Young Turks to power had also precipitated matters, since these adopted a policy of pin-pricks against Italian interests in Libya which was bound to produce exasperation in Italy; so that when Giolitti launched his well-prepared campaign he had far greater support from public opinion that Crispi had ever enjoyed for the Abyssinian adventure. The war dragged on for over a year, having led in its later stages to the occupation by Italy of twelve of the Ægean islands, now collectively known as the Dodecanese. Finally Turkey, already menaced in other quarters, recognized in the Treaty of Ouchy [October, 1912] Italy's annexation of Tripoli and Cyrenaica.

When the war was over the Italians may well have thought that they could rest on their achievements, having vindicated their country's position as a Great Power and readjusted the Mediterranean balance in her favour. But it was not to be. The Balkan Confederation against Turkey had been formed during 1912, and the outcome of the Balkan Wars, by aggrandizing Serbia and Greece at the expense of Bulgaria and Turkey, was to set the Central Empires scheming for redress on the grand scale. Already in 1913 Austria sounded Italy as to whether she would support her in an attack on Serbia, and only the firm refusal of Giolitti and his Foreign Minister, the Marquis of San Giuliano, postponed the outbreak of war for another year. In March, 1914, Giolitti gave place to a Ministry of the Right, led by the able and much-respected Antonio Salandra, but the majority in the Chamber remained Giolittian, and Giolitti's Foreign Minister retained his portfolio in the new Government until his death some seven months later. When therefore the European crisis came with the Austrian ultimatum to Serbia on July 24th, only one thing was clear—that Italy, which had not been consulted by Austria before the despatch of the ultimatum, was not bound by the *casus fœderis* to support her Teutonic allies. Salandra announced her neutrality at the opening of hostilities, thereby freeing a large number of French troops on the Alpine frontier to take part in the defence of their country against Germany.

But neutrality alone was not sufficient to maintain the good name of Italy either in the eyes of Italians themselves or among the nations of the world. A strong current of public opinion immediately formed itself in favour of intervention, not on the side

of the Triple Alliance, but on that of the Triple Entente. Nationalists, Reformists, Socialists, and a section of the Liberals ranged
themselves in unwonted alliance to promote the cause, while Giolitti and his majority in the Chamber, supported by large sections
of the commercial and business interests, stood for neutrality. All
through the winter of 1914—1915 the controversy raged, while
the serious deficiency in military stores and artillery, judged by
the standards set in France during that winter, was partly but
insufficiently rectified by General Cadorna. In the spring of 1915
the crisis approached. For many weeks Baron Sidney Sonnino
(who had succeeded San Giuliano at the Foreign Office) carried on
his elaborate negotiations with Vienna, demanding the Trentino,
Gorizia and the northern Dalmatian islands, with the autonomy of
Trieste, as the 'compensation' due to Italy under Art. VII. of the
Triple Alliance. But while feeling in the country rose steadily in
favour of war, Austria, with fatal obstinacy, allowed every favourable moment to pass. The Austrians were not to know that direct
negotiations were proceeding simultaneously with the Entente for
Italy's participation in the war on the side of Great Britain, France,
and Russia.

Baron Sonnino, a man whose inflexibility of purpose and immense staying-power, combined with a clear if limited vision, were
to impress themselves deeply on the conduct of affairs in Italy,
felt that if the heavy responsibility of guiding his country into the
war were laid upon him, he must see to it that she should emerge
from the ordeal with the full security to North and East which
she had never yet possessed. He therefore stipulated with the
Entente that in the event of victory Italy's Alpine frontier should
be carried to the Brenner Pass, and that on the north-east she
should receive Trieste, Istria, the islands of Cherso and Lussin, and
a narrow strip, some 110 kilometres long, of the northern portion
of Dalmatia. Further south, the islands of Curzola were also to go
to Italy to remove the naval menace from her own indefensible
eastern coast. The islands of the Dodecanese were to be formally
annexed. But the little port of Fiume, in spite of its Italian population, was to be left, at Russia's express desire, to the future Croatia.
A Treaty embodying these conditions was signed in London on
April 26th, 1915, between Italy on the one hand and Great Britain,
France, and Russia on the other, and has become known as the
Pact of London.

These terms, as the reader of today can easily perceive, were
designed to complete Italian unity and to protect her frontiers

against the Austrian Empire, the survival of which was not then doubted by Italian statesmen. They were kept secret—even it seems from Giolitti—until the Russian Soviet Government, late in 1917, discovered and published them. When therefore certain active sections among the Italian people began to take matters into their own hands, in the month of May, they were ignorant of the precise bargain made on their behalf by their Foreign Minister. But the treatment of Belgium by Germany had already made a profound impression on them; the call of the 'unredeemed' Italians of Trento and Trieste affected them powerfully, and they watched with growing anger the attempts of Prince von Bülow, Germany's Special Envoy, to negotiate with the Opposition when he found Salandra and Sonnino deaf to his belated promises of concessions at Austria's expense. Then, on May 8th, came the news of the sinking of the *Lusitania*, and simultaneously the public became aware of the intrigues of Herr Erzberger with the Giolittians in the Chamber for the overthrow of Salandra's Government by refusing credits for the war. It was the culminating moment. In the famous Days of May (Giornate di Maggio) the mob descended into the market-place and overruled the Parliamentary majority. Signor Salandra had actually resigned on May 13th, foreseeing an adverse vote in the Chamber, but the mass demonstrations that took place throughout the country on the two following days convinced the King that Italy was ready to confirm the decision he had already made the previous month. On the 16th he reinstated Salandra in office; on the 20th the Chamber, overborne by this combination of Court and mob, endowed the Government with the full powers for which they asked by 407 votes to 74, and at midnight on the 23rd Italy declared war on Austria. Nothing could more fitly symbolize the fact that this, to the Italian of those days, was to be the last War of the Risorgimento, than the vast procession, many scores of thousands strong, which filed past the British Embassy on that memorable Sunday [May 23rd] headed by a slender band of old men clad in Garibaldian red shirts. As the throng surged around the British Ambassador,[1] clasping his hand and even pressing his cheek, the unspoken thought was written on the faces of those simple folk, that as England had stood by Italy then, so Italy would now march side by side with England.

A War of Risorgimento it appeared at least to the more intelligent and patriotic section of the population, but Italy suf-

[1] Sir Rennell Rodd.

fered far more than either France or England from the cleavage
of opinion symbolized by the state of the Chamber, in which, as
we have seen, more than half the Deputies had been neutralist.
Apart from certain groups, the Socialists, unlike their brethren in
France and Germany, were against the war; the Church, and with
it a section of the aristocracy, was more in sympathy with the
political ideals of the Central Powers than with the democratic
aims proclaimed by the Allies; and the peasant, little instructed in
politics or in the affairs of the outside world, found himself taken
from his home and exposed to sufferings undreamed of before,
in a cause which he but little understood. Yet his patient valour
made possible the gradual advance of the Italian armies on the
Isonzo front; the taking of Gorizia [August, 1916], and the pressing
back of the Austrian forces a year later on the blood-soaked Carso
and on the Bainsizza plateau,—a success which seemed to promise
an advance towards Laybach. Even so the cost of these twenty-
eight months of incessant fighting had been appalling, and was the
more severely felt as the value of Italy's contribution seemed
hardly to be appreciated in allied countries. Then, when the
Italian effort was spent and a deadlock seemed to have been
reached, a thrust made by certain fresh German divisions in the
quiet sector of Caporetto, where a couple of semi-mutinous bat-
talions from Turin had sought to fraternize with the enemy, suddenly carried all before it. The Italian front was pierced and
turned, and a general retreat became inevitable. But as those
agonizing days wore on and the advance of the Austro-Germans
became ever more menacing, the spirit of the Italian people
rallied and the country settled down to resistance with a grim
determination unseen since the beginning of the war. At the
Piave River, emerging from the Alps along the skirts of Monte
Grappa and the Montello, and covering Venice by a very narrow
margin, the troops were halted and reorganized, while five British
and six French divisions[1] were hurried to Italy to lend support.
These troops, however, did not reach their positions on the Piave
until December, so that the Italian armies, hastily reinforced by
the levies of the youngest class, bore the full brunt of the Austrian
attack between Brenta and Piave during November, and showed
by their heroic stand that no invasion of the Lombard Plain would
be permitted. Behind these lads the population worked and endured privations both of food and fuel with a stoic patience, until
at last, in June, 1918, the tide of victory turned. Repulsed in their
six-days' attempt to cross the Piave, the Austrian forces, fifty-nine

[1] Gradually reduced in 1918 to three and two respectively.

divisions strong, fell back on the defensive, while in France and in the Balkans those victorious advances began which might not have taken place for another year if the main Austrian army had not been held in Italy. Then, last of all, the Italian troops themselves moved forward, and pressed the Teutonic forces back over the mountains and the river. The colossal victory of Vittorio Veneto[1] reversed the racial tendencies of fifteen centuries, and the Italians found themselves reoccupying both the Roman city of Trieste and the great highway to the north down which Barbarossa had been wont to ride with his feudal host. On November 3rd, 1918, the armistice was signed which ended Italy's three and a half years of war.

But if the losses and sacrifices of these years had been almost greater than any country so newly knit together and so relatively poor as Italy could have endured, the miseries of the first two years of peace left a still more bitter impression upon the minds of the people. When the Delegates to the Peace Conference met in Paris, Italy found her now greater claims in the Adriatic opposed by no less a champion than President Wilson, whose uncompromising pronouncements in favour of Yugoslav rights, while those of the Germans in Czecho-Slovakia, the Ruthenians in Poland and the Magyars in Roumania went unnoticed, caused profound mortification amongst Italians. At one moment, during the peace negotiations, the Italian Delegation withdrew from Paris, and the whole country applauded their action. At another, the American Ambassador in Rome, Mr. Nelson Page, hastened to Paris with the object of placing certain considerations before his chief, but was never granted an audience by the President, and after a long period of fruitless waiting withdrew and soon afterwards sent in his resignation. At length, however, the Treaty of St. Germain was signed between the Allies and Austria, confirming the dismemberment of the Empire and allotting to Italy the Trentino and South Tyrol; but the Italian frontier as against the new Kingdom of Yugoslavia was left to be settled by direct negotiation between the two parties. Before, however, these negotiations could be opened, the poet-leader Gabriele D'Annunzio had created a 'new fact' by taking forcible possession of the port of Fiume, at the head of a band of mutinous soldiers, adventurers, and

---

[1] 51 Italian divisions, 3 British, 2 French, 1 Czecho-Slovak and 1 American regiment were engaged against 73 Austrian divisions. On November 4th, General Diaz reported that 300,000 prisoners had already been taken and 'not less than 5,000 guns.'

patriots, who in the general disillusion rallied gladly to his leadership. Inspired by a profound dislike and distrust of the Allies and of all politicians, D'Annunzio remained as the thorn in the side of the negotiators throughout the year 1920, ruling his little republic in the name of Italy and resisting all attempts at compromise. In the end, however, he was obliged to yield to a display of force. Signor Orlando, who had been Prime Minister at the time of Caporetto and the Armistice, had given place to the Radical Nitti in June, 1919, and Nitti, after an unsuccessful attempt to settle the Adriatic question on moderate lines, had fallen a victim to internal difficulties in June, 1920. The way was thereby cleared for the return of Giolitti, who was determined to effect a settlement at all costs. President Wilson was by this time removed from the scene; France and England were sincerely in favour of any reasonable settlement, and it was in a serener atmosphere than any yet experienced that the plenipotentiaries of Italy and Yugoslavia met at Rapallo in November, 1920. The result of their labours was the so-called Treaty of Rapallo, by which in return for the renunciation of Dalmatia, Italy secured a good strategic frontier on the eastern side of Istria, the town and district of Zara and two of the larger islands in the north and two in the centre of the Dalmatian archipelago. The Italians of the coast towns were to be allowed to claim Italian citizenship, and the independence of Fiume and its district—the ancient *corpus separatum*—was recognized by both parties. This last condition, however, implied the expulsion of D'Annunzio, a feat which was duly accomplished in the last days of December, 1920, by General Caviglia and a mere threat of force.

But even so the vicissitudes of Fiume were not yet at an end. The little port, whose commerce had already been extinguished by D'Annunzio's occupation, remained silent and grass-grown under the new régime of the 'Free State.' It was to no one's interest to use it, and the realities of the situation were at last recognized in the agreement concluded between the Italian and Yugoslav Governments at Rome on January 27th, 1924, by which the city, port and territory of Fiume were annexed to Italy, and the adjoining harbour of Porto Barros to Yugoslavia. Thus, after five years of controversy, the two most important provisions of the Treaty of London were reversed by mutual consent. Dalmatia, with its Slavonic population, was exchanged for Fiume, and Italy included within her frontiers almost all her scattered *irredenti*.

The difficulties and disillusions of these years in the field of foreign politics were matched by equally disastrous experiences at home. Industries wholly unsuited to the country had been forced on Italy by the war, and these could not survive the restoration of peace. Their cessation produced wide unemployment and misery, much intensified by the rise in prices consequent on the depreciation of the *lira*, which during the war had been artificially kept steady by international agreement. These causes combined to produce a profound discontent among the masses and to turn their eyes towards Russia, where the Dictatorship of the Proletariat was in full progress. In 1919 and 1920 some people feared that Italy came near to following in Russia's footsteps. Strikes for ever-increasing wages to match the ever-increasing rise in prices followed each other in quick succession, and acquired a definitely political colour with the postal and railway strikes of the early part of 1920. Signor Nitti's Government, much in awe of the 156 Socialists returned at the Election of November, 1919, temporized and tried to buy off the strikers by concessions and amnesties; but the situation rapidly deteriorated; the budget showed a deficit of 14 milliards of *lire*, and Nitti, after two previous attempts at resignation, finally abandoned his impossible task in June, 1920. He was succeeded, as we have seen, by Giolitti, whose principal achievements were the evacuation of Albania by Italian troops; the gradual abolition of the bread subsidy, which was costing the nation six milliards of *lire* per annum; the Treaty of Rapallo; and the masterly inactivity with which he watched the industrial crisis of August—September, 1920, known as the Occupation of the Factories. This was originally a movement of resistance by the great Metallurgical Trade Union to a threatened lock-out by the employers in the engineering factories of Milan, but it spread sporadically through Lombardy and Piedmont and even to other parts of Italy. In some workshops arms were stored and the red flag was flown, but since the authorities sent no troops against the men, little blood was shed. After a few weeks the movement collapsed owing to the inability of the strikers to conduct the business side of the undertakings, to replenish stores or to effect sales. Giolitti was much blamed for his failure to provide police protection for the factories, some of which were seriously damaged, and for the settlement which he finally negotiated, involving some recognition of the principle of control by the workers; but in reality the failure of the experiment itself had made a deep impression, which was augmented by a very unsatisfactory report of the situation in Russia received from delegates whom the Italian Socialists had sent to investigate conditions there. The result was a deep cleavage in the Socialist party, an end to all hopes of revolution, and a definite tendency towards reaction.

In the meantime a new movement had been gathering strength which was destined to carry out, though in an opposite sense, the revolution dreamed of by the Communists. After Caporetto the patriotic parties in the Chamber had formed an alliance to which they gave the name of *Fascio Parlamentare*, in allusion to the *fasces* or bundles carried by the Roman lictors. The name then spread to certain groups throughout the country, formed to counteract the defeatism which had so nearly brought about disaster, and was finally adopted by a leader of remarkable antecedents and strong personal ascendancy, Benito Mussolini, who organized the first of his *Fasci di Combattimento* in March, 1919. An ex-editor of a Socialist newspaper, a man of the people and a Republican, Mussolini had yet changed his mind in time to support the war and had himself been wounded. The ideals of these earliest *Fascisti* consisted in a kind of patriotic Socialism, equally directed against war profiteers and industrialists on the one side and against Communist strikers or town-councillors on the other. Basically, perhaps, it was just a rude attempt to capture power with whatever policy. Mussolini was a believer in swifter methods than those of law and liberty, and his followers succeeded, when once they took cruel and violent action on a large scale in the autumn of 1920, in breaking the Socialist monopoly of local government.

Their leader himself hovered between Socialism and Nationalism, but the force of circumstances drew him irresistibly towards the latter, with its inevitable concomitant of an alliance with the bourgeois and capitalist classes; yet he exacted his price for the alliance in the shape of a paper pledge in favour of the Eight Hours Day. From the autumn of 1921 onwards he acted definitely in harmony with the Nationalist party, while his followers, increasing in numbers and in organization, routed the Communists in the countryside and exemplified once more the truth of that terrible saying of Villani's: 'It is the custom in the cities of Lombardy for men to assemble and fight on the piazza of the commonwealth.' But the new militia claimed to fight in the name of order and discipline and of the doctrine that work alone must be Italy's salvation, and if their methods seemed sometimes to belie these ideals, it was the view of many competent observers that nothing but violence would have met the case. As time went on, however, it became apparent that Italy was suffering from a still deeper ill than that of these civil broils. For the central government seemed to have abdicated its powers, and as Bonomi followed Giolitti and

Facta followed Bonomi, the hand of authority grew ever feebler and Parliament fell into ever greater disrepute. It was Italy's fate that at this juncture no inheritor of Cavour's tradition arose to uphold the authority of law and to show that strong government was compatible with liberty of speech and person. Italy drifted instead towards her old ideal of the *Capitano del Popolo*. The growing paralysis of the central government at length offered Mussolini his supreme chance. In October, 1922, his Black-shirts converged upon Rome, and nothing but military action could have stemmed the tide. The King refused to authorize such action; Mussolini was summoned from Milan, and this ex-Republican, who only a month before had announced his acceptance of the Monarchy, received from Victor Emanuel the seals of office. The Fascist Revolution was accomplished—big with new and perhaps unhappy destinies for Italy.

To appraise the value of so recent and so complex a phenomenon is not yet within the power of the historian. It may, however, be recorded here, in bare outline, that the avowed object of the Fascist State was to root out all traces of what, in Fascist eyes, was the corrupt and inefficient Liberal-Democratic régime that preceded it, so that a progressive modification of the *Statuto* of 1848 took place until no vestige of a freely-elected Parliament, or liberty of speech, person or press remained to the Italian subject. The whole basis of the State was shifted; it was no longer democratic, but corporative. Every trade and profession was—in theory—organized in a hierarchy of *syndicates*, which were the sole legally recognized bodies in the labour world and were based on the principle that labour is the first duty of the citizen, and were entitled in return to the protection of the State. The Syndicates were even entrusted with the fundamental constitutional right of nominating the preliminary list of members of the new *Parlamento*; but the supreme power in the State was in reality vested in the *Capo dello Stato* (Head of the State) assisted by the Ministers and by the Fascist Grand Council. The position of the latter was regulated by a law of November, 1928. It consisted of some eighty members, most of whom were appointed for three years by Signor Mussolini, while a few held seats for life and a few were *ex-officio* members. Their function was to draw up the final list of 400 candidates for Parliament from among the 1,000 names handed in by the Syndicates; the list thus purged was then submitted to the national electorate—a restricted body composed only of those who were registered members of some Syndi-

z

cate—and voted upon Yes or No, no opposition list of candidates being allowed. To the Grand Council also belonged the task of supplying a vacancy in the Headship of the State, should such arise, by submitting a list of names to the King. The Parliament thus elected formed, with the Senate, the legislative authority in the State.

So vast and comprehensive a change as this, though inspired by the will of a single man, could not have been accomplished without the active co-operation of the people. The disappointments of the after-war period prepared the mass of Italians to accept with relief a strong and despotic government, and to give free rein to the pent-up forces of nationalism which the war and the struggle against Communism had engendered. The watchwords of Fascism were order, discipline, and the immolation of self in the service of the State; it had no use for a liberty which had become licence, or for a democratic form of government which was borrowed from overseas and seemed to have proved itself unsuited to the Italian temperament. Hence the gradual encroachment of the hand of authority on every department of life; the permeation of schools and universities by the Fascist rule, to the exclusion of all other ideals; the attempt at suppression of the Masonic Order and of the criminal Mafia in Sicily; an enhanced perception of the glory and dignity of Italy's great past, so that ancient buildings were treated with a new veneration and a fresh impulse was given to achæological research. Emigration was checked and an energetic campaign carried on for the development of the country's own resources and the restriction of imports from abroad. A high birth-rate was enjoined and the high destinies awaiting Italy's large and growing population preached in vague but resounding phrases by the national press.

But if the Fascist revolution was no doubt inspired by genuine ideals, it was as ruthless as any mediæval or renaissance tyrant in its methods of imposing them upon the recalcitrant. Being the child of violence and an avowed disbeliever in liberty and tolera- tion, it suppressed opposition by violent means, and not least by the impunity granted, through a long series of outrages, to Fascist murderers and bullies. A state of terror was thereby created which enforced silence upon opponents; but hatred remained, and a very bitter colony of anti-Fascist émigrés was domiciled in France. Thus was the current of Italian life divided, and the undoubted progress which Fascist energy and courage brought to the country was crossed by the shadow of a deep domestic rancour. The name of the Risorgimento was often invoked by Fascist orators, but the voice of Camillo di Cavour was heard no more in Italy.

Yet the great task to which Cavour had set his hand in vain in the months before his death was accomplished by his more fortunate successor. Mussolini's attitude towards the Church had, since his rise to power, been unexpectedly friendly. The crucifix was hung once more in the schools and religious instruction admitted to the curriculum within a few weeks of the march on Rome, and the suppression of the Masonic Order in 1926 produced a still closer *rapprochement*. As the destruction of the old Liberal and anti-clerical parties proceeded step by step, Mussolini felt himself strong enough to approach the crucial task. Negotiations for the definite settlement of the Roman question were opened in the strictest secrecy in August, 1926, between a single representative on either side—Monsignor Pacelli for the Vatican and Sig. Domenico Barone for the Italian Government. The two conditions laid down by the Vatican and accepted by Mussolini were, first, the reconstitution of a small Pontifical State, with the manifest and visible sovereignty of the Pontiff, and, secondly, the possibility of conferring on the religious marriage ceremony the full status of the civil rite. From these two germs sprang the Lateran Treaty, dealing with the territorial sovereignty of the Pope, and the Concordat, regulating the relations between the Catholic Church and the Kingdom of Italy. A settlement was at one time endangered by the dispute which arose in 1928 over Mussolini's suppression of the Catholic Boy Scouts—for the control of youth is a cardinal point in Fascist doctrine—but the forces in favour of reconciliation were strong enough to surmount the check. The two treaties, with a financial agreement liquidating the sums due from State to Pope under the Law of Guarantees, were signed on February 11th, 1929, by Cardinal Gasparri for the Church and Benito Mussolini for the Kingdom. Article 26 of the Treaty runs of follows:—

The Holy See considers that the agreements signed offer an adequate guarantee for assuring to it, together with the requisite liberty and independence, the pastoral administration of the Roman Diocese and of the Catholic Church throughout Italy and the entire world, and it declares the Roman Question to be definitely and irrevocably settled and therefore eliminated, and recognises the Kingdom of Italy under the Monarchy of the House of Savoy, with Rome as the capital of the Italian State.
Italy, on her part, recognises the State of the Vatican City under the sovereignty of the Supreme Pontiff.

After an interval of three months, during which the first election conducted on the system described above had been held, and all the forces of the Church had been mobilized in favour of the official List, the Treaty and Concordat were submitted to the Chamber and passed by 357 votes to 2. But it was noteworthy that in his speech on that occasion Mussolini gave deep offence at the Vatican, and incidentally much satisfaction to the anti-clerical remnant, by his references to the statue of Giordano Bruno, which would stay where it was in the Campo de' Fiori, and to that of Garibaldi on the Janiculan, whose horse's head would not be deflected an inch in its gaze towards St. Peter's. He even claimed that Garibaldi's great spirit was now placated, and that today the olive branch which Cavour had so ardently desired from the Vatican might be laid on the tomb of the great architect of Italian unity. Perhaps, however, he forgot Cavour's famous phrase, 'A Free Church in a Free State.' Freedom and power were given to the Church by the Lateran Treaty of 1929, as anyone may see who peruses the clauses of the Concordat, but Mussolini himself would have scorned the idea that a Free State had given them. Not a Free, but a Fascist State. From that antithesis might yet spring strange vicissitudes for the people of Shelley's 'sacred Italy.'

Epilogue

THIS reconciliation with the Church was perhaps Mussolini's most incisive and successful stroke of policy, and in the eyes of the Catholic population it must have removed any lingering scruples over the ethics and doctrine of his movement. The subsequent elections of 1929 appeared to give him an almost unanimous vote of confidence. By this time most non-Fascist groups and organisations had either been reconciled by skilful politics or ended by force. Mussolini used to boast of his admixture of the carrot and the stick; but the carrot predominated. Of course he developed all the usual apparatus of secret tribunals and penal settlements, and he had a dozen or more separate and even rival police forces working for different departments of state. But this persecution was more humane and more incompetent than its counterpart in Germany. There was nothing remotely like Hitler's slave camps and gas chambers. Racial persecution was not introduced until 1938, and even then was partial and ineffective. A few of the liberals went into exile, others were imprisoned, but the great majority went on living their ordinary lives without much let or hindrance.

On the whole, people seem to have been glad to sacrifice the trappings of freedom for what Fascism offered in the way of order and glory—until the suspicion grew that these too were but trappings. Inroads were made, little by little, upon the practice of representative government. Parliament was gradually altered out of recognition and given less and less work to do. Local elected councils and trial by jury were abolished. So far as possible this was done by degrees, so that people would not see quite how the old type of liberal government was giving way to a dictatorship. A revolution was thus effected almost unconsciously, and the irony of the situation was that so many future victims were deluded into helping the process. At first liberals and Christian Democrats even sat in the cabinet, and eleventh-hour converts from communism and socialism were soon numbered among the party bosses. For Mussolini tried to offer something to everyone: reconciliation to the Church, abolition of strikes to employers, a living wage to the poor, law and order to the many, corruption and profitable disorder to a select few, bread and circuses to everyone, and for good measure a glamorous policy of imperialist expansion to attract all true patriots.

Trying to please everyone is a difficult game to continue for long, and the inner contradictions would not stay hidden. For instance, it was not possible to plan for war at the same time as to mend Italy's economic situation and restore prosperity. Nor was it possible to find a social programme that would satisfy both Right and Left at once. Most people were pleased in theory at the restoration of order and authority in the life of the nation, but employers had not meant this to put an end to the system of free enterprise, nor did the workers like the loss of their union rights. The Church was glad to have confirmation of its privileged position in the state, but then the demands of a totalitarian system were bound to conflict with the Papal interest in education and the direction of consciences. Loyal monarchists were torn between the beneficial conservatism of the régime and its contemptuous disregard of the reigning monarch. The nationalists were over-joyed to find Italy once more feared in Europe, but had not bar-gained on paying the price of submission to Germany: for Musso-lini had to let Germany annex Austria, and this brought back a strong state to the other side of the Brenner frontier and so undid the one important gain to Italy from the war of 1915—18.

These internal contradictions were not haphazard, they were in a real sense typical of Fascism, as they were one reason for Mussolini's only partial success. Contrary to what one might have expected, there was no consistent theme except opportunism running through his policy and beliefs. In his time he had been a pacifist as well as a militarist, an opponent of imperialism as well as its champion, a republican as well as a monarchist, a revolutionary socialist as well as the man who saved Italy from revolutionary socialism, a notorious anti-clerical as well as the architect of the Vatican treaty. Frequent 'changes of guard' in the Fascist party were the outward sign of many inner changes of policy, according to whether he was more anxious at any one moment to make Fascism seem conservative or radical. In foreign policy, relations with Germany oscillated more than once between friendship and hostility. Sometimes there was good reason for these changes. But all too often they seem to have been made irresponsibly, for insufficient reason or no reason at all. The dictator was chiefly concerned to see that his movement should seem to be dynamic, at whatever cost in consistency. Putting the stress on action for its own sake, he was trying to cover up the fundamental lack of positive aim in what had been a mere con-quest of power. In the long run this irrationality and irresponsibility was to serve him ill, but it fooled most of the people for most of the time.

A further paradox is that his new experiment in dictatorship turned out to be so inefficient. In attempting to justify his conquest of power it was easy to make large claims about restoring order and efficiency; but these claims were more easily said than made good. No expense was spared to make the main tourist trains run on time, and to drain those marshes near Rome that visitors might happen to hear about; but this was politically rather than economically effective, and an ostentatious expense over such window-dressing could by no means entirely conceal the onset of financial ruin. An adverse balance of trade continued, if it did not become worse; unemployment can have improved but little, despite the half-hearted attempt to bring in a planned economy; there was a real decline in the standard of living of the people. The more important problems of the country were barely touched. Fascism failed to make much impression on the 'southern problem'. It even added to the scourge of overpopulation, by making emigration more difficult and encouraging very large families. The irritant German and Slav-speaking minorities in the north remained unabsorbed, despite the use of ugly means of coercion. Some success was registered against the *mala vita* of gangsterism, but only by setting a thief to catch a thief and leaving the country possessed of seven devils instead of one. Fascism did not even succeed in tapping those subterranean stores of oil and methane which after 1945 were to bring about a second industrial revolution. Vital resources were squandered in unprofitable prestige ventures in Africa; and, although Italy was made more self-sufficient in foodstuffs and armament production, this was only at a prohibitive cost in subsidies which the nation could not afford.

Perhaps a certain degree of incompetence is a corollary of totalitarianism. Mussolini so relied on his own intuition, and so despised his fellow Italians, and so feared to have subordinates who might criticise or have views of their own, that he centralized power more and more in his own person. The drawback here was that his own most notable attributes were not those of an administrator: they belonged to the mob leader and ruthless conqueror of power. The intuition upon which he depended was unreliable and changeable. He had small patience with the detailed administration of a department, let alone of all the four or five ministries he might hold himself. In this single fact lies one important reason why a régime which believed so dogmatically in war did so little to make ready for the wars it provoked. Whether in munitions production, in organization of the armed services, in capacity for civilian mobilization, this totalitarian country proved to be immeasurably behind the democratic countries. Corruption flourished in a society which had so many controls and yet so little control. It was a society in which honest criticism was not encouraged, and in which the vast bureaucratic organization of the corporative system and the Fascist party were an expensive and unproductive burden on the state. By the early nineteen-thirties, most of the pre-1922 officials had been succeeded by party hacks and placemen who knew little about commanding an army or conducting foreign policy. The time had come when the inherent flaws began to crack the structure of this clay-footed colossus.

The conquest of Abyssinia in 1935—6, in defiance of the League of Nations, provided a last moment of illusory success. It rallied opinion at home, just as it frightened opinion abroad, and Mussolini took the occasion to defy the scoffers and declare that the Roman Empire was in being once again. This was to challenge an unwelcome comparison. His victory, moreover, though it seemed decisive enough, was hollow and dangerous. It ruined his earlier attempt to line up Italy with the western democracies in the 'Stresa front', and forced him instead to join Hitler and allow the Austrian *Anschluss*. It also encouraged him to think that he was a great war leader, not to say that he had an instinct for generalship that obviated any need for military training; and the success of mustard gas against ill-armed tribesmen gave him the idea that the capacity of Italy for aggrandizement was unlimited. In 1936 he therefore sent his troops to help Franco in Spain; in 1937 he withdrew from the League of Nations; in 1938 he took over Albania, and so stirred up a hornets' nest in the Balkans that would soon be about his head. He followed this in 1939 by making the axis more solid and signing a treaty with Germany. So doing he threw away Italy's arbitral position of holding the scales in the balance of power. The one policy for such an essentially weak nation was to keep her independence between rival power groups, and this was precisely how Mussolini had managed to appear important at the time of the Munich agreement in 1938. But once he had signed the Pact of Steel, Italy was despite all appearances a satellite of Germany, having to fight for interests that were not hers, exploited, yet also despised by her ally for being so weak.

When war broke out in September, 1939, Italy did not fight at once. Although war—or, rather, a successful and glorious war—

was what Mussolini ardently wanted of everything in the world, he feared his own unreadiness and the humiliation of following decisions made without consultation in Berlin. Only the following Spring, when France was already defeated, did he brace his courage to risk a short war in order not to be excluded from the peace treaty which seemed so near. In his state of exalted megalomania he was not likely to listen to his army leaders or anyone else, even if there had been people so bold and well-informed as to offer him advice. The result was that Italy suffered a resounding defeat at the hands of Greece in the Autumn of 1940, and then in 1941 lost almost all of her African empire. She was reduced to begging the Germans to come in and take over the Balkans and North Africa, and of course in the process they took over the mainland of Italy as well. It is ironic that Fascism, with all its talk about national dignity and prowess, should have been the government that not only ceded Trieste once more to the Germans, but opened the Italian peninsula to another series of invasion and counter-invasion. After defeat in battle and years of foreign occupation, Italy was to be left poorer and weaker than ever, and more exposed to communist revolution than she had been in 1922.

Not even Mussolini's artificially inflated reputation could survive such a calamity. In 1943 he was deposed—not by the anti-Fascists, nor by the army, nor even in the first instance by the king, but by fair-weather trimmers inside the Fascist party itself who had been his willing accomplices in time of success. The king only waited for this chance to assert his authority again, and appointed Marshal Badoglio to form a new government. An armistice was signed with the Allies, but only after an unfortunate delay which allowed the Germans to strengthen their position in Italy. For twenty months after that the country was once again the battleground of Europe, its land wasted, its cities destroyed. Worse than this, a civil war broke out which divided families and friends and left a legacy of hatred behind. In 1945 during the last stages of this civil war, Mussolini, who had been first arrested by the king and then brilliantly recaptured by the Germans, was taken and summarily executed by the partisans. His corpse, and that of his mistress, were hung upside down before the public gaze in the Piazza Loreto in Milan.

The evil that this man did lives after him. But luckily the vigour and diversity of Italian life had been only cut back, not killed, by the Fascist revolution. Those who were left of the old liberal leaders came home from exile and hiding, and new and more radical forces appeared at once on the political scene. As the monarchy had been too much compromised with Fascism, a republic was proclaimed, and a new constitution came into operation in 1948. Elections in that year gave an outright majority to a centre party which tried to combine in itself both Catholicism and democracy; but there was also a strong and uncompromising opposition from the extreme Left, and it was the conflict between these two which now became the central issue of politics. Stimulated by this challenge, and given much generous help from America, Italians set about picking up the threads of their political and economic life.

Year of Accession	BISHOPS OF ROME	EMPERORS	Year of Accession
A. D.			B. C.
		Augustus.	27
			A. D.
		Tiberius.	14
		Caligula.	37
		Claudius.	41
42	St. Peter (according to Jerome).		
		Nero.	54
67	Linus (according to Irenaeus, Eusebius, Jerome).		
68	Clement (according to Tertullian and Rufinus).	Galba, Otho, Vitellius, Vespasian.	68
78	Anacletus (?).		
		Titus.	79
		Domitian.	81
91	Clement (according to some later writers).		
		Nerva.	96
		Trajan.	98
100	Evarestus (?).		
109	Alexander (?).		
		Hadrian.	117
119	Sixtus I.		
129	Telesphorus.		
		Antoninus Pius.	138
139	Hyginus.		
143	Pius I.		
157	Anicetus.		
		Marcus Aurelius.	161
168	Soter.		
177	Eleutherius.		
		Commodus.	180
		Pertinax.	193
		Didius Julianus.	193
		Niger.	193
193	Victor (?).	Septimius Severus.	193
202	Zephyrinus (?).		
		Caracalla, Geta.	211
		Opilius Macrinus, Diadumenian.	217

Year of Accession	BISHOPS OF ROME	EMPERORS	Year of Accession
A. D.			A. D.
		Elagabalus.	218
219	Calixtus I.		
		Alexander Severus.	222
223	Urban I.		
230	Pontianus.		
235	Anterius or Anteros.	Maximin.	235
236	Fabianus.		
		The two Gordians, Maximus Pupienus, Balbinus.	237
		The third Gordian.	238
		Philip.	244
		Decius.	249
251	Cornelius.	Hostilian, Gallus.	251
252	Lucius I.	Volusian.	252
253	Stephen I.	Aemilian, Valerian, Gallienus.	253
257	Sixtus II.		
259	Dionysius.		
		Gallienus alone.	260
		Claudius II.	268
269	Felix.		
		Aurelian.	270
275	Eutychianus.	Tactitus.	275
		Florian.	276
		Probus.	276
		Carus.	282
283	Caius.		
		Carinus, Numerian.	284
		Diocletian.	284
		Maximian, associated with Diocletian.	286
296	Marcellinus.		
304	Vacancy.		
		Constantius, Galerius.	305
		Severus.	306
		Constantine (the Great).	306
		Licinius.	307
308	Marcellus I.	Maximin.	308
		Constantine, Galerius, Licinius, Maximin, Maxentius, and Maximian reigning jointly.	309
310	Eusebius.		
311	Melchiades.		
314	Sylvester I.		
		Constantine (the Great) alone.	323
336	Marcus I.		

Year of Accession	BISHOPS OF ROME	EMPERORS	Year of Accession
A. D.			A. D.
337	Julius I.	Constantine II., Constantius II., Constans. Magnentius.	337
352	Liberius.	Constantius alone.	353
356	Felix (Anti-pope).	Julian.	361
		Jovian.	363
		Valens and Valentinian I.	364
366	Damasus I.	Gratian and Valentinian I.	367
		Gratian and Valentinian II.	375
		Theodosius.	379
384	Siricius.	Arcadius (in the East), Honorius (in the West).	395
398	Anastasius I.		
402	Innocent I.	Theodosius II. (E).	408
417	Zosimus.		
418	Boniface I.		
418	Eulalius (Anti-pope).		
422	Celestine I.	Valentinian III. (W).	424
432	Sixtus III.		
440	Leo I. (the Great).	Marcian (E).	450
		Maximus, Avitus (W).	455
		Majorian (W).	455
		Leo I. (E).	457
461	Hilarius.	Severus (W).	461
		Vacancy (W).	465
		Anthemius (W).	467
468	Simplicius.	Olybrius (W).	472
		Glycerius (W).	473
		Julius Nepos (W).	474
		Leo II., Zeno, Basiliscus (all E).	474
		Romulus Augustulus (W).	475
		(End of the Western line in Romulus Augustus).	476
		(Henceforth, till A.D. 800, Emperors reigning at Constantinople).	

Year of Accession	POPES	EMPERORS	Year of Accession
A. D.			A. D.
483	Felix III.*		
		Anastasius I.	491
492	Gelasius I.		
496	Anastasius II.		
498	Symmachus.		
498	(Laurentius, Anti-Pope).		
514	Hormisdas.		
		Justin I.	518
523	John I.		
526	Felix IV.		
		Justinian.	527
530	Boniface II.		
530	(Dioscorus, Anti-pope).		
532	John II.		
535	Agapetus I.		
536	Silverius.		
537	Vigilius.		
555	Pelagius I.		
560	John III.		
		Justin II.	565
574	Benedict I.		
578	Pelagius II.	Tiberius II.	578
		Maurice.	582
590	Gregory I. (the Great).		
		Phocas.	602
604	Sabinianus.		
607	Boniface III.		
607	Boniface IV.		
		Heraclius.	610
615	Deus dedit.		
618	Boniface V.		
625	Honorius I.		
638	Severinus.		
640	John IV.		
		Constantine III., Heracleonas, Constans II.	641
642	Theodorus I.		
649	Martin I.		
654	Eugenius I.		
657	Vitalianus I.		
		Constantine IV. (Pogonatus).	668
672	Adeodatus.		
676	Domnus or Donus I.		
678	Agatho.		
682	Leo II.		

* Reckoning the Anti-pope Felix (A.D. 356) as Felix II.

Year of Accession	POPES	EMPERORS	Year of Accession
A. D.			A. D.
683(?)	Benedict II.		
685	John V.	Justinian II.	685
685(?)	Conon.		
687	Sergius I.		
687	(Paschal, Anti-pope).		
687	(Theodorus, Anti-pope).		
		Leontius.	694
		Tiberius III.	697
701	John VI.		
705	John VII.	Justinian II. restored.	705
708	Sisinnius.		
708	Constantine.		
		Philippicus Bardanes.	711
		Anastasius II.	713
715	Gregory II.		
		Theodosius III.	716
		Leo III. (the Isaurian).	718
731	Gregory III.		
741	Zacharias.	Constantine V. (Copronymus).	741
752	Stephen (II.).		
752	Stephen II. (or III.).		
757	Paul I.		
767	Constantine (Anti-pope).		
768	Stephen III. (IV.).		
772	Hadrian I.		
		Leo IV.	775
		Constantine VI.	780
795	Leo III.		
		Deposition of Constantine VI. by Irene.	797
		Charles I. (the Great). *Following henceforth the new Western line).*	800
		Lewis I. (the Pious).	814
816	Stephen IV.		
817	Paschal I.		
824	Eugenius II.		
827	Valentinus.		
827	Gregory IV.		
		Lothar I.	840
844	Sergius II.		
847	Leo IV.		
855	Benedict III.	Lewis II. (in Italy).	855
855	(Anastasius, Anti-pope).		
858	Nicholas I.		
867	Hadrian II.		
872	John VIII.		

Year of Accession A. D.	POPES	EMPERORS	Year of Accession A. D.
		Charles II., the Bald (W. Frankish).	
		Charles III., the Fat (E. Frankish).	875
882	Martin II.		881
884	Hadrian III.	*Interval from 888.*	
885	Stephen V.		
891	Formosus.	Guido (in Italy).	891
		Lambert (in Italy).	894
896	Boniface VI.	Arnulf (E. Frankish).	896
896	Stephen VI.		
897	Romanus.		
897	Theodore II.		
898	John IX.		
		*Lewis (the Child).**	899
900	Benedict IV.		
		Lewis III. king of Provence (in Italy).	901
903	Leo V.		
903	Christopher.		
904	Sergius III.		
911	Anastasius III.	*Conrad I.*	911
913	Lando.		
914	John X.		
		Berengar (in Italy).	915
		Henry I. (the Fowler) of Saxony.	918
928	Leo VI.		
929	Stephen VII.		
931	John XI.		
936	Leo VII.	*Otto I. (the Great),*	
939	Stephen VIII.	crowned E. Frankish	
941	Martin III.	king at Aachen.	936
946	Agapetus II.		
955	John XII.	*Saxon House.*	
		Otto I., crowned Emperor at Rome.	962
963	Leo VIII.		
964	(Benedict V., Anti-pope?).		
965	John XIII.		
972	Benedict VI.		
		Otto II.	973
974	(Boniface VII., Antipope?).		
974	Domnus II (?).		
974	Benedict VII.		

* The names in italics are those of East Frankish or German kings who never made any claim to the imperial title.

Year of Accession	POPES	EMPERORS	Year of Accession
A. D.			A. D.
983	John XIV.	Otto III.	983
985	John XV.		
996	Gregory V.		
996	(John XVI, Anti-pope?).		
999	Sylvester II.		
		HenryII. (the Saint).	1002
1003	John XVII.		
1003	John XVIII.		
1009	Sergius IV.		
1012	Benedict VIII.	*House of Franconia.*	
1024	John XIX.	Conrad II. (the Salic).	1024
1033	Benedict IX.		
		Henry III. (the Black).	1039
1044	(Sylvester, Anti-pope).		
1045	Gregory VI.		
1046	Clement II.		
1048	Damasus II.		
1048	Leo IX.		
1054	Victor II.		
		Henry IV.	1056
1057	Stephen IX.		
1058	Benedict X.		
1059	Nicholas II.		
1061	Alexander II.		
1073	Gregory VII. (Hildebrand).	(Rudolf of Swabia, rival).	1077
1080	(Clement, Anti-pope).		
		(Hermann of Luxemborg, rival).	1081
1086	Victor III.		
1087	Urban II.		
		(Conrad of Franconia, rival).	1093
1099	Paschal II.		
1102	(Albert, Anti-pope).		
1105	(Sylvester, Anti-pope).		
		Henry V.	1106
1118	Gelasius II.		
1118	(Gregory, Anti-pope).		
1119	Calixtus II.		
1121	(Celestine, Anti-pope).		
1124	Honorius II.		
		Lothar II. (of Saxony).	1125
1130	Innocent II.	*House of Swabia or*	
	(Anacletus, Anti-pope).	*Hohenstaufen).*	
1138	(Victor, Anti-pope).	*Conrad III.	1138

* Those marked with an asterisk were never actually crowned at Rome.

AA

Year of Accession	POPES	EMPERORS	Year of Accession
A. D.			A. D.
1143	Celestine II.		
1144	Lucius II.		
1145	Eugenius III.		
		Frederick I. (Barbarossa).	1152
1153	Anastasius IV.		
1154	Hadrian IV.		
1159	Alexander III.		
1159	(Victor, Anti-pope).		
1164	(Paschal, Anti-pope).		
1168	(Calixtus, Anti-pope).		
1181	Lucius III.		
1185	Urban III.		
1187	Gregory VIII.		
1187	Clement III.		
		Henry VI.	1190
1191	Celestine III.		
		*Philip, Otto IV. (rivals).	1197
1198	Innocent III.		
		Otto IV. (House of Brunswick).	1208
		Frederick II.	1212
1216	Honorius III.		
1227	Gregory IX.		
1241	Celestine IV.		
1241	Vacancy.		
1243	Innocent IV.		
		(Henry Raspe, rival).	1246
		(William of Holland, rival).	1246-7
		*Conrad IV.	1250
1254	Alexander IV.	Interregnum.	1254
		*Richard (earl of Cornwall), *Alfonso (king of Castile) (rivals).	1257
1261	Urban IV.		
1265	Clement IV.		
1269	Vacancy.		
1271	Gregory X.		
		*Rudolf I. (of Hapsburg).	1273
1276	Innocent V.		
1276	Hadrian V.		
1277	John XX. or XXI.		
1277	Nicholas III.		
1281	Martin IV.		
1285	Honorius IV.		
1289	Nicholas IV.		

* Those marked with an asterisk were never actually crowned at Rome.

Year of Accession	POPES	EMPERORS	Year of Accession
A. D.			A. D.
1292	Vacancy.	*Adolf (of Nassau).	1292
1294	Celestine V.		
1294	Boniface VIII.		
		*Albert I. (of Hapsburg).	1298
1303	Benedict XI.		
1305	Clement V.		
		Henry VII. (of Luxemburg).	1308
1314	Vacancy.	Lewis IV. (of Bavaria). (Frederick of Austria, rival).	1314
1316	John XXII.		
1334	Benedict XII.		
1342	Clement VI.		
		Charles IV. (of Luxemburg). (Günther of Schwartzburg, rival).	1347
1352	Innocent VI.		
1362	Urban V.		
1370	Gregory XI.		
1378	Urban VI. (Clement VII., Antipope). Beginning of the Great Schism.	*Wenzel (of Luxemburg).	1378
1389	Boniface IX.		
1394	(Benedict, Anti-pope).		
		*Rupert (of the Palatinate).	1400
1404	Innocent VII.		
1406	Gregory XII.		
1409	Alexander V.		
1410	John XXIII.	Sigismund (of Luxemburg). (Jobst, of Moravia, rival).	1410
1417	End of the Great Schism. Martin V.		
1431	Eugene IV.		
		*Albert II. (of Hapsburg).†	1438
1439	(Felix V., Anti-pope).		
		Frederick III.	1440
1447	Nicholas V.		
1455	Calixtus IV.		

* Those marked with an asterisk were never actually crowned at Rome.
† All the succeeding Emperors, except Charles VII. and Frances I., belong to the House of Hapsburg.

Year of Accession	POPES	EMPERORS	Year of Accession
A. D.			A. D.
1458	Pius II.		
1464	Paul II.		
1471	Sixtus IV.		
1484	Innocent VIII.		
1493	Alexander VI.	*Maximilian I.	1493
1503	Pius III.		
1503	Julius II.		
1513	Leo X.		
		‡Charles V.	1519
1522	Hadrian VI.		
1523	Clement VII.		
1534	Paul III.		
1550	Julius III.		
1555	Marcellus II.		
1555	Paul IV.		
		*Ferdinand I.	1558
1559	Pius IV.		
		*Maximilian II.	1564
1566	Pius V.		
1572	Gregory XIII.		
		*Rudolf II.	1576
1585	Sixtus V.		
1590	Urban VII.		
1590	Gregory XIV.		
1591	Innocent IX.		
1592	Clement VIII.		
1604	Leo XI.		
1604	Paul V.		
		*Matthias.	1612
		*Ferdinand II.	1619
1621	Gregory XV.		
1623	Urban VIII.		
		*Ferdinand III.	1637
1644	Innocent X.		
1655	Alexander VII.		
		*Leopold I.	1658
1667	Clement IX.		
1670	Clement X.		
1676	Innocent XI.		
1689	Alexander VIII.		
1691	Innocent XII.		
1700	Clement XI.		
		*Joseph I.	1705
		*Charles VI.	1711
1720	Innocent XIII.		
1724	Benedict XIII.		

* Those marked with an asterisk were never actually crowned at Rome.
‡ Crowned Emperor, but at Bologna, not at Rome.

Year of Accession	POPES	EMPERORS	Year of Accession
A. D.			A. D.
1730	Clement XII.		
1740	Benedict XIV		
		*Charles VII. (of Bavaria).	1742
		*Francis I. (of Lorraine).	1745
1758	Clement XIII.		
		*Joseph II.	1765
1769	Clement XIV.		
1775	Pius VI.		
		*Leopold II.	1790
		*Francis II.	1792
1800	Pius VII.		
		ABDICATION OF FRANCIS II.	1806
1823	Leo. XII.		
1829	Pius VIII.		
1831	Gregory XVI.		
1846	Pius IX.		
		GERMAN EMPERORS.	
		William I.	1871
		Frederick.	1888
		William II.	1888
1878	Leo XIII.		
1903	Pius X.		
1914	Benedict XV.		
1921	Pius XI.		
1939	Pius XII.		

* Those marked with an asterisk were never actually crowned in Rome.

This table is reproduced, by kind permission of the author's heirs and of Messrs. Macmillan & Co Ltd, from Bryce : *The Holy Roman Empire*—which will explain some slight discrepancies between this table and the text.

Index

GEORGE ALLEN & UNWIN LTD
London: 40 Museum Street, W.C.1

Auckland: 24 Wyndham Street
Sydney, N.S.W.: Bradbury House, 55 York Street
Cape Town: 58–60 Long Street
Bombay: 15 Graham Road, Ballard Estate, Bombay 1
Calcutta: 17 Chittaranjan Avenue, Calcutta 13
New Delhi: 13–14 Ajmere Gate Extension, New Delhi 1
Karachi: Haroon Chambers, South Napier Road, Karachi 2
Toronto: 91 Wellington Street West
São Paulo: Avenida 9 de Julho 1138–Ap. 51

RICHARD THE THIRD
Paul Murray Kendall

This can be called the first real biography of a notorious but actually unknown King, one of the most controversial figures in English history. Previous works, whether frankly popular or of scholarly stamp, have been largely devoted to arguing a "case" either for or against King Richard. They have too often relied, if ardently defending him, on wishful speculation or have followed the Tudor tradition of history, now no longer tenable, of showing him to be the ruthless villain of Shakespeare's melodrama.

This biography offers an impartial study of Richard's enigmatic character and turbulent career. Based almost wholly upon the Pre-Tudor historical sources of Richard's own day, it includes much entirely fresh material as well as information unobtainable when the Gairdner biography was published. It removes Richard from the shadow of misrepresentation and rumour. It artfully shapes Richard's life into a drama of tragic passion and violence, complex in thematic development and fascinating in its psychology. It evokes the neglected but colourful times in which Richard lived and the array of great figures whose lives touched his—Warwick the Kingmaker, Margaret of Anjou, Louis the Eleventh, Edward the Fourth, Caxton, Jane Shore, Henry Tudor, and many others. A special section has been devoted to what is perhaps the most famous, and bitterly disputed, murder mystery in English annals— that of the "little Princes in the Tower."

This is one of the most readable works of history that has ever come into its publisher's hands. The author is an American professor of English Literature, who after several years of research in his home country, spent a year and a half in England seeking further material.

Sm. Royal 8vo   30s. net

ENGLISH RADICALISM: THE ORIGINS
S. Maccoby

In the three volumes which have already appeared under the title of *English Radicalism*, Dr. Maccoby's success in combining new ranges of sources with the old has been widely accepted. With the help of a Leverhulme Fellowship, he has been able to turn, in this volume, to the origins of modern "popular" politics in the first half of George III's reign. A further volume is being prepared under the title of *English Radicalism from Paine to Cobbett* which will take the story of "popular" politics on from 1785 to 1832. Such a volume would complete what might be called a History of the British Left from 1762 to 1914.

Demy 8vo   45s. net

THE PATH TO ROME

Hilaire Belloc

It is nearly half a century since *The Path to Rome* was written, but its high place among English books of travel was never more secure. Described long ago as "quite the most sumptuous embodiment of universal gaiety and erratic wisdom that has been written," there is now scarcely a prose anthology that does not contain some passage from its fascinating pages. For who, having once read them, will ever forget the lines which describe the first vision of the Alps from the Weissenstein, or the crossing of the Brienzergrat, or the forced march from Belinzona to Milan on eight francs, or the many adventures on the long road through Italian plains and hills, or the wine that was drunk and the meals consumed in so many humble inns, or the folk encountered on the way? For this tale of a journey on foot from Toul in Lorraine to the Eternal City, by the straightest possible line, is rich in every page with wisdom and the joy of living; it is a book of which you never tire and to which you will return again and again.

Cr. 8vo   12s. 6d. net

A HISTORY OF SWITZERLAND

Charles Gilliard

In Switzerland people of three races, two religions and four languages live peaceably side by side. The evolution of this model pacifist Confederation is a story of extraordinary fascination and is told in this concise history, in a way admirably suited for the general reader. The author gives a lucid and straightforward account of the Republic with the emphasis on the constitutional development rather than on battles and national figures.

Lg. Cr. 8vo   8s. 6d. net

THE EMPEROR CHARLES THE FIFTH

Royall Tyler

in Preparation
Sm. Royal 8vo.   About 40s. net

A HISTORY OF EUROPE

Henri Pirenne

"A model of descriptive and objective commentary, so objective that it seems to be itself a part of history."— F. M. POWICKE in *The Manchester Guardian*.

"A very great book."—*Liverpool Daily Post*.

"A measured and comprehensive outline of European history from the Barbarian Invasions to the abdication of the Emperor Charles V . . . it is deserving of careful study ; and throughout it is illuminated by brilliant historical insight and quiet humour."— *Church Times*.

"A work of detachment, concentration and memory . . . proving, yet again, that the chains of the body are often wings to the spirit . . . His view . . . is magnificent and highly individual."—I. K. SUMMERHAYES in *Time and Tide*.

Demy 8vo   35s. net

THE FIRST EUROPE

C. Delisle Burns

"A book of great interest and great importance. It deals with the period from 400 to 800 A.D., which is very little studied, and on which very few good books exist. Yet in this period were founded the institutions of mediæval Europe, many of which persisted till quite modern times. The subject is treated with a wealth of knowledge, but not with the aloofness of mere erudition ; everything is related to human problems which are still important at the present day. The conflict of an old and feeble civilization with the vigorous and brutal barbarians, with the consequent changes in the lives of ordinary men and women ; the transition from an urban slave-economy built on imperial trade to a rural serf-economy in which almost all production was for local needs ; the decay of culture, the growth of anarchy, and the gradual emergence of new centres of social cohesion ; all this is better told than in any other book known to me. To anyone who wishes to understand Europe, both mediæval and modern, the book is invaluable."
—BERTRAND RUSSELL.

Sm. Royal   25s. net

A HISTORY OF THE HOMELAND

Henry Hamilton

"It has a freshness that is exhilarating, and it throws new light on the whole period with which it deals, by the admirable way in which the problems of the age are seen from quite new angles." —H. J. LASKI.

"I know no other book which so well deserves to be called 'Social History'."—J. A. LAUWERYS.

Demy 8vo   18s. net

THE MONGUL EMPIRE

Michael Prawdin

"It has the rare merit of being both scholarly and exciting. The narrative traces in a detailed but absorbing manner the rise of the nomadic power under Jenghiz Khan and his early successors, then its decline, the momentary rally under Tamerlane, and its final submergence. The entire world comes on to his canvas, romantic and fantastical persons pass in our view, and at the conclusion we realize that we have seen the whole of what Marco Polo saw only in part."—MAURICE COLLIS in *Time and Tide*.

Demy 8vo   35s. net

THE SPIRIT OF RUSSIA

T. G. Masaryk

Pre-eminent among the theoreticians and leaders of democracy, Thomas Masaryk speaks with authority still on a number of questions that trouble the world to-day. Early in life he became a close student of Russian affairs and *The Spirit of Russia* was the result. It was republished in 1930 and 1933 with new historical material. This is now translated for the first time. There is an urgent need to understand present-day Russia and Masaryk adds greatly to our understanding of the origins.

Demy 8vo   60s. net the set of 2 volumes

THE BRITISH WORKING CLASS
READER, 1790 — 1848

R. K. Webb

At the time of the French Revolution the upper and middle classes discovered that the working classes could read and, in their view, were reading the wrong things. Making the fullest use of original research on the material held by the great provincial libraries, Dr. Webb studies their efforts to deal with this challenge. After a consideration of the extent of literacy, he examines the early attempts to influence working class readers and then analyses the more positive approach adopted after 1820. Following a general analysis of this movement, in terms of attitudes, machinery, and impact, there are three detailed studies of attempts at indoctrination connected with important causes of social tension : the agricultural disturbances of 1830, the new poor law of 1834, and the trade union movement.

Demy 8vo   18s. net

CHARLES I AND THE PURITAN
UPHEAVAL

Allen French

For many years historians have considered religious feeling as the prime motive for the emigration of the Puritans. Recent studies have tended to give much more prominence to economic factors. Allen French's study shows clearly that the religious conviction was undoubtedly the main motive, but the Puritans were in addition seeking security from mental hardships of many other kinds.

Carefully examining all the available papers at the Public Records and other contemporary sources, the author builds up an excellent picture of England before the Civil War, particularly as it might have appeared to the type of man who emigrated to New England. Then through a series of case histories the author describes the sort of man who emigrated and why he did so.

The wealth of evidence from original documents is clearly arranged and while the book is not a superficial study it is extremely readable. It is a refreshing reassessment of the period.

Sm. Royal 8vo   30s. net

MEMBERS OF THE LONG PARLIAMENT

D. Brunton and D. H. Pennington

"Very important. . . . Henceforth no one can set out to write seriously on the origins of the Civil War without studying it with care."—G. M. TREVELYAN in *The Sunday Times*.

"No previous work," writes Professor Tawney in his Foreword, "has examined in detail the membership of the House of Commons which entered and emerged from the Civil War ; nor . . . is it easy to point to one providing for any period before the nineteenth century information comparable in range and precision with that here supplied."

Demy 8vo   21s. net

UNIVERSITY REPRESENTATION IN ENGLAND, 1604—1690

Millicent Barton Rex

This work is a history of university parliamentary representation in England from its beginning in 1604 to the close of the Convention Parliament of 1688-89. A careful analysis is made from time to time to determine the trends of university politics and personnel throughout the great events of the century. Such matters as royal domination, and freedom of election in the university constituencies, contributions made by university members to public service and to learning (or their failure to contribute) are constantly kept before the reader. It deals with university representation as part of the history of a century that is one of the most notable in England's constitutional development.

Demy 8vo   30s. net

GEORGE ALLEN AND UNWIN LTD.